Annual Review of Cultural Heritage Informatics

Annual Review of Cultural Heritage Informatics

2012–2013

Edited by Samantha K. Hastings

facet publishing

Published by Facet Publishing,
7 Ridgmount Street, London WC1E 7AE
www.facetpublishing.co.uk

Facet Publishing is wholly owned by CILIP: the Chartered Institute of
Library and Information Professionals.

First published in the USA by Rowman & Littlefield, 2014.
This UK edition 2014.

British Library Cataloguing in Publication Data
A catalogue record for this book is available from the British Library.

ISBN 978-1-78330-026-6

Text printed on FSC accredited material.

Printed and bound in the United Kingdom by CPI Group (UK) Ltd,
Croydon, CR0 4YY.

Contents

List of Figures

List of Tables

List of Articles by Section with Abstracts

BEST PRACTICES

Digital Preservation: Whose Responsibility?

Michèle V. Cloonan, Dean Emerita and Professor, Simmons Graduate School of Library and Information Science

Martha Mahard, Professor of Practice, Simmons Graduate School of Library and Information Science

Abstract

Preservation seeks to ensure the memory of civilizations and the longevity of oral and recorded information. This paper suggests that the preservation of digital cultural heritage is inherently pluralistic in the sense that many preservation perspectives are held by increasingly diverse groups of people. Digital preservation activities are becoming increasingly distributed, decentralized, and ad hoc while incorporating new forms of social networking. Thus, traditional models of preservation programs, which depend on extant institutional structures, may no longer be effective. The reasons for this shift are explored and new preservation perspectives are suggested.

Facilitating Discovery and Use of Digital Cultural Heritage Resources with Folksonomies: A Review

Daniel Gelaw Alemneh, Digital Libraries Services, University of North Texas Libraries

Abebe Rorissa, Department of Information Studies, University at Albany, State University of New York (SUNY)

Abstract

The increase in the number and heterogeneity of digital resources has led cultural heritage institutions to develop tools, workflows, and quality-assurance mechanisms that allow effective digital resource management. In their quest for better discoverability of existing digital resources, cultural heritage institutions attempt to enrich traditional catalogs and enhance metadata with additional user-supplied terms and descriptions such as folksonomies. The current landscape in the use of folksonomies by cultural heritage institutions is reviewed and emerging trends in this area identified. Strengths and limitations of folksonomies vis-à-vis traditional indexing and taxonomies are explored with a particular emphasis on the history of cultural heritage information retrieval, including a consideration of the potential benefits and controversies surrounding user-supplied tags or keywords as complements to established controlled vocabularies. By providing high-level descriptions and representations, such topical and natural approaches to the subject matter in a digital collection may empower users of digital libraries of cultural heritage resources and promote diverse, collaborative online environments.

Experiments in Cultural Heritage Informatics: Convergence and Divergence

Jeannette A. Bastian, Graduate School of Library and Information Science, Simmons College, Boston

Ross Harvey, Graduate School of Library and Information Science, Simmons College, Boston

Abstract

We typically think that the major challenges for digitization, convergence, and digital preservation are technological. However, cultural and professional issues predominate and are more difficult to overcome. This observation is reinforced by research on the convergence of cultural heritage institutions conducted since 2009 by faculty at the Graduate School of Library and Information Studies at Simmons College in Boston. Grounded in the emerging field of cultural heritage informatics, that research is described with a focus on the Simmons Digital Curriculum Laboratory, the digital convergence projects negotiated and completed by faculty and students, and the lessons learned from those projects. The problems encountered are outlined, including concerns about controlling public access, communication difficulties, staff layoffs, lack of technical skills, lack of strategic vision, and constraints arising from organizational hierarchies. Based on the findings, the trajectory for convergence is evaluated.

DIGITAL COMMUNITIES

Web Representation and Interpretation of Culture: The Case of a Holistic Healing System

Hemalata Iyer, Associate Professor, Department of Information Studies, University at Albany, State University of New York

Amber J. D'Ambrosio, Assistant Professor, Special Collections Librarian and Archivist, Dixie State University

Abstract

Ayurveda, a holistic healing system deeply rooted in its indigenous culture, is being practiced within a different cultural milieu in the United States. The healing system has undergone a cultural shift away from its religious origins on U.S. websites, and the transplanted cultural context impacts the meaning and interpretations drawn from its digital representations. Utilizing Stuart Hall's approach to representation in media as a framework, representations of Ayurveda in a sample of U.S. websites are analyzed. The significance and the methods used to legitimize Ayurveda, the cultural symbols employed, the philosophy and purpose of the websites, and the viewer's perception of the representations are examined. The authors explore whether representations translated on both symbolic and linguistic levels may surmount the problems and issues arising from varying cultural maps.

Knitting as Cultural Heritage: Knitting Blogs and Conservation

Jennifer Burek Pierce, Associate Professor, School of Library and Information Science, The University of Iowa

Abstract

Knitting has existed as a means of constructing fabric for thousands of years around the globe. Digital resources, including blogs and other social media platforms, now document the nature of the fiber craft. Intended for any number of purposes, a legion of online outlets depict what twenty-first-century knitters do, what materials they employ, who will receive the work they have done, how they have learned a technique, and how they feel about their endeavors. As social media facilitate intense interactions between knitting writers and knitting readers, knitting forms a significant element of cultural heritage, with social, technological, and economic effects, making it a phenomenon that merits recognition as an enduring aspect of cultural heritage. Employing the historical and discursive analysis articulated by Chartier, three prominent knitting blogs and their cultural discourse are explored. Misunderstood as an old-fashioned activity, this examination of digital materials associated with the fiber craft reveals a cultural heritage meriting and awaiting digital preservation.

EDUCATION

Developing Twenty-First-Century Cultural Heritage Information Professionals for Digital Stewardship: A Framework for Curriculum Design

Mary W. Elings, Archivist for Digital Collections of The Bancroft Library at the University of California, Berkeley, Adjunct Professor, School of Library and Information Science, the Catholic University of America

Youngok Choi, Assistant Professor, School of Library and Information Science, the Catholic University of America

Jane Zhang, Assistant Professor, School of Library and Information Science, the Catholic University of America

Abstract

As digital stewardship emerges as a concept of professional roles and responsibilities due to digital convergence, Library and Information Science (LIS) educational programs need to provide students with appropriate educational programs to take on new responsibilities and roles in all aspects of digital resources management. The Cultural Heritage Information Management (CHIM) concentration at the Department of Library and Information Science of the Catholic University of America prepares twenty-first-century cultural heritage information professionals to develop and curate sustainable digital collections, meeting the research and educational needs served by libraries, archives, museums, and other cultural heritage institutions. The program of study supporting the development of five core competencies is described with an emphasis on courses providing a foundation in digital stewardship concepts. The learning activities, exploratory projects, and collaborations with digital curation and preservation professionals designed to prepare students for twenty-first-century digital stewardship of cultural heritage resources are highlighted.

Local History and Genealogy Collections in Libraries: The Challenge to Library and Information Science Educators

Rhonda L. Clark, Department of Library Science, Clarion University of Pennsylvania

James T. Maccaferri, Department of Library Science, Clarion University of Pennsylvania

Abstract

In the digital age, local history and genealogy collections held by libraries present new opportunities for programming, reference, delivery, outreach, and collaboration. Especially in smaller libraries, without adequate educational and research support, those opportunities may not be embraced as focal points for library services. The question of whether the North American library and information science field provides adequate education and resources to support professionals embracing local collection management within the scope of their duties is explored. Answering that question begins with a discussion of the challenges identifying libraries holding local history and genealogy collections. Existing instructional support for professionals managing local collections is surveyed and periodical literature related to local studies librarianship since 2000 is reviewed. Suggestions for new directions in research, education, and collaboration are offered.

FIELD REPORTS

Initiatives in Digitization and Digital Preservation of Cultural Heritage in Ethiopia

Abebe Rorissa, Associate Professor, Department of Information Studies, College of Computing and Information, University at Albany, State University of New York
    Teklemichael T. Wordofa, Addis Ababa University
    Solomon Teferra, Addis Ababa University

Abstract

A diverse nation of over ninety million people who speak more than eighty different languages, Ethiopia has a rich and unique history as well as cultural heritage. Due to a number of factors, its rich cultural heritage is neither adequately preserved nor widely accessible. A potential solution is digitization, which could serve to rectify both these problems. Although some institutions in the country initiated digitization of cultural heritage resources, the full picture of the initiatives in digitization and digital preservation of cultural heritage in Ethiopia is not clear. To address this gap in the literature and assess what has been achieved so far, as well as plans for the future, we conducted a cross-sectional survey of twenty-two institutions, which is the first such comprehensive study of its kind. Our results revealed that 64% of the institutions either have digital collections of cultural heritage resources or are engaged in digitization activities that relied heavily on internal and external funding, including funding from international donors. Only a fraction (29%) of those institutions have an explicit use policy and track the usage of their digital collections. Among those institutions that neither have digital collections nor are engaged in digitization activities, most have plans for digitization in the next four years. Lack of funding and skilled human resources are the top two most cited reasons for lack of digitization efforts and are consistent with reasons often cited by similar institutions in other countries. Based on the results, we offer recommendations on the path forward so that cultural heritage institutions in Ethiopia might achieve the ultimate goal of digital preservation as well as serve their users effectively and efficiently.

Creating the Online Literary and Cultural Heritage Map of Pennsylvania

Alan C. Jalowitz, Editor, Pennsylvania Center for the Book

Steven L. Herb, Director, Pennsylvania Center for the Book, Affiliate Professor of Education (Language and Literacy Education), College of Education, Penn State

Abstract

Launched in January 2000 as an online literary map project of the Pennsylvania Center for the Book, the Online Literary and Cultural Heritage Map of Pennsylvania encompasses 1,150 biographies and 285 featured essays accompanied by digital image, audio, and video data. Displaying the contributions of over nine hundred authors, including a high percentage of Penn State students, the Map draws over fifty-two thousand average page views per month. The evolution of the project is traced from the founding of the Pennsylvania Center for the book in 1989, through the early focus on literary heritage and involvement of students in the development of materials, to the Map's expansion into the broader realm of cultural heritage. Project managers describe the challenges of defining project scope; establishing standards; balancing usability and available technologies; rights management issues; and planning for ongoing maintenance, upgrades, and migration to new platforms and functionality. From established foundations of solid editorial care and judicious additions to text, audio, image, and video data, future creative plans for the Map are discussed.

The Community Heritage Grants Program in Australia: Report of a Survey

Sigrid McCausland, Joint Secretary at International Council on Archives Section on Archival Education and Training, Lecturer in Information Management at School of Information Studies, Charles Sturt University

Kim M. Thompson, Lecturer at School of Information Studies, Charles Sturt University

Abstract

The Community Heritage Grants (CHG) program is a small annual competitive grant scheme funded and administered directly by the Australian Government to support the management of cultural heritage at the local level. Grants fund significance assessment, preservation, and training projects in a wide range of cultural institutions, including archives, galleries, genealogical and historical societies, museums, and public libraries, among others. By the close of 2011, the program had disbursed over $4 million in funds to 888 community organizations. This paper reports on a project undertaken in 2012, Assessing the Impact of Community Heritage Grants, the focus of which was a survey of CHG applicants and recipients in regional New South Wales (NSW), Australia. The survey was designed to assess the impact of the grants on the organizations that applied for them and to document their concerns for the future of the collections they manage. The paper concludes with reflections on relationships between central government agencies and grassroots organizations as evidenced in the CHG program and offers suggestions for further research into the delivery of grant programs to local cultural heritage organizations in Australia.

Toward a Study of "Unofficial" Museums

Cheryl Klimaszewski, Fellow, Doctoral Student, Rutgers School of Communication and Information

James M. Nyce, Ball State University, Department of Anthropology

Abstract

The peasant is an important national symbol in Romania for both historical and ideological reasons. Since the 1989 revolution, a large number of rural, "unofficial" museums founded by amateur museum proprietors opened their doors to showcase peasant life in situ. Developing a better understanding of these local, "unofficial" museums may help ensure their role in the global network of cultural heritage production and preservation. Work toward a plan for the study of unofficial museums draws from field work and extant literature while considering these institutions within a library and information science (LIS) context. After an introduction situating the local, "unofficial" museum in the larger context of cultural heritage and museums in Romania, the collections, ethnic groups represented, physical spaces housing the collections, and the kinds of visitors who view the collections are described. Collection development practices and the construction of narratives around the collections are discussed and contrasted with official museum practices. Areas for further research into unofficial, local museums in Romania and elsewhere are mapped.

TECHNOLOGY

Ghosts of the Horseshoe, a Mobile Application: Fostering a New Habit of Thinking about the History of University of South Carolina's Historic Horseshoe

Heidi Rae Cooley, Assistant Professor, Media Arts, the Department of Art, University of South Carolina

Duncan A. Buell, Professor, Department of Computer Science and Engineering, University of South Carolina

Abstract

Ghosts of the Horseshoe is a mobile interactive application deploying game mechanics, augmented reality, and Global Positioning System functionality. Drawing
on American Pragmatist Charles Sanders Peirce's notion of habit-change, Ghosts
was designed to generate awareness of and questioning about the historic grassy
space at the center of the University of South Carolina campus that is surrounded
by the remains of the original South Carolina College (1801–1865). Participants
enter into a relation with history and the historical enslaved persons who built
and maintained the Horseshoe through their mobile micro-screen "window" onto
the past—one whose real-time image responds to touch, gesture, and location.
The interaction opens moments of empathic identification and the opportunity
to think differently about the place and work of history. Ghost's technology and
content are described, and the application's use as an enabler of citizen archeology
is highlighted. Augmented reality applications like Ghosts that invite historical
reflection and sensitivity to place are surveyed.

Tune In, Turn On, Drop Out: Section 108(c) and Evaluating Deterioration in Commercially Produced VHS Collections

Walter Forsberg, Research Fellow, Moving Image Archiving and Preservation Program, New York University Libraries
Erik Piil, Digital Archivist at Anthology Film Archives, Video Preservation Technician at DuArt Film and Video

Abstract

Analog videotape, an imperfect moving image technology format since its introduction, is reaching the end of its life cycle. However, large quantities of out-of-print
and irreplaceable VHS titles still comprise significant portions of library and archival
collections and circulations. Given the need to preserve this content, this study investigates the use of the "dropout" metric (counts of disruptions in the video signal)
for determining whether libraries and archives can invoke their rights of reproduction under the United States Copyright Act. Videotape technology and deterioration
problems are explained and prior deterioration studies are reviewed. Dropout tests of
four pairs of commercially produced VHS titles are conducted and relationships between videotape deterioration as measured by dropout counts, circulation statistics,
and manufacturing quality control standards are evaluated. Offering noninvasive
evidence of videotape deterioration, quantified dropout counts appear to provide
libraries and archives with an objective measure to meet the vague "deterioration"
standard of the Copyright Act.

REVIEWS

The Devils You Don't Know: The New Lives of the Finding Aid

Sheila O'Hare, Assistant Professor, School of Library and Information Management, Emporia State University

Ashley Todd-Diaz, Assistant Professor, Curator of Special Collections and Archives, University Libraries and Archives, Emporia State University

Abstract

The nature and purpose of the "finding aid" in cultural heritage institutions has become the focus of considerable scholarly examination. As much of the literature of 2012 devoted to the subject indicated, finding aids are still at the heart of the cultural heritage enterprise, but questions surround their future design and ultimate relevance in the digital era. This review of the 2012 literature on topics related to finding aids and associated access tools considers the future of the finding aid from four perspectives: reassessment of the traditional functions and meanings of the finding aid; online finding aid design and usability; efforts to make the "invisible" work of cocreators or information professionals in describing, organizing, and presenting resources apparent; and the impact of new developments, including interactive content and linked data.

If You Build It, Will They Come? A Review of Digital Collection User Studies

Ashley Todd-Diaz, Assistant Professor, Curator of Special Collections and Archives, University Libraries and Archives, Emporia State University

Sheila O'Hare, Assistant Professor, School of Library and Information Management, Emporia State University

Abstract

As more and more cultural institutions have begun curating digital collections, it is a priority to examine how users are interacting with digital objects. Recent scholarship has focused on data (e.g., web analytics, use statistics, number of citations) and user feedback to gauge how often users are accessing digital collections and to what extent they are using the objects—considering that viewing, downloading, and citing are all different activities. This article reviews studies focusing on digital collection use in practice published in 2012. Generally, access and use numbers appeared to be fairly low. However, results also uncovered intriguing trends, including the impact of promotion and collection location on number of views and citations of digital materials in historical research over the last decade. The challenges still confronting the accessibility and usability of digital collections are explored.

Memories of a Museum Visit

Carol Lynn Price, Doctoral Student, School of Library and Information Science, University of South Carolina

Book reviews: Falk, John H. & Dierking, Lynn D. (1992) *The Museum Experience*, Whalesback Books: Washington D.C. and Falk, John H. & Dierking, Lynn D. (2013) *The Museum Experience Revisited*, Left Coast Press, Inc.: Walnut Creek, California

Acknowledgments

The idea for this first volume of the *Annual Review of Cultural Heritage Informatics* (ARCHI) was created in a phone conversation with Charles Harmon, editor at Rowman & Littlefield, as we discussed the need for something centered on cultural heritage and related fields for library and museum professionals and scholars. Thank you for the phone call, Charles.

We wouldn't have the volume without the contributors, and what a great group we have included here. Thank you one and all for stepping forward and helping us build this content. I think you will agree that we've ended up with a complementary set of great articles.

Next, the editorial board played an important role in this process as advisors and as peer reviewers. A list of the board members and their affiliations reflects the diversity of the group that helped build a bridge across several disciplines. Your assistance was instrumental in getting this volume to press.

My name is the one listed as editor but the entire faculty and staff of the School of Library and Information Science at the University of South Carolina helped produce ARCHI. We are very fortunate to have a great copyeditor among us, and Karen Miller deserves all the praise and credit for that task as well as for the introductions to each section. Karen, your expertise and willingness to help is greatly appreciated!

Finally, thank you dear readers for all of the good work you do to protect, preserve, and provide access to our cultural heritage.

Introduction

Welcome to the first *Annual Review of Cultural Heritage Informatics*, or ARCHI, as we are affectionately calling this publication. This series looks at how we access, store, and preserve our cultural heritage from a variety of perspectives. It is published by a partnership between Dr. S. K. (Sam) Hastings, director of the School of Library and Information Science at the University of South Carolina, and Charles Harmon, executive editor of Rowman & Littlefield.

The mission for ARCHI is to provide an annual compilation of research and practices in this nascent and growing field as an important contribution to our scholarly knowledge, to keep it timely, international, and of interest to scholars from a variety of disciplines. ARCHI is the first review of research and best practices in cultural heritage and related fields, filling a void for introducing and publishing excellent research across disciplines and from different perspectives. The development of scholarship in this area is crucial to building a corpus of work that reflects the challenge of working in a field that continues to stretch and grow from issues of concern to archives, libraries, and museums to issues of concern to every discipline. Providing access and preventing obsolescence of our cultural heritage is important to every science, every area of study, and every student of life.

The articles selected for this issue were solicited through several listservs and professional conferences. The letters of intent were vetted by our editorial board, and invitations to submit papers were sent in spring 2013. The board suggested categories or sections for organizing the issue and reviewed the final papers. The papers were returned to the authors after careful copyediting (by Karen Miller) for final approval. Sections include: Best Practices, Digital Communities, Education, Field Reports, Technology, and the beginnings of a Review section. We plan to add reviews of conferences, professional activities, books, and film (if applicable) to the review section for the next issue. Each section has an introduction and each article has an abstract. Karen Miller, Dr. Jennifer Arns, and Dr. Elise Lewis all contributed to these introductions.

The authors for Volume I hold a variety of positions in several disciplines including:

- Archivists and digital archivists for film archives
- Computer science faculty
- Curators of special collections and archives
- Education, language, and literacy faculty and administration
- Lecturers in information management and information studies
- Library and information science faculty and administration
- Librarians from digital library services, special collections, and international university libraries
- Media arts faculty
- Moving image archiving and preservation programs
- practitioners

We are very proud to present this first of a series. Sometimes it seems that the first is always most challenging, so we are looking forward to working on the second volume with plans to publish articles from 2014 in early spring 2015. Any comments, suggestions, or submissions should come directly to Sam at hastings@sc.edu.

Please enjoy, and take the time to read each article, as they not only tell a story as a collection but share some of the challenges and best practices in our field. Remember, if we don't provide access in perpetuity to our cultural heritage we may not have it in the future. It is up to us to organize and preserve these precious artifacts, objects, and distributed digital content.

Part I

BEST PRACTICES

BEST PRACTICES: INTRODUCTION

A common theme of the articles included in the Best Practices section is the increasingly converging, distributed, and pluralistic nature of digital cultural heritage. New perspectives addressing the constraints of traditional preservation and access methodologies are suggested. The question of whether institutional cultures represent major challenges to digitization, convergence, and preservation is explored.

In "Digital Preservation: Whose Responsibility?" Michèle V. Cloonan (dean emerita and professor, Simmons Graduate School of Library and Information Science) and Martha Mahard (professor of practice, Simmons Graduate School of Library and Information Science) suggest that preservation of digital cultural heritage is inherently pluralistic, with diverse groups of people holding varying preservation perspectives. With digital preservation activities becoming increasingly distributed, decentralized, and ad hoc while incorporating new forms of social networking, traditional models of preservation programs may no longer be effective. The reasons for this shift are explored and new preservation perspectives are suggested.

As part of the increasingly distributed nature of digital cultural heritage, Daniel Gelaw Alemneh (Digital Libraries Services, University of North Texas Libraries) and Abebe Rorissa (Department of Information Studies, University at Albany, State University of New York) explore the use of folksonomies by cultural heritage institutions. In "Facilitating Discovery and Use of Digital Cultural Heritage Resources with Folksonomies: A Review," the authors identify emerging trends in this area and consider the potential benefits and controversies surrounding user supplied tags or keywords as complements to established controlled vocabularies. The authors suggest that, by providing high-level descriptions and representations, such topical and natural approaches to the subject matter in digital collections may empower users and promote diverse, collaborative online environments.

Jeannette A. Bastian (professor at the Graduate School of Library and Information Science, Simmons College, Boston) and Ross Harvey (formerly of the Graduate School of Library and Information Science, Simmons College, Boston) comment in "Experiments in Cultural Heritage Informatics: Convergence and Divergence" that the major challenges for digitization, convergence, and digital preservation are cultural and professional in nature rather than technological. The authors describe their research on the convergence of cultural heritage institutions conducted in the context of the Simmons Digital Curriculum Laboratory and the digital convergence projects negotiated and completed by faculty and students. The trajectory for convergence is evaluated based on their findings.

1

Digital Preservation: Whose Responsibility?

Michèle V. Cloonan and Martha Mahard

ABSTRACT

Preservation seeks to ensure the memory of civilizations and the longevity of oral and recorded information. This paper suggests that the preservation of digital cultural heritage is inherently pluralistic in the sense that many preservation perspectives are held by increasingly diverse groups of people. Digital preservation activities are becoming increasingly distributed, decentralized, and ad hoc while incorporating new forms of social networking. Thus, traditional models of preservation programs, which depend on extant institutional structures, may no longer be effective. The reasons for this shift are explored and new preservation perspectives are suggested.

INTRODUCTION

Preservation seeks to ensure the memory of civilizations and the longevity of oral and recorded information. The need for the preservation of documents has been recognized for nearly three thousand years, beginning with such early texts as the Bible. Recognition of the importance of preservation is manifest in many historical texts that talk of preserving history, documents, ideas, and the oral and written record, though only rarely do early writers propose strategies for achieving the longevity of cultural heritage.

By the beginning of the twentieth century, a broader view of preservation was emerging. For example, in the United States the importance of preserving parks and historic buildings was acknowledged and acted upon in the nineteenth century.[1] Later, in 1906, the Antiquities Act was passed to protect Native American archaeo-

Figure 1.1.

logical sites on federal lands. Meanwhile, in Brussels, at the International Congress of Archivists and Librarians, Paul Otlet and Robert Goldschmidt proposed microform (*livre micrographique*) as a way to record and store documents efficiently.[2] The Hague Convention for the Protection of Cultural Property in Case of Armed Conflict emerged as a result of two peace conferences held in The Hague in 1899 and 1907. Subsequent revisions of the Convention were made in 1954 and throughout the rest of the twentieth century. These events were, perhaps, rehearsals for the even larger world stage on which digital preservation is now played (see Figure 1.1).

A CONSIDERATION OF TERMINOLOGY

The conservator is a technical specialist who treats objects. A preservationist is a managerial specialist (Association of North American Graduate Programs in Conservation [ANAGPIC], 2000, p. 68). These distinctions were reinforced and formalized in 1981 when the School of Library Service at Columbia University and the Conservation Center at the Institute of Fine Arts at New York University created graduate training programs, one for conservators of library and archival *materials*, the other for preservation administrators ("Columbia Programs," 1981).

Since then, libraries and archives have continued to distinguish between the managerial and treatment components of preservation.

The Columbia conservation program was designed for library and archival *materials*. Librarians refer to the items in their collections as *materials*, archivists as *records*, and museums call them *objects*. These distinctions sometimes point to the different ways in which we preserve and conserve things. A treatment decision for a book that is to be checked out of the library is different from that of an object that will only rarely be handled. In a library most items are mass-produced rather than unique; exhibits are usually of special collections and archival items. Records are usually one-of-a-kind documents that have historical and/or legal significance. A document tends to be part of a *fonds*, which is a body of records that originate from an organization, family, or individual. In museums, objects are usually one of a kind. Staff in museums, libraries, and archives, using variant terminology, think of the kinds of materials they oversee in different ways, and the preservation of their holdings, likewise, is handled with different uses, needs, and audiences in mind.

Although we have chosen to use the term *preservation* to encompass all media, scholars like Ross Harvey tend to use terms such as *stewardship* and *curation* to represent a broad vision of care and management of digital objects. In this paper, *preservation* will be the term we use to describe global activities with *curation* and *stewardship* reserved for more specific digital activities (see also Lazorchak, 2011). We have chosen to use *preservation* for the sake of historical continuity since we are talking about past practices as well as future directions.

THE PAST AS PRELUDE

Conservation and preservation became academic fields only in the twentieth century. Several developments led to their professionalization:

1. Research scientists were hired in museum conservation labs: the Berlin Royal Museums (1888), British Museum (1920), and Fogg Art Museum, Harvard University, were three of the first museums to incorporate science and research into conservation work.
2. Professional journals were established: *Technical Studies, in the Field of the Fine Arts*, which was published by the Fogg from 1932 to 1942, was the first; today there are hundreds of journals, newsletters, listservs, and blogs across several preservation-related fields.
3. Graduate programs were established. In 1960, New York University established an art conservation program, the first in the States. Four years later, Columbia University established a program in historic preservation. Some twenty years later, Columbia established graduate programs in libraries and archives conservation and preservation. (Graduate programs in moving image archive studies

were established over the past decade. More recently, certificate programs in digital curation and stewardship have been introduced. If history is any indication, such offerings may eventually become degree programs.)

4. Promulgation of international charters established the notion of world heritage. This has extended to digital heritage, of which two examples are the UNESCO *Guidelines for the Preservation of Digital Heritage* (2003) and *The Memory of the World in the Digital Age: Digitization and Preservation* (2012–2013).

5. Professional associations for library, archive, and museum professions provide preservation advocacy. At its first General Conference in 1948, the International Council of Museums "recommended that UNESCO should extend the scope of action of the Museums Division into a new Museums and Monuments Division" (Jokilehto, 2009, p. 26). Others include the American Library Association Preservation Policy statement adopted in 1991, and the Society of American Archivists 1996 statement on the preservation of digitized reproductions.

The ways in which we think about digital preservation build on numbers one through five, above. However, some new contexts and conditions for preservation have also emerged. These include:

6. The ownership of digital cultural heritage, which may include digital surrogates of analog originals or born-digital objects, is not always clear.

7. Intellectual property issues relating to ownership and fair use are complex and constantly changing.

8. There are changing notions of what collections are, and an ever-increasing community of content creators. Heritage institutions are focusing more on users than ever before. There are so many standards and the landscape changes so rapidly that it is hard to know who is using what and what a particular institutional strategy should be. To wit: In 1990 *The American Archivist* published an article compiled for the SAA Task Force on Archival Standards by Victoria Irons Walch, "Checklist of Standards Applicable to the Preservation of Archives and Manuscripts." More than one hundred fifty standards related in some way to archival preservation appear on this list. These included standards developed by the International Organization for Standardization; the American National Standards Institute as well as ANSI-accredited standards developing organizations; other technical and professional associations such as the American Library Association, the Research Libraries Group, and the American Institute for Conservation of Historic and Artistic Work; and U.S. Federal Agencies, including the Library of Congress. To compile a similar checklist today that would include digital preservation standards would be daunting, as standards have multiplied and proliferated at a staggering rate. Of course, the pace at which technology changes means that traditional methods of standards development are unable to keep up with the developments in

the field. In many areas professionals are relying on discipline-specific "best practice" guidelines. The Digital Preservation Coalition offers helpful advice on navigating the current landscape of standards and institutional strategies (Digital Preservation Coalition [DPC], 2012). How do we balance the incontrovertible need for standards with the ever-increasing need for access to big data, for example?

9. No cultural heritage institution can achieve digital preservation alone. While collaborative approaches to preservation—such as microfilming and digitization projects—have been around for many decades, these approaches must now include an ever more diverse group of stakeholders, including users.[3]

THE PRELUDE HAS PASSED

One theme that has emerged in the literature in recent years is that librarians, archivists, and museum professionals have to focus less on perfection and more on access. The reason is simple: there is so much digital information being created that we can no longer impose the standards that we used for organizing and preserving analog materials. Paul Conway (2013) addressed this issue in a recent article he titled "Preserving Imperfection: Assessing the Incidence of Digital Imaging Error in HathiTrust." Mark A. Greene and Dennis Meissner (2005) advocated for less processing of archival collections in "More Product, Less Process: Revamping Traditional Archival Processing." In a study on the impact of information technology on museum workers, one of the findings was that there is a tension between access to collections on the web and the accuracy of information about them (Duff et al., 2009).

Libraries, archives, and museums gather, organize, steward, and display objects, and engage and converse with their users and visitors. While these cultural heritage institutions act to ensure the sustainability of their collections, they approach it in distinctly different ways. We must reconcile these differences and advocate for collaboration to care for all collections. We must consider differences and commonalities between practices in museums, archives, and libraries. In so doing, we hope to encourage a holistic view of preservation issues that transcends institutional boundaries.

Collections, whether digital or analog, are given meaning by institutions. Museums focus on exhibition and education, libraries on organization and dissemination, and archives on reliability and authenticity of records. Though these central aims may be somewhat different, museums and libraries are currently grappling with the notion of collections in a digital world. Libraries, archives, and museums are rethinking the role of users—who no longer have to walk through our doors to access our collections. Museums are reporting their efforts to accommodate the so-called paradigm shift from the old object-centric, inward-looking institution to the more outward-facing, visitor-centered, and even performative experience. In some ways this is a similar game-changing notion to the idea that a library collection may not be made up of physical objects but may be more about access than ownership.

The fundamental shifts that are taking place in cultural heritage institutions will affect ways we think about—and carry out—preservation. For example, while research libraries presumably are responsible for preserving collections "for the ages," will that responsibility be lessened as an increasing percentage of collections are no longer owned? Will there be two preservation models, one for legacy collections and one for digital collections? Who will carry out which responsibilities?

Perhaps preservation in a museum setting versus preservation in a library setting can be likened to the old quip that Britain and America are two countries divided by a common language. Libraries preserve materials for *access* while museums preserve objects for display and study, not generally for *use*. Like all generalizations, there are notable exceptions. The National Museum of the American Indian (NMAI) shows how conservation and documentary research can be integrated into museum activities. The following description taken from the NMAI website proves this point:

> Although maintained as four discrete components, the Object, Photo Archive, Media Archive, and Paper Archive collections are deeply intertwined since each contains items that relate to one another: *Photo and Media Archives* include images of objects in use in Native communities or excavation contexts and the *Paper Archive* includes fieldnotes and documentation for all aspects of the combined collections. Through implementation of its Collecting Plan, NMAI hopes to expand the scope of the collections and continue its historically significant work in documenting indigenous lives and perspectives—through objects, diverse media, and other means—while simultaneously *increasing the integration of the collections* with one another *and making them more applicable to museum programs and accessible to external users.*

CONSERVATION

Considered one of the premier facilities in the conservation field for work with Native Americans on ethnographic and archaeological materials, the Conservation Office has a permanent staff of conservators, a mount-maker, and a management support assistant that is regularly augmented by Mellon fellows, interns, and contractors, making for a staff size that ranges from twelve to fourteen people at any one time.

Recent NMAI Conservation Office activities include *conservation research projects*; the documentation, [and] treatment [of] mountmaking [for] objects on exhibit at the . . . museum . . . ; *interviews with contemporary Native American artists, . . . documentation and archiving processes . . . collaborative investigations*: DNA analysis of hair on Salish blankets; technical study of Andean . . . ceremonial drinking vessels; identification, properties and use of Native Alaskan cultural material made of gutskin, experimentation with new materials and techniques in mannequin making, and evaluation of materials for mount-making, storage, and exhibition casework. (National Museum of the American Indian [NMAI], 2013a, 2013b; italics added.)

NMAI collections are actively used by tribes, so conservators must decide on treatments that will facilitate use. NMAI demonstrates new directions for the conservation field in which a community of users may play a dynamic role in conservation. In the case of Native Americans and First Nations, there are many historical, political, social, and cultural issues to consider. Two conservators, Sherelyn Ogden (2004) and Miriam Clavir (2002), have explored these issues in depth as well as the resulting changes in institutional practices. So for most kinds of collections—libraries, archives, or museums—it may be possible, practical, and even necessary to engage the institution's users in decision making with respect to the acquisition, display, use, conservation, and preservation of its holdings.

When a museum has a library and archive, conservators must understand critical differences in making treatment decisions. When and how should a book be rebound? What are the treatment issues for a *fonds* as opposed to those for an individual document? How much and what type of cosmetic treatment is to be given to an object that will be displayed or exhibited? And just what are the distinct differences in displaying documents, books, paintings, and other objects?

The NMAI model could be successfully applied to digital objects; it could encourage those responsible for preservation to work closely with the creators of digital information from the outset to work out how digital collections will be transferred to institutional collections, rights issues, and sustainable formats. Increasingly, content is created by groups of people through social media. Archiving social media will necessitate new models for long-term preservation. Who owns content? Who keeps it?

In 2010 Twitter signed a deal with the Library of Congress giving the library access to contents dating back to the company's inception in 2006. Since then the library has struggled to keep up with four hundred million daily tweets and has yet to develop a satisfactory or scalable method of providing access to the information in the more than thirty terabytes amassed so far. The deal with Twitter was presented as in line with the Library's mission "to collect the story of America and to acquire collections that will have research value" (Allen, 2013).

As the twentieth century ended, libraries and archives were already grappling with efforts to archive parts of the web. Some early efforts were undertaken at the national level led by Australia (1996) and Sweden (1996). The University of North Texas developed the CyberCemetery for defunct government websites. Other projects began as ad hoc efforts in response to local or national events. Many projects such as the UCLA Online Campaign Literacy Archive and the Library of Congress's September 11 Archive developed strategies that combined desktop web-capture programs supplemented by manual file downloading. New technology, unavailable at the start of many such projects, will allow for more automated workflows and improved sustainability. As yet, however, human intervention for selection and access remain essential (Niu, 2012a).

Organizations such as the Internet Archive (IA), also begun in 1996, are becoming increasingly important players in digital preservation, as are service providers like IA's Archive-It and the California Digital Library's University of California Curation Center Web Archiving Service (WAS). The Internet Archive in partnership with Archive-It maintains pages for "Global Events" and "Spontaneous Events" where it collects web pages and social media documents from natural disasters (the Haiti earthquake), tragedies (the Boston Marathon bombing), and protest movements (Occupy Movement, 2011–2012). Institutions frequently step forward to begin the capture of web content related to events and then continue to maintain some responsibility for these resources with the help of the Internet Archive. For example, Virginia Polytechnic Institute, itself the site of a tragic shooting in 2007, had within a matter of days archived more than two hundred Twitter and RSS feeds relating to the Boston Marathon bombing. At Northeastern University in Boston a website called *Our Marathon* has been established, partnering with the Internet Archive and the Digital Public Library of America. Other web-content collections are less event-driven and more systematic perhaps, but the problem remains one of responsibility. Collecting around a topic without objects to preserve physically still remains a challenge that involves human and financial resources. How will such efforts be sustained?

Within institutions, there are several current models for preservation, some of which are departmental, but in some institutions, preservation is often a distributed activity. That is, there do not tend to be preservation managers and preservation departments. The activities may take place throughout the museum in the IT department, registrar's offices, security departments, circulation, exhibition preparation units, curatorial departments, and elsewhere. The museum library may have responsibility for overseeing library-specific preservation concerns such as stacks maintenance, rebinding, and rehousing of items.

The literature on library preservation management is voluminous, as are the number of publications on each aspect of preservation. Less has been written on preservation in the museum and archives literature. Therefore, the comprehensive and centralized preservation programs that have existed in research and university libraries since the late 1970s offer one model of how collections are preserved.

New models for preservation are emerging, and the literature does not yet reflect a full range of preservation approaches. The International Council on Museums (ICOM), International Committee for the Training of Personnel (ICTOP), has issued guidelines for museum professional development (International Council on Museums [ICOM], 2010). The document identifies five competencies for museum professionals: "Management," "Information and Collections Management and Care," "Public Programming," "Museology," and "General" (see table 1.1). Preservation is not singled out as a core competency because its activities are distributed across the ICOM/ICTOP competencies. We think that this is an approach that has relevance for the preparation of all professionals who may work on preservation initiatives.

This schema is useful in several ways. It demonstrates that in museums, preservation activities are distributed throughout. It also suggests that graduates of museum studies programs have been introduced to preservation principles in their degree programs. However, museums employ professionals who have many other credentials; how and where do *they* learn about preservation? Many of these issues overlap those in the archives and library realms. This integration of preservation into the overall

Table 1.1.   Preservation-Related Topics Appearing in the ICTOP Guidelines for Professional Development

I. General
Environmental audits and sustainable practices

II. Museology
Issues in museum practices
   Physical access
   Repatriation of cultural patrimony, human remains, funerary goods
Legal context for practice
   Cultural heritage conventions
   Copyright and artists' rights
   Artistic freedom of expression

III. Management
Architecture
   Environmental controls

Financial planning and management
   Risk Management

IV. Public Programming
Exhibitions
   Lighting
   Design and installation
Visitor Service and public relationships
   Preservation requirements of collection and structure
   Education

V. Information and Collections Management and Care
Collections
   Agents of deterioration: physical, chemical, and biological factors
   Collection issues
   Preventive care
   Copies/reproductions/digitization
   Copyright
   Environmental monitoring and control
   Packing and transporting
   Pest Management
   Principles of conservation/restoration
   Properties of materials, implications for preservation

curriculum is highly desirable. Ideally the notion of digital stewardship should be incorporated under almost every area in the schema.

While libraries, museums, and archives will need to preserve their collections in traditional ways, they must also adapt to the preservation needs of new technologies. And because of the evolution of technology, it is probably no longer possible to consolidate the various functions of preservation into one department or program. Although in the past it has worked well in libraries to have a centralized department, today you could never have all of the experts that you need in one unit, nor can a museum preservation expert know all that needs to be known to protect all the analog and digital materials held by the museum or to know other issues related to preservation. For example, in large institutions you may have attorneys on staff. Legal issues surrounding preservation such as copyright and artistic freedom of expression must be attended to in libraries, archives, and museums. Each institution has its own prevalent issues: in libraries, it is copyright and site licensing; in archives, ownership and retention schedules for records; in museums, it is ownership, provenance, publication rights for images, deaccessioning of objects, and so on. There is no need for a person to work in a single department, nor can one person know all that is required to preserve what needs to be saved.

DIGITAL PRESERVATION

Over the past fifteen years, there have been ample opportunities for libraries, archives, and museums to collaborate in the digital environment. They now share collections and cocurate exhibitions online, and collaborate in a number of other ways as well. However, there have often been obstacles to collaboration because libraries, archives, and museums have different ways of describing and cataloging their collections. Differences in practices, vocabularies, and online systems in use have created interoperability issues.

How do we preserve our digital content, particularly in light of some of these basic differences across our fields? The challenges of digital preservation are similar for all of us: *records that are born digital or converted to digital form need to be continuously sustained to assure long-term access to them.* There are many components of digital preservation: technical, organizational, legal, fiscal, and so on. Content creation, integrity, and maintenance must conform to standards and best practices. There must be sustainable economic models on which digital preservation actions can rest. It is important for librarians, archivists, and museum professionals to work toward a common vocabulary and common practices in much of what they do if they want to create commonalities in their operations—commonalities that will enhance overall cataloging and preservation activities.

Digital preservation "combines policies, strategies and actions that ensure access to digital content over time. The goal . . . is the accurate rendering of authenticated content over time" (Association for Library Collections & Technical Services

[ALCTS], 2009). As with the preservation of our physical heritage, digital preservation must remain focused on future users and how they will require access to information. Best practices for required functionality are evolving but more remains to be done (Niu, 2012b).

SUSTAINABILITY AND STEWARDSHIP

In the Getty publication *Values and Heritage Conservation*, published just over a decade ago, the editors suggested that "Underpinning this research is the assumption that heritage is an integral part of civil society. . . . Conservation shapes the society in which it is situated, and in turn, it is shaped by the needs and dynamics of that society" (Avrami, Mason, & de la Torre, 2000, p. 3). At the heart of sustainability is *stewardship*, the belief that resources can be managed through successive generations. Indeed, stewardship is commonly used in the environmental community.

In 2010, the European Commission (EC) passed the Europe 2020 strategy to "generate smart, sustainable, and inclusive growth" in the European Union (European Commission, 2010, p. 10). Three interrelated priorities were established:

- Smart growth
- Inclusive growth
- Sustainable growth

Sustainable growth considers climate change and energy. The 2020 strategy seeks to reduce greenhouse gas emissions at least 20% from 1990 levels, derive 20% of energy from renewable sources, and realize a 20% increase in energy efficiency.

While this will affect libraries, archives, and museums in Europe soon, there is a move toward sustainability in the United States, too. Since the 1990s, conservation scientists, such as Donald K. Sebera and James M. Reilly, have advocated for new environmental management approaches. Reilly now focuses on sustainable preservation practices, offering workshops and tools through the Image Permanence Institute at the Rochester Institute of Technology. The impetus for these changes is coming from the conservation and preservation fields as well as from directors of cultural heritage institutions. Museums, libraries, and archives, if they are responsible, will work together to create environmental sustainability as well as preservation-level sustainability for their collections. As we mentioned above, this will take intra-institutional collaboration and mutual understanding of the different realms of activities in cultural heritage institutions.

In the recently concluded study "Framing the Digital Curation Curriculum" conducted in Europe, a framework was developed that used the concept of lenses through which to consider what skills were needed at various managerial and operational levels. The three levels are: executive, manager, and practitioner. The executive level takes a strategic view of digital curation—"To understand the emerging challenges in digital curation for the cultural heritage sector, and to make informed funding decisions to meet these challenges." The managerial lens incorporates planning, executing, and monitoring digital curation projects. This also includes recruiting and supporting project teams and working with a variety of internal and external stakeholders. The practitioner lens refers to planning and technical skills, and working on interdisciplinary teams to carry out digital projects. We recommend that people read the entire study, in which the authors consider how we impart these skills to students. Of relevance to this discussion is that these lenses illustrate how there needs to be engagement at every stage of the organization for institutions to successfully carry out and sustain digital programs (DigCurV, 2013).

The Art Institute of Chicago's Sam Quigley, a long-time leader in museum technology, conducted a survey of nine major art museums in the United States in 2004 to find out about digital preservation policy development, particularly with respect to born-digital works of art. The survey found that none of the respondents had a policy specifically for digital preservation, but most had "well considered procedures" for creating and managing digital assets. Most respondents admitted to little preparation, active planning, or written policies on digital preservation. These institutions had written policies in a variety of other areas including deaccessioning and codes of ethics. About half had written policies on intellectual property and records management. The museums themselves realize the value of institutionally adopted policies in this arena. Two examples cited in support of this were uniform procedures and financial planning. To move forward we must find a way to "transcend the procedures," as Quigley observes (Quigley, 2004). As one of Quigley's respondents pointed out, in the end, the primary goal is the effective management and preservation of all of our collections.

CLOSING THOUGHTS

How do we ensure that adequate coordination takes place to insure the preservation of our heritage? It is not certain that we can. The increasing breadth and complexity of preservation—and the increasingly broad stakeholder groups—will demand new and flexible institutional and global approaches. These approaches will need to be decentralized, ad hoc, and increasingly open to new forms of social networking. Digital collections transcend traditional boundaries. Preservation must include many stakeholders. It is inherently pluralistic and no one perspective will suffice.

NOTES

This paper draws on two presentations that the authors prepared for the following conferences: "Bridges and Boundaries Conference," Reinwardt Academy for Cultural Heritage, Amsterdam, School of the Arts, September 13–15, 2012; and "Art Museum Libraries Symposium: Volume II," Phillips Library of the Peabody Essex Museum, Salem, MA, September 20–21, 2012.

1. For example, in 1875, Yellowstone National Park was established—an acknowledgment that the U.S. government had responsibility for preserving national lands. In 1910 the Society for the Preservation of New England Antiquities (SPNEA) was founded by William Sumner Appleton, and others. Similar movements were taking place in Europe.

2. International Congress of Archivists and Librarians, Brussels, August 28–31, 1910.

3. See Figure 1, "Preservation Principles and Practices Applicable to Analog and Digital Materials" in Harvey and Mahard (2013, p. 10). The general principles for digital preservation include: collaboration, advocacy, active managed care, and so on.

REFERENCES

Allen, E. (2013, January 4). Update on the Twitter archive at the Library of Congress. [Web log comment]. Retrieved from http://blogs.loc.gov/loc/2013/01/update-on-the-twitter-archive-at-the-library-of-congress/

Association for Library Collections & Technical Services (ALCTS). (2009). Definitions of digital preservation. Retrieved from http://www.ala.org/alcts/resources/preserv/2009def

Association of North American Graduate Programs in Conservation (ANAGPIC). (2000). *North American graduate programs in the conservation of cultural property: Histories, alumni.* Buffalo, NY: ANAGPIC. Retrieved from https://www.ischool.utexas.edu/~anagpic/histalum_full.pdf

Avrami, E., Mason, R., & de la Torre, M. (2000). *Values and heritage conservation: Research report.* Los Angeles, CA: The Getty Conservation Institute. Retrieved from http://www.getty.edu/conservation/publications_resources/pdf_publications/values_heritage_research_report.html

Clavir, M. (2002). *Preserving what is valued: Museums, conservation, and First Nations.* Vancouver, BC: University of British Columbia Press.

Columbia programs announced. (1981, February). *Abbey Newsletter, 5*(1). Retrieved from http://cool.conservation-us.org/byorg/abbey/an/an05/an05-1/an05-103.html

Conway, P. (2013). Preserving imperfection: Assessing the incidence of digital imaging error in HathiTrust. *Preservation, Digital Technology & Culture, 42*(1), 17–30.

DigCurV. (2013). *The executive lens.* Retrieved from http://www.digcurv.gla.ac.uk/executiveLens.html

Digital Preservation Coalition (DPC). (2012). *Institutional strategies—Standards and best practice guidelines.* Retrieved from http://www.dpconline.org/advice/preservationhandbook/institutional-strategies/standards-and-best-practice-guidelines

Duff, W., Carter, J., Dallas, C., Howarth, L., Ross, S., Sheffield, R., & Tilson, C. (2009). The changing museum environment in North America and the impact of technology on museum work. In *Proceedings: Cultural heritage on line. Empowering users: An active role for user communities.* Florence, Italy, December 16, 2009. Retrieved from http://www.rinascimento-digitale.it/eventi/conference2009/proceedings-2009/duff.pdf

European Commission. (2010). *Communication from the Commission. Europe 2020: A strategy for smart, sustainable and inclusive growth.* Retrieved from http://eur-lex.europa.eu/LexUriServ/LexUriServ.do?uri=COM:2010:2020:FIN:EN:PDF

Greene, M. A., & Meissner, D. (2005, Fall/Winter). More product, less process: Revamping traditional archival processing. *American Archivist, 68*(2), 208–63.

Harvey, R., & Mahard, M. (2013). Mapping the preservation landscape for the twenty-first century. *Preservation, Digital Technology & Culture, 42*(1), 5–16. doi: 10.1515/pdtc-2013-0002

International Council of Museums, International Committee for the Training of Personnel (ICOM). (2010). *ICOM curricula guidelines for museum professional development.* Retrieved from http://museumstudies.si.edu/ICOM-ICTOP/comp.htm

Jokilehto, J. (2009). ICCROM's first fifty years. *Museum International, 61*(3), 26–35. doi: 10.1111/j.1468-0033.2009.01690.x

Lazorchak, B. (2011, August 23). Digital preservation, digital curation, digital stewardship: What's in (some) names?" *The Signal: Digital Preservation.* Retrieved from http://blogs.loc.gov/digitalpreservation/2011/08/digital-preservation-digital-curation-digital-stewardship-what's-in-some-names

National Museum of the American Indian (NMAI). (2013a). Collections. Retrieved from http://nmai.si.edu/explore/collections/

National Museum of the American Indian (NMAI). (2013b). Conservation. Retrieved from http://nmai.si.edu/explore/collections/conservation/

Niu, J. (2012a, March/April). An overview of web archiving. *D-Lib magazine, 18*(3/4). Retrieved from http://www.dlib.org/dlib/march12/niu/03niu1.html

Niu, J. (2012b, March/April). Functionalities of web archives. *D-Lib magazine, 8*(3/4). Retrieved from http://www.dlib.org/dlib/march12/niu/03niu2.html

Ogden, S. (2004). *Caring for American Indian objects: A practical and cultural guide.* St. Paul, MN: Minnesota Historical Society.

Quigley, S. (2004). *Digital preservation policy development in art museums: A survey of nine art museums in the USA* [PowerPoint slides]. Retrieved from www.museumcomputernetwork.org/old-conferences/ …/sq.pps.ppt

2

Facilitating Discovery and Use of Digital Cultural Heritage Resources with Folksonomies

A Review

Daniel Gelaw Alemneh and Abebe Rorissa

ABSTRACT

The increase in the number and heterogeneity of digital resources has led cultural heritage institutions to develop tools, workflows, and quality-assurance mechanisms that allow effective digital resource management. In their quest for better discoverability of existing digital resources, cultural heritage institutions attempt to enrich traditional catalogs and enhance metadata with additional user-supplied terms and descriptions such as folksonomies. The current landscape in the use of folksonomies by cultural heritage institutions is reviewed and emerging trends in this area identified. Strengths and limitations of folksonomies vis-à-vis traditional indexing and taxonomies are explored with a particular emphasis on the history of cultural heritage information retrieval, including a consideration of the potential benefits and controversies surrounding user-supplied tags or keywords as complements to established controlled vocabularies. By providing high-level descriptions and representations, such topical and natural approaches to the subject matter in a digital collection may empower users of digital libraries of cultural heritage resources and promote diverse, collaborative online environments.

INTRODUCTION

Today's cultural heritage institutions may still be located within a physical facility with four walls, but the resources that they collect, process, manage, and disseminate, and the services that they deliver, are increasingly accessible through online and distributed means. A review of the current landscape in digital libraries in terms of best practices and emerging trends shows that there is no shortage of opinions on the roles of information environments that evolved from local resource repositories to global gateways for access.

In this age of growing interdisciplinarity and constant changes in users' requirements, access to digital content in general, and digital cultural heritage resources in particular, relies on a seamless discovery process that offers all possible options to users. Many patrons of today's libraries are individuals who are members of Generation Y; they have grown up expecting rapid delivery of information via the latest technologies. The successful curation of cultural heritage resources in an information environment requires efforts across their entire life cycle to ensure that they are created, managed, preserved, and made accessible in a manner that today's users expect.

Trends and Current Practice

The digital environment has introduced new resource types, new partners, and new user expectations into the current information landscape. As research and scientific inquiry depends on both the availability of heterogeneous resources and their easy and continuous accessibility, enabling knowledge creation and facilitating long-term access to information resources becomes critical. As illustrated in figure 2.1, when building digital collections, digital curators need to be aware of and consider various factors as well as value-added services that facilitate management of the digital content in terms of making them more visible, accessible, usable, reusable, interoperable, and persistent.

Cultural heritage digital resources demand a more specialized treatment and characterization that can help to better capture their semantics and relations as well as the underlying contents and concepts. Seamless access to trustworthy and meaningful digital resources requires cultural heritage institutions to identify, preserve, and make accessible significant digital content and also to capture the relationships of these artifacts to the contexts within which they were created and curated. People, institutions, places, and events are all important constituents. Although different metadata elements are often mutually complementary, good subject or keyword terms help users find what they are seeking, even when they are not aware of their needs.

To deliver a richer user experience, it is critical to ensure the quality of the keywords and taxonomies used to describe heterogeneous digital resources within digital libraries. Various emerging (Web 2.0 and/or 3.0) applications, driven by semantic web technologies such as the web ontology language (OWL), the resource description framework (RDF), semantic web rules language (SWRL), and other families of World Wide Web Consortium (W3C) specifications offer powerful data organization, combination, and query capabilities.

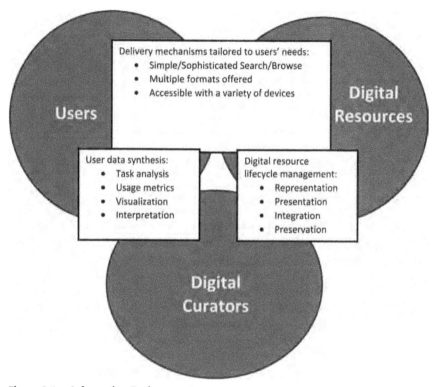

Figure 2.1. Information Environment

INDEXING AND REPRESENTATION

Cultural heritage institutions exist to connect users with resources and information. In a traditional library, for example, a card or online catalog is merely one aspect of finding and accessing holdings, albeit an essential one. In the same way, for digital libraries, metadata records allow users to gain access to the digital resources. Successful metadata, indexing, and taxonomies add value—allowing users to explore and delve deeper than with a traditional static representation.

An index term is a systematic representation of an information-bearing object (text, image, audio, video, etc.) that points users to specific items on topics of interest. In other words, it is an information retrieval tool. As noted by Caropreso, Matwin, and Sebastiani (2001), one of the key issues for information retrieval (IR) and all other content-based text management applications is document indexing.

The generation of accurate indexing terms (i.e., an accurate representation of an information-bearing object) is fundamental to the discovery, use, and reuse of digital resources. Indexing enhances the accessibility and value of a resource, provided that it is based on a thorough analysis of the resource. A good index helps users find what they need, even when they are not sure of what they are looking for.

To fully understand what a good index is, it is necessary to be both micro- and macro-minded. On the micro level, we concern ourselves with the specific mechanics of creating an index term. On the macro level, indexing could be thought of as part of a larger context of an information retrieval system. At the basic level, retrieval of information involves the user expressing an information need in the form of an information retrieval request or query with terms from the common vernacular and matching requests with stored records.

Different metadata elements describe different characteristics or aspects of an object or digital resource. However, users are interested in the contents and the subjects rather than in what the objects are. The most useful metadata about a digital object are the subjects (or keywords), since they explicitly describe what the object is about. To describe digital resources accurately, metadata creators and catalogers try to follow (as closely as possible) the thinking of an object's creator/author, and also anticipate what the users might want to discover and how they will want to retrieve the object. Otherwise, the descriptions or subject headings will be ineffective. Wichowski (2009) noted that in the rapidly growing information environment, unidentified and unorganized content, however useful it may be, is at risk of being rendered unfindable, and thus obsolete.

A number of researchers, Bates (1998), Peterson (2006), and Spiteri (2007), among others, analyzed content indexing (especially subject indexing) and described the general behavior of users' information seeking and their queries. Most of them agree that the two major reasons why users experience problems with subject access are the quality and application of subject index on the one hand and the complexity of knowledge and information literacy skills required for successful subject access on the other. To maintain the consistency of search results and high recall of available resources, it is critical to ensure the quality of the keywords and taxonomies used to index heterogeneous digital resources within digital libraries, especially those at cultural heritage institutions.

Thesaurus and Controlled Vocabularies

Libraries have been developing various systems for creating and managing controlled vocabularies for use in digital library initiatives. A thesaurus can be a useful tool for both organizers/indexers and users/searchers. Thesauri are types of controlled indexing vocabularies in which index terms are restricted to a predetermined set of terms. A standard thesaurus is constructed and managed as a set of terms. Links between concepts in the subject domain can be expressed by their semantic relationships (USE, USE for, broader/narrower, and related terms). This semantic index approach offers the potential for searcher and indexer to speak the same language and for a user to be guided to useful terms when searching a particular collection for a particular purpose.

Essentially, the purpose of most thesauri is to have "a manipulative system." However, too much control will make the device nonmanipulative and thus defeat its purpose. Empowering end users in searching heterogeneous collections requires a complex knowledge organization system. Thesauri need to be constructed and maintained in a manner that is consistent with a set of standards, which themselves are prone to ambiguous interpretations. However, most commentators agree that existing thesauri are lacking in sound semantics and structural consistency.

Having said that, selecting terms from a controlled vocabulary ensures indexing consistency and enhances retrieval precision across all digital resources. In this regard, controlled terms provide a broad navigational tool for browsing through digital content and digital library collections. Users can drill down through subordinate subject terms to find other content within that subject category. Such an approach promotes consistency and enhances a digital library user's ability to find and use available digital resources.

Considering the complexities and multifaceted issues involved in determining the level of indexing term quality, traditional approaches may not adequately address the diverse users' requirements and needs. It is critical for digital libraries to assess the practice that shapes the generation of subject terms and determines the effectiveness of subject and keyword access. Some (e.g., Fox, 2006) have long advocated the introduction of user-centered indexing by involving end-users and others in the process of organizing information resources by capturing index terms that may be of use in meeting their future information needs. User-centered indexing is now a reality, thanks in part to the increase in Web 2.0 social networking and tagging, where users are not only creators of content, but have also assumed the role of indexer (Peters, 2009; Rorissa, 2010).

Folksonomy

A folksonomy is a system that allows users to tag their own and/or others' digital resources using natural-language words. It is closely associated with social or collaborative tagging of online resources by a community of users. The term was originally coined by Thomas Vander Wal (2005) and represents a merging of the terms "folk" and "taxonomy."

As seen in figure 2.2, the different functionality of tagging, ranging from the personal vocabulary to its social dimensions can help users to find objects on the web that are of interest to them. Knowing the attributes of the person doing the tagging and having some indication of how the tags are to be utilized are both important to understand their overall functionality. In this regard, folksonomies and tagging can provide connections across disciplines and can supplement or make up for missing terms in a standard system or taxonomy. For instance, health informatics professionals can discern valuable information from health workers (who have domain knowledge) with different experiences and backgrounds when an object is tagged by both communities using their own differing terms of practice.

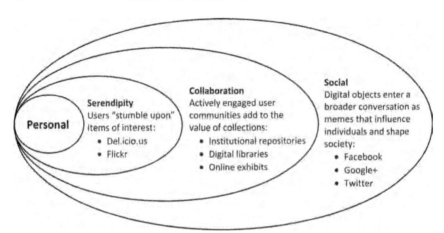

Figure 2.2. Functionality of Folksonomy

In a socially constructed metadata paradigm, users not only search/browse, access, and use content but also proactively participate in its production and description by tagging, rating, reviewing, highlighting, and recommending. Table 2.1 lists some of the popular sites that employ folksonomies. A number of libraries are using these sites to post tag clouds on their websites (Rethlefsen, 2007; Smith 2008).

There are small but growing initiatives in various cultural heritage institutions that have effectively engaged the user community, from transcribing content to correcting OCR output. For example, the Library of Congress is using Flickr for tagging its photograph collection (Cormode & Krishnamurthy, 2008; Steele, 2009). The library hopes allowing people to create tags will help to identify new information and enrich the descriptions for many of the old photos, which came to the library with "scanty descriptions" (Library of Congress, 2012).

Tapping into user knowledge does not mean that the information professionals curating a collection in a production environment would be able to step back from the collection after the core metadata was added. A number of cultural heritage institutions have recognized that fact. For instance, at the University of North Texas Libraries, the metadata set typically includes the more complex notion of the subject and keyword application. Where possible, the subject element is taken from a relevant controlled vocabulary (such as LCSH or TGN). In addition, in order to facilitate browsing, at least one (mandatory) subject must be chosen from the University of North Texas Libraries Browse Subjects, UNTL-BS list. This locally developed list (served on an in-house database) supports the browse feature of The Portal to Texas History. However, considering the various limitations and restrictions of the controlled subject terms, staff who enter data are encouraged to identify and apply terms that are not currently included in the UNTL Browse Subjects and propose them for addition to the list (UNT Libraries, 2013a; 2013b).

This raises the question of whether information retrieval is significantly improved by user-supplied tags and folksonomies and professionally applied keywords in ad-

Table 2.1. Popular Sites Employing Folksonomies

Site Name	Web Address	Description
Bibsonomy	http://www.bibsonomy.org	A system for sharing bookmarks and lists of literature
BlinkList	www.blinklist.com	A tool to "blink" web pages in one click from any browser
Citeulike	www.citeulike.org	A service for managing and discovering scholarly references
Del.icio.us	http://del.icio.us	A tool to save and organize the links found on the web
Diigo	https://www.diigo.com/	A web annotation, social bookmarking & research tool
Flickr	http://www.flickr.com	An online photo sharing and management application
Frassle	http://www.frassle	A source for information about (publishing) blogs
LibraryThing	www.librarything.com	An application for storing and sharing book catalogs/metadata
Scuttle	http://sourceforge.net/ projects/scuttle/scottle/	A system that allows multiple users to store, share, and tag their favorite links online
Tagzania	www.tagzania.com	Helps to create and share maps (tagging the planet)
Technorati	http://technorati.com	A blog search engine that indexes more than a million blogs
YouTube	www.youtube.com/	A video-sharing website

dition to traditional indexing methods (Van Damme, Hepp, & Siorpaes, 2007; Syn & Spring, 2013). A continuous assessment and better understanding of the virtues of tags and folksonomies in information representation, organization, and retrieval as well as their shortcomings vis-à-vis conventional indexing methods is necessary in order to seek answers to this and similar questions (Bar-Ilan, Shoham, Idan, Miller, & Shachak, 2008; Wolfram, Olson, & Bloom, 2009). This review is an attempt to keep the discussion going so as to seek clearer answers and consensus.

With respect to indexing and retrieval of cultural heritage collections, folksonomies and social tagging could even play a unique role because the indexing of cultural heritage items could be enhanced by tags supplied by users who are more knowledgeable about the items and their associated local history and language (Matusiak, 2006). In their search for better discoverability for existing digital resources, various types of cultural heritage institutions have attempted to enrich the traditional catalog and metadata of digital collections with additional user-supplied terms and descriptions, not to mention folksonomies, including moving image archives (Andreano, 2007), museum items (Chun, Cherry, Hiwiller, Trant, & Wyman, 2006; Trant, 2006), general archival materials (Evans, 2007), and art collections (Efron, Organisciak, & Fenlon, 2011; Fry, 2007).

Even though they have been in existence for some time, discussion about the pros and cons of folksonomies, as well as comparison to traditional information organization systems, is ongoing. There are both critics and proponents. Trant (2009) and Golder and Huberman (2006) were among the first authors to identify the negatives and positives of folksonomies and social tagging. First of all, unlike formal taxonomies and classification schemes where there are multiple kinds of explicit relationships (e.g., broader, narrower, and related terms) between and among terms, there are no clearly defined relations between and among the terms in a folksonomy. In addition, in folksonomies and social tagging systems, the semantic relations between words and their referents is imperfect (Golder & Huberman, 2006). Although folksonomies serve as classification systems, they are different from traditional controlled vocabularies such as thesauri and taxonomies where terms have hierarchical relationships (Gruber, 2005). Also, most critics point to the fact that an uncontrolled vocabulary leads to less effective information retrieval.

On the other hand, proponents argue that it is user-friendly and enables personalized information indexing and retrieval by users. In addition, as folksonomies are in a continual state of flux, they are better able to accommodate current terminology and concepts than traditional indexing tools and systems for the organization, management, and retrieval of digital library collections. Because social tagging and folksonomies are products of actions by users (who can also possibly be multicultural and multilingual) they can also be ideal test beds for cross-language retrieval of cultural heritage resources. Another benefit of folksonomies and tags is that they can be used to filter results of queries during retrieval to increase precision and decrease recall. They are also ideal tools for navigation and browsing—especially when retrieval systems organize their output and query results as tag clouds (Golder & Huberman, 2006; MacGregor & McCulloch, 2006; Matusiak, 2006).

In the emerging state of cultural abundance, as some commentators noted (e.g., Peterson, 2006; Spiteri, 2007; and TechSmith, 2008; among others), both approaches share a basic problem—the potential users of information are either fully or partially disconnected from the process of information indexing and organization. They believe combining both traditional indexing systems with folksonomies is the solution for delivering a richer user experience of digital libraries, including those of cultural heritage collections, while leveraging the benefits of composite applications, mashups, and service-oriented architectures. Many commentators (Weidner & Alemneh, 2013; Zhao, Liu, Tang, & Zhu, 2013; Hillmann, Dushay, & Phipps, 2004) also cautioned that involving all possible stakeholders and building a dedicated group of contributors requires an investment of repository staff time, as well as strategies for promoting data ownership, ensuring quality, and producing seamless integration.

SUMMARY

In the increasingly self-structured Web 2.0 environment, it is clear that traditional user experience and access methods will be of limited utility. However, it is unclear whether cultural heritage institutions are well-equipped to appeal to current users who have unprecedented access to cultural resources in a distributed and networked information environment.

In this brief paper, we presented the current landscape and emerging trends in indexing resources in digital libraries. We also reviewed the potentials of and controversies surrounding folksonomies versus taxonomies. Both topical and natural approaches to the subject matter in a digital collection provide high-level descriptions and representations. Such a combination of techniques will add value and enhance a digital library user's ability to find, access, use, and reuse available digital objects. Considering the emerging applications, combining the strengths of the two approaches indeed offers powerful information organization, management, and retrieval capabilities.

REFERENCES

Andreano, K. (2007). The missing link: Content indexing, user-created metadata, and improving scholarly access to moving image archives. *The Moving Image: The Journal of the Association of Moving Image Archivists, 7*(2), 82–99.

Bar-Ilan, J., Shoham, S., Idan, A., Miller, Y., & Shachak, A. (2008). Structured versus unstructured tagging: A case study. *Online Information Review, 32*(5), 635–647.

Bates, M. J. (1998). Indexing and access for digital libraries and the Internet: Human, database, and domain factors. *Journal of the American Society for Information Science, 49*(13), 1185–1205.

Caropreso, M. F., Matwin, S., & Sebastiani, F. (2001). A learner-independent evaluation of the usefulness of statistical phrases for automated text categorization. In A. G. Chin (Ed.), *Text databases and document management: Theory and practice* (pp. 78–102). Hershey, PA: Idea Group Publishing.

Chun, S., Cherry, R., Hiwiller, D., Trant, J., & Wyman, B. (2006). Steve.museum: An ongoing experiment in social tagging, folksonomy, and museums. In J. Trant & D. Bearman (Eds.), *Museums and the web 2006: Selected papers from an international conference* (pp. 93–107). Toronto, ON: Archives & Museum Informatics.

Cormode, G., & Krishnamurthy, B. (2008). Key differences between Web 1.0 and Web 2.0. *First Monday, 13*(6). Retrieved from http://www.uic.edu/htbin/cgiwrap/bin/ojs/index.php/fm/article/viewArticle/2125/1972

Efron, M., Organisciak, P., & Fenlon, K. (2011). Building topic models in a federated digital library through selective document exclusion. *Proceedings of the American Society for Information Science and Technology, 48*(1), 1–10.

Evans, M. J. (2007). Archives of the people, by the people, for the people. *The American Archivist, 70*(2), 387–400.

Fox, R. (2006). Cataloging for the masses. *OCLC Systems & Services, 22*(3), 166–172.

Fry, E. (2007). Of torquetums, flute cases, and puff sleeves: A study in folksonomic and expert image tagging. *Art Documentation: Journal of the Art Libraries Society of North America, 26*(1), 21–27.

Golder, S. A., & Huberman, B. A. (2006). Usage patterns of collaborative tagging systems. *Journal of Information Science, 32*(2), 198–208.

Gruber, T. (2005). Ontology of folksonomy: A mash-up of apples and oranges. Retrieved from http://tomgruber.org/writing/ontology-of-folksonomy.htm

Hillmann, D., Dushay, N., & Phipps, J. (2004). Improving metadata quality: Augmentation and recombination. In *Proceedings of the 2004 international conference on Dublin Core and metadata applications: Metadata across languages and cultures, 11–14 October 2004.* Singapore: Dublin Core Metadata Initiative. Retrieved from http://dcpapers.dublincore.org/pubs/article/view/770

Library of Congress (2012, July 23). *Prints & photographs reading room: Library of Congress photos on Flickr.* Retrieved from http://www.loc.gov/rr/print/flickr_pilot.html

MacGregor, G., & McCulloch, E. (2006). Collaborative tagging as a knowledge organisation and resource discovery tool. *Library View, 55*(5), 291–300.

Matusiak, K. K. (2006). Towards user-centered indexing in digital image collections. *OCLC Systems & Services, 22*(4), 283–298.

Peters, I. (2009). *Folksonomies: Indexing and retrieval in Web 2.0.* Berlin, Germany: De Gruyter Saur.

Peterson, E. (2006). Beneath the metadata: Some philosophical problems with folksonomies. *D-lib Magazine, 12*(11). Retrieved from http://www.dlib.org/dlib/november06/peterson/11peterson.html

Rethlefsen, M. L. (2007, September 15). Tags help make libraries Del.icio.us: Social bookmarking and tagging boost participation. *Library Journal, 132*(15)26–28.

Rorissa, A. (2010). A comparative study of Flickr tags and index terms in a general image collection. *Journal of the American Society for Information Science and Technology, 61*(11), 2230–2242.

Smith, G. (2008). *Tagging: People-powered metadata for the social web.* Berkeley, CA: New Riders.

Spiteri, L. F. (2007). The structure and form of folksonomy tags: The road to the public library catalog information. *Technology & Libraries, 26*(3), 13–25.

Steele, T. (2009). The new cooperative cataloging. *Library Hi Tech, 27*(1), 68–77.

Syn, S. Y., & Spring, M. B. (2013). Finding subject terms for classificatory metadata from user-generated social tags. *Journal of the American Society for Information Science and Technology, 64*(5), 964–980.

TechSmith. (2008). *UX 2.0: Any user, any time, any channel.* Retrieved from http://download.techsmith.com/morae/docs/UserExperience2_0.pdf

Trant, J. (2006). Exploring the potential for social tagging and folksonomy in art museums: Proof of concept. *New Review of Hypermedia and Multimedia, 12*(1), 83–105.

Trant, J. (2009). Studying social tagging and folksonomy: A review and framework. *Journal of Digital Information, 10*(1). Retrieved from http://journals.tdl.org/jodi/article/view/269

Tunkelang, D. (2009). *Faceted search.* Synthesis lectures on information concepts, retrieval, and services. San Rafael, CA: Morgan & Claypool.

UNT Libraries. (2013a). *Input guidelines for descriptive metadata.* Retrieved from http://www.library.unt.edu/digital-projects-unit/input-guidelines-descriptive-metadata

UNT Libraries. (2013b). *Controlled vocabularies: Home.* Retrieved from http://digital2.library.unt.edu/vocabularies/

Van Damme, C., Hepp, M., & Siorpaes, K. (2007). FolksOntology: An integrated approach for turning folksonomies into ontologies. In *Proceedings of ESWC 2007,* 71–84. Retrieved from http://www.heppnetz.de/files/vandammeheppsiorpaes-folksontology-semnet2007-crc.pdf

Vander Wal, T. (2005). Off the top: Folksonomy entries. Retrieved from http://www.vander wal.net/random/category.php?cat=153

Weidner, A., & Alemneh, D. (2013). Workflow tools for digital curation. *Code4Lib Journal, 20.* Retrieved from http://journal.code4lib.org/articles/8419

Wichowski, A. (2009). Survival of the fittest tag: Folksonomies, findability, and the evolution of information organization. *First Monday, 14*(5). Retrieved from http://firstmonday.org/htbin/cg

Wolfram, D., Olson, H. A., & Bloom, R. (2009). Measuring consistency for multiple taggers using vector space modeling. *Journal of the American Society for Information Science and Technology, 60*(10), 1995–2003.

Zhao, Y., Liu, J., Tang, J., & Zhu, Q. (2013). Conceptualizing perceived affordances in social media interaction design. *Aslib Proceedings, 65*(3), 289–303.

3

Experiments in Cultural Heritage Informatics

Convergence and Divergence

Jeannette A. Bastian and Ross Harvey

ABSTRACT

We typically think that the major challenges for digitization, convergence, and digital preservation are technological. However, cultural and professional issues predominate and are more difficult to overcome. This observation is reinforced by research on the convergence of cultural heritage institutions conducted since 2009 by faculty at the Graduate School of Library and Information Studies at Simmons College in Boston. Grounded in the emerging field of cultural heritage informatics, that research is described with a focus on the Simmons Digital Curriculum Laboratory, the digital convergence projects negotiated and completed by faculty and students, and the lessons learned from those projects. The problems encountered are outlined, including concerns about controlling public access, communication difficulties, staff layoffs, lack of technical skills, lack of strategic vision, and constraints arising from organizational hierarchies. Based on the findings, the trajectory for convergence is evaluated.

INTRODUCTION

For the past four years, faculty at the Graduate School of Library and Information Science (GSLIS) at Simmons College in Boston have been conducting research and experiments in the digital convergence of cultural heritage institutions.[1] Anticipating that most of our challenges would be technical ones, we hired programmers, built a grant-funded virtual laboratory and developed and supported open-source tools.

Although these ventures were successful in addressing many of the digital challenges, we discovered that our major issues were not technical at all, but rather cultural, professional, and organizational. In this paper we point to these issues by describing our research and experiments, the obstacles we encountered, and the successes we achieved. We conclude with an analysis of the challenges of digital convergence based on our experiences.

Although libraries, archives, and museums—philosophically, intellectually, and often even physically linked for decades—have long been grappling with the chaotic and complex realities of connecting and converging, today's digital technologies can finally turn visions of connecting and converging into reality. But in practice, despite the facts that recent research has produced a substantial body of digital convergence theory and that a growing number of major public and private institutions are committing to implementing convergence models, the many obstacles to convergence are often overwhelming. In 2011, the National Library and the National Archives of the Netherlands announced plans to integrate into one organization, thereby following the paths of national libraries and archives in Canada, New Zealand, and Ireland. Their formal integration acknowledges the less formal truths that library, archival, and museum materials have always coexisted in single organizations—although, generally, this coexistence has not been convergence. By integrating formally, these institutions have made a commitment to overcome the many challenges of convergence. For cultural heritage institutions that are less visible and less well-resourced than the integrating national institutions, many of which may have an equally critical public mandate to provide access to their holdings, the challenges are formidable, overwhelming, and sometimes seemingly impossible to overcome. In the management of digital materials, divergence has been the norm of training, organization, arrangement, purpose, and territorial control. Libraries, archives, and museums have separately developed their own digital asset management systems, metadata, organizing principles, and procedures appropriate for their conceptions of their particular audience.

Our research interests were multipronged. On the one hand, they were driven by a pedagogical interest in identifying and experimenting with a theoretical infrastructure that would accommodate digital convergence; on the other, they were driven by a wish to better understand the dichotomy between the current technical ability to achieve convergence in digital practice and the many stumbling blocks and challenges encountered, particularly by small and medium-sized cultural heritage institutions. We undertook a series of initiatives that combined a cultural heritage curriculum with practicums that directly addressed convergence in small and medium-sized cultural heritage institutions with which we sought partnerships. Through these practical experiments in convergence we were able to make some preliminary assessments about the requirements for convergence, future possibilities, and the role of technology.

CONVERGENCE

Much has been written about the convergence of cultural heritage institutions over the past decade. A leading theorist in this area writes: "While the traditions and historical areas of expertise in archives, libraries, and museums may differ, the new challenges facing all collecting cultural institutions are best addressed in concert, in an interdisciplinary forum that explores multiple solutions and takes advantage of many skills" (Trant, 2009, p. 377). Collaboration is an essential element in achieving convergence. Practitioners and theorists alike agree that "incorporating collaboration into the underlying work culture is foundational to realizing that institution's potential and achieving its mission" (Waibel, 2010, p. 4). Although collaboration may be an essential ingredient in the digital convergence recipe, other elements are equally crucial. Not only do these include a strong understanding of the potential of technology and digital curation, but they also embrace leadership and organizational skills, as well as an appreciation of the theoretical constructs underlying the separate but related disciplines of archives, libraries, and museums.

In our research at Simmons College we defined convergence in terms of the institution; a converging cultural heritage institution is one that combines library, archival, and museum material, and is working toward implementing a set of standards and best practices that unites traditional theory and operations within these three disciplines. There are many reasons why libraries, archives, and museums are finding the concept of convergence attractive. The potential for federated searching across collections, the economic leverage of joint infrastructure investments for both physical and digital content creation as well as digital asset management, working in a common collaborative context, sharing organizational concerns, and the opportunity to identify gaps in collections are just a few of the attractions. An overarching public mandate for seamless access to collections and the potential for users to add value to digital objects through enhancements and combinations (such as mashups) are primary motivators.

The driver for convergence, we contended, is the use of technology for the representation, documentation, archiving, preservation, and communication of cultural heritage knowledge. The outcome is the creation of new relationships and new knowledge by bringing digital data sets representing social and cultural activity together in novel ways.

While libraries, archives, and museums share many concerns, roles, and missions, they come from distinct and different traditions. Not the least of the differences is in professional education. The education of librarians, archivists, and museum professionals is typically undertaken in separate library science, public history, or museum studies programs. Each profession has its own established standards of professional practice, such as metadata schemas, search and data management tools, and policies on access, which have resulted in some profound differences in organizational and professional culture. As they carry the distinctions of practice from their professional education into their careers, professionals may also become obstacles to crossing disciplinary boundaries and convergence.

CULTURAL HERITAGE INFORMATICS

To ground our experimentation, we sought a theoretical framework and pedagogy that offered a broad vision of cultural heritage institutions, looking beyond the silos of traditional information practice toward the confluence of a wide variety of data in virtual and physical forms. We found that theoretical and pedagogical foundation in the concept of cultural heritage informatics. Cultural heritage informatics, a relatively new discipline arising from convergence, emphasizes collecting, managing, supporting, reconciling, merging, and making accessible digital data across a broad spectrum of libraries, archives, and museums. It can be particularly applicable and effective in institutions that combine the responsibility of a library, an archive, and a museum, but is also surprisingly challenging. Cultural heritage informatics offers an overarching context for the seamless connecting and merging of a wide variety of materials within and across traditional cultural heritage information institutions.

The phrase "cultural heritage informatics" seems to have struggled over the past two decades to gain currency. It embraces digital convergence, cultural heritage information technology, digital curation, and a wide range of practices and theories. The word "informatics" is increasingly used in combination with other words to express the application of information technology and information science to the data and objects of different disciplines, as in, for example, health informatics, archaeological informatics, social informatics, and community informatics. Jennifer Trant and David Bearman were among the early users of the term, beginning in the early 1990s through their series of conferences, International Cultural Heritage Informatics Meetings (1991–2007), and the ongoing Museums and the Web conferences beginning in 1997. On their Archives and Museum Informatics website they define informatics as "the interdisciplinary study of information content, representation, technology and applications, and the methods and strategies by which information is used in organizations, networks, cultures and societies" (Archives & Museum Informatics, 2013).

The working definition that we have devised to guide our set of cultural heritage informatics experiments at Simmons College follows similar lines. It asserts that the term *cultural heritage informatics* generally refers to the intersection between computer science and cultural heritage, to the application of information technology to the legacies of the past that are found in cultural heritage institutions, such as libraries, archives, and museums. Cultural heritage informatics focuses on the use of technology for the representation, documentation, archiving, preservation, and communication of cultural heritage knowledge.

More specifically, cultural heritage informatics is the study and creation of the additional cultural value that is achieved by linking disparate digital data sets, stored either locally or remotely and organized according to accepted standards of description, arrangement, and metadata for archives, records, museum objects, or library materials. It encompasses the appraisal of data and data sets for enduring value in the context of cultural heritage, and explores the creation of new relationships and new knowledge by bringing digital data sets representing social and cultural activity together in novel ways. It is also concerned with the policy, social, economic, organizational, and legal issues of digital culture and heritage from the many perspectives of stakeholders such as heritage institutions and other cultural participants. The scope of cultural heritage informatics includes standards, metadata, and every phase of the application of information technology, including data capture, preservation, data processing, reconstruction, visualization, and documentation, as well as the dissemination of the output of these technical processes to cultural heritage communities and the general public.[2]

Are the differences in the cultural heritage disciplines of libraries, archives, museums, and other cultural arrangement constructs sufficient to demand different approaches, as is demonstrated in the distinction between, for example, health informatics and bioinformatics? Or is there enough common ground, with common theory and common approaches, to enable the identification of a universally applicable cultural heritage informatics? Is there really such a construct as cultural heritage informatics? Or is it just a convenient conflation of related disciplines? Is there a unique cultural heritage informatics approach, or just linked data? Do librarians, archivists, and museum curators talk to each other in meaningful ways to encourage a fruitful cultural heritage informatics approach? Or is every group a law unto itself? These are some of the questions that we attempted to address.

THE PROCESS

The research team at Simmons College, which included faculty and students, worked with partners in cultural heritage institutions throughout New England. The team had two curriculum-related goals: to design a cultural heritage informatics curriculum for students in the GSLIS program; and to provide experiential learning for students by working with partners on actual convergence projects. In this way, the curriculum combined classroom learning and experimentation in a laboratory setting with practical experience. The team has undertaken three main activities: designing appropriate coursework, constructing a virtual laboratory using open-source applications as an experimentation space for digital projects (see http://gslis.simmons.edu/dcl/), and collaborating with six different cultural heritage institutions on digital convergence projects. Conclusions drawn from this collaboration form the basis of this chapter.

THE DIGITAL CURRICULUM LABORATORY

A Digital Curriculum Laboratory (DCL) anchors the entire convergence research project. This virtual space provides integrated access to digital content, content management tools, standards, and curriculum-based scenarios, and allows experimentation with a wide range of open-source applications relevant to digital convergence. Developed by the Simmons faculty and supported by external funding,[3] the DCL facilitates scenario-building, problem-solving, evaluation, and tool utilization by making it possible for students to apply and assess a variety of online archival and preservation procedures and techniques. The DCL was envisioned as an open-access space containing a variety of digital content; providing an array of digital asset management systems for describing, preserving, and managing this content; offering sets of descriptive, content, structure, and data value standards; and providing an evolving set of instructional learning modules and exercises. These are used to prepare students for today's professional environment in cultural heritage institutions. The DCL was also envisioned as a permanent curriculum tool to facilitate experimentation with digital materials in a variety of venues and contexts. It was expected that students would bring digital issues from our partner sites into the DCL where they could test possible solutions.

OUR PARTNERS

In selecting institutional partners, we had a wide choice in terms of size and focus of the institution. Cultural heritage institutions abound in New England, which comprises the six states on the northeast coast of the United States and was the site of some of the earliest European settlements in the 1600s. People in New England are proud of their heritage, and even the smallest town generally boasts a local historical society with a mixture of artifacts, records, books, and paintings, often located in a historic house with appropriate gardens and landscaping. The cultural heritage institutions of New England offer real-world laboratories for experiments in cultural heritage informatics, and they also present all the issues and challenges of digital convergence inherent in small under-resourced institutions. Some of these small and often struggling institutions, whose collections are relatively hidden and whose operations lack resources, have the greatest need for creative and innovative solutions to the challenges of digital convergence.

The cultural heritage institutions with whom we collaborated demonstrate a wide variety of aims, activities, scopes of collections, and technological expertise, and a significant diversity in size. All of them, to varying extents, contained museum, library, and archival materials and were actively creating digital assets. Teams of students worked on aspects of creating appropriate digital convergence models that would fit each of the institutions. We initially formed partnerships with six institutions: one public library with a special collection; one historical society; three museums, each with a special focus; and one umbrella organization for historic houses throughout New England. Each of these organizations was well-established and had collections that spanned many decades or centuries; each included library, museum, and archival materials that coexisted side-by-side; each generally organized these materials using separate systems; and, importantly, each desired to improve access through digital convergence and was creating digital assets to achieve this goal.

WHAT WE ENCOUNTERED

Since the practicum projects provided data that directly addressed digital convergence, three of them will be briefly described, with a focus on the sites, the specific digital experiment, the results, and the many and unexpected issues encountered. Among these issues were concerns about controlling public access, communication difficulties, key personnel at the sites being laid off, lack of necessary technical skills, lack of strategic vision, and constraints imposed by existing and ingrained organizational hierarchies. The issues led us to recognize the critical importance of understanding the policy, social, economic, organizational, and legal issues of digital culture and heritage from the perspective of the heritage institutions and other cultural participants.

Our initial expectation was that technical issues would impede convergence, especially difficulties relating to interoperability among systems and metadata. For example, one of our partners is a well-resourced library in a large well-resourced museum, which had been formed by the amalgamation of two libraries with long histories. We suspected that there would be issues to resolve arising from the use of different metadata sets from disparate library-based systems and museum systems, and that a lack of interoperability between museum and library catalog applications would pose problems. Our suspicions were confirmed, but probably of greater significance were cultural aspects of the broader institutional context; although the museum talks to the library, the museum considers the library a junior partner and their communication is often at cross-purposes, which stymies any significant progression toward convergence and collaboration that might benefit the patrons of the library and its parent museum.

Practicum Project 1

Our major success story was the collaboration with the Gropius House at Historic New England. Historic New England (2008) defines itself as a "museum of cultural history that collects and preserves buildings, landscapes, and objects dating from the seventeenth century to the present and uses them to keep history alive and to help people develop a deeper understanding and enjoyment of New England life and appreciation for its preservation." Centered in Boston, Historic New England operates thirty-nine historic houses scattered throughout New England. Among these is the Gropius House, designed and built by architect and Bauhaus founder Walter Gropius in 1939 as his family home when he moved to Massachusetts to teach architecture at Harvard's Graduate School of Design. Gropius died in 1969, entrusting the distribution of his estate to his widow Ise Gropius. In 1979 Ise gave the house and grounds to Historic New England (then the Society for the Preservation of New England Antiquities), though she continued to live in the house until her death in 1983. The Gropius House opened as a museum in 1985 and has become Historic New England's most popular site. Preserved intact, the Gropius House includes furniture, artwork, books, clothing, and archival materials—all the impedimenta of family life. Gropius and his wife also designed the gardens, and the Japanese Garden and sculpture installations have been maintained as they left them.

Five teams of students worked on projects at the Gropius House between the fall semester of 2010 and the spring semester of 2013. In the spring of 2012 one team had the opportunity to interview Gropius's daughter, Ati Gropius Johansen. In preparation for her visit to Historic New England in Boston the team focused on one room in the house, Ati's bedroom, which contained a wide variety of objects, artwork, clothes, and books. The project involved researching and describing materials in the bedroom, linking images of the items to their descriptions, and creating an online exhibit. Using audio and video clips of their interview with Ati Gropius Johansen the students were also able to link objects in the online exhibit to the interview in a dynamic fashion. The descriptions of the objects that the students added to the Historic New England database used that organization's prescribed metadata schema. To manage the objects in the online exhibit the students experimented with content management systems to find the best option. They also experimented with digital mapping of the room within the wider context of the Gropius House. The final exhibit provides a model for Historic New England in working with its other sites.

This collaboration was a convergence success story for the students and for the site, where the exhibit seamlessly moves through different formats and media to deliver a single integrated information experience. Few issues arose from the use of information technology at this site, which has an effective systems librarian/archivist (the very job title illustrates convergence) who is a recent graduate from Simmons GSLIS and was very willing to work with our student team. The systems librarian/archivist and the senior curator with whom the students worked had agreed on an integrated vision of how their collections should be described, displayed, and accessed, and Historic New England had the organizational infrastructure and will to implement the vision.

Practicum Project 2

At the other end of the spectrum of success is a less well-resourced institution, a museum of American textiles, costume, and material culture that combines museum, archives, and library roles around the mission of telling America's story through these materials. In spite of this avowed mission, the museum website presence is entirely separated from its library, which contains an internationally authoritative collection in a wide variety of formats documenting the textile and clothing industry.

We were aware from the start of our collaboration that information technology issues would be significant. Yet, technological incompatibilities were only a reflection of deeper structural issues. This institution relies heavily on a proprietary application that, for primarily financial reasons, has not been updated for some years. Projects initially identified as appropriate for collaboration included planning the migration of a large collection of digitized images stored on obsolete technology and mapping the metadata for these images into a standardized metadata schema. Other projects included using the DCL to create an Omeka digital exhibit to exemplify how unique objects in the collection could be enhanced and displayed through the versatility of free and open-source software.

We eventually realized that the technological issues at this site were the result of unequal access and competition for resources and could not, therefore, be addressed solely by technological solutions such as the applications provided in the DCL. The information technology issues, challenging enough in themselves, were trumped by economic realities. Major staff layoffs took place just as the student team and museum staff were finalizing the projects. The few remaining library and archives staff, accustomed to years of financial vagaries, depend on the museum's board to find a solution and seem not to have any sense of control over the problem-solving process. While the staff at the institution were eager to cooperate on a convergence project, the lack of funding and support for the library and archives and the lack of an overall vision for collaboration and convergence were obstacles that goodwill could not overcome. For the students, outdated technology and the failure to upgrade installed systems were challenges that could not be offset by their great willingness to help find solutions. As the problems did not lie in the technological sphere but in the organizational context that encompassed it, the students could not provide the answers. Professional consultants, with much more training and experience, might be able to identify these broader issues and make recommendations, but would not necessarily be able to effect the organizational change that might bring the solutions.

Practicum Project 3

Lying somewhere in between on our success spectrum is a public library with a special collection. Founded in the late nineteenth century, this renowned colonial history collection begins with the first European settlements in the 1600s and focuses on the Revolutionary events of the late 1700s in this region. The collection also boasts a rich collection of primary sources on the literary history of the area, including materials on the transcendentalists and their heirs. The initial convergence project was the linking of a series of fourteen paintings to related holdings within the collection. The students would scan the selected artwork, select an appropriate digital asset management system after experimenting with several in the DCL, describe the artwork, enter descriptions into the selected system, and finally link these to related library sources, creating navigation between the exhibit and website.

Although this project ran into technology issues similar to those experienced in several of the other projects, the overarching obstacles were the lack of communication about expectations between the library personnel and the students, and the self-consciously deliberate focus of the institution. For reasons related to their view of the context of the collection and their particular vision of the intended users of the collection, the librarians in the special collection were more interested in using the virtual site to market their physical site rather than for describing and providing on-line access to what was held at that physical site. For this reason, they permitted only a limited amount of information on the website and restricted linking to digitized components of their collections. Additionally, although the students created a model for the project, they were unable to actually link to the site's website due to technical incompatibilities that were not made clear when the project was initiated. These technologies offered by the site and by the students were not incompatible with the vision of each group, but they were incompatible with one another. The students completed their tasks and created a prototype but were unable to realize the dynamic website they had envisioned. Although the perspective and expectations of the site were perfectly rational in the context of the expected uses of the collections, they had not been sufficiently communicated to the students, who were not sufficiently experienced to recognize purposes for digital collections beyond those they had been introduced to in their training and course work. While a more limited convergence project could have been designed to meet the needs of this site, more discussion and analysis, as well as a better articulation of the overall vision, would have helped to make this project more successful.

LESSONS

The three examples given here illustrate that, although many of the convergence problems seemingly centered on technical issues, the larger, overarching obstacles were not technical. Rather, they stemmed from the organizational culture at the sites, from competing interests between creators and preservers, and differing access and preservation philosophies. Although the practicums were not the focus of the study, but rather part of the case study methodology and data gathering, relationships between the student teams and the sites often contributed to the dissonance. The mismatch between expectations of partner sites on the one hand and student teams and faculty on the other, inadequate communication, and insufficiently defined outcomes, demonstrated the difficulties of cooperative projects—even when all parties were trying to make things work. Specific examples of the problems encountered were: concerns about controlling public access, communication difficulties between students and site staff, key personnel at sites being laid off, lack of necessary technical skills at the sites, lack of strategic vision in some institutions, and constraints imposed by existing and ingrained organizational hierarchies.

In terms of the technical issues, we were surprised by the lack of technical expertise at many of the sites, particularly in the light of their eagerness to pursue technology and convergence options. At one site, for example, the institution's accountant handled the information technology operation, providing trouble-shooting measures and occasional support. We observed a lack of understanding of and interest in open-source software, some of which (Omeka, for example) is well supported and very effective. Many sites remained wedded to outdated software, posing a significant challenge not only to site staff but also to the students. File-naming conventions were generally haphazard and, where they did exist, were not adhered to. One site consciously preferred HTML over the XML-based Encoded Archival Description (EAD) for its finding aids, limiting future options requiring interoperability that the institution might seek to pursue.

As already mentioned, one of the larger overarching obstacles we encountered was the organizational culture at the sites. Existing and ingrained organizational hierarchies imposed constraints. There were few integrated data systems and generally a resistance to change. This was exemplified at one site where the lack of collaboration between the constituent parts of the institution was a significant impediment to convergence and efficiency. Digital images were created and managed in at least four different sections of the institution, each of which used different workflows, file-naming conventions, metadata standards, hardware, and software. Although the staff recognized the need to standardize and centralize its disparate and disorganized image collections for more functional use, their recognition had not translated into any action. Consequently, the staff faced difficulties when trying to locate a digital image file and wasted considerable time in searching the institution's multiple systems; effort was wasted in redigitizing images that had already been digitized; and, because no one had institution-wide oversight of digitizing policy and workflow documentation, collection material was digitized to inadequate and varying standards.

A prevalent example of the mismatch between the expectations of partner sites and of the student teams and Simmons faculty was the inability of the technical infrastructure at several of the sites to support the scope of the proposed solutions. The lack of technology resources and expertise at the sites often meant that there was a knowledge gap, and it became apparent that, in some instances, the questions raised during initial discussion with the partners had not been understood. Although Simmons faculty attempted to clearly define expectations with all partner sites well before the students participated, differences in expectations persisted.

The discrepancy between expectations arose in part from inadequate communication and is the second critical nontechnical factor we identified. We observed shortcomings in communication between sites and students and internally within the sites. Changing expectations during the project contributed to the effects of inadequate communication. At one site it quickly became apparent that one section of that site had not communicated what it was doing to another section, causing problems for students who needed to work with both sections to complete the project as initially defined. Another example of inadequate communication within sites was the lack of documentation about procedures; for instance, one site had no documentation about the metadata standards it used or about the servers available and what should be stored on each of them.

The third critical nontechnical factor we identified was the lack of vision and lack of sufficient clarity about desired outcomes, which is related in part to inadequate communication. Although discussions about technology and infrastructure were held with the partner sites at the time of the partner agreements, the inconsistencies and gaps did not become apparent until after the students began working at the sites. Most sites did not have a workable vision that included convergence, and the negative impact of this on all involved in the projects became increasingly apparent as they progressed.

RECOMMENDATIONS

What can be learned from these lessons? Although they are to some extent generic lessons that can apply to all endeavors, aspects of them that are specific to digital converged environments can be identified.

The overriding lesson from our cultural heritage informatics collaboration with partner sites is that developing clear expectations and a vision is crucial. This takes a lot of time, can be frustrating, and requires excellent communication on both sides. In the most successful project with the Gropius House, the staff at Historic New England was very willing to commit significant amounts of time, which resulted in expectations that were articulated clearly and thoroughly and in the availability of staff for consultation when students encountered problems. Another clear lesson is that sites need to be better aware of what is needed to function effectively in the digital environment, in terms of both technical and general requirements. As noted, we frequently observed that the understanding of information technology requirements and possibilities was minimal, resulting in unwillingness to consider new applications and different workflows, or even to upgrade installed applications. Also as noted, most sites did not have a workable vision that included convergence. From these lessons we can identify some recommendations for similar projects in the future.

The first recommendation is that sites need to take time to develop their understanding of what is required to function effectively in a converging digital environment and to seek assistance in developing their abilities to function effectively. This is a significant issue, of course, requiring ongoing action from educators, professional associations, and, indeed, learning by all professionals. For Simmons, any future collaboration in this area will probably involve building in an educational component for personnel at the sites.

The second recommendation is that sites need to develop clear and workable visions of convergence and of what they are aiming to do in a digital environment. This is likely to involve identifying goals that are consistent with their business use cases, developing strategies consistent with these goals, identifying issues either favoring or impeding the implementation of these goals and their sustainability, pursuing behavioral as well as structural modifications to improve end-user interaction, acquiring systems that support the strategies defined, and developing workflows that maintain consistent value and integrity for digital content.

The third recommendation, directly aimed at educational programs contemplating similar practicum projects, is to be very clear about expectations when negotiating specific projects with sites. We intend to develop a scope-of-work form to assist us in negotiating expectations at the start of any new project, noting in detail what we want, what we will use, and what we need.

One common element in all of our collaborations was the use of the DCL, developed as part of this research (http://gslis.simmons.edu/dcl/) and described earlier in this paper. It was fully used by students to investigate possible applications that could be used at the partner sites. As a result of presentations and publications, the DCL is currently of interest to an increasingly wide range of professionals. It is designed for use as a sandbox in which to test applications and software tools for their applicability to a local institution. We suggest that it is a model worth investigating by local consortiums to build and use as a local tool for testing appropriate technical solutions.

CONCLUSION

The call for papers for a recent conference noted specifically that "digital continuity requires meeting technological, legal, economic, political and cultural challenges" and made explicit some of the cultural and professional challenges: "lack of cooperation among Information Technology, legal, archival, library, museum and other professionals or institutions; organizational and institutional culture; competing interests between creators and preservers and between access and preservation philosophies, evolving skill sets, cultural sensitivity" (UNESCO, 2012). We encountered most of these challenges. Despite what we initially considered to be adequate preliminary planning (environmental scans, site visits, profiling, and identifying practicum projects), the implementation of our planning was not entirely successful. The real issues of convergence and digital continuity go beyond translating theory into practice; they also, probably more significantly, call for the recognition and negotiation of the myriad issues and concerns of the cultural heritage institutions themselves. Lack of resources, compartmentalized and siloed mind-sets, and territoriality are but a few of these issues and concerns.

Although not strictly within the scope of this research, it is also worth considering whether convergence is a mandate that is appropriate for all cultural heritage institutions. Cooperation certainly . . . convergence possibly. Myriad factors, including most of those highlighted in this chapter, suggest that there is no "one size fits all" for convergence, and that convergence depends upon a host of considerations, not least of which is the concept of cultural heritage informatics itself. If convergence through cultural heritage informatics is based on technology, but technology is not the major convergence issue, what does this say about convergence? Perhaps it says that, even though all the data are digital, cultural forces for divergence still triumph, and the digitization of the data ultimately does not bridge the different worlds. It may be that in certain circumstances, rather than convergence, the coexistence and linking of data might be more effective both for the institution and its public.

NOTES

1. We gratefully acknowledge the assistance of our colleagues at Simmons College, Michèle Cloonan, Martha Mahard, and Terry Plum in commenting on this paper, which is a significantly revised version of one presented at *The Memory of the World in the Digital Age: Digitization and Preservation—An international conference on permanent access to digital documentary heritage*, Vancouver, September 26–28, 2012, with the title "The Convergence of Cultural Heritage: Practical Experiments and Lessons Learned."

2. We are indebted to our colleagues Terry Plum, Martha Mahard, and Michèle Cloonan for this extended collaborative definition of cultural heritage informatics.

3. In 2009, we received a grant from the National Historical Publications and Records Commission (NHPRC) that directly supported the development of a virtual curriculum laboratory. Simultaneously we received an Institute of Museum and Library Services grant to develop a cultural heritage curriculum. A portion of this grant supported laboratory development.

REFERENCES

Archives & Museum Informatics. (2013). Conferences, consulting, publishing and training for cultural heritage professionals. Retrieved from http://www.archimuse.com/

Historic New England. (2008). *Our mission . . . approved September 24, 2008*. Retrieved from http://www.historicnewengland.org/about-us/mission-and-vision

Trant, J. (2009). Emerging convergence? Thoughts on museums, archives, libraries and professional training. *Museum Management and Curatorship, 24*, 369–386.

UNESCO. (2012). *The memory of the world in the digital age: Digitization and preservation: Call for papers*. Retrieved from http://www.unesco.org/new/fileadmin/MULTIMEDIA/HQ/CI/CI/pdf/mow/call_for_papers_mow_digital_age_en.pdf

Waibel, G. (2010). *Collaboration contexts: Framing local, group and global solutions*. Dublin, OH: OCLC Research.

Part II

DIGITAL COMMUNITIES

INTRODUCTION: DIGITAL COMMUNITIES

Representation of cultural heritage on the web can evolve into "digital communities" where ideas, philosophies, art, and science are shared across cultural boundaries. Cultural heritage professionals are challenged by the articles in this section to: (1) be aware of the role of cultural maps in the creation of meaning from representations, and (2) consider the challenges of preserving cultural discourse.

In "Web Representation and Interpretation of Culture: The Case of a Holistic Healing System," Hemalata Iyer (associate professor, Department of Information Studies, University at Albany, State University of New York) and Amber J. D'Ambrosio (assistant professor, special collections librarian, and archivist, Dixie State University), introduce us to Ayurveda, a holistic healing system deeply rooted in its indigenous culture. Ayurveda has undergone a cultural shift away from its religious origins on U.S. websites, and the transplanted cultural context impacts the meaning and interpretations drawn from Ayurveda's digital representations. Presenting a study of Ayurveda representations in a sample of U.S. websites, the authors explore whether translation of those representations on both symbolic and linguistic levels may surmount the problems and issues arising from varying cultural maps.

Jennifer Burek Pierce (associate professor, School of Library and Information Science, University of Iowa) explores the blogs and other social media platforms documenting the nature of a familiar fiber craft—knitting. In "Knitting as Cultural Heritage: Knitting Blogs and Conservation," Pierce demonstrates that social media facilitate intense interactions between knitting-writers and knitting-readers. Her historical and discursive analysis of three prominent knitting blogs reveals knitting as a significant element of cultural heritage with social, technological, and economic effects. Pierce challenges professionals to consider how knitting's and other cultural discourses might be preserved.

4

Web Representation and Interpretation of Culture

The Case of a Holistic Healing System

Hemalata Iyer and Amber J. D'Ambrosio

ABSTRACT

Ayurveda, a holistic healing system deeply rooted in its indigenous culture, is being practiced within a different cultural milieu in the United States. The healing system has undergone a cultural shift away from its religious origins on U.S. websites, and the transplanted cultural context impacts the meaning and interpretations drawn from its digital representations. Utilizing Stuart Hall's approach to representation in media as a framework, representations of Ayurveda in a sample of U.S. websites are analyzed. The significance and the methods used to legitimize Ayurveda, the cultural symbols employed, the philosophy and purpose of the websites, and the viewer's perception of the representations are examined. The authors explore whether representations translated on both symbolic and linguistic levels may surmount the problems and issues arising from varying cultural maps.

INTRODUCTION

In the past few years the use of Complementary and Alternative Medicine (CAM) has increased considerably. This has been in spite of the advances in health care technology and its use by conventional medicine, otherwise known as biomedicine or allopathy. This continuing trend has implications for consumers and the health care system in the United States. Vibha Bharghava's (2007) study identifies the predictors of demand for CAM, particularly with reference to chiropractic, acupuncture, and massage therapies (Bharghava, 2007). The World Health Organization estimates that approximately 80% of the world's population relies on traditional systems of

45

medicines for primary health care, defining these systems as those in which plants form the dominant component over other natural resources (Mukherjee & Wahile, 2006). One system of alternative medicine used prevalently in the United States is Ayurveda, a system that originated in India. In 2007 the National Health Interview Survey included a comprehensive survey of CAM use by Americans. The results indicated that more than 200,000 U.S. adults had used Ayurvedic medicine in the previous year (Barnes, Bloom, & Nahin, 2008, p. 10). Understanding how a traditional system of medicine from India continues to gain a foothold in the health care decisions of U.S. citizens requires an understanding of its origins, its movement to the United States, and how it is being represented to those choosing to utilize it either in conjunction with or as a replacement for biomedicine. Websites were chosen as the method of representation due to the increasing use of the Internet by the general public to research medical issues and to research how these representations of Ayurveda on the web might impact its use.

The discussion has arisen in recent years over the need for cultural sensitivity in information technology. It confronts the ways in which the development of information technology needs to be aware of the representations of cultures (Mudur, 2001). The Internet makes this issue somewhat more complex, especially in the context of this paper, which does not focus on institutionally produced information technologies but instead examines the representations of a cultural healing system, Ayurveda, through the medium of mostly small-business and independent websites. The focus of the website design may in these cases be more to create representations of Ayurveda and its cultural origins that appeal to the target culture instead of focusing on sensitivity to the culture of origin. To understand how an alternative medical system from another culture is represented on the web and what the implications of such representations might be, cultural theory offers frameworks from which to work.

When discussing representation in the media, Stuart Hall synthesizes a wealth of theories spanning linguistic theory and semiotics and applies the results to media. Theories of representation in the media have a rich theoretical and philosophical background starting with the linguistic theories of Saussure and continuing through Lévi-Strauss, Barthes, and Foucault to develop into the study of semiotics. Hall's explanation of representation assists in understanding how it is operating in the context of this exploration of representations of the Ayurvedic medical system on U.S. websites. In his discussion of the new view of representation, Stuart Hall speaks of representation as constitutive and active. This view acknowledges that there will never be one fixed meaning or interpretation to an event. There can be no distortion of reality in a representation because there is no absolute meaning in the first place. This does not mean that physical reality does not exist but that there is no single interpretation of that physical reality. Meaning is what people make of it, and that remains dependent on the representation of physical reality; meaning comes to exist through the process of representation. Representation, rather than occurring after an event, is a necessary aspect of the event. Essentially, an event does not exist in a meaningful way until it has been represented, and as forms of representation change, so do meanings. As stated above, this does not mean that the physical Ayurvedic texts and practices do not exist but that their meaning does not exist until the information contained within them is represented, and this relies on the cultural context in which they are situated.

Culture enables us to make sense of and give meaning to things and events. It provides our framework for understanding the world and consists of conceptual maps that allow us to make sense of our world. Meaning arises when a group or members of a culture or society share a conceptual map. Without this to provide a context, the world would be unintelligible. When considering a representation, a key component of visual literacy is how expectations contrast with what is in a representation. Absence signifies as much as presence and the meaning lies in the fact that the signifiers subvert expectations. The production of meaning is a process of interpreting a representation; in other words, recognizing expectations and actual presence and absence within a representation and drawing conclusions. This interpretation is dependent on cultural and historical context as stated above. There can be a more or less plausible reading of a representation, but there will never be a "true" meaning as every meaning is dependent on the ever-changing context in which it is positioned. Here then, the cultural context into which Ayurveda has been transplanted impacts the meaning and the interpretations drawn from representations, in this case the contemporary United States. An example of meaning and representation would be the frequent association of alternative therapies with a mythology of nature (Coward, 1989).

AYURVEDA AND ITS PRESENCE IN THE UNITED STATES

Ayurveda originated in India several thousand years ago, independently of biomedicine, and moved to the west in the 1980s. The term *Ayurveda* combines the Sanskrit words *ayur* (life) and *veda* (science or knowledge), and so Ayurveda is often translated as "the science of life." It is one of the oldest systems of medicine in the world. Several practices in Ayurveda predate written records, and these were transmitted to successive generations by word of mouth. The oral and the family lineage traditions are found still in India today. This ancient science of medicine is believed to have come from heavenly origins involving Hindu deities. The Indian legends have it that Ayurveda was passed from Brahma, the creator of the universe, through a succession of deities until it reached Dhanvantari, the Hindu god of medicine, who taught it to Susruta and others for the well-being of the human race. It is part of one of the four Vedas (sacred scriptures of the Hindus), the *Atharvaveda*, which was composed by Lord Brahma before he created the world. Ayurveda was later subdivided into eight parts known as *Angas*, or the classical limb: major surgery (*shalya*), supraclavical surgery (*shalakya*), general medicine (*kayacikitsa*), demonology (*bhutavidya*), pediatrics and obstetrics (*kaumarabhrtya*), toxicology (*agadatantra*), use of organic elixirs (*rasayanatantra*), and the science of fertility and virility (*vajikaranatantra*). According to the National Center for Complementary and Alternative Medicine (NCCAM), the eight branches are: internal medicine; surgery; treatment of head and neck disease; gynecology, obstetrics, and pediatrics; toxicology; psychiatry; care of the elderly and rejuvenation; and sexual vitality (NCCAM, 2009, p. 2).

Two ancient Sanskrit books, *Caraka Samhita* and *Sushruta Samhita*, written over 2,000 years ago, are the main treatises on Ayurveda. The foundational concepts of Ayurveda have to do with three basic ideas: the body's constitution (*prakriti*), life forces (*doshas*), and universal interconnectedness (Valiathan, 2009). Ayurveda envisions the human body as the microcosm and the universe as the macrocosm. As man is a part of all that exists, the human body is attuned to the constituent elements of the universe or the macrocosm. *Panchabhutas* is the Sanskrit word that refers to the five constituent elements in nature: sky (*aakaash*), air (*vaayu*), fire (*agni*), water (*jala*), and earth (*bhoomi*). This underlying synergy with the elements that forms the basis of Ayurvedic therapeutics dictates the choice of food and drugs and the effect that they produce in the body.

The idea of *samya*, or equilibrium, is also very important in Ayurveda. Examples include *dhatu samya*, *dosha samya*, and *ritu samya*. Dhatu samya is balance between the tissues (*dhatus*) such as the muscle, bone, fat, and so on; equilibrium of doshas results in dosha samya; and ritu samya refers to maintaining equilibrium through the three seasonal changes due to the interaction between the body and the environment. Ayurveda recommends food, drinks, and activities to help the body adapt to seasonal changes. It also stresses good conduct to promote overall wellness. In order to have long life and good health, the ancient Ayurvedic medical text, *Charaka Samhita*, prescribes a code of conduct that addresses one's personal life in terms of food, drink, kind of clothing, accessories, hygiene, and so on, and personal virtues such as honesty, courage, modesty, compassion, and kinship with all life and beings. Basically, the *Charaka Samhita* advocates against the overuse, underuse, and/or misuse of the mind and the senses and stresses living in harmony with the environment as the requirement for health and well-being (Valiathan, 2009).

Given the increasing interest in Ayurveda, sociologists, cultural anthropologists, philosophers, medical professionals, and others have examined several different issues relating to Ayurvedic medicine. The *Charaka Samhita* has been critically examined to understand the philosophic presuppositions underlying the medical science. The close relationship between medicine and philosophy has been detailed by Pramod B. Thakar (1995).

The philosophy behind Ayurvedic medicine contrasts with the biomedical view of health. Scholars often define good health as a natural state of being and medicine to be a science concerned with healing and problems of ill health. Ayurvedic medicine, however, presents a very different perspective by advocating overall fitness and by being proactive rather than reacting to illness. In a cross-cultural comparative study of medical systems, Alter (1999) presents an argument that goes beyond the remedial health care approach and challenges some of the most basic ontological assumptions.

By placing equal emphasis on the body, mind, and spirit, Ayurveda endeavors to restore the innate harmony of a person. The primary goal of this system of medicine is prevention and longevity rather than curing diseases. Given the differing philosophies behind the Ayurvedic medical system and biomedicine, the growing interest in the United States, whose medical practices have centered on allopathy increasingly since the early twentieth century (Steuter, 2002), should be explored.

Deepak Chopra, one of the earliest protagonists in the transference of Ayurveda to the United States in the late 1980s, linked Ayurveda to Indian mysticism. However, Sita Reddy (2004) traced the timeline of Ayurveda and found as early as 1995 that the image had started to change. In its transmission to the United States, Ayurveda shifted from being an intertwined system with its origins in the Hindu religion, as detailed above, to a separate field independent of religion. As with all other ancient systems, Ayurveda was also an integral part of a religion, Hinduism, in ancient times. However, in its movement to the United States through the popularity of the New Age movement and to other parts of the world through globalization, Ayurveda seems to have undergone a cultural paradigm shift that has resulted in its dissolution from the holistic, Hindu body of knowledge. This tendency can also be seen with other, similar health practices from India, such as yoga, in their manifestations in the United States.

Many people in the United States are open to embracing ideas that come from another culture. One instance is yoga, which has become popular and is practiced all over the United States as well as other parts of the world. Yoga was an integral part of Hinduism, but in the United States, it is often presented as an independent system with minimal, if any, reference to the culture of origin. Likewise, Ayurveda is often presented in print materials as well as on websites in the United States as "the world's oldest system of healing, one that has been practiced continuously for about three thousand years." Many of these materials and websites deemphasize Ayurveda's Indian origins. This is not to say that it is not referenced at all, but that the information is not privileged in any particular way. By communicating yoga and Ayurveda in this manner, print materials and websites can be seen as representing these products of ancient civilizations as belonging to the human race as a whole. The ancientness of these ideas, thoughts, and methods represented in this manner could be seen as removing boundaries of culture. Representations of Ayurveda on websites can be considered within the context of cultural studies, particularly Stuart Hall's elucidation of representation in the media (Hall, 2011).

METHODOLOGY

Thirty United States websites were used as a sample in this exploratory study. The following open directories on the web were chosen for analysis:

1. From the DMOZ directory, sites were chosen from those listed within "Health: Alternative: Ayurveda": http://www.dmoz.org/Health/Alternative/.

From this directory the sites listed in the categories "clinics and practitioners" and "schools" were selected.

2. From the Yahoo directory, sites listed in the category "Ayurveda" were selected: http://dir.yahoo.com/Health/Alternative_Medicine/?skw=alternative+medicine +web+directory.

3. From the alternative medicine directory, sites from the "Ayurveda: Clinics" category were used: http://www.alternativemedicinedirectory.org/ayurveda -clinics.html.

The first step in the process was to search Google, as it is a popularly used search engine and an average user browsing the web for information on Ayurveda is likely to use it. The following search terms were used to search Google, from which top-ranking sites/directories were randomly selected:

1. The search term "Ayurveda open directory" resulted in a listing and the DMOZ directory was the top-ranking website. The listing had a subheading for "Ayurveda": http://www.dmoz.org/Health/Alternative/.

2. The search term "Ayurveda Medicine Directory" resulted in a listing in which Yahoo directory was first. The Yahoo directory had a subcategory for Ayurveda: http://dir.yahoo.com/Health/Alternative_Medicine/. The alternative medicine health and healing directory was also listed among the top five directories in the results from this search. This also had a subcategory "Ayurveda": http:// www.alternativemedicinedirectory.org/ayurveda-clinics.html. AlternativeMed-icineDirectory.org is a noncommercial directory designed to provide users with the most up-to-date links to reputable alternative medicine and health resources. Yahoo is a general directory used by many.

The rest of the websites consulted were chosen from a separate search rather than from directories. The search "Ayurveda clinics in USA" returned several sites and a random selection was made from the first two pages of results.

While selecting sites from the above sources, only clinics and centers located in the United States were chosen. Exclusively commercial stores were omitted. The data was collected during the months of October and November 2012 and subsequently confirmed in March 2013. Each of the thirty randomly chosen sites was examined to determine the stated objective of the site, evidence of an effort to establish legitimacy, and references to India through language and symbols.

REPRESENTATION OF AYURVEDA ON THE WEB

Sita Reddy (2000) examined clients for New Age holistic healing and noted the different segments of the population open to the New Age phenomenon. Interest in Ayurveda is or can be seen as an offshoot of the New Age movement since it initially came to the United States as a component of the transcendental meditation package that Maharshi Mahesh Yogi offered. It then had a religious, spiritual, and metaphysical flavor to it. Based on the ideological strategies used to represent Ayurveda in magazines and other popular print materials, Reddy identified five potential target groups: educated, liberal environmentalists; transcendentalists; a nonintellectual American middle-class; professionals and executives; and "vulnerable groups" such as women, the elderly, and children (pp. 207–230). Looking at this list suggests that the viewers of Ayurveda websites might be from any portion of the population of the United States with access to the Internet.

With this potential audience for Ayurvedic websites, the objectives of the sites, how they seek to establish legitimacy, and their use of Hindu symbols can be understood as representing Ayurveda in the broad cultural context of the United States.

Philosophy and Purpose

The websites operate as the medium of communication, and the words and images used act as the language communicating the representations of Ayurveda, attempting to determine whether or not any of the concepts conveyed resonate with their viewers. Communication and language complete the circuit of representation and are necessary to find out whether or not concepts are shared within a group. *Language* here refers to the broadest definition of anything that externalizes the meanings we make of the world in a way that can be communicated. The production of meaning does not just happen; it is an act to give meaning to events and communicate that meaning to others.

The philosophy or objective of the website details its purpose for existing and includes a variety of words to represent the purpose of the site and, by extension, Ayurveda. The objectives stated range throughout wellness and health; prevention of diseases; inner and outer beauty; yoga; rejuvenation and detoxification; treatment in general and of specific diseases; the manufacture of medication; education and research; and the transformation of consciousness by body, mind, and soul integration. Website philosophies fall into three broad categories: health and wellness, education and research, and beauty.

Few of the websites represent Ayurveda as a method of healing diseases or treating illnesses, which is the purview of biomedicine. While some sites focus on specific illnesses such as Parkinson's disease, cardiovascular disease, hair loss, and treating cancer together with conventional medicine, the majority deal with general wellness and health. Not many sites address integration or working with conventional medicine, although one of the sites mentions that their goal is "keeping people healthy and working with conventional medicine." None of the sites present themselves as taking the place of or competing with biomedicine. Typically, sites that mention conventional medicine do so in terms of integration and sites concerned solely with Ayurveda focus on overall well-being rather than curing or healing.

Although prevention is implicit in all of the sites that talk about rejuvenation, wellness, and health, they do not explicitly state it. One that does make an explicit statement reads: "Believed to have been gifted to humanity by the devas (celestial beings), it lays as important an emphasis on prevention and maintenance as it does on reversal and eradication of diseased states" (Deva, n.d.). In Ayurveda the integration of body, mind, and spirit is seen as central, and some websites address this by declarations or assertions such as: "Body mind and soul healing"; "facilitates self-healing via the consciousness transformation potential contained in the sage sciences of Ayurveda, Yoga and Vedanta"; "Help people achieve an ideal balance in life, and integration of body mind & spirit"; "beneficial for the integrative health of body, mind and spirit"; and so on. "Living from a foundation of consciousness, integrity, and love, provides a tried and true means for enhancing your wellbeing and spiritual connection"; and natural treatments are also mentioned. Another connected idea is that of holistic health. Some sites allude to "promoting holistic healthcare" as "[this] ancient medical system from India is perhaps the most complete holistic system we have today." These sites mention several of the key ideas behind Ayurveda as detailed in the medical texts, including the focus on holistic health. Rather than waiting until illness or disease occurs, these sites represent Ayurveda as helping people maintain healthy lives, and part of that is looking after more than physical well-being. Yoga is mentioned as one of the aspects that promotes and supports healing and thus is represented as an integral part of Ayurveda. However, none of the sites were exclusively yoga sites nor is it overly emphasized in the sites where it occurs. Yoga has been integrated into Ayurveda on these sites as one aspect of a whole lifestyle to maintain general health and wellness, and the therapies and treatments offered focus on restoring balance to the whole person rather than attempting to combat a specific disease or illness.

Websites that represent themselves as educational focus on teaching Ayurveda practitioners or on teaching workshops on yoga, meditation, or other aspects of following an Ayurvedic lifestyle. There are only a few sites that explicitly state their educational goals, though the majority of them offer workshops. One of the educational sites states that they support "the establishment and growth of Ayurveda as an independent healing profession in the State of California" (California Association of Ayurvedic Medicine, 2006). There are not many sites that emphasize research. One of the sites explicitly asserts that research is their goal: "to conduct scientific research at the highest level, to provide accurate and authentic information to the public regarding Ayurveda, to provide information about the Panchakarma Detoxification Therapy."

Some of the sites also represent Ayurveda as an aid to beauty—an appeal to vanity on a certain level. Reversing the aging process, enhancing beauty, relaxation, bliss, and rejuvenation are often mentioned on the homepages of these sites. A few of them stress inner and outer beauty, for instance: "Lifestyle programs designed to invoke your beauty, everyday self-care, individualistic, enhancing inner beauty." This seems to present Ayurveda as beneficial for appearance as well as health, with the focus moving away from lifestyle and wellness to a more shallow focus on appearance.

These representations might be seen as attempting to engage and identify with the viewer. If the viewer does not identify with an idea, he or she will only understand the meaning in an abstract way, and it will have no claim on him or her. Viewers must be able to imagine themselves in the scenario depicted in order for them to connect with the scenario and draw meaning from it. Who views the website and how they relate to it will determine their interpretation and response. Legitimacy plays a role in this; how the website represents its legitimacy will determine whether or not the viewer will take the information provided seriously or as trustworthy.

Representing Legitimacy

The websites frequently use adjectives such as "authentic." Phrases such as "authentic Ayurveda," "authentic information to the public," and "authentic treatments" are employed to establish credibility. This may be seen as needed, as there could be other sites that may be presenting inaccurate information or making false claims, and since the general public is often not well informed about the different alternative medical practices, they could be exploited by fraudulent sites. The idea of authenticity is by far the most significant factor for potential users. Some sites authenticate or substantiate their claims of offering authentic Ayurvedic treatment by emphasizing their educational background, their training under established Ayurvedic practitioners and leaders, and the preparation of medicines using herbs from India among other methods.

It seems important for many of these organizations to legitimize first themselves and second the system of medicine. They feel a need to engage with existing cultural ideologies that dictate how legitimacy is established. Dowling and Pfeffer (1975, p. 122) define organizational legitimacy as "the congruence between the values associated with the organization and the values of its environment." The efforts toward legitimization by Ayurvedic websites can be understood in light of this definition as their attempts to align their values with those of their environment and its culture, in this case, the United States. Therefore, the gestures toward legitimacy will be different based on the location of the practitioner and the audience they wish to reach. Values align closely with culture, so the efforts made toward legitimizing an organization will seek to align with a particular culture. As Ayurveda originates in India and the organizations examined in this study are located in the United States, the efforts to legitimize Ayurveda in the United States will understandably have to vary in some manner from legitimization efforts within the indigenous culture.

Aligning values is not the only effort that has to be made to establish legitimacy. Analyzing literature on legitimacy and performance in the context of organizations, Cho and Roberts (2010) have pointed out that

> because the organization's goal is to project a positive image and enhance its reputation, it will undertake certain legitimate-looking activities, but also communicate those activities to its stakeholders and the general public in order to meet those societal expectations

and satisfy the public's demands. It will be in the organization's interests to control the responsive treatment and conduct of the stakeholders and relevant publics. (p. 6)

Though Cho and Roberts are writing with accounting firms specifically in mind, their overall meaning applies to efforts by Ayurvedic organizations to legitimize themselves to their audience. Efforts toward legitimization only have meaning once they have been effectively communicated to their intended audience and are only effective if they convey the message the organization wishes to have received by the audience. In this case, efforts at communicating legitimacy occur via the images and messages of the organizational websites.

Given the twofold nature of establishing legitimacy detailed here, it is worth acknowledging what type of authenticity is considered necessary as well as how it is expressed to the intended audience. Considering that the websites chosen originate in the United States, claims of legitimacy need to align with the cultural values of Americans. The primary medical system in the United States is biomedicine, often referred to as conventional medicine. The use of the phrase "conventional medicine" to describe biomedicine automatically positions it against some other system that is "unconventional." CAM is defined as "a group of diverse medical and healthcare systems, practices and products that are not part of conventional medicine" (NCCAM, 2008). Thus Ayurveda can be seen as standing in opposition to biomedicine in a Derridian dichotomy. With this in mind, perhaps one of the most effective means of legitimizing Ayurveda for at least the large portion of the population in the United States that subscribes to the biomedicine/alternative medicine dichotomy would be to eliminate opposition by means of integration. This is not to say that integration is undertaken solely on behalf of achieving or conveying legitimacy, but that where integration occurs it could be seen as offering legitimacy. Several sites studied mention the use of both Ayurveda and biomedical diagnostic tools, and in some at least one of the primary practitioners holds both an MD in biomedicine as well as a PhD in Ayurvedic medicine. Integrating conventional medicine with Ayurveda does provide some legitimacy to Ayurveda and as such a few sites do take this approach and state that their doctors are both conventional and alternative medical practitioners.

The methods by which the websites communicate their legitimacy in relation to biomedicine include listing the qualifications of the doctors, such as degrees and certifications. Biomedicine requires the completion of medical training in accredited institutions that results in the conference of degrees and certifications. This process and the resultant qualifications operate as the signifier for the legitimacy of biomedical professionals and organizations. By listing such qualifications, Ayurveda websites position their legitimacy in the same vein as that established by conventional medicine. Reference to accredited bodies serves the same function for Ayurveda websites. One website states the qualifications and qualifies them with reference to the accrediting bodies: "They are the accrediting body for the state of California and affiliated with the International Association of Yoga Therapists and National Ayurvedic Medical Association (NAMA)." Another method aligned with conventional medicine's signification of legitimacy is reference to the prestige and reputation of the institution where the practitioner trained, such as, "Trained at Mahrishi University of Valkenburg in Holland."

One other interesting means of signifying legitimacy aligns with both the indigenous cultural tradition of passing knowledge of the medical system from a teacher to a student and the biomedical tradition of studying under medical professionals who have made significant contributions. It is a type of prestige by association, or legitimacy by association. The Ayurveda websites communicate this type of legitimizing information by mentioning that practitioners trained under well-known Ayurveda doctors. In the case of practitioners in the West, one sees well-known Ayurveda doctors such as Vasant Lad, Deepak Chopra, and others being mentioned.

Other more general methods of signifying legitimacy also exist on the websites of Ayurveda organizations. The organization will mention the date of origin or the number of years in operation if the number demonstrates they have withstood the test of time and possess the experience of that timeframe. If practitioners of Ayurveda incorporate the principles and practices of the medical system into their own lives, they also make sure to mention that. Practicing what one preaches is a way of validating one's commitment to the ideology underlying the medical practice. Medical practitioners often speak about the "Ayurvedic lifestyle" they live. Images, videos, and interviews with practitioners demonstrating their participation in the lifestyle serve to establish their legitimacy within this framework.

With reference to the herbs used by and sold by Ayurvedic practitioners, the method of authentication revolves around established regulatory institutions. The presence of the Food and Drug Administration in the United States gives rise to an expectation that items for consumption, particularly for medicinal purposes, have been examined and monitored by a regulating agency. In the context of this cultural value, Ayurvedic organizations that promote or distribute herbal supplements and treatments feel the need to establish the legitimacy of their products. The FDA does not typically regulate or approve herbal supplements, so other methods of establishing legitimacy appear on the websites. They mention access to the highest-quality herbal supplements, direct from India, or refer to organic, self-grown, and hand-prepared medicine intended to work alongside allopathic medicine. Some organizations describe themselves as being licensed preparers of Ayurvedic medicines, relying on the legitimacy conferred by the idea of licensing by a regulatory agent. They might also mention that it conforms to ISO 9001–2000 standards—the presence of a standard lending once again validation from the sense of regulation and control. Websites might also provide the source of their herbs and why they approach it that way, claim to have strict quality-control standards in place, describe how they are processed, claim them to be verified by modern technology, or provide lengthy descriptions. These methods rely on disclosure to offer a sense of possessing the relevant information and making a decision based on access to that information. It might be seen as offering a sense of empowerment to the audience.

However, the prevalence of Indian/Hindu symbols and metaphors for life and spirituality on many of the websites suggests that positioning Ayurveda in relation to biomedicine is either not the appropriate method of legitimization for some audiences or else cannot be the sole method. These efforts would suggest that positioning Ayurveda in relation to its indigenous culture offers another form of authentication. Indian/Hindu symbols and metaphors operate as one method of communicating a message of validity to the viewer and also largely facilitate the representation of Ayurveda on these websites.

Cultural Symbols

There are several views on the attributes of symbols. They are seen as having "innate power" in the magical sense. On the other hand, they are also perceived as being socially determined and acceptable. These two ideas contradict each other. Seen from another perspective symbols are characterized by their naturalness within the culture. For example, the banyan tree, which is a tropical tree commonly found in India, and fire are both very powerful and popular symbols in India. A number of symbols significant to Hinduism appear on the websites analyzed here. Among them are fire; the banyan tree; the lotus flower; hands; and the god of medicine, Dhanvantri. *Agni* (fire in Sanskrit) is connected with "*samskaras*, the rites marking out the life stages from conception to death" (Smith, 1990, p. 130); fertility; spiritual power; and with Indian mythology as well. The banyan tree is the national tree of India. The roots sprout into more trunks and branches. Because of this characteristic and its longevity, the banyan tree is considered immortal and sacred. The lotus, though it has its roots in marshy soil, rises up and blooms in pristine purity. Possibly it alludes to a purer state of mind being conducive to good health.

Another noticeable trend in the imagery of the websites is the depiction of hands in a variety of gestures. The Sanskrit word *mudra* refers to a gesture, usually of the hands, that is believed to channel reflexes and energy flow and reflexes to the brain; mudras are also associated with healing and channelling energy for better health. The Hindu deity Dhanvantri is considered to be the first proponent of Indian medicine. He is worshipped as the god of health and healing and has four hands. He holds a pot with rejuvenating nectar (*amrita* in Sanskrit) in one hand and medicinal herbs in another. His role in the Hindu religion associates him naturally with medicine, healing, and rejuvenation of the body, mind, and spirit.

All of these images associate Ayurveda with its indigenous culture of origin to one extent or another. Many of them operate on a subtler level than others. The banyan tree, fire, and hands might not necessarily bring India to a viewer's mind unless they already possess significant knowledge of Indian culture. Images of Dhanvantri and the lotus may have a more prevalent role in the shared concept map of people in the United States. Likely, the viewer will not know who Dhanvantri is, but they will be able to associate the icon of a man with four hands as not belonging to the cultural symbolism of the United States per se. The lotus also has a fairly well established association with Asia, provided that the viewer recognizes the type of flower depicted. These symbols have the potential to locate Ayurveda within its culture of origin, and by extension offer it the legitimacy of association with an ancient system of healing, but they may be overlooked by those unfamiliar with them.

VIEWERS AND THEIR PERCEPTIONS

In her discussion of target groups for Ayurveda in print materials in the United States, Sita Reddy (2000) mentions the characteristics of some of these groups and what their needs might be as audiences. For example, the nonintellectual segment of the American middle-class often seeks relief from stress and may be more concerned with the legitimacy of Ayurveda because of their pragmatic nature. This group will also tend to see India as an alien place. Therefore, like the consumers of Ayurvedic print materials, their interpretation of Ayurveda websites is likely to vary significantly from professionals and executives who value capitalist success and the portion of the middle class that wants a middle way with success in the traditional and modern sense. For these groups, Ayurveda contributes to the distinctly American consciousness that understands health as leading to success in their terms (Reddy, 2000). The interpretations of these groups will vary from the transcendentalists and educated liberals who value Ayurveda largely for its culture of origin and the philosophies of that culture.

Given the various meanings and interpretations that might arise from a viewer's experience with Ayurveda websites, the pros and cons of the methods of representation should be considered. Whether or not a viewer chooses to make use of Ayurveda may in large part be determined by their interpretation of the website they consult. As meaning varies by individual, each website will be interpreted differently depending on the person viewing it and their own background and cultural framework. One person might interpret the presence of Indian and Hindu symbols and images as conveying legitimacy by connecting the system of medicine to its culture of origin while another might find them alienating or confusing. Some sites have few, small, or subtle references to Hindu or Indian culture while others have more overt images and language. Some explanation of Ayurveda and reference to India is standard with all sites, but the degree to which it is made obvious varies. Some sites may represent Ayurveda in a fashion that appeals more strongly to certain people while other sites may attract a different group of viewers. However, on the whole the variety of representations should construct a position of identification with a wide audience.

Meaning also depends on engaging with the image and forming a position of identification with the image. Viewers need to be able to imagine or place themselves within the image or idea that is being represented to them. Focus on relaxation, images of people receiving massages with their eyes closed, flowers, plants, soothing colors, rejuvenation, and health might all be interpreted positively by a society with high stress, such as the nonintellectual, pragmatic middle-class mentioned by Reddy.

This audience probably will not respond as favorably to websites where the colors and images emphasize the Hindu origins of Ayurveda heavily. The appeal of relaxation, rejuvenation, and beauty seem the most prevalent on sites offering treatments and lifestyle workshops. These seem to represent Ayurveda as a means of combating stress and imbalances in everyday life. More so than emphasizing the cultural origins of Ayurveda in order to appeal to the viewer, these sites want to engage with their sense of something out of sync in their lives. The history of Ayurveda or other references to it, such as mantras or explanations of the origins of treatments, appears in secondary pages, but the homepages emphasize calm and relaxation.

Some of the images of people relaxing show them receiving specific Ayurvedic treatments such as *shirodhara*, where the person administering the treatment wears what appears to be traditional Indian garb. Websites with more explicit references to the "foreign" nature of the treatments may appeal more to the transcendentalists and educated liberals and those who embraced the New Age movement. The treatments offered by these websites often walk a line between embracing the indigenous culture and appealing to a group of people who might be uncomfortable with the Sanskrit names. The services described range from familiar English words such as *massage, cleanse, anti-aging, integrative health, consultations,* and *lifestyle regimen,* to those of more obviously Indian origin: *abhyanga, shirodhara, panchakarma, kaya kalpa* and *dosha* testing.

How a person determines the legitimacy of a website will also vary based on their frame of reference. Those with a more liberal viewpoint might not be concerned about how Ayurveda websites position themselves in relation to biomedicine and its established methods of conveying legitimacy. However, the nonintellectual middle class in their pragmatism will likely value Ayurveda in relation to biomedicine and how the website expresses its authenticity following accepted practices established by conventional medical organizations. Educated liberals and those with a wholehearted belief in this system of medicine will not necessarily avoid a website with such methods of establishing legitimacy and may still value some aspects of these efforts, but they will likely seek out the information on the website establishing its validity in relation to its cultural origins and traditions.

MEDICAL PLURALISM

While the relative nature of representation and interpretation makes it impossible to fix on a single perception of Ayurveda conveyed by these websites, the range of representations on the web with aspects that will appeal to one audience or another provide this system of medicine with a wide and potentially receptive audience. According to a 2009 Pew Internet report, 83% of people who use the Internet have consulted it at least once for medical information of some nature, and 35% of these looked specifically for information on alternative treatments or medicines (Fox & Jones, 2009, pp. 8, 54). In a study of alternative medicine clients and practitioners,

Barrett and colleagues (2003) discovered that most of the individuals interviewed seemed to be searching for an integrated solution to their health problems. They expressed a desire for a holistic, individualized, and empowering approach and were willing to combine different treatments to combat illness or achieve better health. These results suggest that rather than relying solely on biomedicine, many people in the United States opt for medical pluralism.

Medical pluralism appears to be the standard around the world. Many ethnographic studies have examined why people make the choices they do from among the different therapeutic options available to them (Doron & Broom, 2010; Foster, 1978; Janzen & Arkinstall, 1978; Waxler, 1984). These studies demonstrate that individuals move through several healers or doctors on their path to treatment and health (Kleinman, 1980; Nichter & Nordstrom, 1989; Nordstrom, 1988). These individual choices often result as much from the broader sociocultural context as from medical consequences and information, much as with the interpretations of medical systems. These factors influence the manifestation of medical pluralism. In the indigenous culture where this alternate system of medicine originated, medical pluralism takes the form of options between the various streams within the said system of medicine. For instance, one could opt for the path of yoga or for herbal therapeutics in Ayurveda. Likewise, it could take the form of medical options between two alternative medical systems, often those that emerged from the same roots and that have similar philosophic foundations, such as Ayurveda and Siddha medicine in India.

In the United States such a trend toward medical plurality is visible and has been acknowledged and studied (Wade, Chao, Kronenberg, Cushman, & Kalmuss, 2008; Goldstein, 2004; Kaptchuk & Eisenberg, 2001). With reference to where Ayurveda is practiced, it can be found in the *Ashrams* (spiritual and religious resorts), massage spas, Ayurveda doctors, clinics, and other places, each having their take on the different aspects of this system of alternative medicine. With this in mind, it is necessary to be aware of the social concerns in medical interaction. Barrett and colleagues (2003) argue that many individuals seek alternative medicine because they find the practitioners spend time with their patients and show empathy. The individuals interviewed appreciated the more well-rounded approach of alternative medicine, particularly that it considered their social, emotional, and psychological well-being in conjunction with their physical health. They also praised the individualized treatments and the feeling of being personally involved in their own health (Barrett, Scheder, Appelbaum, & Rabago, 2003, p. 941). However, as mentioned above, the interviewees in the study often relied on both conventional medicine as well as alternative medicine. Conventional medicine catered to their desire to utilize the socially accepted, "legitimate" form of medicine, while alternative treatments provided for their emotional and psychological need to feel in control of their own bodies and well-being. These reasons for choosing medical pluralism center more on the social and cultural context of the clients and on the ways in which they perceive alternative medicine benefitting them, and the benefits they value do not center solely on the effects of treatment.

When individuals make medical choices based on more than actual results and are influenced equally by social factors, the representations and interpretations of medical systems can play a pivotal role in their decision-making process. Ayurveda's presence on the web plays a role in its inclusion in medical decisions made by citizens of the United States. The more broadly the representations appeal to the population—and it does seem to be a large swath of the demographic that utilizes Ayurveda according to Reddy—the more heavily it will be integrated into the health care decisions of the population. The focus on individualized treatments, rejuvenation, and a holistic view of wellness in combination with the ways in which these websites legitimize Ayurveda in the context of conventional medical practices and the indigenous culture all play a role in how people perceive this system of medicine. With this in mind, the ways in which Ayurveda is represented on the web can be seen as playing a significant part in the medical decisions of people within the United States and the degree to which they will turn to medical pluralism to satisfy more than just their need for physical health. In Lupton's words, "The linguistic and visual representations of medicine, illness, disease and body in the elite and popular cultures and medico-scientific texts are influential in the construction of both lay and medical knowledges and experiences of these phenomena" (Lupton, 2003, p. 83).

CONCLUSION

With this in mind, it is possible to see how the representation of a cultural phenomenon such as Ayurveda on the web can impact its interpretation by a target culture not its own but also be subject to the varying cultural maps of individuals within the culture. According to Hannerz (1997), expanded "traffic in culture" through cultural exchange has resulted in the world increasingly becoming one in more than just an economic or political sense (p. 107). However valid his argument is for a certain portion of the world's population, such a cultural exchange cannot happen equally and at the same time for every individual. It may be increasingly the case, but it is by far not universally the situation for the majority of people, even among those with ready access to information technology and the Internet. Rather, increased exposure to other cultures through the medium of the web should highlight the degree to which cultures do not share conceptual maps. Not all cultural references and images on a website will be understood in the same manner, if at all. In conjunction with this, when one culture represents another online or through some other information technology medium, a degree of sensitivity in representing that other culture is required. Without the awareness of the limitations of cultural maps and sensitivity to cultural representation, websites and information technology run the risk of missing their target audience and offending members of the culture represented. Inevitably, information technology plays a necessary role in accepting the notion of cultural relativism. Translation needs to occur on the symbolic level as well as on the linguistic level (Hall, 1997).

REFERENCES

Alter, J. S. (1999, February). Heaps of health, metaphysical fitness: Ayurveda and the ontology of good health in medical anthropology. *Current Anthropology, 40*(Sl), S43–S56.

Barnes, P. M., Bloom, B., & Nahin, R. L. (2008, December 10). Complementary and alternative medicine use among adults and children: United States, 2007. *National Health Statistics Reports*, 12. Retrieved from http://nccam.nih.gov/sites/nccam.nih.gov/files/news/nhsr12.pdf

Barrett, B., Scheder, J., Appelbaum, D., & Rabago, D. (2003). Themes of holism, empowerment, access, and legitimacy define complementary, alternative, and integrative medicine in relation to conventional biomedicine. *Journal of Alternative and Complementary Medicine, 9*(6), 937–947.

Bharghava, V. (2007). *Demand for complementary and alternative medicine: An economic analysis* (Doctoral dissertation). Retrieved from ProQuest Dissertations & Theses Full Text. (3268905)

California Association of Ayurvedic Medicine (2006). *About CAAM: What is CAAM?* Retrieved from http://www.ayurveda-caam.org/about/

Cho, C. H., & Roberts, R. W. (2010). Environmental reporting on the Internet by America's toxic 100: Legitimacy and self-presentation. *International Journal of Accounting Information Systems, 11*(1), 1–16.

Coward, R. (1989). *The whole truth: The myth of alternative medicine.* London: Faber and Faber.

Deva, A. (n.d.). *Arunachala yoga & Ayurveda.* Retrieved from http://yogarasayana.com/about/

Doron, A., & Broom, A. (Eds.). (2010). Health and healing in South Asia. Special issue. *South Asian History & Culture, 1*(2).

Dowling, J., & Pfeffer, J. (1975). Organizational legitimacy: Social values and organizational behavior. *Pacific Sociological Review, 18*(1), 122–136.

Foster, G. (1978). Medical anthropology and international health planning. In M. H. Logan, & E. E. Hunt (Eds.), *Health and the human condition* (pp. 301–313). North Scituate, MA: Duxbury Press.

Fox, S., & Jones, S. (2009, June). *The social life of health information: Americans' pursuit of health takes place within a widening network of both online and offline sources.* Washington, DC: Pew Internet & American Life Project. Retrieved from http://www.pewinternet.org/~/media//Files/Reports/2009/PIP_Health_2009.pdf

Goldstein, M. S. (2004). The persistence and resurgence of medical pluralism. *Journal of Health Politics, Policy and Law, 29*(4/5), 925–945.

Hall, S. (1997). The work of representation. In S. Hall (Ed.), *Representation: Cultural representations and signifying practices* (pp.13–74). London: Sage Publications.

Hall, S. (2011, June 23). Representation and the media: Parts 1–4 [Video files]. Retrieved from http://www.youtube.com/watch?v=6sbYyw1mPdQ

Hannerz, U. (1997). Scenarios for peripheral cultures. In A. D. King (Ed.), *Culture and globalization and the world system: Contemporary conditions for representation of identity* (pp. 107–127). Minneapolis, MN: University of Minnesota Press.

Janzen, J. M., & Arkinstall, W. (1978). *The quest for therapy in lower Zaire.* Berkeley, CA: University of California Press.

Kaptchuck, T. J., & Eisenberg, D. M. (2001). Varieties of healing. 1: Medical pluralism in the United States. *Annals of Internal Medicine, 135*(3), 189–195.

Kleinman, A. (1980). *Patients and healers in the context of culture*. Berkeley, CA: University of California Press.

Lupton, D. (2003). *Medicine as Culture: Illness, disease and body in Western societies* (2nd ed.). London: Sage Publications.

Mudur, S. P. (2001) On the need for cultural representation in interactive systems. In R. A. Earnshaw (Ed.), *Frontiers of human-centered computing, online communities and virtual environments* (pp. 299–310). London: Springer-Verlag.

Mukherjee, P. K., & Wahile, A. (2006). Integrated approaches towards drug development from Ayurveda and other Indian system of medicines. *Journal of Ethnopharmacology, 103*(1), 25–35.

National Center for Complementary and Alternative Medicine (NCCAM). (2008). *CAM basics—Complementary, alternative, or integrative health: What's in a name?* Retrieved from http://web-beta.archive.org/web/20070104172944/http://nccam.nih.gov/health/whatiscam/

National Center for Complementary and Alternative Medicine (NCCAM). (2009, July). *Backgrounder—Ayurvedic medicine: An introduction*. Washington, DC: National Institutes of Health, U.S. Department of Health and Human Services. Retrieved from http://nccam .nih.gov/sites/nccam.nih.gov/files/D287_BKG.pdf?nav=gsa

Nichter, M., & Nordstrom, C. (1989). A question of medicine answering: Health commodification and the social relations of healing in Sri Lanka. *Culture, Medicine, and Psychiatry, 13*(4), 367–390.

Nordstrom, C. (1988). Exploring pluralism: The many faces of Ayurveda. *Social Science and Medicine, 27*(5), 479–489.

Reddy, S. (2000). *Reinventing medical traditions: The professionalization of Ayurveda in contemporary America* (Doctoral dissertation). Retrieved from ProQuest Dissertations & Theses Full Text. (9965551)

Reddy, S. (2004). The politics and poetics of "magazine medicine": New age Ayurveda in the print media. In R. D. Johnston (Ed.), *The politics of healing: Histories of alternative medicine in twentieth-century North America* (pp. 207–229). New York, NY: Routledge.

Smith, D. (1990). Aspects of symbolism of fire. In K. Weiner (Ed.), *Symbols in art and religion: Indian and comparative perspectives* (pp.129–139). London: Curzon Press.

Steuter, E. (2002). Contesting the rule(s) of medicine: Homeopathy's battle for legitimacy. *Journal of Canadian Studies, 37*(3), 92–111.

Thakar, P. B. (1995). *The philosophic foundations in ancient Indian medicine: Science, philosophy and ethics in Caraka-samhitā* (Unpublished doctoral dissertation). Boston College, Chestnut Hill, MA.

Valiathan, M. S. (2009). The Ayurvedic view of life. *Current Science, 96*(9), 1186–1192.

Wade, C., Chao, M., Kronenberg, F., Cushman, L., & Kalmuss, D. (2008). Medical pluralism among American women: Results of a national survey. *Journal of Women's Health, 17*(5), 829–840.

Waxler, N. E. (1984). Behavioral convergence and institutional separation: An analysis of plural medicine in Sri Lanka. *Culture, Medicine, and Psychiatry, 8*(2), 187–205.

5

Knitting as Cultural Heritage

Knitting Blogs and Conservation

Jennifer Burek Pierce

ABSTRACT

Knitting has existed as a means of constructing fabric for thousands of years around the globe. Digital resources, including blogs and other social media platforms, now document the nature of the fiber craft. Intended for any number of purposes, a legion of online outlets depict what twenty-first-century knitters do, what materials they employ, who will receive the work they have done, how they have learned a technique, and how they feel about their endeavors. As social media facilitate intense interactions between knitting writers and knitting readers, knitting forms a significant element of cultural heritage, with social, technological, and economic effects, making it a phenomenon that merits recognition as an enduring aspect of cultural heritage. Employing the historical and discursive analysis articulated by Chartier, three prominent knitting blogs and their cultural discourse are explored. Misunderstood as an old-fashioned activity, this examination of digital materials associated with the fiber craft reveals a cultural heritage meriting and awaiting digital preservation.

INTRODUCTION

Knitting represents an enduring part of the "intimate relationship between textiles and society" (Siegelaub, 1997, p. 9). It is a means of forming fabric from a strand of fiber and sticks made of anything from precision machine-tooled metal, to pencils, to rolled tubes of paper and glue (Signature Needle Arts, n.d.; Zimmermann, 1973; Pearl-McPhee, 2005, p. 303). The exact historical origins of knitting are unknown,

63

but textual references and disintegrating garments indicate that it has existed as a means of constructing fabric for thousands of years around the globe (Rutt, 1989; Turnau, 1991). The spread of knitting and its eventual status as domestic labor, Barber (1994) contends, stems from the earliest years of human civilization, when fiber craft underwent a transition from being a "plaything" that occupied leisure time to a means of improving the lot of family and community (p. 103). By the nineteenth century, directions for creating textiles and newly possible photographic representations with the potential to inspire craftspeople provided a "major stimulus in the formation of public collections and museums" and was "linked to the growing need to develop and expand public education" (Siegelaub, 1997, p. 12).

Knitting plays a role in that long history, yet its story is far from whole, as historians observe, because the craft has long been taught face-to-face and most resulting fabrics are intended for the hard uses of daily wear. As Gordon (2010) explains in a study of the Scottish fisherman's gansey:

> The people who made the original garments for their intended purposes are no longer alive, and the community, of which they are a product, has all but dissolved. The knitting and wearing of traditional ganseys began to die out in the 1930s and became a rarity after the Second World War. Some collection and documentation work was carried out in the 1950s while the generation for whom making them was a part of everyday life still held such knowledge in their heads. Until then, the patterns were not usually written down, an example of what is now defined as "intangible cultural heritage. (p. 99)

Gordon's history of the gansey outlines key challenges to understanding the roles of knitting and hand-knitted garments in actual, lived experience, and she articulates both the gaps in the historical record and the myths that have grown up in their stead. Among her conclusions, presented almost incidentally, is the idea that while knitting and its artifacts may endure, their use might become entirely separated from their origins. To understand the practice of knitting requires attention to what has happened at particular times and in particular places. We must, according to Gilbert (2012), look to the evidence of artifacts to "highlight gaps in written documents," as materiality is "important . . . for the study of those aspects of life taken for granted at the time, the things that 'go without saying' and leave no other record" (pp. 90–106).

Although knitted garments inevitably wear out, hand-knitting endured for centuries as a dominant means of constructing clothes, and in recent decades, it has seen a resurgence. In the 1960s and 1970s, figures like Elizabeth Zimmermann popularized knitting in the United States by introducing an invigorating sensibility that was both pragmatic and personal; later, in the early years of the twenty-first century, the Stitch 'n Bitch phenomenon made knitting the slightly edgy activity of hip young women (Parks & McFarland, 2011/2012; Stoller, 2004). The late twentieth-century popularity of knitting has extended into the twenty-first century, and its history has undergone a fundamental change.

Digital resources, including blogs and other social media platforms, now document the nature of knitting. Intended for any number of purposes—self-expression, publicity, sharing, or instruction—a legion of online outlets depict what twenty-first-century knitters do, what materials they employ, who will receive the work they have done, how they have learned a technique, and how they feel about their endeavors. Such outlets do all this and more, as social media facilitate intense interactions between knitting writers and knitting readers, generating and collocating testimonials to the bonds among members of the fiber community (Davies, 2013a; Pearl-McPhee, 2013). Further, where practices once would have been understood as part of a particular culture or place, distribution of patterns via the Internet means that the ideas of a lone Finnish designer can manifest on the needles of thousands of knitters around the world (Valimaki, 2011). The available texts suggest that knitting forms a significant element of cultural heritage, with social, technological, and economic effects, making it a phenomenon that merits recognition as an enduring aspect of cultural heritage.

How should the emerging history of hand-knitting in the twenty-first century be preserved? And when it is preserved, as is done by the British Library with designer Kate Davies' blog and other publications (Davies, n.d.), what is it that is being saved? What, in other words, is the significance of the proliferating discourse on knitting, preserved either institutionally or through various sorts of self-curation? While common sense might hold that these digital resources comprise a self-referential conversation about craft, analysis of a collection of texts indicates that knitters' discourse directs our attention to ideas about numerous causes and concerns: local economies and small businesses, social activism, and the history of knitting, both in terms of one's personal actions and the implications of the craft's revived popularity. The text and images that twenty-first-century knitters publish online reveal that, collectively, knitting functions as a trope of conservation. It is not simply a history of a handcraft that is preserved in contemporary discourse on knitting; instead, knitters simultaneously advance the idea that characteristically local places and other phenomena that support the public good must be maintained as a community's cultural heritage.

METHODOLOGICAL CONSIDERATIONS

Discourse analysis has seen some vogue in Library and Information Science (LIS), where the ideas of Michel Foucault and other postmodern theorists have been its starting point. In the late twentieth century, discourse analysis was adopted as a theoretical approach to research invested in creating equitable information environments. This approach has produced a distinctive set of theoretically aligned publications. Adler (2012), Budd (2006), and Frohmann (1994) see discourse analysis as a means of critically evaluating the language and the norms that constitute professional practice. Frohmann (1992) also suggests its utility to visual as well as textual analysis.

The ways discourse analysis has been applied to problems in the field suggest both its utility and its limitations in considering cultural heritage. Discourse analysis gives attention to language arising from cultural conditions (Budd, 2006; Adler, 2012).

Frohmann (2001) and Wiegand (1999) have linked how we understand the history of the profession with concepts found in Foucault's work, like his notion of archeology. Other much-cited studies draw on discourse analysis to examine the tensions between popular perceptions of the profession and its discursive practices (Radford & Radford, 2001). Some proponents set aside truth claims in favor of attention to these matters of perception. Budd (2006) observes that discourse analysis is far from prescriptive, though like any mode of serious study, has recognizable elements and rigor. The benefit, Wiegand (1999) has argued, comes from placing LIS scholars in dialogue with other fields. These studies view the institutional setting of the library as their subject matter, particularly the power relations inherent in different facets of professional work. They do not necessarily chart a course for understanding a culture that is taking shape largely outside this context, even though its constitutive materials are also represented with words and images.

Although Budd and Raber (1996) indicate that discourse analysis can be used to examine information in context and one book-length study applies many of its precepts to knitting (Turney, 2009), some scholars in the field have turned to critical discourse analysis as information available via the Internet becomes more prevalent. Critical discourse analysis presents further permutations of scholarly attention to language, replacing concerns inherent in face-to-face exchanges with the ones that accrue in digital contexts. Linked to the work of Bakhtin, critical discourse analysis enables critiques of "structures of power" (Blackledge, 2012, p. 618) and may involve awareness of how "texts relate to other texts, and [how] they relate to the social and historical conditions of their production" (Blackledge, 2012, p. 617). This historicism, however, is limited and not a universal feature of critical discourse analysis. At root, critical discourse analysis and the related techno-critical discourse analysis (Brock, 2013) resemble the antecedent Foucauldian approach in their determined interest in elements of identity, such as race, class, and gender.

Scholars interested in cultural heritage, where materiality is integral to research and professional ends, require a theoretical framework that accounts for texts and objects as part of the cultural record. Because collection management and preservation of materials are concerned with contemporary use and conservation of the historical record alike, analysis should respond to the documents and materials of interest, rather than theoretical imperatives. Further, newer translations of his writings have spurred questions about the research once believed to ground Foucault's explanatory concepts and suggest the imperative for new approaches to scholarly study when language forms the remaining historical record of a specialized discourse (Pierce, 2011).

When materials described as born-digital texts document cultural heritage, web ethnography may seem, at first glance, like a natural alternative or supplement to discourse analysis. Web ethnography, however, approaches digital documents with less interest in the historical contexts integral to making decisions about preservation (Blommaert & Huang, as cited in Blackledge, 2012). boyd (2009) disavows geography as "the defining framework of culture" (p. 27), but elsewhere (Baym & boyd,

2012) returns to themes of unstable boundaries and power inequities created by levels of technological skill rather than connecting online discourses to material culture.

The links Cloonan and Harvey (2007) articulate among preservation, history, and memory, however, prefigure theoretical and scholarly work on aspects of cultural heritage. To understand what one scholar has called "the material texture of the past" involves connections between artifacts and discourse (Gibbons, as quoted in Barry, 2013). In essays collected in *On the Edge of the Cliff*, Chartier (1997) argues that "experience is not reducible to discourse" (p. 20). Instead, he directs theoretical attention to "the challenge facing historians today: to link the discursive construction of the social to the social construction of discourse" (p. 25). Chartier's imperatives include the interpretation of texts in relation to one another for the purpose of constructing knowledge of lived experience.

Researchers relying on Foucault tend to set aside truth claims, which are essential when cultural heritage is at stake, according to Chartier (1997):

> If we give up striving for truth, an ambition that may be out of all measure but that is surely fundamental, we leave the field open to all manner of falsification and to all the forgers who betray knowledge and therefore hurt memory. (p. 27)

This sentiment parallels the concerns of Cloonan (2007) regarding the ethical imperatives that gird preservation. Chartier (1997) seeks instead "new foundations to the critical realism of historical knowledge" (p. 27). Those foundations involve awareness of "the linguistic, conceptual, and material resources available" to the individuals whose texts we study (p. 77). History takes narrative form, he argues, and these narratives are "the result of establishing relations among data arranged by the operation of knowing" (p. 45).

The priorities for historical and discursive analysis articulated by Chartier can guide the analysis of texts found online as well as in the archives. In adopting and adapting his agenda, we align our scholarly attention with the profession's responsibilities for the preservation of cultural heritage. Further, the methodological values of the sort of scholarship advocated by Chartier focus on the aims and ideas given voice in contemporary discourse on knitting, rather than subordinating their words to the precepts of postmodernism. It is not the fancy dress of theory that will indicate the importance of the cultural heritage of knitting; it is the words, powerful and poignant, of knitters themselves.

THREE PROMINENT KNITTING BLOGS: ANALYSIS AND COMMENTARY

Scholarship tends to focus on the artifacts of knitting—garments and even public art known as yarn bombing—so that studies considering knitters' information needs and their thought processes are exceptions, rather than the norm (Haring, 2011; Prigoda & McKenzie, 2007; Rosner & Ryokai, 2009). The contemporary discourse that has evolved around knitting, however, complements and interprets the artifacts, revealing their connections to different communities. Attention to the discourse of knitters is essential to understanding the intersections of digital and material culture that shape knitting today.

The sheer number of knitting blogs, in tandem with the nature of the Internet, indicates the proliferation of online resources that discuss knitting, whether as a personal exploration of the subject or in some more broadly conceived way. The blogs of prominent knitwear designers, primarily in the United Kingdom and North America, including Canada, and the digital trail left by amateur knitters offer cues to the meaning and the significance of the largely self-curated contemporary information about knitting. It is possible to identify the leading voices in this vast, online conversation, and the blogs selected for discussion in this essay result from an analysis that identifies prominent knitters and assesses their influence (Pierce, 2012/2013). The vast readership of these blogs should suggest that the online conversation they promote is a complex and dynamic one, too. Chartier's methodological guidance suggests that considering these texts in relation to each other, comparing their accounts, permits understanding of their subject matter.

A sumptuous example of digital media on knitting is found in the work of Jared Flood, founder of Brooklyn Tweed, which began as a blog and PDF pattern-purchasing site and has become a multi-purpose fiber studio. Brooklyn Tweed now produces American-made wool and publishes the work of multiple designers. The most recent texts that represent these projects to the public are digital *Look Books*, with skilled photography in carefully chosen venues, schematics and design specifications, as well as links to online purchasing information.

For all their commercial intent, the *Look Books* and other digital media at Brooklyn Tweed simultaneously evoke the importance of locally made products and the history of the places where production occurs. Brooklyn Tweed yarns are touted as "grown in the USA," and their manufacture by a "historic Harrisville, New Hampshire" mill is given prominence in product descriptions (Brooklyn Tweed, n.d., para. 1). As the yarn debuted in 2011, Flood's blog featured a virtual tour of the mill and the process of turning fleece into workable fiber for knitters (Flood, 2011). In this five-part photo essay, Flood created a tribute to the mill that produces the wool under his brand, documenting the tools that have been used in this kind of work for years.

The series of posts on wool manufacture is one of many that link fiber craft and place. The BT Fall 2012 *Look Book*, for example, was photographed at Suceries de la Montagne outside Quebec, a site Flood hoped readers would see as evoking a "story of Woods & Wool" (2012b, p. 4). An accompanying photo essay filled pages with images of the site as it reflected the Canadian "sugaring tradition" (Flood, 2012a, p. 28). At the same time that it acknowledges the history that foregrounds contemporary knitting, Flood's work evokes the beauty and the importance of place that many knitters regard as defining features of the craft in the twenty-first century.

Kate Davies, a historian turned knitwear designer, lives in and writes from Edinburgh. The blog, now at an eponymous URL (http://katedaviesdesigns.com/), devotes attention to yarns from native sheep and regional producers; designs inspired by regional figures or places; and the local sites, whether shops or walking trails. A recent blog post, for example, details a visit to a place associated with the founding of utopian socialism and an eighteenth-century cotton mill (Davies, 2013b); these features factor in the city's recognition as a world heritage site. In her attention to other historical phenomena that document the culture of the United Kingdom, she has written of one historic artifact, "It is . . . a massive conveyer of meaning" (Davies, 2013c, para. 13). The sentiment stands true of her work as a whole.

Davies's other publications, especially her patterns, commemorate the people and places that shaped the heritage of the country. Much as her blog and the individual patterns sold there evoke the local landscape and her environs, her *Colours of Shetland* (Davies, 2012) features ten knitting patterns that have their inspiration in landmarks and historic figures. In addition to naming patterns for people and places, her book and blog include essays explaining the geographic features, historic figures, and flora and fauna. Each design, then, is a testimonial to the past and the people who have shaped the place where she lives. In her own work, as well as that of the knitters who follow her blog and make garments from her patterns, these defining features of cultural heritage are remembered.

Similar themes are evident in Stephanie Pearl-McPhee's *Yarn Harlot* blog, written primarily from her home in Toronto, Canada. The *Yarn Harlot* (http://www .yarnharlot.ca/blog/) has published continuously at its current site since January 2004 and earned numerous awards, including top honors from the Canadian Blog Awards and the Blogger's Choice Awards. One academic treatise on knitting has pronounced it, unequivocally, the most popular knitting blog going, and a review of one of Pearl-McPhee's first books claimed the site saw 20,000 hits per day (Turney, 2009, p. 151; "Review," 2007).

Pearl-McPhee is known for her passionate voice, technical skills, and advocacy for charities, public libraries, and local yarn shops and bookstores. A theme that recurs in her writing is the importance of collective action—of individuals who work together toward a common end. Rather than celebrating the grand gesture, Pearl-McPhee holds that what an individual does matters. Knitting, according to her, is an activity that brings people together in the interest of connecting and helping others. In one blog post last July, Pearl-McPhee (2012a) wrote about the selfless nature of the knitting community:

> Knitting teaches you that one small action does matter. That one small action, like knitting a stitch, isn't unimportant. It's vital. One small action repeated many times is a sweater. . . . Our whole group sees that one small thing—put together with many other things can create something enormous, and wonderful, and magical. Why are knitters like this? Because they knit, and they have learned everything they need to know about little things mattering. Knitters produce, rather than taking or simply consuming. (para. 5)

This manifesto encapsulates the values she sees in knitting and in community.

She articulates notions of culture and heritage that entail social attitudes and actions, values made manifest through actions large and small. It is a feeling that has won a following. Pearl-McPhee's fans not only support her—and here support should be understood broadly, to include both the purchase of her books and the intense, emotional connection they evince in posting to her blog and attending her readings—they give their time, attention, and resources to the causes with which she is involved. In the summer of 2012, many cheered at the sidelines and contributed to the fund-raising goals of the bicycling team she participated in to raise funds for an AIDS charity. These individual acts were documented with commentary and photographs via her blog as well (Pearl-McPhee, 2012b). Much as she asks others to be conscious of the need to support the places and the events that make their communities distinctive and welcoming places, she devotes space on her blog to recording the actions that others take toward these ends.

At present, the vast majority of these digital documents are protected only to the extent that individual site owners and platform providers continue to maintain the material. Yet if library and information professionals participate in the core goal of conservation—"to preserve the material evidence of our past so we can learn from it today and appreciate it in the future" (American Institute for Conservation of Historic and Artistic Works, n.d., para. 2)—developing strategies and partnerships for the preservation of online information resources on knitting matters. When these resources are simply the province of individuals or individual organizations, the discourse and the knowledge they represent are likely to be accessed only by proponents of knitting, despite the range of content they represent.

The preservation and utility of these discourses, then, has to do with ideas and endeavors beyond women's historical craft work. While the texts generated by knitters discuss pattern and fiber attributes, as well as the pleasure that writers find in knitting and design, the writers are not simply members of knitting communities. They are activists for causes, from AIDS support to historic conservation, and these other issues signal the nature of what is needed in terms of conservation and preservation of these discourses. In addition to identifying documents as a discourse on craft, they must also be linked to collections that will be consulted by researchers on subjects like social justice, philanthropy, woman-owned businesses, and historic preservation. Assigning these descriptive attributes and directing researchers to these texts, however, would come about through institutional rather than individual curation. Like the CAMEO database that "increases access to formerly obscure information" and "creates a historical context" for the artifacts it records (Derrick, 2004), institutional conservation and preservation of knitting texts would authenticate and promote information, ensuring its continued availability and broader use.

CONCLUSION: CONSERVATION AND THE DISCOURSE OF KNITTING

Knitting, a practice sometimes described in a self-deprecating manner as simple work with two sticks and a string, is nonetheless not a simplistic undertaking. Its little-understood history suggests its larger significance and indicates that its proponents have always adapted new information and communication technologies to share ideas about their craft. In the twenty-first century, knitting has become important as both leisure and commercial activity. It can be a small business enterprise, a leisure activity that is personally and emotionally satisfying, or a means of connecting to the past or a community. Discussions of knitting invoke its status as a historic handcraft, its proponents' reliance on their own energy and local resources in lieu of big-box consumption, the historic mills that continue to produce wool, and the distinctive places where designers' work is photographed to create images for patterns and marketing purposes. The contemporary cultural heritage of knitting as reflected in online environments is oriented to questions about what will endure and suggests that knitting itself serves as a conservation trope.

The contextual history provided by pattern books augments this conclusion, further illuminating what knitting has meant over the years. It has been a compulsory activity and one that has been a means of earning a living by providing luxury goods to the monarchy and those of means (MacDonald, 1990; National Society for Promoting the Education of the Poor, 1832). It has demonstrated patriotism (Royal Air Force Comfort Committee, ca. 1939). At times, knitting has been seen as a means of making fashion affordable or of creating flattering garments (Gauguin, 1845; Koster & Murray, 1952). It has become an art form, a way of expressing visions of beauty and color or social critique (Fassett, 1988; Hemmings, 2010). In other words, knitting is protean, reflective of its era and culture.

Discussions of how to regard and preserve digital cultural heritage have been proffered but are far from settled (Cameron & Kenderdine, 2007). Cloonan (2007) has urged library and information professionals to consider the implications of issues like the conservation of born-digital materials and "prospective" conservation that anticipates the potential interests of the future (p. 144). Contemporary knitting is an area that presents exactly these challenges. To understand knitting as a component of cultural heritage means we must collect a variety of texts and artifacts, both digital and material. The idea of collecting these ephemeral, every-day resources may seem outside most institutional missions, yet if we attend to the words of prominent members of the knitting community and explore the effect of their writings and photography on others, we find stories of cultural significance.

The knitted object may testify to its creator's skills or a wearer's life, but its contributions to the discourse of intention and significance are limited. The documents that explain how and why people knitted must be preserved, as well as artifacts that survive an infant's wearing or other daily use. The documents we have make plain that the reasons knitting was important in one era may change in the next. Given recent developments in the history of knitting that make the blog and the digital image so important to its overall practice, understanding the cultural heritage of this fiber craft commits us to digital as well as material conservation.

Some proponents and scholars of knitting have argued that the craft is misunderstood as an old-fashioned and unfashionable activity (Newington, 2010; Turney,

2009). Examination of digital materials associated with prominent knitters signal that practicing this craft is something quite different. In a commentary on knitting as art, Hemmings (2010) calls attention to the ways fiber artists have used the craft and how through their work "knitting is revealed to be a significant tool for the structuring of both thinking and making" as a preliminary to the need "to reconsider what we thought we knew knitting to be" (p. 9). Digital texts likewise point toward another sort of reconsideration. In knitting blogs, we see that in the here and now, knitters use their craft to advocate for the conservation of their communities, their history, and their capacity to create a good life for all. Documenting and preserving knitters' words are the only ways to move past extant notions of knitting as a fusty antiquarianism and ensuring its real legacy will be understood.

ACKNOWLEDGMENTS

Research for this chapter, chiefly access to texts held at the National Library of Art at the Victoria and Albert Museum and the British Library, was funded by an Arts & Humanities Initiative award from the University of Iowa. Additional support came from a research fellowship awarded by Winterthur Museum, Garden, and Library. The author also wishes to acknowledge the work of Beth Kamp in preparing the manuscript for publication.

REFERENCES

Adler, M. A. (2012). Disciplining knowledge at the Library of Congress. *Knowledge Organization*, *39*(5), 370–376. Retrieved from http://www.isko.org/ko.html

American Institute for Conservation of Historic and Artistic Works. (n.d.). *About AIC*. Retrieved from http://www.conservation-us.org/index.cfm?fuseaction=page.viewpage&pageid=489

Barber, E. J. W. (1994). *Women's work: The first 20,000 years; Women, cloth, and society in early times*. New York, NY: W. W. Norton.

Barry, D. (2013, March 15). History evergreen. *New York Times*, p. AR1.

Baym, N. K., & boyd, d. (2012). Socially mediated publicness: An introduction. *Journal of Broadcasting & Electronic Media*, *56*(3), 320–329. doi:10.1080/08838151.2012.705200

Blackledge, A. (2012). Discourse and power. In J. P. Gee & M. Handford (Eds.), *Routledge handbook of discourse analysis* (pp. 616–627). New York, NY: Routledge.

boyd, d. (2009). How can qualitative Internet researchers define the boundaries of their projects: A response to Christine Hine. In A. Markham & N. Baym (Eds.), *Internet inquiry: Conversations about method* (pp. 26–32). Retrieved from http://www.danah.org/papers/EthnoBoundaries.pdf

Brock, A. (2013, February). *Cultural critical informatics: Twitter as black discourse*. Paper presented at Black Geek Week, University of Illinois Champaign-Urbana.

Brooklyn Tweed. (n.d.). *Yarn*. Retrieved from http://brooklyntweed.net/yarn.html

Budd, J. M. (2006). Discourse analysis and the study of communication in LIS. *Library Trends*, *55*(1), 65–82. doi:10.1353/lib.2006.0046

Budd, J. M., & Raber, D. (1996). Discourse analysis: Method and application in the study of information. *Information Processing and Management, 32*(5), 217–226. doi: http://dx.doi .org/10.1016/S0306-4573(96)85007-2

Cameron, F., & Kenderdine, S. (Eds.). (2007). *Theorizing digital cultural heritage: A critical discourse.* Cambridge, MA: MIT Press.

Chartier, R. (1997). *On the edge of the cliff: History, language, and practices.* (L. G. Cochrane, Trans.). Baltimore, MD: Johns Hopkins University Press.

Cloonan, M. (2007). The moral imperative to preserve. *Library Trends, 55*(3), 746–755. doi:10.1353/lib.2007.0003

Cloonan, M., & Harvey, R. (2007). Preserving cultural heritage: Introduction. *Library Trends, 56*(1), 1–3. doi:10.1353/lib.2007.0046

Davies, K. (n.d.). About. Retrieved from http://katedaviesdesigns.com/about/

Davies, K. (2012). *Colours of Shetland.* Kate Davies Designs.

Davies, K. (2013a, March 20). Still making. [Web log comment]. Retrieved from http:// katedaviesdesigns.com/2013 /03/20/still-making/

Davies, K. (2013b, April 2). New Lanark, the egg, and the naming of things. [Web log comment]. Retrieved from http://katedaviesdesigns.com/2013/04/02/new-lanark-the-egg-and -the-naming-of-things/

Davies, K. (2013c, April 9). A kiss from France. [Web log comment]. Retrieved from http:// katedaviesdesigns.com/2013/04/09/a-kiss-from-france/

Derrick, M. (2004, May 3). CAMEO: A free Internet reference on materials used in the production and conservation of historic and artistic works. *First Monday, 9*(5). doi: http:// dx.doi.org/10.5210%2Ffm.v9i5.1143

Fassett, K. (1988). *Kaffe Fassett at the V&A: Knitting and needlepoint.* London: Century.

Flood, J. (2011, March 9). Building heathers: Mill tour part 1 of 5. [Web log comment]. Retrieved from https://brooklyntweed.net/blog/?p=575

Flood, J. (2012a). Gone Sugarin'. *BT Fall '12 Look Book,* 28–34. Retrieved from https:// brooklyntweed.net/btfall12lookbook.html

Flood, J. (2012b). Outpost. *BT Fall '12 Look Book,* 4. Retrieved from https://brooklyntweed .net/btfall12lookbook.html

Frohmann, B. (1992). The power of images: A discourse analysis of the cognitive viewpoint. *Journal of Documentation, 48*(4), 365–386. http://dx.doi.org/10.1108/eb026904

Frohmann, B. (1994). Discourse analysis as a research method in library and information science. *Library & Information Science Research, 16*(2), 119–138. http://dx.doi.org/10.1016/0740 -8188(94)90004-3

Frohmann, B. (2001). Discourse and documentation: Some implications for pedagogy and research. *Journal of Education for Library and Information Science, 42*(1), 12–26. Retrieved from http://www.jstor.org/stable/40324034

Gaugin, J. (1845). *The lady's assistant for executing useful and fancy designs in knitting, netting, and crochet work.* London: I. J. Gauguin & Ackerman & Co.

Gilbert, R. (2012). A knitted cotton jacket in the collection of the Knitting and Crochet Guild of Great Britain. *Textile History, 43*(1), 90–106. http://dx.doi.org/10.1179/174329 512X13284471321325

Gordon, J. (2010). Maritime influences on traditional knitwear design: The case of the fisherman's gansey: An object study. *Textile History, 41*(1), 99–108. http://dx.doi.org/10.1179/ 174329510x12670196126728

Haring, K. (2011). Morse code knitting. In G. Joseph-Hunter, P. Duff, & M. Papadomano-laki (Eds.), *Transmission arts: Artists and airwaves*. New York, NY: PAJ Publications.

Hemmings, J. (2010). Rethinking Knitting. In J. Hemmings (Ed.), *In the loop* (pp. 8–9). London: Black Dog.

Koster, J., & Murray, M. (1952). *Knitted garments for all*. London: Odhams Press, Ltd.

MacDonald, A. (1990). *No idle hands: The social history of American knitting*. New York, NY: Ballantine Books.

National Society for Promoting the Education of the Poor in the Principles of the Established Church of England and Wales. (1832). *Instructions on needle-work and knitting, as derived from the practice of the central school of the national society for promoting the education of the poor in the principles of the established church, in the sanctuary, Westminster*. London: Roake and Varty.

Newington, L. (2010). Knitting has an image problem. In J. Hemmings (Ed.), *In the loop* (pp. 26–31). London: Black Dog Publishing.

Parks, K., & McFarland, C. (2011/2012, Winter). Stitch by stitch: The life and legacy of Elizabeth Zimmermann. *Wisconsin Magazine of History*, *95*(2), 39–60. Retrieved from http://www.wisconsinhistory.org/wmh/

Pearl-McPhee, S. (2005). *At knit's end: Meditations for women who knit too much*. North Adams, MA: Storey Publishing.

Pearl-McPhee, S. (2012a, July 26). With love. [Web log comment]. Retrieved from http://www.yarnharlot.ca/blog/archives/2012/07/26/with_love.html

Pearl-McPhee, S. (2012b, August 7). A very long bike ride. [Web log comment]. http://www.yarnharlot.ca/blog/archives/2012/08/07/a_very_long_bike_ride.html

Pearl-McPhee, S. (2013, April 3). Endings and beginnings. [Web log comment]. Retrieved from http://www.yarnharlot.ca/blog/archives/2013/04/03/endings_and_beginnings.html

Pierce, J. Burek (2011).*What adolescents ought to know: Sexual health texts in early twentieth-century America*. Amherst, MA: University of Massachusetts Press.

Pierce, J. Burek (2012/2013). [Study of online knitting/fiber arts community]. Unpublished raw data.

Prigoda, E., & McKenzie, P. (2007). Purls of wisdom: A collectivist study of human informa-tion behaviour in a public library knitting group. *Journal of Documentation*, *63*(1), 90–114. doi:10.1108/00220410710723902

Radford, G. P., & Radford, M. L. (2001). Libraries, librarians, and the discourse of fear. *Library Quarterly*, *71*(3), 299–329. Retrieved from http://www.jstor.org/stable/4309528

Review: *At knit's end: Meditations for women who knit too much*. (2007, August 27). *Publishers Weekly*, *254*(34), 86. Retrieved from http://www.publishersweekly.com/978-1-59887-520-1

Rosner, D. K., & Ryokai, K. (2009). Reflections on craft: Probing the creative process of everyday knitters. *Proceedings of the Seventh Annual ACM Conference on Creativity and Cog-nition*, Berkeley, CA, 195–204. doi:10.1145/1640233.1640264

Royal Air Force Comforts Committee. [ca. 1939]. *Knitting for the R.A.F.* [booklet]. General Collection. National Art Library, Victoria and Albert Museum, London.

Rutt, R. (1989). *A history of hand-knitting*. Loveland, CO: Interweave Press.

Siegelaub, S. (Ed.). (1997). *Bibliographica textilia historiae: Towards a general bibliography on the history of textiles based on the library and archives of the Center for Social Research on Old Textiles (CSROT)*. New York, NY: International General.

Signature Needle Arts. (n.d.). *Our Story*. Retrieved from http://www.signatureneedlearts.com/our_story/

Stoller, D. (2004). *Stitch 'n bitch: The knitter's handbook*. New York, NY: Workman Publishing Company.

Turnau, I. (1991). *History of knitting before mass production*. (A. Szonert, Trans.). Warsaw: Institute of the History of Material Culture, Polish Academy of Sciences.

Turney, J. (2009). *The culture of knitting*. New York, NY: Berg/Oxford.

Valimaki, V. (2011). *Color affection* [knitting pattern]. Retrieved from http://www.ravelry .com/patterns/library/color-affection

Wiegand, W. A. (1999). Tunnel vision and blind spots: What the past tells us about the present; reflections on the twentieth-century history of American librarianship. *Library Quarterly, 69*(1), 1–31. Retrieved from http://www.jstor.org/stable/4309267

Zimmermann, E. (1973). *Knitting without tears*. New York, NY: Fireside Books.

Part III

EDUCATION

INTRODUCTION: EDUCATION

The authors of "Developing Twenty-First-Century Cultural Heritage Information Professionals for Digital Stewardship: A Framework for Curriculum Design" unintentionally validated the inclusion of an Education section in this volume:

> As digital stewardship is emerging as a concept of professional roles and responsibilities due to digital convergence, Library and Information Science (LIS) educational programs need to provide students with appropriate educational programs to take on new responsibilities and roles in all aspects of digital resources management.

In their article, Mary W. Elings (archivist for digital collections of the Bancroft Library at the University of California, Berkeley, adjunct professor, School of Library and Information Science, The Catholic University of America), Youngok Choi (assistant professor, School of Library and Information Science, The Catholic University of America), and Jane Zhang (assistant professor, School of Library and Information Science, The Catholic University of America) describe the Cultural Heritage Information Management (CHIM) concentration at the School of Library and Information Science of the Catholic University of America. Developed around five core competencies, CHIM prepares twenty-first-century cultural heritage information professionals to develop and curate sustainable digital collections meeting the research and educational needs served by libraries, archives, museums, and other cultural heritage institutions.

In "Local History and Genealogy Collections in Libraries: The Challenge to Library and Information Science Educators," Rhonda L. Clark and James T. Maccaferri of the

Department of Library Science, Clarion University of Pennsylvania, explore the question of whether the library and information science field provides adequate education and resources to support professionals managing local collections. Clark and Maccaferri provide a survey of existing instructional support for professionals managing local collections, review periodical literature related to local studies librarianship since 2000, and offer suggestions for new directions in local collections research, education, and collaboration.

6

Developing Twenty-First-Century Cultural Heritage Information Professionals for Digital Stewardship

A Framework for Curriculum Design

Youngok Choi, Mary W. Elings, and Jane Zhang

ABSTRACT

As digital stewardship emerges as a concept of professional roles and responsibilities due to digital convergence, Library and Information Science (LIS) educational programs need to provide students with appropriate educational programs to take on new responsibilities and roles in all aspects of digital resources management. The Cultural Heritage Information Management (CHIM) concentration at the Department of Library and Information Science of the Catholic University of America prepares twenty-first-century cultural heritage information professionals to develop and curate sustainable digital collections, meeting the research and educational needs served by libraries, archives, museums, and other cultural heritage institutions. The program of study supporting the development of five core competencies is described with an emphasis on courses providing a foundation in digital stewardship concepts. The learning activities, exploratory projects, and collaborations with digital curation and preservation professionals designed to prepare students for twenty-first-century digital stewardship of cultural heritage resources are highlighted.

INTRODUCTION

Digital technology has changed how people search for, access, and interact with information in the twenty-first century. Such digital technology enables users to actively embrace digital resources in their research, teaching, and daily activities. In particular, it is reported that scholars in humanities and social sciences actively use digital resources in their teaching and research (Harley, 2007; Sinn, 2012). As digital collections have become vital resources for scholarly and social endeavor, cultural heritage institutions such as libraries, archives, and museums (LAMs) put more effort into making their collections broadly available online by undertaking digitization programs, acquiring born-digital materials, and employing digital strategies (Smithsonian, 2009, 2010; Stack, 2010, 2013). Building, managing, and sharing digital collections is now an essential activity at such institutions. As one museum recently characterized this trend, digital is a "Dimension of Everything" (Stack, 2013).

Development and management of digitized and born-digital collections bring changes to resource management and professional practice. Success in creating and managing digital collections requires competencies in acquisition and curation of objects, information, and data; information organization; information services and outreach; strategic planning; project management; the ability to collaborate with partners across departmental, institutional, and disciplinary boundaries; and expertise in digital technologies (Sula, 2013). In other words, the development and management of cultural heritage digital content should be concerned not simply with capturing objects or technical considerations, but with presenting information as accurately, authentically, and engagingly as possible; disseminating information as widely as possible in a sensitive, safe, and durable manner; and providing an effective and inspirational learning environment that best communicates the collections' intended purposes. In doing so, cultural heritage professionals must have the capacity to think critically about the meanings and implications of digital content to advance institutional cultures, methods, and relationships with audiences, and thus, improve cultural heritage in general for use (Cameron & Kenderdine, 2007). This range of professional responsibilities and roles involving the collection, selection, management, long-term preservation, and accessibility of digital assets has been represented as "digital stewardship" (Bastian, Cloonan, & Harvey, 2011; Cloonan & Mahard, 2010). Even the Library of Congress's National Digital Information Infrastructure and Preservation Program (NDIIPP) uses the term "digital stewardship" in the National Digital Stewardship Alliance initiative (NDSA, n.d.), to stress management of digital content for current and long-term use via collaboration.

As digital stewardship emerges as a concept of professional roles and responsibilities due to digital convergence, Library and Information Science (LIS) educational programs need to provide students with appropriate educational programs to take on new responsibilities and roles in all aspects of digital resources management. Several LIS schools have offered new curricula, specializations, and continuing education programs to meet this need (Kim, 2012; Marty & Twidale, 2011). These include a cultural informatics concentration and museum libraries certificate at Pratt Institute's School of Information and Library Science, curriculum development at Simmons College (Cloonan & Mahard, 2010), the cultural heritage information program of study at the University of South Carolina,[1] the digital curation curriculum at the University of North Carolina at Chapel Hill, and data curation specialization at the University of Illinois, Urbana-Champaign.[2] More specialized curricula are necessary to help students gain expertise in related areas. Another example is the recently launched concentration in Cultural Heritage Information management (CHIM) for the Master of Science in Library and Information Science program at the Department of Library and Information Science of the Catholic University of America (CUA-DLIS).

The CHIM concentration at CUA-DLIS prepares twenty-first-century cultural heritage information professionals to develop and curate sustainable digital collections that address research and educational needs being served by LAM institutions. As researchers involved in digital humanities and social sciences computing increasingly work with digital collections as their primary research resources, preparing students to create, manage, preserve, and promote digital collections that meet the research needs of these growing fields is critical (Sula, 2013).

This paper begins with an overview of the CHIM curriculum that looks at how this program of study prepares students to become competent information professionals in the converging LAM environment, and highlights the growing importance of digital technology competencies in this area. The paper then focuses on the design of two of the digital courses in this curriculum—Digital Curation and Digital Collections in Libraries, Archives, and Museums (DCLAM)—and describes how this curriculum framework educates students in twenty-first-century digital stewardship in LAMs and prepares them to advance the mission of cultural heritage institutions in the digital age.

CURRICULUM DESIGN

As the practices of libraries, archives, and museums converge, the need to educate a new generation of information professionals prepared to succeed in these cultural heritage institutions becomes clear. The Cultural Heritage Information Professionals Workshop in 2008 (http://chips.ci.fsu.edu), for example, brought together professionals in the field to identify and make recommendations to address this issue. Researchers (Ray, 2009; Trant, 2009) have called for changes to the education system to produce professionals ready to address new challenges in managing cultural heritage information. Marty (2005, 2006, 2007a, 2007b) discusses the skills required of today's museum professionals in areas including technology application, user interface design, user services, and information literacy. A survey of museum professionals on perceptions of necessary knowledge and skills echoes Marty's discussion on important knowledge and skills required in museum fields (Duff, Cherry, & Sheffield, 2010). Many practitioners and LIS educators also emphasize that an educational program should focus not only on digital conversions, processes, and preservation, but also on systematic evaluation and assessment to advance services and facilitate broader use in different contexts across institutional types (Chowdhury, 2010; Institute of Museum and Library Services [IMLS], 2003, 2006; Evens & Hauttekeete, 2011; Mallan & Park, 2006; Manzuch, 2009; National Initiative for a Networked Cultural Heritage, 2002). In short, a curriculum for cultural heritage information management should strike a fine balance between technology, user needs and services, preservation, and management.

In addressing such educational needs, the Department of Library and Information Science at the Catholic University of America (CUA) recognized the importance of offering guidance in course selection to LIS students who are interested in this career path in LAMs. Based on a long tradition of offering an education in CHIM, the school reshaped its curriculum to guide students to build knowledge and skills critical to take responsibilities for digital convergence in LAMs.

The curriculum as a concentration for cultural heritage information management was officially introduced in 2012 and was built on the Department of Library and Information Science (DLIS) at the Catholic University of America in its long tradition of offering courses in cultural heritage information management including special collections, archives management, preservation, art and museum librarianship, and rare book librarianship; and public programs; outreach; and digital exhibits in libraries, archives, and museums. A concentration, Cultural Heritage Information Management (CHIM), focuses on a critical and theoretical appraisal of the specific roles that cultural heritage institutions play in the interpretation, representation, preservation, and use of collections implementing emerging digital technology, and ensures that students gain appropriate knowledge and skills via classroom learning and practical experience to become competent information professionals in the field of cultural heritage information management. The envisioned competencies[3] that students can obtain through the CHIM curriculum include:

- A competency, "contextual foundations," which represents knowledge and understanding of the culture, context, and collections of cultural institutions; being able to articulate the interrelationship among libraries, archives, museums, and cultural heritage institutions; and understanding the management of nonprofits and the challenges faced by these institutions.
- A competency, "resource management and digital curation," which implies fluency in the theory, standards, and best practices of information selection, acquisition, disposal, organization, evaluation, storage, preservation, and conservation of cultural resources in all formats, including digital, within libraries, archives, and museums. The curriculum ensures students obtain planning and management skills in the activities of resource management and curation.
- A competency, "information organization," which defines an understanding of conceptual frameworks for organizing and retrieving information resources, including metadata schemas, classification systems, taxonomies, standardized terminologies, controlled vocabularies, standards for data sharing, and approaches for interoperability. Students will be capable of developing information representations of archival and cultural resources, and have expertise in metadata standards, classification schemes, taxonomy, and controlled vocabularies.
- A competency, "information service provisions," which characterizes the skills of students to analyze the needs of users so as to design and evaluate products

and services to meet those needs and advance their institution's missions and values. Students will be able to demonstrate their ability to develop new programs and strategies/activities to enhance user experience.

- A competency, "digital technology," which requires students to demonstrate utilization of technological tools for the delivery of content and services, and understand digital technologies and their potential for advancing the mission of cultural heritage institutions. Based on this competency of digital technology, students will be able to apply technology for the preservation of cultural heritage resources and develop the ability to manage projects involving digital technologies.

The five competencies are closely related and represent interconnected components of professional work that are manifested in LAM collaboration and convergence. Along with four core courses for a master's degree in LIS, a set of specialized courses were formed to foster the development of competencies in the five areas. Among the specialized courses, two new courses—LSC677 History and Theory of Cultural Heritage Institutions and LSC648 Digital Curation—were developed as a new addition to the concentration in fall 2011 and offered in spring 2012. These two courses lay the foundation for the CHIM concentration. Other specific courses in the CHIM concentration include LSC615 Metadata, LSC635 Use and Users of Libraries and Information, and LSC652 Foundations of Digital Libraries, which gives students an opportunity to build a digital collection using a digital content management system based on best practices in digitization projects and digital libraries. Additional electives recommended in this concentration are available on the department's website.[4] One of these electives is LSC878 Digital Collections in Libraries, Archives, and Museums (DCLAM), which has been offered since 2010.

In addition to multiple courses for students to obtain the competencies, the CHIM concentration also offers a practicum for experiential learning at many cultural institutions in the Washington metropolitan region. Art Museum of the Americas, Corcoran Gallery of Art/College of Art & Design, and the National Museum of Women in the Arts are the private cultural institutions that partner with DLIS. Federal partners include Library of Congress, National Agricultural Libraries, National Library of Medicine, and the Smithsonian Institution. These partners hold invaluable cultural heritage resources and artifacts in diverse subject areas, have deep and extensive expertise in the management and organization of cultural heritage information, and offer rich experiential learning opportunities for students. Students would complete 120 hours of practicums on projects such as resource management, digital content creation, preservation, and service delivery at partner institutions under the supervision of professionals.

Building on a foundation of traditional professional training, the CHIM curriculum prepares professionals to work in the increasingly digitally oriented field of cultural heritage information. Through core and specialized courses, as well as electives, students are given a foundation to take on new responsibilities and roles in the area of digital stewardship. Two of these courses: Digital Curation and Digital

Collections in Libraries, Archives, and Museums, are examples of how this curriculum framework educates students and prepares them to work in cultural heritage institutions in the digital age.

DIGITAL CURATION

The digital curation course is a recent addition to the DLIS CHIM curriculum. As described in the course syllabus, the course provides an overview of digital curation as a lifecycle management strategy to manage, evaluate, collect, organize, preserve, share, and support the use and reuse of digital assets. The course introduces digital curation models, infrastructures, standards, initiatives, and technical tools; and covers the concepts and skills involved in creating and managing an integrated and sustainable digital cultural heritage repository as a trusted body of digital information for current and future use. The goals and objectives are to prepare students, upon completion of the course, to be able to:

- Understand the digital curation lifecycle concept and its application;
- Explain, evaluate, and use online tools to create data management plans;
- Familiarize with digital curation technical environments and have hands-on experience using digital curation tools and explaining how to use them;
- Conduct research to find out current professional practices and solutions for curatorial challenges in an institutional or personal digital curation context; and
- Analyze digital curatorial challenges and think innovatively for theoretical, practical, or technological solutions.

The course was designed on the basis of an emerging concept and practice of digital curation that has been introduced into the curriculum of library and information science education.[5] To achieve the course goals and objectives, several approaches are incorporated into the course delivery and requirements. This section describes details of how the course is in line with the foundation of digital curation concepts and approaches adopted to maximize student learning experiences.

Digital curation lifecycle serves as the core thread that guides the course content delivery in our digital curation course. After a brief introduction to digital curation, the course starts with a close observation of several conceptual models that explicate the theory and practice of digital curation and preservation. The body part of the course content focuses on key functional components as identified in major conceptual digital curation lifecycle models such as the Reference Model for an Open Archival Information System (OAIS) (Consultative Committee for Space Data Systems [CCSDS], 2012) and the DCC Curation Lifecycle model (Digital Curation Center [DCC], 2004–2013a). It covers topics such as data creation and management, digital appraisal and acquisition, digital repository infrastructures, digital preservation strategies and solutions, data representation and contextualization, and data use and reuse. The lifecycle approach helps students to establish a holistic perspective when thinking about and dealing with digital curation and preservation issues.

The curation lifecycle approach is also adopted in the course requirement and assignment design. In building data management plans based on funding agencies' requirements, students need to think conceptually from data creation, format, and dissemination to data storage, preservation, and access. Before selecting digital curation tools for review and demo, students are required to review tools and categorize them according to their curatorial functions in the curation lifecycle. In seeking innovative ideas and solutions for digital curation and preservation challenges, students are asked to identify the challenges in the context of a conceptual digital curation program in a cultural heritage information management setting. In their group digital preservation outreach workshop, students presented four modules of digital preservation strategies for college students, systematically progressing from importance of digital preservation, content selection, storage options, and personal digital collection management.

The curation lifecycle approach is an effective way to educate graduate-level professionals who need not only to know "how to," but also to understand "why" so as to survive in the emerging digital work environment. As one of the students commented:

> It was rewarding when everything started to click. When, for example, I realized how long-tail graphs spoke to preservation strategies or how you could use the DROID file format identification tool and PREMIS entities to feed into DCC Lifecycle Model activities. My own work is preservation-based, and it was giddying to realize I've been producing Archival Information Packets (AIP) all along without realizing it. The Digital Curation course speaks to me in many avenues of my life, relating to lessons learned in other classes at CUA, to both my professional and personal lives. Other students in the class say they've had similar awakenings throughout the semester. (Marcou, 2012)

Digital curation education is also about technology as the digital curation and preservation community is constantly building, testing, and using technical tools. One big challenge that digital curation educators confront is how to incorporate a large quantity and a wide variety of open source software tools into a time-constrained classroom teaching and learning schedule. A module-based or project-based approach to introducing students to digital curation technical tools has been experimented with in digital curation educational programs.[6] However, the module-based or project-based approach would be challenging in introducing students to various tools available and used in the entire lifecycle. To help students to achieve a maximum exposure to technical tools, we have adopted a participatory approach. For example, the tool review and mini-tutorial assignment requires students to briefly review a list of more than seventy tools that the instructor has provided with descriptions and links on the course management site. After the review, students provide oral reports on the digital curation functions the tools support in the curation lifecycle. The process provides them with an overview and basic characterization of existing tools. Students then select from the existing list or other sources two to three tools for a thorough review and write a short review report. Through describing, comparing, and contrasting the functionality of the tools, they get to know the tools beyond a simple impression or click. Each student eventually selects one tool to further explore its functionality. They download and test the software until they gain a comfortable use experience of the tool. Based on their experience, each of them produces a short written tutorial to explain how to use the tool and provides a live demo in class to their fellow classmates. The step-by-step instructions each provides in their written tutorial are voluntarily posted on the course site so that students can learn from other's work if they are interested in the tools after they watch the live demos. Tools selected by students include TimelineJS, Google Refine, MUSE, Zotero, Social Safe, Viewshare, Bulk Rename Utility, Vimeo, Omeka, MP3TAG, MetaArchive, DROID, Dioscuri, DSpace, Xena, WebCite, Greenstone, Mendeley, and ArchiveFacebook.

The participatory approach helps to magnify students' collaborative learning experience. Having students become familiar with a specific tool and teach the tool for peers is encouraging and effective to build students' confidence. An important trait of cultural heritage professionals in the digital environment is having the ability to select and test tools and teach others how to use them. Willingness to learn and to challenge oneself with new technology is essential and should be incorporated into digital curation education.

In addition to theoretical models and technical skills, the design of the course requirements also strives to achieve the goal of encouraging students to think innovatively for theoretical, practical, and technological solutions when challenged with digital curation issues. Students are required to complete a digital curatorial scenario research. For a cultural heritage information setting they have selected, students use the digital curation lifecycle concept as a guide to describe a conceptual digital curation program covering major components and curatorial activities. They then consult current literature or professionals to identify a challenging digital curatorial scenario in their information setting and conduct research on current practices and existing solutions. Based on their research, each of them proposes one nontraditional, innovative idea on how to solve the curatorial challenge from one or more aspects (theoretical, practical, or technological). Students are evaluated on the basis of completeness of program lifecycle description, appropriateness of curatorial scenario identification, sufficient coverage of literature, and originality of ideas.

We have also collaborated with digital curation and preservation professional communities in the region and invited guest speakers from the Library of Congress's National Digital Information Infrastructure and Preservation Program (NDIIPP), the National Archives' Electronic Records Archives (ERA), and the Tessella Digital Preservation team. In collaboration with the National Digital Stewardship Alliance (NDSA) Outreach Working Group and CUA Mullen Library, students in the 2012 class held an open workshop to help undergraduate students learn how to curate their personal digital collections in honor of ALA Preservation Week. The success of outreach activities requires substantial efforts in collaboration, coordination, and interaction with professional institutions and potential audience.

To achieve the desired learning goals for in- and out-of-class learning activities, the instructor needs to plan carefully in the design and implementation of the course. In its first two offerings for the past two years, the digital curation course at CUA-DLIS-CHIM has benefited from some unique approaches, as described in this section, which help achieve its educational goals. To effectively integrate digital curation education into our cultural heritage information management program, we have more to do and will continue to explore and experiment in this exciting new field.

DIGITAL COLLECTIONS IN LIBRARIES, ARCHIVES, AND MUSEUMS

Digital Collections in Libraries, Archives, and Museums (DCLAM) is a featured course in the CHIM program. Taught in the weeklong summer institute, this course provides students with a practical overview of digital collections from creation to dissemination to preservation, as well as looking at cross-domain institutional conditions—past, present, and future—that influence collection access. The course addresses the information needs of digital information creators, users, and researchers in the cultural heritage sector. It gives students a broad understanding of how and why digital collections are created, managed, and preserved within the full digital curation lifecycle. Students learn about digital curation trends, tools, policies, and standards.

The course puts particular emphasis on building digital collection for use and reuse. Lectures and case studies demonstrate how digital collections can be developed to serve the growing needs of digital humanists and digital social scientists to reuse digital data and objects. Increasingly, researchers are relying on digital collections and digital collection information (metadata) as a basis of their research (Sula, 2013). As more and more researchers base their analysis on the "behind-the-scenes" information associated with a digital resource, such as descriptive and administrative metadata, twenty-first-century cultural heritage information professionals will need to fully address reusability issues. Challenges and solutions, such as structured metadata designed to answer new research questions, application layer access to digital collections and metadata, and support for the creation of new knowledge and scholarship, are integrated into the course plan.

This course was specifically designed to prepare cultural heritage information professionals in the area of digital collections development and digital curation across the LAM domains. The DCLAM graduate level course was first delivered in 2004 with a curriculum focus on the full lifecycle of digital collections in libraries, archives, and museums from conception to end-user access and long-term preservation. In each subsequent year, the course curriculum has remained focused on the lifecycle of digital collections within the three main cultural heritage communities, and as new tools, standards, models, and processes emerged, they were incorporated into the curriculum to keep the course relevant in a rapidly evolving environment.

The original faculty, Günter Waibel and Mary W. Elings, developed the DCLAM curriculum based on a workshop delivered at the Museum Computer Network Annual Meeting in September 2000. Having worked on cross-community digital collaborations as part of their work at the University of California, the instructors had an understanding of the points of commonality and dissonance across the fields. It seemed clear that the information needs and digital collection development processes were more in parallel across the LAMs than not. The subsequent DCLAM course was designed to help students gain competencies needed to be information professionals within these organizations by pointing to the areas of both intersection and diversion. Now in its ninth year as an intensive summer institute (from 2004 to 2009 at Syracuse University and 2010 to 2013 at CUA), the DCLAM course is now among the featured offerings in the new CHIM curriculum.

The DCLAM course offers broad coverage of all the CHIM competency areas, builds knowledge and skills, and fosters collaboration. The principal method of course presentation is by lecture, along with participatory discussions, in-class individual and group presentations, and readings. Taking advantage of the proximity to the Library of Congress and Smithsonian, students experience a digitization facilities tour and invited lecturers who bring expert domain knowledge of digitization, web strategies, and digital repository to the lecture portion.[7] The goals for learning include students gaining an understanding of:

- Challenges and solutions in creating digital collections;
- Library, archive, and museum practices and perspectives;
- The use of standards for scalable digital initiatives, integration among different institutions, and long-term data retention;
- Standards relevant to digitization, collection description, data exchange, and digital preservation;
- The broader information context within which cultural institutions are situated; and
- Digital collections as primary resource collections for digital scholarship.

The DCLAM design aligns with the continuum approach in the DigCurr I curriculum (Lee, 2009). This approach pays holistic attention to the full span of design, creation, management, use, and reuse of digital objects. DCLAM expands the focus on digital objects, looking more broadly at digital collections (collections of digital objects) through this lens.

The course is designed to cover a number of competency areas defined in the CHIM curriculum. These competencies also cover some of the DigCCur I competencies, including mandates, values, and principles; functions and skills; professional, disciplinary, institutional, organizational, and cultural contexts; types of resources;

prerequisite knowledge; and transition points in the information continuum. The competencies are addressed across the course's four major topical areas: Library, Archive, Museum (LAM) Convergence; Creating Digital Collections; Managing Collections; and Aggregating Digital Collections.

In the LAM convergence section, students gain an understanding of stakeholders involved, the history of the institutions and the professionals in them, the work contexts that surround them (professional, disciplinary, cultural, and organizational), and the types of resources they provide access to. This provides students with knowledge and understanding of the culture, context, and collections of cultural institutions, as well as their interrelationships. This is done through discussion and lectures covering the mission of each institution, the formal training of professionals, stances on access to collections, and the principles by which information is organized; and compares these across the three contexts. The course explores the historical and contextual foundations of these three communities, looking at past development through recent trends and toward convergence as framed in "Beyond the Silos of the LAMs" (Zorich, Waibel, & Erway, 2008). The class considers the current conditions and challenges that are influencing collection access online, the drivers behind digitization and collaboration, and what we can learn from each other as our communities converge in the networked age.

In the Creating Digital Collections section, students are introduced to the digital curation lifecycle. Like the Digital Curation course discussed in the previous section, the DCLAM course uses the DCC Curation Lifecycle Model (DCC, 2004–2013b) as a framework for discussing the lifecycle of digital collections. The course uses the full lifecycle actions, occasional actions, and sequential actions to frame the broader context of creating, managing, and aggregating digital collections. Students learn about resource management and become familiar with the theory, standards, and best practices associated with curating digital collections. The class discusses the concepts surrounding the creation of digital collections, including the departments, roles, and workflows involved in the process. Students are introduced to digital capture and project specifications (including relevant standards and best practice guidelines), project management theory and practice, in-house versus outsourcing (pros/cons and costs), and traditional digitization versus mass digitization. To balance theory and practice, students are exposed to firsthand experiences through a lecture and tour by a domain expert.

The course also teaches students about information organization concepts and tools, including digital asset management systems; digital preservation conceptual models, systems, tools, and best practices; metadata schemas; and standards for interoperability, illustrating these through case studies. The course spotlights the growing needs of research data (e.g., data management plans) and born-digital materials in these contexts with the goal of creating durable, sustainable, and useable digital collections.

The section on managing digital collections expands further on concepts related to information organization. Students explore the broad LAM metadata landscape and then focus on descriptive metadata standards and schema, emphasizing the need for standards to support data sharing, discoverability, and interoperability of resources, as well as hands-on exercises using standardized terminologies and controlled vocabularies. This is a springboard for a further discussion of how collections are disclosed into different environments (including as linked data) and how the metadata standards used can influence our ability to share digital collections beyond institutional walls, both physical and virtual.

Emphasis is placed on theory and practice employed in creating digital collections that can support the growing needs of digital scholars. The rapidly emerging fields of digital humanities and digital social sciences are being built on digital information, such as digitized texts, maps, born-digital content (e.g., Twitter archive), census data, databases, and so on. Information professionals are being called upon to create and organize these resources, as well as provide access to them in ways that often go beyond traditional online means (Sula, 2013). Research has pointed to building digital collections, supporting use of those collections, and preserving those collections as key functions of information professionals in this area (Zorich, 2008).

The last major section of the course, Aggregating Digital Collections, supports the CHIM information service provisions competency. Students explore local sharing, community sharing, and cross-community aggregations of digital collections. These are then contrasted against global information and social hubs like Flickr, Wikipedia, Twitter, Pinterest, and others. Students analyze, compare and contrast approaches, and prepare individual presentations. They also look at how these venues can provide user-generated metadata and extend the reach of collections online, and how these sites enhance user experiences. This exercise is put into the context of how these services meet the needs of online users and advance the mission and values of an institution, highlighting the aspect of trust among various stakeholders.

All sections of the course are supplemented with targeted readings, as well as an expanded bibliography including relevant reports, best practice guidelines, handbooks, and tutorials. Throughout the course, discussions and presentations give students the opportunity to expand on their own thoughts, question assumptions, and think critically about the meanings and implications of digital collections in these contexts. At the end of the week, students participate in a collaborative learning experience to synthesize and present on the content of the course. In a compressed format, this exercise helps them to review the course content, fill in gaps, learn from their peers, and work together as a cohort.

The student learning experience appears to have benefited from the course design. By drawing from both theory and practice in the field, encouraging discussions, providing supplementary readings, requiring individual and group presentations, bringing in outside practitioners and seeing the work firsthand, students learn practical application of the information delivered. As one former student commented in a 2010 course evaluation, "This course was excellent—the technical issues of digitization, as well as the ethical, social, and political issues were touched on—the importance of collaboration and providing access to information across disciplines. I thought the readings were wonderfully paired with each class day. . . . Thanks for a great class!" The course design strives to balance theory and practice through lectures, discussion, and exposure to real-world experiences. This is highlighted in two other remarks from a student in 2010: "It's great to have this integrated with all the theory in a real way—that we can take away & make things happen," and "We learned about how these concepts worked in the real world, sort of a 'where the rubber meets the road' experience."

As more and more research is done using digital collections (images, text, and data sets) and metadata, the DCLAM course design seeks to prepare students to work as professionals in supporting this work, building digital collections for research, and, with the digital curation course, managing those collections over the long term. Digital scholarship (digital humanities and social sciences) is driving the need for new knowledge, skills, and abilities in this area (Sula, 2013). The DCLAM design emphasizes how collections can be created, developed, used, reused, and remixed, and how they serve as the basis for creation of new digital scholarship.

CONCLUSION

Collections of cultural heritage institutions hold great social and historical value. Such cultural resources are the "intellectual capital of our information society" (Cameron & Kenderdine, 2007). Cultural heritage institutions are continuing to adopt emerging digital technologies to activate, engage, and transform their resources for the future and to provide access to them in new ways, which is necessitating a shift in organizational practice. Initiatives such as the Biodiversity Heritage Library, The Digital Public Library of America, and Europeana, are examples of digital LAM convergence.[8] These large-scale aggregations of digital collections characterize a move toward a LAM environment where digital is a "Dimension of Everything" (Stack, 2013). With this trend, LIS schools need to produce a new generation of cultural heritage information professionals to shape the future of the profession. The CHIM concentration offered at the Department of Library and Information Science at the Catholic University of America, can provide the educational opportunities and guidance for LIS students who want to pursue careers and succeed as information professionals in cultural heritage institutions in today's network environment. The design of the CHIM curriculum provides a framework for digital stewardship that will prepare information professionals to fulfill their roles in the expanding digital sphere that LAMs are seeking to occupy.

ACKNOWLEDGMENT

The Department of Library and Information Science at the Catholic University of America received a Laura Bush 21st Century Librarianship grant in June 2012 from the Institute of Museum and Library Services (IMLS; http://www.imls.gov/). The grant supports a cohort of seventeen students to complete the CHIM program to become a next generation of information professionals working in LAMs. Dr. Youngok Choi, one of the authors of this chapter, is the Principal Investigator of the CHIM IMLS grant project. The authors would like to thank the IMLS for their support for this emerging curriculum.

NOTES

1. See FastTrack Cohort: Cultural Heritage Institutions program of study, School of Library and Information Science, University of South Carolina, http://www.libsci.sc.edu/fasttrack/culturalheritage.htm.

2. See Data Curation Education Program (DCEP), Graduate School of Library and Information Science, University of Illinois at Urbana-Champaign, http://cirss.lis.illinois.edu/CollMeta/dcep.html.

3. A competency is defined as a set of knowledge, skills, and experience for competent work performance.

4. Courses listed for CHIM curriculum are available at the department's website. See http://lis.cua.edu/MSinLS/coursesStudy/CHIM.cfm.

5. For instance, the Digital Curation Curriculum (DigCCurr I) project at the University of North Carolina at Chapel Hill identifies twenty-four high-level digital curation functions or function categories on the basis of digital curation lifecycle in its six-dimensional matrix of digital curation knowledge and competencies (Lee, 2009). The Data Curation Education Program at the University of Illinois at Urbana-Champaign develops a master-level data curation specialization in "the active and ongoing management of data through its lifecycle of interest and usefulness to scholarship, science, and education" (http://cirss.lis.illinois.edu/CollMeta/dcep.html).

6. Popular models established in recent years include the construction of digital curation virtual labs, such as the Digital Curriculum Laboratory (DCL) at Simmons College (Harvey & Bastian, 2011) and the Digital Archaeology Lab at the School of Information at the University of Texas at Austin (DAL), https://www.ischool.utexas.edu/about/labs/digital_archaeology_lab.

7. Expert guest lecturers have included Steve Puglia, manager of Digital Conversion Services at the Library of Congress; Günter Waibel, director of the Digitization Program Office, Office of the Chief Information Officer, Smithsonian Institution; Michael Edson, director of Web and New Media Strategy, Smithsonian Institution; Ching-hsien Wang, Library and Archives Systems Support Branch, OCIO, Smithsonian Institution; Nancy E. Gwinn, director of the Smithsonian Institution Libraries, Smithsonian Institution; and Alan Newman, chief of Digital Imaging and Visual Services, National Gallery of Art.

8. Biodiversity Heritage Library, http://www.biodiversitylibrary.org/; Europeana, http://www.europeana.eu/; Digital Public Library of America, http://dp.la/ (which launched in April 2013).

REFERENCES

Bastian, J., Cloonan, M., & Harvey, R. (2011). From teacher to learner to user: Developing a digital stewardship pedagogy. *Library Trends, 59*(4), 607–622.

Cameron, F., & Kenderdine, S. (2007). Introduction. In F. Cameron & S. Kenderdine (Eds.), *Theorizing digital cultural heritage: A critical discourse* (pp.1–18). Cambridge, MA: MIT Press.

Chowdhury, G. (2010). From digital libraries to digital preservation research: The importance of users and context. *Journal of Documentation, 66*(2), 207–223.

Cloonan, M., & Mahard, M. (2010). Collaborative approaches to teaching digital steward-ship: Classroom, laboratory, and internships. Paper presented at IFLA-ALISE-EUCLID Conference, Cooperation and Collaboration in Teaching and Research: Trends in LIS Education, Borås, Sweden, August 8–9.

The Consultative Committee for Space Data Systems (CCSDS). (2012, January). *Recommendation for space data system practice: Reference model for an Open Archival Information System (OAIS)*. Washington, DC: CCSDS. Retrieved from http://public.ccsds.org/publications/archive/650x0m2.pdf

Digital Curation Center (DCC). (2004–2013a). *The DCC curation lifecycle model.* Retrieved from http://www.dcc.ac.uk/resources/curation-lifecycle-model

Digital Curation Center (DCC). (2004–2013b). *What is digital curation?* Retrieved from http://www.dcc.ac.uk/digital-curation/what-digital-curation

Duff, W. M., Cherry, J. M., & Sheffield, R. (2010). Creating a better understanding of who we are: A survey of graduates of a museum studies program. *Museum Management and Curatorship, 25*(4), 361–381.

Evens, T., & Hauttekeete, L. (2011). Challenges of digital preservation for cultural heritage institutions. *Journal of Librarianship and Information Science, 43*(3), 157–165.

Harley, D. (2007). Use and users of digital resources: A survey explores scholars' attitudes about educational technology environments in the humanities. *Educause Quarterly, 30*(4), 12–20.

Harvey, R., & Bastian, J. A. (2011). Out of the classroom and into the laboratory: Teaching digital curation virtually and experientially. *IFLA Journal, 38*(1). Retrieved from http://conference.ifla.org/past/ifla77/217-harvey-en.pdf

Institute of Museum and Library Services (IMLS). (2003, October). *Assessment of end-user needs in IMLS-funded digitization projects.* Retrieved from http://www.imls.gov/assets/1/AssetManager/userneedsassessment.pdf

Institute of Museum and Library Services (IMLS). (2006, January). *Status of technology and digitization in the nation's museums and libraries.* Retrieved from http://www.imls.gov/assets/1/AssetManager/Technology_Digitization.pdf

Kim, J. (2012). Building rapport between LIS and museum studies. *Journal of Education for Library and Information Science, 53*(2), 149–161.

Lee, C. (2009, June 18). *Functions and skills (dimension 2 of matrix of digital curation knowledge and competencies).* DigCCurr I, School of Information and Library Science, University of North Carolina at Chapel Hill. Retrieved from http://www.ils.unc.edu/digccurr/digccurr-functions.html

Mallan, K., & Park, E. (2006). Is digitization sufficient for collective remembering? Access to and use of cultural heritage collections. *The Canadian Journal of Information and Library Science, 30*(3/4), 201–220.

Manzuch, Z. (2009). Monitoring digitization: Lessons from previous experiences. *Journal of Documentation, 65*(5), 768–796.

Marcou, K. (2012, June 8). Canned preserves: Reaching out from the classroom and be-yond. [Web log comment]. *The Signal: Digital Preservation.* Retrieved from http://blogs.loc.gov/digitalpreservation/2012/06/canned-preserves-reaching-out-from-the-classroom-and-beyond/

Marty, P. F. (2005). So you want to work in a museum . . . Guiding the careers of future museum information professionals. *Journal of Education for Library and Information Science, 46*(2), 115–133.

Marty, P. F. (2006). Finding the skills for tomorrow: Information literacy and museum information professionals. *Museum Management and Curatorship, 21*(4), 317–335.

Marty, P. F. (2007a). The changing nature of information work in museums. *Journal of the American Society for Information Science and Technology, 58*(1), 97–107.

Marty, P. F. (2007b). Museum professionals and the relevance of LIS expertise. *Library & Information Science Research, 29*, 252–276.

Marty, P. F., & Twidale, M. B. (2011). Museum informatics across the curriculum: Ten years of preparing LIS students for careers transcending libraries, archives, and museums. *Journal of Education for Library and Information Science, 52*(1), 9–16.

(NDSA) National Digital Stewardship Alliance. (n.d.). Retrieved from http://www.digital preservation.gov/ndsa/

National Initiative for a Networked Cultural Heritage (2002). *The NINCH guide to good practice in the digital representation and management of cultural heritage materials*. Retrieved from http://www.nyu.edu/its/humanities/ninchguide/

Ray, J. (2009). Sharks, digital curation, and the education of information professionals. *Museum Management and Curatorship, 24*(4), 359–368.

Sinn, D. (2012). Impact of digital archival collections on historical research. *Journal of the American Society for Information Science and Technology, 63*(8), 1521–1527.

Smithsonian Institution. (2009, July 30). *Web and new media strategy*. Retrieved from http://www.si.edu/content/pdf/about/web-new-media-strategy_v1.0.pdf

Smithsonian Institution. (2010). *Creating a digital Smithsonian: Digitization strategic plan*. Retrieved from http://www.si.edu/content/pdf/about/2010_SI_Digitization_Plan.pdf

Stack, J. (2010). *Tate online strategy 2010-2011*. Retrieved from http://www.tate.org.uk/research/publications/tate-papers/tate-online-strategy-2010-12

Stack, J. (2013). *Tate digital strategy 2013–15: Digital as a dimension of everything*. Retrieved from http://www.tate.org.uk/research/publications/tate-papers/tate-digital-strategy-2013-15-digital-dimension-everything

Sula, C. A. (2013). Digital humanities and libraries: A conceptual model. *Journal of Library Administration, 53*(1), 10–26.

Trant, J. (2009). Emerging convergence? Thoughts on museums, archives, libraries and professional training. *Museum Management and Curatorship, 24*(4), 369–387.

Waibel, G., & Erway, R. (2009). Think global, act local—Library, archive and museum collaboration. *Museum Management and Curatorship, 24*(4), 323–335.

Zorich, D. M. (2008). *A survey of digital humanities centers in the United States*. Washington, DC: Council on Library and Information Resources. Retrieved from http://www.clir.org/pubs/reports/pub143/reports/pub143/pub143.pdf

Zorich, D., Waibel, G., & Erway, R. (2008). *Beyond the silos of the LAMs: Collaboration among libraries, archives, and museums*. Dublin, OH: OCLC Research. Retrieved from http://www.oclc.org/research/publications/library/2008/2008-05.pdf

7

Local History and Genealogy Collections in Libraries

The Challenge to Library and Information Science Educators

Rhonda L. Clark and James T. Maccaferri

ABSTRACT

In the digital age, local history and genealogy collections held by libraries present new opportunities for programming, reference, delivery, outreach, and collaboration. Especially in smaller libraries, without adequate educational and research support, those opportunities may not be embraced as focal points for library services. The question of whether the North American library and information science field provides adequate education and resources to support professionals embracing local collection management within the scope of their duties is explored. Answering that question begins with a discussion of the challenges identifying libraries holding local history and genealogy collections. Existing instructional support for professionals managing local collections is surveyed and periodical literature related to local studies librarianship since 2000 is reviewed. Suggestions for new directions in research, education, and collaboration are offered.

INTRODUCTION

Local history and genealogy collections are ubiquitous. They exist across a variety of organizations, such as special collections in academic institutions, public libraries, archives, historical societies, heritage clubs, genealogy clubs, and museum libraries. Their unique resources may be supplemented from the record-keeping of municipalities, businesses, churches, service organizations, and cemetery associations. In any given community, the bulk of local collections may lie in one organization, such as a public library or county historical archive, whereas the neighboring community may find their most utilized resources in completely different information settings from these; such variations are common and their patterns unpredictable.

In the Internet age, another layer of digitized local resources now exists through a robust growth in proprietary and nonprofit sites, not to mention the multitude of online user-input resources that are increasingly available. As noted in a recent study by Lisa Given and Lianne McTavish, "the lines between libraries, museums, archives, and related institutions have become blurred in the last decade," and this impression may be born out "particularly in the eyes of citizens who may be unfamiliar with the divided territory that has come to shape traditional approaches to gathering and providing access to cultural materials" (2010, p. 22). Indeed, in the digital age, local digitized collections may span multiple institutions, which provide varying support roles; for example, as financial backers, catalogers, or collection managers.

When considering the scope and role of local collections in libraries, the digital era provides multiple opportunities for delivery of such materials, even if a large physical collection is not present. Such facts may suggest new opportunities for programing, reference, and outreach for libraries of all sizes, but particularly for those small public libraries that previously did not embrace their local collections as focal points for library services. In light of such opportunities, questions arise as to how local collections in libraries are recognized as a part of library resources. Additionally, a concern must be voiced as to how well library and information science programs prepare graduate students to work with local collections and to envision opportunities for outreach, collaboration, and service.

The following chapter questions whether the library and information science field in the United States and Canada is providing adequate education and resources to support professionals who find local collection management or reference to constitute a part of their job requirements. Challenges in identifying which libraries are collecting and delivering local collections will be discussed at the outset. Because of the important role played by professional organizations in defining standards and protocols, relevant organization materials in the library and information field will be assessed, as well as available instructional writings for librarians to support collection care.

Also key in understanding the development of local collection education is an investigation of whether scholars in the library and information fields are carrying out adequate research to support such education. An assessment of published articles from the year 2000 will be carried out for the major library and information science databases. The goal of the literature review is not an exhaustive analysis, but rather a starting point for understanding the most important challenges in accessing this literature, as well as the dominant categories of information.

IDENTIFYING LOCAL COLLECTIONS IN LIBRARIES

Examples of established local special collections abound in a wide variety of U.S. and Canadian libraries. In one small sample region of western Pennsylvania, for example, major local collections easily can be found, such as the Pennsylvania Department of the Carnegie Library of Pittsburgh (www.carnegielibrary.org/locations/pennsylvania/) and the Heritage Room at the Erie County Public Library in Erie, PA (www.erielibrary.org/services/genealogy/), as well as examples of well-developed collections and genealogical indexes in small libraries, such as those at the Eccles-Lesher Memorial Library in Rimersburg, PA (http://eccles-lesher.org/Collections.html#Anchor-Local-11481). Within such collections, a wide variety of resources exist, from standard county histories, to local family genealogies, to archival documents, photographs, and artifacts. Yet this ideal of well developed, accessible, local collections, many staffed with librarians or archivists trained in the care and reference of their resources, is often not realistic, particularly for smaller and rural libraries. The question of how many local collections exist in libraries and what depth of resources, staffing, and training they possess should receive more attention from the library community. It is difficult to discuss collection size and staffing in an aggregate sense, as there are no easy methods for tracking and measuring these collections.

Standard reporting by libraries that appear as data sets at the Institute of Museum and Library Services (IMLS) website, for example, provide detailed information on certain aspects of public libraries, such as staffing and funding. The IMLS questionnaire, however, does not ask about collections to a level that would identify local collections. There are questions on numbers of public programs provided, which could be understood to include those on local history and genealogy, but the only specific type of programming requested outside of the general number are those for children and young adults (Institute of Museum and Library Services, 2012, pp. 65–67, items 600–605).

The well-known reference work *American Library Directory* (2012), shows a category for reporting special collections in all types of libraries surveyed. Unfortunately, the names and types of special collections are self-reported by those filling out the survey at each library, with no suggested controlled vocabulary, so use of the paper volumes requires actual hand counting of the many variations submitted to represent similar concepts. The online version has a field for "special collection," but it has no method for reporting a list of all libraries that have input text into that field (www.americanlibrarydirectory.com/help.asp). Use of the database advanced search reveals that the "special collection" field allows only text searches (and no Boolean), which require a knowledge of the phrases used by each library that are reported in the print version. If one were patient enough to compile these phrases, the results would still yield only rough numbers of total local collections from the perspective of the reporting library. With no definitions of "special collection," one librarian may perceive this category as intended only for rare items, whereas another may input the titles of particular local collections, and still another could input a general descriptor, such as "local history collection."

A major directory focusing on historical collections and genealogy libraries is the *Directory of Genealogical and Historical Societies, Libraries and Collections in the US and Canada* (Carson, 2012). The mammoth reference is updated biannually and does include information on the local history and genealogy collections of libraries. It exists only in paper format, however, so similar problems exist with regard to use for aggregate studies, but the information is updated regularly through direct contact with libraries. It would be useful to have electronic access to its dataset to more easily study trends and to derive research samples sets. Without such aggregate data, it is difficult to provide convincing arguments for funding, rationales for course development, and support for planning documents.

INSTRUCTIONAL SUPPORT FOR LIBRARY LOCAL COLLECTIONS

Historically, the library profession has recognized local collections, particularly genealogy ones, as existing under the umbrella of reference services. The need for continuing training support for this area of reference is seen by the regular offering of the Reference and User Association (RUSA) online course, Genealogy 101, which teaches "tools for assisting patrons with family history research. The goal of the class is to give students confidence and skill in assisting family history researchers" (www .ala.org/rusa/development/genealogy101). Training sessions on genealogy resources are also common offerings of state libraries and regional library associations in recognition of the need to deliver reference services in this area of growing public interest.

Further RUSA commitment to developing local history and genealogy support can be seen in the variety of committees and awards developed under the History Section, which creates publications and awards, and provides leadership for local history and genealogical concerns of ALA members. In particular, the section supports a number of committees related to the topic, including the Genealogical Publishing Company Award Committee, the Genealogy and Local History Discussion Group, the Genealogy Committee, the Genealogy Preconference Planning Committee, the Historical Materials Committee, and the Local History Committee (www.ala.org/rusa/contact/rosters).

Under the leadership of the RUSA History Section and its various committees on genealogy and local history collections, three sets of guidelines are provided, including a broad set for establishing local history collections. These guidelines note the need for dialogue among various cultural organizations that have a vested interest in local history collections, such as historical societies, museums, academic libraries, archives, and government agencies. They also emphasize the need for clear collection development policies and acquisition/de-acquisition procedures. Of note, the guidelines specifically designate the responsibility to "collect, process, maintain, and provide access to the local history collection" to professional staff, noting that they may be "assisted by trained paraprofessionals and volunteers" (Reference and User Services Association [RUSA], 2012, sec. 4.6).

RUSA guidelines for developing core genealogy collections are very specific about recommended holdings. Revised most recently in 2007, they dictate the following:

Genealogy collections should include: family histories and genealogies of local families; pedigrees and/or compilations of family group sheets of local families (originals or copies thereof); vital records when available; federal and state census for the local community; probate and will records; land records; county, city, and state maps; cemetery records; information on local churches; naturalization records; military records; local newspapers; county histories; and indexes to the preceding items. The items may be available and provided in various formats, including microform, print, and digital. Collections should also include manuals and handbooks of how to do genealogy research. (RUSA, 2007b, sec. 3.2)

These guidelines also indicate that genealogy reference should be provided by professional reference librarians (sec. 4.1).

The final set of guidelines are for the development of a "unit or course of instruction in genealogical research at schools of library and information science," which recognize the importance of providing courses that can prepare librarians to deliver basic genealogical reference (RUSA, 2007a). It would seem reasonable, therefore, to assume a strong role for library and information science master's programs in teaching about local collections, yet such an assumption may only hold true, at least in the majority of programs, when preparing students for work in large archival, museum, or special collection settings. Even within the introduction to the RUSA guidelines, it is indicated that "the majority of schools of library and information science offer very little about this subject" (par. 1). Indeed, according to course listings on the websites of U.S. and Canadian ALA-accredited master's programs in library and information science, only five schools listed a three-credit course that focused specifically on genealogy or on genealogy/local collection reference as a part of their regular course offerings. Clearly, the goal of providing trained reference librarians for such collections is falling short. It might be argued that this goal needs reconsideration in recognition of the hybrid nature of the work and library staffing realities, but for such a debate to commence, more data on local collection staffing and staff training is needed.

Besides RUSA, other ALA-affiliated organizations speak to the tools needed to work in local collections. The Association of College and Research Libraries (ACRL), Rare Books and Manuscript Section (2008) completed "Competencies for Special Collections Professionals." ACRL and the Society of American Archivists (SAA) issued a "Joint Statement on Access to Research Materials in Archives and Special Collections Libraries" (ACRL & SAA, 2009). In addition, the SAA recognizes the need for support of library special collections processing through its Public Library Archives/Special Collections Roundtable (PLASC). Launched in 2011, its mission is to:

encourage advocacy for and education about archival, manuscript, local history, genealogy, and other historic and special collections within public libraries of all sizes. The Roundtable provides an arena for discussion and dissemination of best practices of the archival, library, museum and history fields; and works to support the informational, historical, and cultural interests which converge in public library archives and special collections. (SAA, n.d.)

Considering the overlap between archives and local library work, could archival courses be considered preparation for library local collections? While it is certainly true that major aspects of local collection organization and representation can be covered by archival offerings in MLIS programs, the more advanced courses covering the intricacies of processing and representation generally are not in the course plan of the student preparing for a career in the general library setting. In addition, such courses understandably should offer viewpoints specific to the archival profession on collection processing, which may overlook approaches commonly found in the library setting (and in settings of library/historical society collaboration), such as local indices and collection management software often used for item-level processing (i.e., Past Perfect software). Entry-level archival and preservation courses, if taken by the generalist, can be very helpful, but do not answer all of the specific needs of the local library collection setting.

While it is also likely the case that many schools offer the occasional special-topics course to cover reference for local collections, sporadic offerings do not allow for student planning of the "coherent program of study," included in the American Library Association's *Standards for Accreditation of Master's Programs in Library & Information Studies* (2008, p. 8, sec. II.4). Such an approach also fails to demonstrate a dedicated effort to promote local resource librarianship as an integral part of expected responsibilities in a library setting.

One also could argue the importance of coursework that highlights cross-institutional elements of local collection administration. Indeed, the increasing number of library and information science courses in museum informatics, aimed to accentuate common issues of information processing and public service goals of archives, libraries, and museums (Marty & Twidale, 2011), would be highly relevant for the local collection librarian. Such courses, along with organizing information classes such as metadata and indexing, can provide students specific skills and a general platform to understand collection issues, but more specific aspects of genealogy reference and library special collection processing are also necessary to prepare librarians for work with local collections.

Finally, it could also be argued that coursework on digitization and repository architecture apply to the local collection; indeed, they often center on resources from such collections. Such courses are important when considering the role of digitization on raising awareness of collections. Collaborations across the historical, museum, archive, and library fields are common for digital projects, from the flagship collections of American Memory at the Library of Congress, to the "do-it-yourself" websites of small library collections. Funding for digitization has proven to be widespread, with national grants from the IMLS that support collaborative efforts for large-scale projects like Maine Memory Network (n.d.) and Library Services and Technology Act monies distributed in many states through competitive digitization grants.

It is worth asking, however, if courses on digitization fit into a structured program that prepares students for a genre of resources, as opposed to orienting students toward special projects that live outside of related educational objectives such as reference, preservation, collection development, and outreach. In addition, the training of librarians and other information professionals should not assume a work goal for large, urban environments nor extensive archival or museum collections. Students who want to work in local collections within rural settings require the training needed for organizing, preserving, representing, and delivering various materials, as well as a broad education to anticipate their other work duties in a general library environment. The ability to communicate effectively and to recognize issues of territoriality and competition within local collection environments can be as important as the understanding of technical processes for successful digitization and migration of local collection information.

In sum, coursework for the master's degree in library and information science can provide the basics of local collection care and processing if students are careful about how they construct their programs. Professional directives call for more courses in genealogy and local history reference, while collection education should include a wide variety of processing methods and platforms, to reflect the diversity of likely collaborative community partners involved in providing care in any local setting.

As noted above, local collection care can occur in many settings; only small parts of these collections live in libraries. Their use often occurs across varied cultural institutions within one community. Professional organizations from outside library and information science, therefore, can also provide directives and best practices for library local collections. From the arena of the historical museum and historical society, for example, the American Society for State and Local History (AASLH) has long produced succinct, quality publications outlining methods of organizing and delivering local collections to the public (http://aaslh.org/leaflets.htm). Public historians should be highly involved in the debate on how to collaborate effectively with local resources, particularly in areas dealing with oral history projects. The strong kinship among archival studies, museum studies, and public history also suggests the appropriateness of collaboration. Certainly AASLH publications suggest an affinity with collections care and the technical leaflets included in their newsletter add a practicality to the field in line with the historian/interpreter to the populace.

AASLH recommendations raise a valuable topic of concern when curating local special collections in libraries: that of systematic representation models. The organization has for years encouraged members to use Past Perfect museum software as a cataloging and processing tool. The software provides a broad range of tracking features, from acquisition/donation to delivery via an optional online exhibit (www.PastPerfect.com). Past Perfect, once a museum staple, now is a favorite for small historical societies with budgets too small to support larger programs and volunteer staffing too inexperienced for open-source programs such as ArchivesSpace. One can hope that judicious use of programs such as Past Perfect may help replace the patchwork quilt of home-grown resource representations that are all too common in local collections. Yet the learning curve on Past Perfect for volunteers and even library professionals is notable, especially if one aims to adhere to specific controlled vocabularies. Also, in library settings, such programs would likely only be used for particular resources, like photo collections. This raises the question of representation models for library local special collections. The increased description available in Resource Description and Access (RDA) shows promise for local collection authority work. More discussion of how to use standard library cataloging and indexing methods should be developed in instructional literature for the local collection manager, as well as full discussions of varying metadata schemas for digital objects.

INSTRUCTIONAL LITERATURE ON LOCAL COLLECTIONS

Basic reference entries on local collections reflect an understanding of the collaborative nature of these collections. Articles in the online edition of the *Encyclopedia of Library and Information Sciences* (Bates & Maack, 2009), for example, include a wide range of concepts related to the topic. "Genealogical Literature and Its Users" focuses on the process of conducting genealogical research, user behavior, and resources. While the role of particular institutions in housing and providing access to such resources is acknowledged, genealogy is clearly perceived as a self-standing area of user inquiry and resource expertise. The role of libraries is important, but certainly no more so than genealogical societies, historical societies, and the growing influence of online databases (Molto, 2009).

Likewise, in the article "Oral History in Libraries and Archives," methods for collecting and curating oral history records are explored as a topic that exists within, but also beyond any one type of cultural memory institution. The importance of regional and national professional associations is discussed as vital to the development of the field, while the roles of government and university-based projects are deemed to be those leading the field. Of course libraries and historical societies are noted for their significant projects and archives for forging new standards for oral history cataloging (Hansen, 2009).

Instructional monograph literature on organizing and maintaining local studies collections was defined early on by British librarians. Dixon (2001, pp. xv–xvi) dates the emergence of this literature to the World War I period, with the first significant monograph on the subject appearing in 1939. According to Dixon, it was not until the 1960s that local studies emerged as an academic discipline in the United States and elsewhere (pp. xvi–xvii). Noteworthy British contributions include the manuals by Hobbs (1948; revised by Carter, 1962) and Dewe (2002), to which should be added Dixon's (2001) bibliography. U.S. publications include volumes by Thompson (1978), Phillips (1995), and Roberts (2007). Also often cited in American literature are two articles on local collection establishment in libraries by Carvalho (1987–1988) and the North Carolina Library Association (1988).

Phillip's full-length treatment of the topic provides a list of "core" materials, including standard publications in local history such as city directories, histories, newspapers, maps, personal papers, and organizational records (1995). The bulk of the work addresses preservation, organization, representation, and outreach. The work is thoroughly grounded in archival practice and, as such, is especially conducive to supporting such resources in academic special collections or large public library settings. Shorter treatments of the subject, such as Carvalho's "Organizing a Local History Collection in a Small Public Library," reveal the rich potential for local collections, including a wide array of candidates for inclusion, ranging from publications, to archival documents, to manuscripts and ephemera (Carvalho, 1987–1988). Carvalho emphasizes the need to work with other organizations to determine whether a collection should be established and to assess collecting priorities carefully.

Roberts's *Crash Course in Library Gift Programs* (2007) echoes this concern by noting some of the challenges faced by public libraries when presented with local materials. The work is clearly aimed at an audience needing basic-level assistance in collection organization, representation, preservation, and marketing, and warning against taking items that are not appropriate for the library setting. Indeed, without clear collecting guidelines, local gifts to libraries may include objects best housed in a museum or historical society, such as artwork, textiles, tools, and assorted antiques associated with the people and organizations of their towns and regions. Roberts does well to note that librarians are not always prepared for the responsibility of a local collection, but she also points out the enormous potential for creating ties with the public and for preserving important documents.

The instructional works on local collections and related areas for U.S. local studies collections emphasize practical issues of processing (usually archival) and outreach. Works such as *Developing Local History Programs in Community Libraries* (Conrad, 1989) emerge from predictable presses, in this case, the ALA. Thompson's (1978) work was published by the AASLH, while Phillips's (1995) was from Libraries Unlimited. These general works focus on the areas regularly noted to be a part of local collection care, such as collection organization and preservation; specialized areas such as oral history; and specific resources, such as newspapers and genealogical materials.

Single-volume treatments of related areas to local history, such as genealogy, abound. There are several guides to genealogy resources aimed at the reference librarian (Dowell, 2011; Moore, 1998; Simpson, 2008; Swan, 2004). The vast literature on genealogy for the lay person and enthusiast attests to its popularity as a pastime and as a potential area of growth for library services. Hundreds of general help volumes and thousands of region-specific resources are available to the researcher. The popularity of Ancestry.com and other online digitized collections raises major questions and opportunities for local studies librarianship. In a world where public domain fully digitized county histories can now be linked to web-based pathfinders, the role of the local collection onsite has changed. Newspapers in particular are an area of contention. The situation for local libraries that own a microform copy of their historical newspaper but cannot afford to provide digitized access to their patrons through a vendor, such as archives.com, presents challenges for successful, modern genealogical reference work.

Instructional materials emerging in recent years recognize some of these same challenges to continuing local collection care. The compilation, *Preserving Local Writers, Genealogy, Photographs, Newspapers, and Related Materials* (Smallwood & Williams, 2012) provides a fresh approach to specific issues for local collections, including clear discussion of how to establish collaborations with other institutions. Kate Theimer's *Web 2.0 Tools and Strategies for Archives and Local History Collections* (2010) challenges archivists and librarians to update their attitudes and practices regarding patron interaction with collections. The introduction in particular notes changes in the archival working environment, including a profound difference in the ways that users discover the archive's holdings and their expectations regarding access, both in terms of speed and format. The user is also less experienced, resulting in an increase in the workload for archivists (pp. 2–3). Peter Reid's *The Digital Age and Local Studies* (2003) explores new avenues for providing access to genealogy and local history materials electronically—understanding the mind-set of the new local studies patron to the library setting.

Richard Cox's work on *Documenting Localities* (1996) raises a number of important questions and issues to archivists, but the thoughtful discussion provides a model to those working with local collections in any setting. The work is the most comprehensive study to ask not just "how," but "why." Emphasizing both the importance of valuing and preserving the local context, but also the need to create rational, professional standards for appraisal and collection development, the work reminds those in local history collections of the need to evaluate the goals, trajectories, and shifting audiences for their resources.

ASSESSMENT OF ARTICLE LITERATURE

An examination of published articles by library professionals may shed more light on the development of local studies librarianship in the United States. While emphasis varies, all of these works define the field in terms of the materials collected, user services, marketing and outreach, administration, relationships with other depositories, preservation, organization, and, more recently, information technology. The following review will use these categories.

Before considering the periodical literature published since 2000 in detail, it is worth discussing the major serials in which this literature appears. An analysis of the entries in Dixon (2001) shows considerable scattering. The 1,027 articles cited appear in 248 serials, of which sixteen (those with ten or more articles) account for 45% of the articles. Of these, the most important by far is *Local Studies Librarian*, which is published by the Chartered Institute of Library Professionals (CLIP) and indexed by

Library, Information Science & Technology Abstracts (2004 to present) but not *Library Literature & Information Science.* Electronic full-text is not available, and, according to WorldCat (www.worldcat.org/), only five U.S. or Canadian libraries have holdings for it. Of the remaining fifteen serials, only three (*Illinois Libraries, Library Journal,* and *Library Trends*) are published in the United States. Looked at another way, thirteen of the titles are library journals, one focuses on archives, and two on history.

Analysis of the serial literature since 2000 shows much the same story, although the results are not entirely comparable, since Dixon (2001) does not supply a literature search methodology. For the current study, *Library Literature & Information Science* was searched using the controlled vocabulary terms "local history materials" and "cataloging of local history materials." Searches were limited to materials in English published from 2000 to the present. A total of 266 articles published in 119 different serials were found. Fourteen titles (those with 5 or more articles) accounted for 28% of the total. Of the 266 articles, only 70.3% deal with local studies in the United States and Canada. Next, *Library, Information Science & Technology Abstracts* (LISTA) was searched using the same limits as the above search. The controlled vocabulary terms are the same as for *Library Literature*: "local history materials" yielded 27 resources, 13 of which deal with local studies in the United States and Canada. This was reduced to only 4 (15%) once duplicates from the *Library Literature* search and news items were excluded. "Cataloging of local history materials" brought four hits, only one of which was relevant to local studies in the United States and Canada, and it had already been retrieved in the *Library Literature* search. LISTA is an EBSCO index and, as such, its records include vocabulary terms from the other indexes in which the same records appear. This led to a third search using the controlled vocabulary term, "local history" while excluding records also indexed with "local history materials." This search produced 89 additional resources, none of which were duplicated by any of the previous searches. Winnowing out brief news items and those dealing with local history outside of the United States and Canada netted 13 resources (15%).

Library and Information Science Abstracts (LISA) was searched using its controlled vocabulary terms, "local history" and "local history materials," with the same search limits as the *Library Literature & Information Science* search. Of the 150 resources retrieved, 28 (19%) dealt with the United States and Canada, only a few of which were duplicated by previous searches.

It should be noted that none of the indexes searched for this study cover all of the titles included in Dixon (2001); nevertheless, it is clear that the serial literature on local studies collections is very scattered, especially with regard to local studies librarianship in the United States and Canada. There is no single serial that local-studies librarians can consult for the latest research and news, and any attempt to keep current would require access to specialized indexing services, such as those referenced above. *Library Literature* indexes the most titles covering local history studies (154), with LISTA close behind (141) and LISA a distant third (93). Search results suggest that *Library Literature*'s coverage is better; but inconsistencies in indexing and the fact that no one index covers all the relevant serials mean that a comprehensive search requires the use of all three. The following analysis considers articles published from 2000 to the present dealing with local studies in the United States.

Local Studies Materials

With the exception of oral histories, there is but one article each on artifacts (Cunniffe, 2004), church records (Baranowski, 2007), sound recordings (Hooper, 2011), motion pictures (Tomkins and Martin, 2007), and photographs (Austin, 2003). Baranowski (2006) considers American Legion posts as sources of local history resources. Lear (2005) sees a library's own history as an asset on multiple grounds, including as a source for local history. Eight articles appeared on oral history, all of which describe specific projects (see, for example, Cherry, 2004).

User Services

Very little has been done with regard to the unique aspects of user services for local studies collections except for the use of information technology. Hewitt and Horowitz (2007) and Lack and Milbury (2006) show how they used databases to improve access, while King, Tipton, and Hill (2005) used open source technology to create an online research portal. Thom and Hansom (2000) discuss the effect of a digitization project on reference services in a large public library, concluding that these services will change but not decrease.

Marketing and Outreach

Despite its seeming importance in this age of funding shortfalls, only six articles considered marketing and outreach. Staley (2004) gives an example of programming in connection with a notable local event, while Yesson and Jones (2001) describe a university's efforts at K–12 outreach. "Getting the Word Out on Your Hidden Treasures" (2005) speaks to the uniqueness of local studies collection; Bridges (2010) describes an exhibit organized for the Mississippi Heritage trust; Tuzinski (2011) seeks to mobilize school librarians to lead school-wide local history initiatives; and Kennedy (2010) shows how Preservation Week can be used to promote interest in family and local history. Harden (2001) describes how a Colorado public library saw creating a local history collection as part of its outreach efforts. Similarly, Pierce (2003) discusses the role of local history and genealogy services in sustaining the economic health of the community.

Relationships with Other Depositories

The institutional perspective on local studies tends to focus on the role of archives, either by themselves (Horton, 2001) or as part of other institutions (Feil, 2008;

Archives 2011), and building effective relationships with other institutions (Galan, 2003; Austin, 2004; Tonta, 2008). Another theme is the relevance of local studies collections (Lloyd, 2007; Marquis & Waggener, 2011). Examples of the types of collaboration that are possible are provided by Lawton and Lawton (2009), who review a collaboration between a public and an academic library to provide instruction on house and property history research, and by Shires (2004), who argues that librarians and teachers need to work together in the design and use of digital history resources. Bell and Gaston (2004) show how a college found partners to preserve the history of Florida's black junior colleges.

Preservation

In evaluating the local studies literature on preservation and conservation, one must keep in mind that local studies depends greatly on the general literature on this subject—including the many manuals and guides that are available. Setting aside those articles that are derivative in nature or describe specific collections and institutions, there are four that deal with the broader issues of preserving cultural collections. All of them appeared in a special issue of *Library Trends*. Cloonan and Harvey (2007) take a broad view of the changing philosophies, legalities, and techniques of preserving cultural heritage. Cloonan (2007) uses five cases studies to highlight the historical, political, and professional paradoxes inherent in cultural preservation and emphasize the need for "greater community input." Ogden (2007) considers the trend in museums to consider the intangible as well as tangible nature of cultural objects in making preservation decisions. Smith (2007) explores the societal value of preserving cultural resources and how the concept of "value" differs with respect to digital information. Finally, Allen and Johnson (2008) consider the challenges of preserving digital local news, while McCormick (2007) describes a Canadian project to preserve audiovisual materials.

Organization

Despite its seeming importance, cataloging and classification, or, if one prefers, metadata, has received relatively little attention. The seven articles on this topic are brief (about less than three pages) and tend to focus on specific projects. If there is a trend otherwise, it is to consider vocabulary issues (Symonds, 2008; Lourdi, Papatheodorou, & Doerr, 2009) and/or metadata for digital collections (Cronin, 2008). Dragon (2009) discusses name authority control in a local digitization project. Sowers (2003) advances the use of analytical indexing to improve access to local and family history materials.

Information Technology

By far the greatest attention is being paid to the role of information technology in local studies. Reference to this has already been made in preceding sections. This section will deal primarily with digitization. Despite the relative vastness of this literature, it consists almost exclusively of descriptions of specific projects, often at the state level and sometimes with multiple articles devoted to the same project (for example, the Colorado Digitization Project). Although descriptive rather than evaluative, a meta-analysis of this growing literature would shed light on the goals and methods of these projects and perhaps lead to the identification of model projects. Standing out among the evaluations of specific projects are Matusiak (2006), who looks at information-seeking behavior with respect to local history digital image collections; Bond (2004), who describes the use of streaming audio for an oral collection; Shires (2002), who makes a case for digitizing fiction to complement historical resources; Baker (2007), who discusses the financial and social barriers to building digital collections; Nickerson (2004), who discusses online multimedia exhibits; and Lira (2000), who looks at the challenges of "born-digital" primary sources. Litzer and Barnett (2004) consider usage statistics of locally digitized materials, and Jeng (2008) evaluates the New Jersey Digital Highway, which includes local history materials. Zampaglione and Bennett (2012) discuss what they see as a pilot program to enable library systems to develop online obituary archives to counter the possible loss of cultural, genealogical, and personal information as newspapers start charging to run obituaries. Henderson (2001) describes the creation of an online index to a large local newspaper clippings file. Hall (2000) reports on a project to convert audiotapes of oral history interviews to digital files stored on CD-ROMs. Finally, Balas (2000) suggests organizations to which small public libraries can turn for information and advice on whether or not to digitize local history collections.

Related Areas

If one moves the literature review beyond those items specifically cataloged as "local history" or "local history materials," there exists a multitude of possible related areas, each with many articles of interest to the local studies librarian. It falls outside of this review to provide a full, systematic analysis of these areas, but searches in *Library Literature and Information Science Full-Text* for articles on "genealogy" from 2000 provide some useful examples of the types of resources available to the practitioner or researcher interested in this specific aspect of the local collection. For example, two studies investigate genealogical user behavior (Darby & Clough, 2013; Duff & Johnson, 2003). Tucker investigates services for family history in libraries and archives (2006) and Lenstra reports on innovative collaborations in public libraries and other institutions to allow the public to help create digital memory projects (2012).

Finally, it is worth noting that the professional writing on local studies crosses so many discipline and thematic boundaries, it is easy to overlook writings of relevance that may have been catalogued from the perspective of its home discipline or topical area, while ignoring overt connections to the local collection. By using subject searches for main topic areas, such as "metadata" and by narrowing with keywords, the breadth of the field becomes evident. Take, for example, a recent study of retrieval and consistency in digitized postcard collection metadata (Noone, 2010) that failed to show up in local collection cataloging searches. The task of maintaining a comprehensive grasp of all literature produced on topics of interest to the local studies researcher is monumental.

EVALUATION AND CONCLUSION

The literature on local studies reviewed is more notable for what it does not tell us than for what it does. Actual research is rare, with the result that numerous basic questions remain unanswered, including the state of the field in terms of number and distribution of repositories, collection composition and size, staffing, and services. The scattered nature of the serial literature makes it difficult if not impossible for practitioners to keep abreast of developments. Conversely, the literature on technological aspects of local collections, from metadata to digitization to Web 2.0, shows great promise for development in the field if practitioners can continue to work toward collaboration in local studies librarianship.

It is also evident that library and information science education for local collections should be improved in order to meet the needs of libraries holding such collections and in order to provide support to reference librarians who are questioned on the use of online resources and databases. There should be greater emphasis on the creation of reference courses in local collection subject matter, more courses for the generalist to learn to manage local collections, and more innovation in delivering models for multiorganization collaboration, including, but certainly not limited to, centralized digital delivery of resources. Such collaborations are booming, often as a result of grant funding, but the educators in library science programs should take a greater role in researching and evaluating these vibrant activities and their influence, particularly in settings often overlooked in research, such as small and rural public library collections for local history and genealogy. And, a final note, the wealth of professional writings on local studies collections are by no means fully available to those who need them the most—local studies librarians. Perhaps a fitting goal in creating new research to improve library services to the patrons of local collections in libraries should include an emphasis on open access resources that resonate with the collaborative evolution of the local studies world.

REFERENCES

Allen, R. B., & Johnson, K. A. (2008). Preserving digital local news. *Electronic Library*, *26*(3), 387–399.

American Library Association (ALA). (2008). *Standards for accreditation of master's programs in library and information studies.* Retrieved from www.ala.org/accreditedprograms/sites/ala .org.accreditedprograms/files/content/standards/standards_2008.pdf

American library directory. (2012). Medford, NJ: Information Today. Retrieved from www .americanlibrarydirectory.com/

Archives. (2011). *Library Administrators Digest, 46*(2), 12.

Association of College & Research Libraries (ACRL), Rare Books and Manuscript Section. (2008). *Guidelines: Competencies for special collections professionals.* Retrieved from www.ala .org/acrl/standards/comp4specollect

Association of College & Research Libraries (ACRL) & Society of American Archivists (SAA). (2009). *ACRL/SAA joint statement on access to research materials in archives and special collections libraries.* Retrieved from www.ala.org/acrl/standards/jointstatement

Austin, D. (2003). CITY2000: A holistic approach to administering image resources. *Journal of Library Administration, 39*(2/3), 5–13.

Austin, D. (2004). Transcending boundaries: Cross-disciplinary images in the library. *Art Documentation, 23*(1), 14–17.

Baker, S. K. (2007). New opportunities for research libraries in digital information and knowledge management: Challenges for the mid-sized research library. *Journal of Library Administration, 46*(1), 65–74.

Balas, J. K. (2000). Original vs. digital. *Computers in Libraries, 20*(2), 51–52.

Baranowski, R. (2006). American Legion posts. *Public Libraries, 45*(4), 42–46.

Baranowski, R. (2007). Community church records: A local history asset for public libraries. *Public Libraries, 46*(5), 12–17.

Bates, M. J., & Maack, M. N. (Eds.). (2009). *Encyclopedia of library and information sciences* (3rd ed.). Boca Raton, FL: CRC Press. doi:10.1081/E-ELIS3-120043248

Bell, D., & Gaston, B. J. (2004). Collection development: Real steps to include a forgotten group. *Community & Junior College Libraries, 12*(3), 9–16.

Bond, T. J. (2004). Streaming audio from African-American oral history collections. *OCLC Systems & Services, 20*(1),15–23.

Bridges, R. (2010). Historical exhibit viewed at Pascagoula Library. *Mississippi Libraries, 74*(2), 40–41.

Carson, D. C. (2012). *Directory of genealogical and historical societies, libraries and collections in the US and Canada 2012.* Niwot, CO: Iron Gate.

Carter, G. A. (1962). *Local history and the library.* London: Deutsch.

Carvalho, J. (1987–1988). Organizing a local history collection in a small public library. *Public Library Quarterly, 8*(1–2), 109–118.

Cherry, T. K. B. (2004). The North Carolina libraries centennial oral history project. *North Carolina Libraries, 62*(3), 130–139. Retrieved from www.ncl.ecu.edu/index.php/NCL/

Cloonan, M. V. (2007). The paradox of preservation. *Library Trends, 56*(1), 133–147.

Cloonan, M. V., & Harvey, R. (2007). Preserving cultural heritage: Introduction. *Library Trends, 56*(1), 1–3.

Conrad, J. H. (1989). *Developing local history programs in community libraries.* Chicago, IL: American Library Association.

Cox, R. J. (1996). *Documenting localities: A practical model for American archivists and manuscript curators.* Chicago, IL: Society of American Archivists; Lanham, MD: Scarecrow Press.

Cronin, C. (2008). Metadata provision and standards development at the Collaborative Digitization Program (CDP): A history. *First Monday, 13*(5). Retrieved from http://journals .uic.edu/ojs/index.php/fm

Cunniffe, C. (2004). Artifacts from the 20th century. *Information Outlook, 8*(3), 14–19.

Darby, P., & Clough, P. (2013). Investigating the information-seeking behaviour of genealogists and family historians. *Journal of Information Science, 39*(1), 73–84.

Dewe, M. (2002). *Local studies collection management.* Aldershot, UK: Ashgate.

Dixon, D. (2001). *Local studies librarianship: A world bibliography.* London: Library Association.

Dowell, D. R. (2011). *Crash course in genealogy.* Santa Barbara, CA: Libraries Unlimited.

Dragon, P. M. 2009. Name authority control in local digitization projects and the eastern North Carolina postcard collection. *Library Resources & Technical Services, 53*(3), 185–196.

Duff, W. M., & Johnson, C. A. (2003). Where is the list with all the names? Information-seeking behavior of genealogists. *American Archivist, 66*(1), 79–95.

Feil, L. (2008). Are public libraries compatible with archives? *Indiana Libraries, 27*(3), 9–14.

Galan, R. (2003). Texas tides: K-16 collaboration. *Texas Library Journal, 79*(4), 144–146.

Getting the word out on your hidden treasures. (2005). *Unabashed Librarian, 136,* 28–31.

Given, L., & McTavish, L. (2010). What's old is new again: The reconvergence of libraries, archives, and museums in the digital age. *Library Quarterly, 80*(1), 7–32.

Hall, W. (2000). Oral history fast forward: From audiocassette to digital archive. *Colorado Libraries, 26*(4), 9–10.

Hansen, D. G. (2009). Oral history in libraries and archives. In M. J. Bates & M. N. Maack (Eds.), *Encyclopedia of library and information sciences* (3rd ed.) (pp. 4045–4055). Boca Raton, FL: CRC Press. doi: 10.1081/E-ELIS3-120044733

Harden, J. J. (2001). Outreach: Not out of reach, or, gardening tips for growing a local history repository from the ground up. *Colorado Libraries, 27*(4), 19–22.

Henderson, P. (2001). Clippings to computers: The great newspaper migration. *Library Mosaics, 12*(3), 17–18.

Hewitt, J. A., & Horowitz, S. A. (2007). "Documenting the American South" and the public library user: A proposal to improve access for the general public to a database of southern and North Carolina materials. *North Carolina Libraries, 65*(3/4), 70–75. Retrieved from www.ncl.ecu.edu/index.php/NCL/

Hobbs, J. L. (1948). *Libraries and the materials of local history.* London: Grafton.

Hooper, L. (2011). Underwriting history: The role of sound recording collectors in shaping the historical record. *ARSC Journal, 42*(1), 43–49.

Horton, R. (2001). Cultivating our garden: Archives, community, and documentation. *Archival Issues: Journal of the Midwest Archives Conference, 26*(1), 27–40.

Institute of Museum and Library Services. (2012). *Public libraries survey: Fiscal year 2010.* Washington, DC: Institute of Museum and Library Services. Retrieved from www.imls.gov/assets/1/AssetManager/fy2010_pls_data_file_documentation.pdf

Jeng, J. (2008, December). Evaluation of the New Jersey digital highway. *Information Technology & Libraries, 27*(4), 17–24.

Kennedy, T. (2010). Pass it on: Preservation week. *ALCTS Newsletter Online, 21*(1), 18. Retrieved from www.ala.org/alcts/ano/home

King, D., Tipton, J. K., & Hill, H. (2005). KCResearch: Creating a research portal using open source technology. *Public Library Quarterly, 24*(3), 63–73.

Lack, R., & Milbury, P. (2006). Calisphere: Easy access to primary sources. *CSLA Journal, 30*(1), 26–28.

Lawton, J. R., & Lawton, H. B. (2009). Public-academic library collaboration: A case study of an instructional house and property history research program for the public. *American Archivist, 72*(2), 496–514.

Lear, B. A. (2005). The hippest history. *Library Journal, 130*(9), 52–53.

Lenstra, N. (2012). Digital roots: Community approaches to local and family history. *ILA Reporter, 30*(3), 10–13.

Lira, J. A. (2000). Born digital: A new view of primary source materials. *Colorado Libraries, 26*(4), 15–17.

Litzer, D., & Barnett, A. (2004). Local history in e-books and on the web: One library's experience as example and model. *Reference & User Services Quarterly, 43*(3), 248–257.

Lloyd, A. (2007). Guarding against collective amnesia? Making significance problematic: An exploration of issues. *Library Trends, 56*(1), 53–65.

Lourdi, I., Papatheodorou, C., & Doerr, M. (2009). Semantic integration of collection description: Combining CIDOC/CRM and Dublin Core collections application profile. *D-Lib Magazine, 15*(7/8). doi:10.1045/july2009-papatheodorou

Maine Memory Network (n.d.). Our partners: Contributing organizations and communities. Retrieved from www.mainememory.net/our_partners/

Marquis, K., & Waggener, L. C. (2011). Historical collections: Is adding one right for your public library? *Public Libraries, 50*(2), 42–49.

Marty, P. F., & Twidale, M. B. (2011). Museum informatics across the curriculum: Ten years of preparing LIS students for careers transcending libraries, archives, and museums. *Journal of Education for Library & Information Science, 52*(1), 9–22.

Matusiak, K. K. (2006). Information seeking behavior in digital image collections: A cognitive approach. *Journal of Academic Librarianship, 32*(5), 479–488.

McCormick, P. (2007). Preserving Canada's cultural heritage: The AV Trust. *Feliciter, 53*(3), 158–159.

Molto, M. B. (2009). Genealogical literature and its users. In M. J. Bates & M. N. Maack (Eds.), *Encyclopedia of library and information sciences* (3rd ed.) (pp. 1–46). Boca Raton, FL: CRC Press. doi:10.1081/E-ELIS3-120043248

Moore, D. E. (1998). *The librarian's genealogy notebook: A guide to resources.* Chicago, IL: American Library Association.

Nickerson, M. F. (2004). Online multimedia museum exhibits: A case study in technology and collaboration. *Library Hi Tech, 22*(3), 270–276.

Noone, L. (2010). Digital postcard collections: Consistency and retrieval. *PNLA Quarterly, 74*(3), 38–55. Retrieved from http://unllib.unl.edu/LPP/PNLA%20Quarterly/PNLAQ-home.htm

North Carolina Library Association. (1988). Establishing and maintaining a local history collection. *North Carolina Libraries, 46*, 70–84.

Ogden, S. (2007). Understanding, respect, and collaboration in cultural heritage preservation: A conservator's developing perspective. *Library Trends, 56*(1), 275–287.

Phillips, F. (1995). *Local history collections in libraries.* Englewood, CO: Libraries Unlimited.

Pierce, J. B. (2003). History is its own reward back home in Indiana. *American Libraries, 34*(7), 46–48.

Reference and User Services Association (RUSA). (2007a). *Guidelines for a unit or course of instruction in genealogical research at schools of library and information science.* Retrieved from www.ala.org/rusa/resources/guidelines/guidelinesunit

Reference and User Services Association (RUSA). (2007b). *Guidelines for developing a core genealogy collection.* Retrieved from www.ala.org/rusa/resources/guidelines/guidelinesdeveloping

Reference and User Services Association (RUSA). (2012). *RUSA guidelines for establishing local history collections.* Retrieved from www.ala.org/rusa/resources/guidelines/guidelines establishing

Reid, P. H. (2003). *The digital age and local studies.* Oxford, UK: Chandos.

Roberts, E. A. (2007). *Crash course in library gift programs: The reluctant curator's guide to caring for archives, books, and artifacts in a library setting.* Westport, CT: Libraries Unlimited.

Shires, N. P. (2002). The case for digitizing fiction with history. *North Carolina Libraries, 60*(3), 46–52. Retrieved from www.ncl.ecu.edu/index.php/NCL/

Shires, N. P. (2004). To the benefit of both: Academic librarians connect with middle school teachers through a digitized history resources workshop. *Information Technology and Libraries, 24*(3), 142–147.

Simpson, J. (2008). *Basics of genealogy reference: A librarian's guide.* Westport, CT: Libraries Unlimited.

Smallwood, C., & Williams, E. (2012). *Preserving local writers, genealogy, photographs, newspapers, and related materials.* Lanham, MD: Scarecrow Press.

Smith, A. (2007). Valuing preservation. *Library Trends, 56*(1), 4–25.

(SAA) Society of American Archivists. (n.d.). *Public Library Archives/Special Collections Roundtable.* Retrieved from http://saa.archivists.org/4DCGI/committees/SAATBL-PLASC .html?Action=Show_Comm_Detail&CommCode=SAA**TBL-PLASC&

Sowers, B. (2003). Bigger things from smaller packages: Enhancing a catalog with local and family history analytics. *Technicalities, 23*(6), 1, 11–14.

Staley, E. (2004). Programming to promote local history: Remembering the Topeka tornado of 1966. *Public Libraries, 43*(3), 161–164.

Swan, J. (2004). The librarian's guide to genealogical services and research. New York, NY: Neal-Schuman.

Symonds, E. (2008). Controlling the vocabulary: Maintaining consistency across collections. *Visual Resources Association Bulletin, 35*(2), 106–111.

Theimer, K. (2010). *Web 2.0 tools and strategies for archives and local history collections.* New York, NY: Neal-Schuman.

Thom, J., & Hansom, B. (2000). Public service and digitized collections. *Colorado Libraries, 26*(4), 4–7.

Thompson, E. T. (1978). *Local history collections: A manual for librarians.* Nashville, TN: American Association for State and Local History.

Tomkins, J., & Martin, A. (2007). Vancouver in 1907: A case study of archival film as a source of local history. *IFLA Conference Proceedings,* 1–18.

Tonta, Y. (2008). Libraries and museums in the flat world: Are they becoming virtual destinations? *Library Collections, Acquisitions, & Technical Services, 32*(1), 1–9.

Tucker, S. (2006). Doors opening wider: Library and archival services to family history. *Archivaria, 62,* 127–158.

Tuzinski, J. H. (2011). Local history: A peek into the past, an entry into "empowering learners." *Learning & Media, 39*(3), 9–10.

Yesson, L., & Jones, L. (2001). Under construction: the California Heritage Project's K–12 outreach experience at the University of California, Berkeley. *College & Research Libraries News, 62*(3), 296–306.

Zampaglione, T., & Bennett, R. (2012). Electronically preserving obituaries. *Public Libraries, 51*(2), 28–30.

Part IV

FIELD REPORTS

INTRODUCTION: FIELD REPORTS

Our call for papers drew reports of cultural heritage studies from around the world. The *Field Reports* section explores digitization initiatives and cultural heritage projects in Ethiopia, the United States, Australia, and Romania. Whether focused on active digitization programs, cultural heritage preservation, or plans for further studies, these reports will intrigue and inspire cultural heritage professionals.

In "Initiatives in Digitization and Digital Preservation of Cultural Heritage in Ethiopia," Abebe Rorissa (associate professor, Department of Information Studies, College of Computing and Information, University at Albany, State University of New York) and Teklemichael T. Wordofa and Solomon Teferra of Addis Ababa University describe their groundbreaking study of digitized cultural heritage resources in Ethiopia. The authors discuss their findings, including the impediments to digitization efforts and the need for improved access tracking and use policies. Their recommendations will help Ethiopian cultural heritage institutions achieve the ultimate goals of digital preservation and effective, efficient access.

From the other side of the globe, Alan C. Jalowitz (editor, Pennsylvania Center for the Book) and Steven L. Herb (director, Pennsylvania Center for the Book, affiliate professor of Education (Language and Literacy Education), College of Education, Penn State) contributed a report entitled, "Creating the Online Literary and Cultural Heritage Map of Pennsylvania." Launched in January 2000 as an online literary map project of the Pennsylvania Center for the Book, the Online Literary and Cultural Heritage Map of Pennsylvania encompasses 1,150 biographies and 285 featured essays accompanied by digital image, audio, and video data. The evolution of the project is traced, project challenges and solutions are described, and future creative plans for the Map are discussed.

Back across the globe once more, Sigrid McCausland (joint secretary at International Council on Archives Section on Archival Education and Training, lecturer in information management at School of Information Studies, Charles Sturt University) and Kim M. Thompson (lecturer at School of Information Studies, Charles Sturt University) describe their study of the Australian Community Heritage Grants (CHG) program. "The Community Heritage Grants Program in Australia: Report of a Survey" includes assessments of the impact of CHG grants, concerns for the future of the collections, and reflections on relationships between central government agencies and grassroots organizations as evidenced by the CHG program. The authors offer suggestions for further research into the delivery of grant programs to local cultural heritage organizations in Australia.

Our field reports conclude with "Toward a Study of Unofficial Museums" by Cheryl Klimaszewski (fellow, doctoral student, Rutgers School of Communication and Information) and James M. Nyce (Ball State University, Department of Anthropology). Based on field work, a review of the extant literature, and library and information science theory, the authors work toward a plan for the study of unofficial, local Romanian cultural heritage museums. The collections, ethnic groups represented, physical spaces housing the collections, and the kinds of visitors who view the collections are described. Collection development practices and the construction of narratives around the collections are discussed and contrasted with official museum practices. Areas for further research into unofficial, local museums in Romania and elsewhere are mapped.

8

Initiatives in Digitization and Digital Preservation of Cultural Heritage in Ethiopia

Abebe Rorissa, Teklemichael T. Wordofa, and Solomon Teferra

ABSTRACT

A diverse nation of over ninety million people who speak more than eighty different languages, Ethiopia has a rich and unique history as well as cultural heritage. Due to a number of factors, its rich cultural heritage is neither adequately preserved nor widely accessible. A potential solution is digitization, which could serve to rectify both these problems. Although some institutions in the country initiated digitization of cultural heritage resources, the full picture of the initiatives in digitization and digital preservation of cultural heritage in Ethiopia is not clear. To address this gap in the literature and assess what has been achieved so far, as well as plans for the future, we conducted a cross-sectional survey of twenty-two institutions, which is the first such comprehensive study of its kind. Our results revealed that 64% of the institutions either have digital collections of cultural heritage resources or are engaged in digitization activities that relied heavily on internal and external funding, including funding from international donors. Only a fraction (29%) of those institutions have an explicit use policy and track the usage of their digital collections. Among those institutions that neither have digital collections nor are engaged in digitization activities, most have plans for digitization in the next four years. Lack of funding and skilled human resources are the top two most cited reasons for lack of digitization efforts and are consistent with reasons often cited by similar institutions in other countries. Based on the results, we offer recommendations on the path forward so that cultural heritage institutions in Ethiopia might achieve the ultimate goal of digital preservation as well as serve their users effectively and efficiently.

INTRODUCTION

Ethiopia is a diverse nation of over ninety million people where more than eighty different languages are spoken. The country is one of those often thought of as the Cradle of Mankind. It has a rich and unique history as well as cultural heritage. Its monasteries and museums, most of which are scattered all over the country and are at times physically inaccessible, hold unique collections of rare manuscripts that researchers and others could utilize to conduct document-based studies and for other educational purposes. Quite a number of these manuscripts were written in Ge'ez, an ancient language with its own alphabet comparable to some of the well-known writing systems of Sumeria, Egypt, China, Greece, and the Hebrew, Arabic, Latin, and other languages.

Ge'ez played the central role in Ethiopia's status as one of the very few countries in Africa, if not the world, with a rich antique cultural heritage. This ancient language and its alphabet allowed an early proliferation of a print culture, albeit predominantly among religious leaders such as priests and scholars, as well as institutions such as churches and monasteries. For instance, in the words of Ullendorff (1968), the *Kebra Nagast*, or *The Glory of the Kings*, one of the famous manuscripts written in Ge'ez, which describes how Ethiopian emperors have the Solomonic lineage via the meeting between the Queen of Sheba and King Solomon and the conversion of Ethiopians from paganism to Christianity, "is not merely a literary work, but it is the repository of Ethiopian national and religious feelings" (p. 75).

This rich cultural heritage has not been adequately and widely made available and accessible to users within or outside the country and has not been preserved in digital formats. One of the reasons, among others, is that cultural heritage resources such as religious manuscripts and artifacts, some of which date back thousands of years, are scattered around the country in monasteries as well as a few museums. The other main and obvious reason is the country's low economic development coupled with the lack of human and material resources that are crucial to undertake and sustain even the most rudimentary digitization and digital preservation projects.

One of the defining characteristics of the last half of the twentieth century and the more than dozen years of the twenty-first century is the use of information and communication technologies to, among other things, create, manage, access, disseminate, preserve, and use information and cultural heritage resources in digital format. In addition, mobile devices such as smart phones with Internet connectivity have become ubiquitous, even in the poorest of countries. In fact, for the last decade or so, mobile device and phone growth rate on the continent of Africa has consistently been high and the trend will continue for the next three or more years (Elliott, Sieper, Ekpott, & Eyisi, 2012). As a result, users all over the world are increasingly demanding access to these resources in digital format using all kinds of devices, and those in Africa are no exception.

What is more, digitization in general and digitization of cultural heritage in particular is crucial enough that even the European Commission recently urged all its member states to increase digitization activities of cultural heritage, citing the opportunities offered by digitization (Robinson, 2011). Chief among these is the fact that digitization serves dual purposes: accessibility and preservation. In the United States, the Institute of Museum and Library Services (IMLS) often provides funds, through various grant programs, for efforts by cultural heritage institutions, including libraries, to increase their digital collections as well as achieve digital preservation goals. Digital collections of information and cultural resources, especially those in cultural heritage institutions such as museums, archives, monasteries, and the like, have the potential of being accessed and experienced by a wider audience than only those who can visit the cultural heritage institutions. This is especially true for Ethiopia, where most of the institutions, especially the monasteries and churches that hold historical manuscripts and other cultural heritage items, are located in some of the remotest parts of the country and are not easily accessible. In addition, rare items that are sometimes in poor condition can be preserved through digitization for posterity to access and experience.

However, despite the benefits of digitization, although there are institutions in Ethiopia that took the initiative to digitize cultural heritage items and resources as well as preserve them, the amount of these resources in digital format is negligible. Even in a developed nation, let alone a developing country like Ethiopia, digitization is a resource-intensive and costly endeavor that requires a carefully studied and planned-out approach. What is more, the full picture of the initiatives in digitization and digital preservation of cultural heritage in Ethiopia is not clear.

To address this gap in the literature and sensitize the cultural heritage community in Ethiopia as well as other stakeholders about the different approaches to digitization, including recommended courses of action, we conducted a cross-sectional survey of institutions on their digitization and digital preservation initiatives of cultural heritage. We have assessed what has been achieved so far and potential prospects for the future. Our goal was to conduct a systematic and comprehensive survey of the initiatives, the first such comprehensive study of its kind, and present a path forward so that cultural heritage institutions could serve their users effectively and efficiently.

This work is limited to the survey of efforts undertaken in the digitization and digital preservation of cultural heritage within Ethiopia only. In other words, it does not cover efforts that are underway outside the country such as those similar to the ones described in Delamarter (2009), Delamarter and Berhane (2007), and others. We do not leave these out because they are less important, but rather simply to delimit our work.

DIGITIZATION AND DIGITAL PRESERVATION

Digitization

Borgman's (2000) work is one of the sources often cited when tracing the beginning in earnest of digitization of information resources and cultural heritage items such as historical records by universities and other cultural heritage institutions. She puts the date closer to between the late 1970s to the early 1980s. It coincides with the introduction and wider availability of desktop and personal computers. As information and communication technologies became ubiquitous and more afford-able, while at the same time more powerful with respect to their functionalities and capabilities, they led to the increase in digitization activities by information environ-ments and other types of institutions, ushering in the digital age.

By the time Internet connection and the World Wide Web became not just something enjoyed by researchers and students at research and higher learning insti-tutions, but also by households in the early to mid-1990s, digitization and access to digital collections via electronic networks were the norm rather than the exception.

Though some view digitization as a copying activity that is done only to pro-vide easier and wider access to information and cultural resources (Puglia, Reed, & Rhodes, 2005), digitization and digital preservation are increasingly being viewed as intertwined. In fact, Conway (2010) argues that "digital preservation is informed by digital collection building" although it also "encompasses the acqui-sition, ongoing maintenance, periodic transformation, and persistent delivery of digital assets" (p. 65). There is ample evidence to suggest that the principal moti-vating reason for early mass digitization projects by major companies such as the Google Book Search and Microsoft Live Search Books was to help users search and access information resources easily (Rieger, 2008). However, whether the compa-nies and their collaborating institutions intended it or not, it is clear that digital preservation was also an implicit and positive externality. What is more, not only does digitization help improve access, it may potentially help reduce the costs for storage and preservation as well (Rieger, 2008).

Digital Preservation

While it is not clear when and why cultural heritage institutions embarked on preservation of their collections, according to Conway (2010), one of the main events that was the beginning of the preservation revolution, and one that spurred numerous such activities worldwide, was the flooding of buildings that housed cultural heritage collections on the banks of the Arno River in Florence, Italy, on November 4, 1966.

With the advent of information technologies came the next phase in the preser-vation continuum, digital preservation. Conway (2010) argues that, even though "digitization for preservation" and "digital preservation" are very much related, they also have subtle differences. While the former "creates valuable new digital products," the latter "protects the value of those products, regardless of whether the original source is a tangible artifact or data that were born and live digitally" (p. 65). Our own understanding and use of the term "digital preservation" in this work is in the sense that digitization is one of the means by which cultural heritage institutions, or other information environments for that matter, achieve their preservation goals. We believe it is the process by which information artifacts are preserved in digital format, whether they are digitized from physical copies of original items or they were born digital. We see both terms, "digitization for preservation" and "digital preservation" of cultural heritage, as a set of processes and activities that produce digital copies of cultural heritage items for wider access as well as long-term preservation.

RESEARCH DESIGN AND METHODS

Participants

In order to have participants from a cross-section of cultural heritage institutions, we consulted all kinds of lists of such institutions available and accessible to us. The cultural heritage institutions we sought to select included different types of museums, libraries (mainly academic libraries because they predominantly housed and/or managed the bulk of cultural heritage collections and are likely to digitize them as well), archives, broadcasting institutions, and institutions responsible for the care of monuments. We then compiled publicly available contact details, mainly e-mail addresses, of the individuals responsible for cultural heritage management. Our final list contained fifty-five contacts.

Instrument

The survey questionnaire, adapted, in part, from Stroeker & Vogels (2012), was self-administered and had four parts (Part I: Background Information; Part II: Digitization and digital preservation at the cultural heritage institution; Part III: Access to and use of digitized cultural heritage collections at the institution; Part IV: If the cultural heritage institution does not have digital collections, plans for the future) and twenty-four questions covering a number of aspects including: estimated/actual percentage of the cultural heritage collection digitized, estimated cost of digitization, means for monitoring the level of access/use of digitized collections, preservation, and reasons for lack of digitization and digital preservation activities.

Procedures

The URL or Web address for the online survey questionnaire was e-mailed to the potential participants via the e-mail addresses in the compiled contact details at the end of March 2013. Because we did not include any identifying information in the questionnaire and the responses were anonymous, two follow-up e-mails were sent, the first a week after the original e-mail and the second one four weeks later, to all the potential participants, requesting them to complete the questionnaire in case they had not.

RESULTS AND DISCUSSION

Background Information on the Cultural Heritage Institutions

Results are based on twenty-two responses from a total of fifty-five individual cultural heritage institutions that are affiliated with five main groups of parent institutions, namely, academic/educational (e.g., school, college, university, research institute, etc., both government and private; 77.27% of the participants), autonomous cultural heritage institution (e.g., national museum, national archives, national library, etc.; 4.55%), government ministry/department (other than academic/educational institutions and media; 4.55%), international organization (9.10%), and media (TV, radio, newspaper, etc., both government and private; 4.55%). While it is difficult to determine the exact number of cultural heritage institutions in the country, participants of our survey represent a fairly decent percentage of them.

With respect to their type, a significant majority (77.27%) of the cultural heritage institutions were libraries. We deliberately included more libraries in our list of survey participants because, in Ethiopia, traditionally, libraries are primarily the custodians of cultural heritage due to lack of human and other resources and infrastructure at other types of cultural heritage institutions (such as museums, archives, etc.). Figure 8.1 presents the breakdown of the types of institutions of the participants.

Ethiopia has eleven states, called regions and city administrations (henceforth called "states"). Although the majority (77.27%) of the participants' institutions were located in Addis Ababa (due to the fact that it is the capital city and most of the cultural heritage and academic institutions have their headquarters and/or are located there), some were also from Amhara (4.55%); Oromia (4.55%); Southern Nations, Nationalities, and People's (9.10%); and Tigray (4.55%) states.

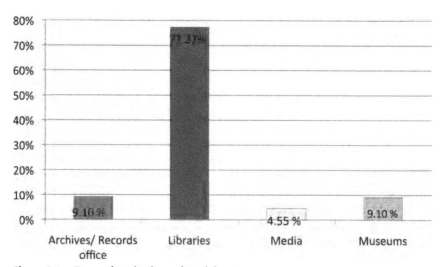

Figure 8.1. Types of Institutions of Participants

In this age of the Internet, for any information environment in general and a cultural institution in particular to broaden its user base and for its collections to be widely accessible, among the first steps it needs to take is establishing a web presence. Thirteen (59.1%) of the twenty-two cultural heritage institutions surveyed had a website. What is more, those institutions from the Addis Ababa City Administration (the country's capital city, which is also a state) were more likely to have a website. This could in part be because they have the necessary skilled manpower as well as better Internet and web infrastructure. It could also be because they are the ones with the higher amounts of annual budgets and larger number of full-time staff.

Tables 8.1 and 8.2 show the annual budgets by type of institution and state of the cultural heritage institutions located in the various regions and city administrations, respectively. In terms of their full-time staff, most of the institutions in Addis Ababa had staff in excess of 35, while the majority of those located in the other states had between 2 and 30 full-time staff. Among the categories of cultural heritage institutions, libraries had the highest number of full-time staff (over 2,000 full time staff), while the least staffed institutions were media, archives, and museums with 150, 279, and 335 full-time staff members, respectively.

Cultural heritage institutions located in Addis Ababa had a minimum of less than 540 U.S. dollars ("USD"; the exchange rate at the time of the survey was, on average, 1 USD = 18.50 Birr) and a maximum of over 540,540 USD in annual budgets, with budgets pretty much covering the entire range in between. The majority of the institutions from the other states had an annual budget of 5,400 USD or less (Table 8.2). While 59.09% of the institutions had budgets less than 54,054 USD, the two top categories of cultural heritage institutions in terms of annual budget were libraries and museums (Table 8.1).

Table 8.1. Annual Budgets of Cultural Heritage Institutions by Type of Institution (n = 22)

| Annual Budget (in Birr) | Type of Cultural Heritage Institution | | | | |
| | Archives[1] | Libraries[2] | Media[3] | Museums[4] | |
	n (%)	n (%)	n (%)	n (%)	Total (%)
< 10,000	0 (0.00)	2 (11.77)	0 (0.00)	1 (50.00)	3 (13.64)
10,000–50,000	0 (0.00)	1 (5.88)	0 (0.00)	0 (0.00)	1 (4.55)
50,000–100,000	0 (0.00)	2 (11.77)	0 (0.00)	0 (0.00)	2 (9.10)
100,000–500,000	0 (0.00)	2 (11.77)	0 (0.00)	0 (0.00)	2 (9.10)
500,000–1 million	0 (0.00)	5 (29.41)	0 (0.00)	0 (0.00)	5 (22.73)
1–10 million	2 (100)	0 (0.00)	1 (100)	0 (0.00)	3 (13.64)
> 10 million	0 (0.00)	5 (29.41)	0 (0.00)	1 (50.00)	6 (27.27)
Total	2 (100)	17 (100)	1 (100)	2 (100)	22 (100)

[1]Archives and records offices; [2]National, higher education, Special, or other types of libraries; [3]TV or radio stations, newspaper publishers, other broadcasting agencies, film institutes; [4]Museums of art, archaeology, history, science, technology, anthropology, ethnology, and other types of museums.

Table 8.2. Annual Budgets of Cultural Heritage Institutions by State (n = 22)

State	Annual Budget (in Birr)							
	< 10,000 n (%)	10,000– 50,000 n (%)	50,000– 100,000 n (%)	100,000– 500,000 n (%)	500,000– 1 million n (%)	1–10 million n (%)	> 10 million n (%)	Total (%)
Addis Ababa	1 (33.33)	1 (100)	1 (50.00)	1 (100)	4 (80.00)	3 (100)	6 (85.71)	17 (77.27)
Amhara	1 (33.33)	0 (0.00)	0 (0.00)	0 (0.00)	0 (0.00)	0 (0.00)	0 (0.00)	1 (4.55)
Oromia	0 (0.00)	0 (0.00)	0 (0.00)	0 (0.00)	1 (20.00)	0 (0.00)	0 (0.00)	1 (4.55)
Southern Nations, Nationalities, and People's	0 (0.00)	0 (0.00)	1 (50.00)	0 (0.00)	0 (0.00)	0 (0.00)	1 (14.29)	2 (9.10)
Tigray	1 (33.33)	0 (0.00)	0 (0.00)	0 (0.00)	0 (0.00)	0 (0.00)	0 (0.00)	1 (4.55)
Total	3 (100)	1 (100)	2 (100)	1 (100)	5 (100)	3 (100)	7 (100)	22 (100)

Digitization and Digital Preservation Activities

The figures for the number of cultural heritage institutions that either have digital collections or are currently involved in collection digitization activities are similar to the figures for those with web presence. Out of the total of twenty-two institutions, fourteen (63.64%) have either digital collections of cultural heritage or are engaged in digitization activities. Once again, the majority of these (85.71%) are from Addis Ababa, followed by those located in Southern Nations, Nationalities, and People's (7.14%), and Tigray (7.14%), respectively. These numbers are understandably low compared to the relatively high level of digitization activities and large digital collections held by, for instance, institutions in European countries (Stroeker & Vogels, 2012).

Mirroring the figures for the number of full-time staff and budget, the top three categories of cultural heritage institutions where the highest percentage of their members either have digital collections and/or are often involved in digitization activities are libraries, archives, and museums. For those institutions with digital collections of cultural heritage, at least 5% of the items in the entire collection and at most 100% are in digital format. Once again, approximately, between 5% and 100% of these are born digital (i.e., items originally created digitally such as digital photos, videos, and sound recordings, for which no physical/analog copies exist). The categories of cultural heritage institutions that have the highest and lowest percentages of their holdings in digital format are libraries and media, respectively. In addition, Tigray and Southern Nations, Nationalities, and People's, respectively are the states where cultural heritage institutions have the highest and lowest percentages of their holdings in digital format. The state with the highest percentage of born-digital collections is Addis Ababa.

It is not surprising that an institution's estimated average annual expenditure on digitization and the percentage of their collections in digital format are somewhat positively correlated. Our findings showed categories of cultural heritage institutions with the highest (or lowest) estimated average annual expenditure on digitization are also those that have the highest (or lowest) percentage of their collections in digital format. For instance, libraries and archives are categories of institutions that spend the highest amounts of their budget on digitization. The bulk of the cultural heritage institutions' annual expenditure on digitization are costs associated with staff, capital, equipment, selection, digital conversion (e.g., metadata enhancement, metadata creation, professional fees, etc.), and digital preservation. The top three expenditure areas on digitization were: staff, equipment, and capital costs, respectively. In terms of funding sources for digitization activities, all of the cultural heritage institutions receive their funding either from internal budgets (50%) or international donors (50%). Commercial trading, public grant/subsidy, private investment, and public/private partnerships were hardly mentioned as sources of funding.

Books (rare and/or others; 57.14% of the fourteen institutions), archival records (35.71%), manuscripts (21.43%), and photographs (21.43%) are the most common types of collection items digitized or being digitized, while drawings, engravings/

prints, serials, maps, microforms/microfilms, and monuments and sites were mentioned by only one institution each. The fact that the majority of the institutions surveyed were libraries could explain this finding. Also, books are items that are relatively less resource intensive to digitize. With respect to the existence of written digitization strategies or written digital preservation strategies, most of the institutions (78.57%) did not have both, while a small minority (28.57%) had written digitization strategies, and only 21.43% had written digital preservation strategies. This is perhaps an area that the cultural heritage institutions need to work on the most so as to ensure that digitization projects are run in a systematic, standardized, and efficient manner. They could also do it under regional or national umbrella organizations and/or consortia to ensure seamless integration of their digital collections as well as resource sharing.

Access to and Use of Digitized Cultural Heritage Collections

Be it cultural heritage or any other resource, preservation is only one of the reasons for digitizing. Beyond preservation, collections of information resources are often digitized so that a larger and more distributed set of users might gain access to and eventually use and/or experience them (especially in the case of cultural heritage). Cultural heritage institutions in Ethiopia that indicated that they have digital cultural heritage items in their collections lack an explicit (written) policy regarding the use of their digital collections (only 28.57% of them indicated they have such a policy). The primary method through which they measure use of digital collections (i.e., count how many times digital metadata and/or digital objects were accessed by users) is through web and database statistics. The type of institutions likely to have explicit use policies and to track use of their digital collections are higher education libraries, perhaps because their digital cultural heritage collections are part of a larger digital library and/or repository. If one of the ultimate goals of digitization of cultural heritage is for the items to be widely accessible and used, then the institutions not only need to institute formal use policy but they also need to track usage of their collections in order to prioritize the types of services they offer.

Plans for and Barriers to Digital Collections and Digitization Activities

The remaining eight cultural heritage institutions (36.36% of the total institutions surveyed) that neither have digital collections nor are currently involved in collection digitization activities have plans to get involved in collection digitization activities, albeit with different planned time frames. The majority of these institutions (60%) plan to digitize their collections within the next three to four years while the remaining 40% indicated plans to initiate digitization in the next two years. A number of possible reasons have been cited, including, but not limited to, lack of funds and/or budget constraints; lack of skilled human resources and professionals (especially ICT professionals); lack of commitment and willingness by management to support digitization projects; digitization not being an institutional priority area; lack of planning of digitization; and lack of appropriate infrastructure.

CONCLUSION AND RECOMMENDATIONS FOR FUTURE WORK

Our findings revealed a picture of digitization and digital preservation of cultural heritage in Ethiopia that is both encouraging and that leaves a lot to be desired. If digitization and digital preservation of cultural heritage, and in turn wider access by users, is to be fully realized in Ethiopia, more concerted efforts are needed in a number of areas. First and foremost, cultural heritage institutions, their parent organizations, the government, and private businesses and/or individuals who have some vested interest in the preservation of the country's precious historical and cultural heritage need to mobilize resources and work together in a coordinated manner. Second of all, they need to devise formal plans and strategies for digitization, preservation, use, and sharing, among other things, of cultural heritage. Lack of planning can lead to digitization and digital preservation efforts that are not only ad hoc, but also inconsistent, as well as not well rooted in the institution's culture and not in tune with how it operates (Cloonan & Sanett, 2005).

In addition, financial support from external sources needs to be sought by the cultural heritage institutions as well as their parent organizations and even the government. Even those cultural heritage institutions in some of the most developed nations cannot sustain cultural heritage digitization projects on their own and have to seek help from private individuals and donor agencies (Robinson, 2011). To achieve their digitization goals, cultural heritage institutions in the country should constantly look for partners, both within and outside the country, that are willing to support their digitization projects by offering to provide access to their digitized collections. In addition, they should forge alliances by forming regional as well as national consortia in order to pool and share resources such as collections, human, technological, and others.

The various higher learning institutions with programs and curricula relevant to cultural heritage and information management and professional organizations should also be brought into the equation when forming the consortia in order to broaden the stakeholder base. Adequately trained professionals are key to the success of any digitization and digital preservation project, especially in this age of ever dynamic and complex technological change that not only requires highly skilled personnel, but also personnel that can tailor the various hardware and software tools to fit local requirements. There are examples where higher learning institutions played a role in designing curricula and training professionals in digital librarianship (e.g., Pomerantz, Wildemuth, Fox, & Yang, 2006). We should also note that training of digitization and digital preservation professionals must be done in parallel with training in traditional preservation techniques and procedures.

The consortia could serve as one of the means by which the cultural heritage institutions might not only attract potential partners but also coordinate their activities so as to alleviate their common digitization and digital preservation challenges. Such an approach has already been tried in digitization and digital preservation efforts by institutions in the United States (Cloonan & Sanett, 2005). Another major and collaborative digitization effort between higher learning institutions, businesses, and other stakeholders that is often cited as an early model is the one by Cornell University, Xerox Corporation, and the Commission on Preservation and Access (CPA) (Commission on Preservation and Access, 1992).

The key to successful digitization efforts, and success in any other human endeavor for that matter, is not to wait for the next big funding or technology or an ideal infrastructure. It is rather to start on a smaller scale and build digital collections up over a reasonable amount of time. This is even more true for cultural heritage institutions in Ethiopia if they are to save the numerous precious manuscripts and other cultural heritage items that are already in poor condition from becoming decomposed due to various weather conditions and other hazards, and, at the same time, take advantage of decrease in cost, at least as far as technology is concerned. Having said that, we believe that cultural heritage institutions, their parent units, and the government should develop short-, mid-, and long-term strategies for dealing with the challenges to digitization and digital preservation of the country's cultural heritage in order to achieve the ultimate goal of providing wider access to current users and future generations.

No two digitization and digital preservation projects are the same. However, when putting together plans and strategies, cultural heritage institutions in the country should pay special attention to and learn from best practices in the areas of digitization and digital preservation, both from within and outside Ethiopia. In addition, plans should not be limited to digital preservation, but should also pay some attention to the physical and environmental conditions of cultural heritage items. In other words, appropriate environmental storage conditions should also be part of the plans and strategies because they are not only essential, but also cost-effective (Reilly, Nishimura, & Zinn, 1995). We acknowledge the fact that cultural heritage institutions may face a dilemma between providing better environmental storage conditions for their precious artifacts and planning to embark on often expensive digitization and digital preservation activities (Conway, 2010). We also recognize that unless proper preservation strategies and plans, digital or otherwise, are put in place, the country may not continue to be one of the richest in cultural heritage and one of which its citizens would be even more proud.

Limitations of the Work

Our work is the first of its kind, but by no means a definitive survey of digitization and digital preservation of cultural heritage in Ethiopia. What is more, the modest level of cultural heritage digitization activities suggests that it should not be the last work of its kind. Further research, preferably longitudinal, is required to keep track of such activities and to suggest ways to improve the level of access to the country's rich cultural heritage.

REFERENCES

Borgman, C. (2000). *From Gutenberg to the global information infrastructure: Access to information in the networked world*. Cambridge, MA: MIT Press.

Cloonan, M. V., & Sanett, S. (2005). The preservation of digital content. *Portal: Libraries and the Academy, 5*(2), 213–237.

Commission on Preservation and Access. (1992). Cornell/Xerox/CPA joint study in digital preservation—progress report number 2. *The Electronic Library, 10*(3), 155–163.

Conway, P. (2010). Preservation in the age of Google: Digitization, digital preservation, and dilemmas. *The Library Quarterly, 80*(1), 61–79.

Delamarter, S. (2009). Catalogues and digitization for previously uncatalogued Ethiopian manuscripts in England and North America. In S. Ege, H. Aspen, B. Teferra, & S. Bekele (Eds.), *Proceedings of the 16th International Conference of Ethiopian Studies, 2–7 July 2007* (pp. 62–69). Norwegian University of Science and Technology, Trondheim. Retrieved from: http://portal.svt.ntnu.no/sites/ices16/Proceedings/Volume%204/Steve%20Delamarter%20 -%20Catalogues%20and%20Digitization.pdf

Delamarter, S., & Berhane, D. (2007). *A catalogue of previously uncatalogued Ethiopic manuscripts in England: Twenty-three manuscripts in the Bodleian, Cambridge and John Rylands University Libraries and in a private collection*. Oxford: Oxford University Press.

Elliott, L. E., Sieper, H., Ekpott, N., & Eyisi, N. (2012). *Grow rich in the new Africa: Navigating opportunities on the continent* (vol. 2). Washington, DC: Conceptualee Publishing.

Pomerantz, J., Wildemuth, B., Fox, E. A., & Yang, S. (2006). Curriculum development for digital libraries. In G. Marchionini, M. L. Nelson, & C. C. Marshall (Eds.), *Proceedings of the 6th ACM/IEEE-CS Joint Conference on Digital Libraries, 11–15 June 2006* (pp. 175–184). New York, NY: Association for Computing Machinery.

Puglia, S., Reed, J., & Rhodes, E. (2005). *Technical guidelines for digitizing archival materials for electronic access: Creation of production master files—raster images*. Washington, DC: Digital Library Federation.

Reilly, J. M., Nishimura, D. W., & Zinn, E. (1995). *New tools for preservation: Assessing long-term environmental effects on library and archives collections*. Washington, DC: Commission on Preservation and Access.

Rieger, O. Y. (2008). *Preservation in the age of large-scale digitization: A white paper*. Washington, DC: Council on Library and Information Resources. Retrieved from http://www.clir .org/pubs/reports/pub141/pub141.pdf

Robinson, F. (2011, October 28). EU calls for digitization of cultural heritage. *Wall Street Journal*. Retrieved from http://online.wsj.com/article/SB10001424052970203554104577 003590312279860.html

Stroeker, N., & Vogels, R. (2012). *Survey report on digitisation in European cultural heritage institutions*. UK: ENUMERATE. Retrieved from http://www.enumerate.eu/fileadmin/ ENUMERATE/documents/ENUMERATE-Digitisation-Survey-2012.pdf

Ullendorff, E. (1968). *Ethiopia and the Bible*. Oxford: University Press for the British Academy.

9

Creating the Online Literary and Cultural Heritage Map of Pennsylvania

Alan C. Jalowitz and Steven L. Herb

ABSTRACT

Launched in January 2000 as an online literary map project of the Pennsylvania Center for the Book, the Online Literary and Cultural Heritage Map of Pennsylvania encompasses 1,150 biographies and 285 featured essays accompanied by digital image, audio, and video data. Displaying the contributions of over nine hundred authors, including a high percentage of Penn State students, the Map draws over fifty-two thousand average page views per month. The evolution of the project is traced from the founding of the Pennsylvania Center for the book in 1989, through the early focus on literary heritage and involvement of students in the development of materials, to the Map's expansion into the broader realm of cultural heritage. Project managers describe the challenges of defining project scope; establishing standards; balancing usability and available technologies; rights management issues; and planning for ongoing maintenance, upgrades, and migration to new platforms and functionality. From established foundations of solid editorial care and judicious additions to text, audio, image, and video data, future creative plans for the Map are discussed.

INTRODUCTION

An online literary map was one of three goals Steven Herb proposed as the focus of the Pennsylvania Center for the Book when it came back to life under the auspices of Penn State University Libraries in 2000. He has often joked since that, if he had really known what that map would entail, he never would have made a public promise to create one. Herb had seen the occasional literary map over the years (oddly, never Pennsylvania's) and was intrigued with the rapidly expanding world of geographic information systems (GIS). If it made sense for all kinds of paper maps to be leaping into the world of computers; why not a literary map? The mission of the Pennsylvania Center for the Book—*to study, honor, celebrate, and promote books, reading, libraries, and literacy to the citizens and residents of the Commonwealth of Pennsylvania*—seemed an ideal match with an online literary map, as did sponsor Penn State's status as a land grant college. Though the Morrill Land-Grant Act of 1862 focused on agriculture and mechanic arts (engineering), the latter part of its charge, "to promote the liberal and practical education of the industrial classes in all the pursuits and professions of life" (*This is Penn State*, 2013), matched the goal of the map best.

The Pennsylvania map we used to create our online version was a generic, public domain, Adobe Illustrator vector base map we had on CD in Penn State's maps library. Original designer, former maps library supervisor Derrick Beckner writes, "I took that, tweaked the colors, masked each county with a smaller version to create the illuminated borders and make each rollover stand out, and tried to give it the classic National Geographic map look. Flash was really the only way to work with graphic-intensive, interactive web pages at the time and worked great with Illustrator files which I had worked with extensively. The rollovers, with photos and text appearing, look . . . quaint . . . in 2013, but it was really cool for 2002 or so" (D. Beckner, personal communication, May 11, 2013).

The first level of the online Literary and Cultural Heritage Map of Pennsylvania[1] contains all sixty-seven of Pennsylvania's counties on one Commonwealth map, with a featured literary or cultural figure, a photograph and note about that figure, the county name, and the county seat. All the information appears as the user rolls over each county. Those featured state-level county figures provide as remarkable a range of reasons for inclusion as the fields from which they emanate. Cultural icons Ben Franklin (Philadelphia) and Fred Rogers (Westmoreland) sit next to Nobel Prize winner Pearl S. Buck (Bucks) and Pulitzer Prize-winning playwright August Wilson (Allegheny).

All manner of writers abound—journalists Nellie Bly (Armstrong) and Grace Greenwood (Beaver); novelists John Updike (Berks) and John O'Hara (Schuylkill); literary critic (Malcolm Cowley); poets Marianne Moore (Cumberland) and H.D. (Northhampton); children's book authors Margaret Sutton (Potter) and Jerry Spinelli (Montgomery); and the king of westerns, Zane Grey (Pike). The father of modern chemistry, Joseph Priestley, is the featured figure from Northumberland County, where he lived from 1794 till his death in 1804. Exactly one hundred years later, America's most famous psychologist, B. F. Skinner, was born in Susquehanna County.

The Literary and Cultural Heritage Map also contains the sixty-seven individual county maps with links for towns wherever a literary or cultural figure is located, as well as third-level maps for Philadelphia, Pittsburgh, and University Park (home to the main campus of Penn State). There is a note and an image for every person located on the map as well as a link to a full biography. The sixty-seven county maps

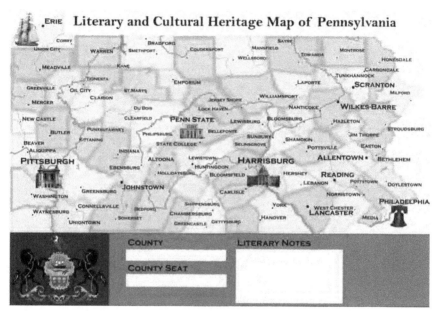

Figure 9.1.   Literary and Cultural Heritage Map of Pennsylvania

Map Image Courtesy of the PA Center for the Book at Penn State University.

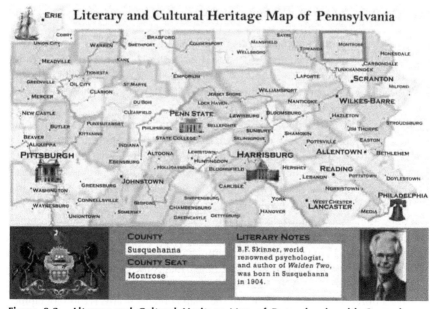

Figure 9.2.   Literary and Cultural Heritage Map of Pennsylvania with Susquehanna County and Featured Cultural Figure B. F. Skinner Highlighted.

Map Image Courtesy of the PA Center for the Book at Penn State University.

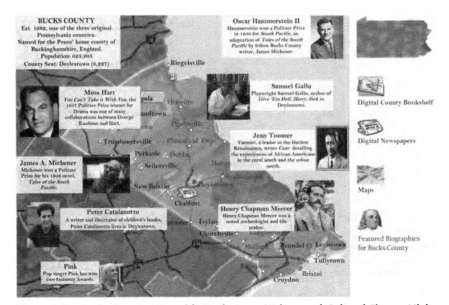

Figure 9.3.   Bucks County Map with Doylestown Writers and Cultural Figures Highlighted

Map Image Courtesy of the PA Center for the Book at Penn State University.

were Digital Elevation Models from the United States Geological Survey (USGS), shaded for elevation with the relevant cities and towns added. Designer Beckner's content partner in the early map years was Pennsylvania Center for the Book web administrator Karen Schwentner. Together they laid the important design foundation that would continue to expand for the next dozen years. One of the recurring early problems was that most computer users really didn't have enough bandwidth to use the very large map!

In 2005 sufficient funding was isolated and stock-piled to support a part-time editorial position for the first time. Alan Jalowitz had just completed his PhD in Comparative Literature the year before at Penn State and shortly after secured an adjunct instructorship in English. His broad background in literature with specializations in German and poetry was an ideal match with our growing content, and his creativity and dedication would have a profound effect on the Map. His editorial position would later be expanded to full-time for three years when additional funding became (temporarily) available. In all, he served as the editor of the Literary and Cultural Heritage Map of Pennsylvania from January of 2005 through June of 2011 when the funding for his position expired. He remains the consulting editor for the Map to this day (Herb & Jalowitz, 2013).

Now a dozen years after its creation, the Map contains nearly 1,150 biographies and 285 featured essays on places, things, and events written by over 900 people, nearly 90% of them Penn State students. It has fully expanded from a literary map to a literary and cultural heritage map and from 2009 to 2012 was page-viewed on average over 52,000 times per month.

The Center for the Book

The story goes, Librarian of Congress Daniel Boorstin wanted to shine a spotlight on the world of the book in the last quarter of the twentieth century, but it is highly unlikely he foresaw what was coming in the world of computers—just a very happy coincidence. In 1977, President Jimmy Carter signed Public Law 95–129, which established the Center for the Book in the Library of Congress to "stimulate public interest and research in the role of the book in the diffusion of knowledge" (Cole, 1993). Since its founding, the Center has established, and sometimes re-established, affiliate centers in all fifty states, the District of Columbia, and the U.S. Virgin Islands.

Pennsylvania Center for the Book 1.0

The Pennsylvania Center came on board as an initiative of the State Library of Pennsylvania in the spring of 1989. In their initial proposal, a strong case was made for Pennsylvania's rich intellectual tradition being an integral part of the nation's heritage, beginning with its namesake and founder, William Penn:

> Penn's literary offering, *No Cross, No Crown*, attests to his mastery of the King's language. Benjamin Franklin, a framer of the U.S. constitution, was a printer, publisher, author, and founder of a lending library. His collection of books was available to Thomas Jefferson as he wrote the Declaration of Independence, and the Library Company of Philadelphia became the de facto Library of Congress during the Constitutional Convention. In addition, many firsts are attributed to Pennsylvania writers such as the first national anthem, "Hail, Columbia," by Joseph Hopkinson; the first American drama, *The Prince of Parthia*, by Thomas Godfrey, Jr.; and the first American fiction, *Wieland* by Charles Brockden Brown. Other famous Pennsylvania authors include Wallace Stevens, John O'Hara, James Michener, W.D. Snodgrass, David Bradley, John Updike, Marianne Moore, H.D., Annie Dillard, and David McCullough. (Parker, 1989, p. 1).

The purpose of that first iteration of the PA Center for the Book was "to enable Pennsylvanians, from beginning readers to scholars, to explore and celebrate the many facets of books: their creation, production, sale, utility, and value" (Parker, 1989, p. 1). The Pennsylvania Center for the Book was the eighteenth state approved as an affiliate center.

Pennsylvania Center for the Book 2.0

The State Library found the going rough and offered the sponsorship of the Pennsylvania Center for the Book to the Penn State University Libraries, but budgetary concerns led them to decline the offer.[2] Several years later, at the behest of John Y. Cole of the national Center for the Book, the earlier Penn State proposal was updated and the Library of Congress approved the new PA Center for the Book to begin operation on January 1, 2000.[3] It promised a focus on family literacy, state sponsorship of at least one national Center for the Book initiative (Letters about Literature), and the creation of an online Literary Map of Pennsylvania.

BEGINNING THE MAP

The earliest steps following Derrick Beckner's design would be to decide who to present on the map and how to present them. Our very small group at the beginning of the process included Steven Herb, who had been named director of the PA Center;[4] Jenny Litz, a full-time staff member who would eventually serve as our web editor; a part time-staff member with a strong interest in literature; and two student assistants. First, we compiled names before ever thinking about criteria. Acknowledging our somewhat unlimited web space and not constrained by paper, we leaned toward inclusiveness rather than exclusivity. An original limit of "at least two authored books" soon became one book, especially when we were attempting to find a representative author for very small, rural counties.[5]

We also began to develop themes for the map—the first three focused on various aspects of Pennsylvania's history: "One State/Many Nations—The People of

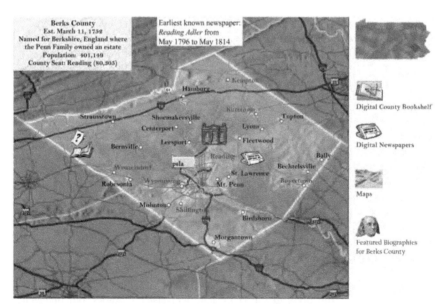

Figure 9.4.   Berks County Map with *Reading Adler* Newspaper Rollover Highlighted

Map Image Courtesy of the PA Center for the Book at Penn State University.

Pennsylvania;" "The Making of Pennsylvania—The History of the State;" and "The Historical Newspapers of Pennsylvania." One remaining feature from those earliest days is the newspaper icon in each county that lists the oldest known newspaper in that county.

Questions often outnumbered answers in the early days of the Map's development. What did we want to include about the literary figures we were selecting— how much information beyond birth, death, and reason for inclusion was required or ideal? Who would write these biographical sketches and how would we present them beyond the simple rollover facts? What were we going to do about famous Pennsylvanians who were not, per se, literary figures, e.g., what if Arnold Palmer had not written a book or two? What about architects, artists, historical figures, home-run hitters, etc.? Even early on, the literary map was calling out for the inclusion of cultural heritage information.

Finding Authors

Given the basic literary idea behind the original project, the question of who to populate the Map with was very easy: authors. Authors of all sorts—famous and obscure, poets and playwrights, novelists and children's book authors. Our first goal beyond the early map themes was to find the literary figures attached to the sixty-seven counties. Some counties like Philadelphia and Allegheny (Pittsburgh) were blessed with multiple candidates to be their "one" representative. We selected the most famous representative for each county, sometimes easily and sometimes not— David McCullough versus August Wilson for Allegheny County, for example. Both men no longer lived in Pittsburgh, but it was Wilson setting all but one of his plays in Pittsburgh that trumped McCullough's more national approach to historical biography, although both could be called the best in their respective fields. Sometimes the choice was an interesting transplant. For example, Abraham Lincoln's selection for Adams County was an acknowledgment of the tremendous significance of the Gettysburg Address. It was exciting to see the variety of our literary representatives growing across vocations and history. And, that was just the first sixty-seven.

One of the natural tendencies of statewide projects such as the Map is to concentrate on one or two primary locations within the state. In our case, the Map could very easily have become what we referred to in-house as "the Pittsburgh and Philadelphia Show."

The 1959 Literary Map of Pennsylvania certainly had a very Pittsburgh/Philadelphia bent. From the very outset of the project, however, we applied the principles of our mission to the scope of the Map project: the Map would strive to cover the entire Commonwealth. To be sure, there is a large amount of content located in Philadelphia and in Pittsburgh; as population centers, such clustering is natural. But our efforts to ensure coverage of all parts of the state have eventually resulted in there being biographies (and features) associated with every one of the sixty-seven counties of Pennsylvania.

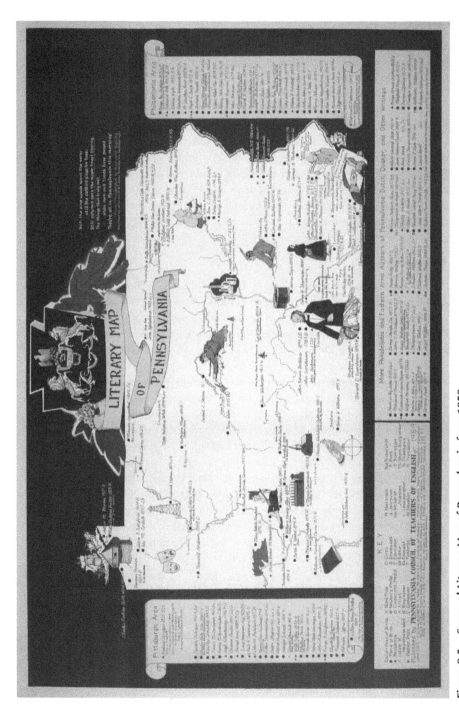

Figure 9.5. Scanned Literary Map of Pennsylvania from 1959
Used by permission of the Pennsylvania Council of Teachers of English.

One of our first standardizations for the map was the creation of a style guide to ensure some uniformity of the approach to biography. Every subject would be listed in the same way including birth date, death date (if applicable), literary vocation, geographic connection to Pennsylvania, keywords—important nouns associated with the subject, and a brief abstract. The first paragraph of the prose section would mention the subject's early life, schooling, and career. Paragraph two, the heart of the biographical sketch, focused on the most important literary or societal contributions, and paragraph three covered current endeavors or the circumstances surrounding the subject's death. Two data-heavy sections followed the biography. One was a "Works" section in which the author's works were listed. If the author had produced more than twelve published works, the writer of the biography would need to select twelve representative works from the author's career. The other data section was the list of "Sources" consulted in the preparation of the biography. This section has no limit to the number of entries; its length depends solely on the nature of the subject and the number of sources available.

In addition to the biographies associated with each particular county, over time we agreed on a standard presentation of links to other stand-alone collections held by Penn State University Libraries. These included links to digitized county histories, newspapers, and maps—topographic and otherwise; for example, the fascinating Sanborn Fire Insurance Maps. Because our portal to that information was *through* a county map, we focused on both geographic connections and geocentric launching points.

Becoming Part of Pennsylvania

The philosophy for inclusion on the Map was constructed over time and became embodied in the style sheet. Our overarching criterion for inclusion was "someone connected with Pennsylvania," and it should be noted that we have never billed figures on the Map as "Pennsylvanians," as that has very different connotations. We have, admittedly, been somewhat broad in our interpretation. Having been born in Pennsylvania became the first principle for selection. It enabled us to place a number of figures on the Map whose subsequent lives would not have allowed us to do so. Prominent among them would be Louisa May Alcott (Duda, 2006), Wallis, Duchess of Windsor (Pavlic, 2007), and Gertrude Stein (Sidorick, 2001). All became permanently connected with other locales, but the Pennsylvania connection also remains prominent—without us they would not be!

We have also included a number of figures on the Map because they died in the Commonwealth. Two noteworthy examples are the actress Eleonora Duse (Kambhampati, 2007) and the poet Edgar Lee Masters (Misko, 2008).

Two other criteria have been somewhat more inclusive than a listing of "Pennsylvanians" would be, if limited to birth or death. We have used education and residence in the Commonwealth with some significance as criteria for inclusion on the Map. John Henry Holliday was born in Georgia and made his fame in the West, but he only became "Doc" Holliday after his time at the Pennsylvania College of

Dental Surgery (Downing, 2010). The novelist Willa Cather, born in Virginia, raised in Nebraska, and living over half her life in New York City, is nonetheless included on the Pennsylvania Map because of the ten years she spent as an editor and critic in Pittsburgh (Gavlock, 2009). Science fiction writer Isaac Asimov conceived and began writing his most important work, *The Foundation* trilogy, while serving at the Naval Shipyard in Philadelphia (Holmes & Homol, 2009).

BROADENING THE SCOPE OF THE MAP

Throughout the summer and autumn of 2005, the director and the editor had a series of conversations in which it became clear that the selection of figures for the Map had been gradually including more and more people whose primary claim to noteworthiness was something other than writing: athletes, artists, musicians, and actors. Rather than viewing this as straying from our original purpose, we felt that the situation presented us with an opportunity to expand the project in new and exciting ways that would also benefit the ultimate users of the site.

Thus, during the autumn of 2005, we decided that while we would continue to encourage the writing of biographies of literary figures, we would also allow the students to write about subjects without literary connections. Thus began the entry of numerous politicians, artists, athletes, and inventors onto the Map over the next several years, and we officially became the Literary and Cultural Heritage Map of Pennsylvania. (Choosing the name was a very arduous process!)

In a parallel move, we also began to develop the feature articles. Our first descriptions of these essays were: "biographies of places, events, and things" related to Pennsylvania culture and history. The first several pieces served as explorations, helping to determine what we wanted from the essays and what we did not. Eventually, as we saw what the feature articles could become, we went back to harmonize the earliest articles in terms of form.

We did not decide to implement the same lengthy style sheet for the features that we did for the biographies. The one exception was the documentation system; that would be common to all essays published on the site. We allowed writers to let the nature of the stories themselves determine the form they would take. Most have a common introductory structure with either interesting anecdotes or quotations, likely in keeping with our request that the features read like an interesting magazine article. This task would require a different tone from the biographies. The feature essays—the creative idea of the editor's—would prove to be hugely popular with student interns.

Feature articles trickled in from our writing interns over the next three years. All told, from the decision to broaden our reach into Pennsylvania's cultural heritage in 2005, until the beginning of 2009, some forty-two feature articles were published on the Map.

The Map's feature holdings increased greatly from the beginning of 2009 because the Center and its editor began to work with other instructors' classes. After a period of exploring how to make the feature articles work in the classroom, one instructor's students generated thirty-two essays that would be published from the first semester alone. The instructor in whose classes we worked praised a number of features of the assignment. It allowed students to have the valuable experience of writing for a "real" audience and there would be consequences for the quality of their writing (publication or rejection). The instructor also enjoyed the fact that the assignment allowed the fulfillment of various pedagogical goals for the class (research, writing, revision, crafting a proper tone, etc.).

Authentic Learning

While our chief concern institutionally in reaching out to various instructors and classes was to secure the production of additional content for the Map, it was accompanied closely by the desire and need to do educational good for the students involved.

Our years of intern supervision gave us certitude that researching, writing, and editing for the Center had been sound educational experiences for the dozens of English and journalism majors who had spent time with us. The Journalism Department answers periodically to outside credentialing organizations who certify the quality of their program. Our writing experiences became an attribute of that certification process. While the English Department did not have such a validating mechanism, their internship coordinator valued the opportunity greatly.

Justifying the writing of biographies, and eventually feature articles, by students whose careers would likely not be primarily focused on writing started by analyzing the core values of the classes we believed might be able to work with us. Each composition class has certain requirements it must fulfill based on improving research skills, the ability to adapt rhetoric to different audiences, and the ability to write persuasively and interestingly for the reader. The nature of the biographical and feature essays let the assignment tick each of these boxes without much debate.

What we came to realize and later to promote was that the assignment was not merely convenient for us and for instructors looking for something "different" to do in the classrooms, but that it also furthered the principles of the Writing in the Disciplines movement that has been reshaping the teaching of writing in college classrooms. Poe, Lerner, and Craig (2010) state that the "[f]irst principles of the WID movement are to model the authentic communication genres and processes of professionals as closely as possible within school contexts" (p. 4). Many of the instructors with whom we have worked have incorporated our partnership to do just this.

For the editing classes with which we worked in the middle years of the project, the instructor incorporated our essays to emulate the processes of actual editors. Each student editor had the opportunity to interact with unknown authors, stimulating the development of tact and empathy that good editors should have.

With the development of the feature articles, we began working with business writing classes. While many business writing courses necessarily focus on the writing of reports, proposals, and memos, the writing of magazine-style, quasi-promotional pieces allowed students to mimic the actual persuasive interest stimulation that businesses of all sorts must engage in.

The necessary "real skill" this assignment promoted in the technical writing classes with which we worked was the notion of translation. The students in these classes were overwhelmingly science and engineering majors, each of whom would have many opportunities to write lab reports and other technical materials for technically oriented readers. Many, though, will also face the challenge of needing to translate their scientific findings to lay audiences, both to provide education and to seek financial support. Students who wrote about patented technological developments or engineering landmarks, among other scientifically based achievements, thus had the very real challenge that many professionals fail at, while doing so in the relatively protected environment of the classroom.

Even the various classes who wrote biographies for the Center had at least one aspect of professional life emulated in their classes: the judgment, and potential rejection, of their work. Unlike, "normal' assignments that are graded, commented upon, and frequently ignored upon their return, the biography essays were part of an additional process, geared to neither the cognitive nor the affective goals of an educational environment, but rather to the potentially harsh judgment of rejection, albeit rejection with a "net" of sorts based on the Center's willingness to continue working with the student toward the eventual acceptance of the essay.

Moreover, each of the assignments, biography and feature, help to develop the socialization function that the Writing the Disciplines movement has begun to stress. Poe, Langer, and Craig (2010) and Carter, Ferzli, and Wiebe (2007), among others, have stressed that an important component of writing in the disciplines is the training in the language of the field. Carter, Ferzli, and Wiebe focus on the socializing role of the lab report in developing not only the scientific mode of expression, but also the development of the scientific mode of thinking and collaboration. Poe, Langer, and Craig do much the same thing with regard to engineering students and their various assignments.

One of the added strengths of these "authentic learning" situations, as some call them, is that not only do they do more good for students, but because they seem more "real" to students, those students tend to be much more motivated to work more diligently on them. Anecdotally, each of the instructors with whom we worked found this to be the case. This was an assignment that excited the student, not simply because of its perceived novelty, but also because of their notions that the assignment was valuable to them both in looks (on a resume) and in substance (forming useful habits of the mind).

Topic Selection

During the "biography only" days, many different resources were consulted to assemble lists of suitable figures for students and interns who worked with us. Searches of *The Dictionary of Literary Biography* database using state of birth located many Pennsylvania writers. We also used a publication issued in conjunction with the 1959 Literary Map of Pennsylvania to cull researchable authors. Lists of notable citizens from various towns and counties, as well as notable alumni of the various colleges in the Commonwealth were perused through various search engines. We even sent letters to the public relations offices of the more than 100 colleges in Pennsylvania asking for their input on the matter.

As we began to add feature articles to the Map, we undertook similar research to assemble lists of possible topics for students and interns to pick from or to inspire them. Some topics, of course, were obvious: Frank Lloyd Wright's Fallingwater (Gutmann, 2006), Philly Cheesesteaks (Ferguson, 2008), and numerous others. Others were generated by searching various sites devoted to tourism in various regions in the state. With the feature articles, we encouraged the students and interns proposing topics for essays. We particularly urged them to consider writing about something "back home," especially if home was a less-populated county.

Some special lists had to be created as our pool of writers developed. While the instructor of technical writing classes had heard a number of good things from her colleagues about the assignment, she justifiably wanted to make sure that the writing could be as relevant as possible both to her courses and to the subject areas of the students. It then seemed wise to focus searches on inventions and architecture, subjects that covered much of the territory. Wikipedia was helpful, providing state-sortable lists of the American Society of Civil Engineers' Historic Civil Engineering Landmarks and the American Chemical Society's National Historic Chemical Landmarks. The reference book, *Famous First Facts*, was also exceptionally helpful (Kane, Anzovin, & Podell, 2006). The book is exactly what the title implies, and included an index that sorted the "famous first facts" by state and towns within the state. (Having Ben Franklin pictured on the cover was a Pennsylvania bonus!)

DISPLAYING THE MAP—DILEMMAS AND OPPORTUNITIES

Maps have traditionally been confronted with problems associated with how they display the portion of the world they attempt to cover. Our electronic Literary and Cultural Heritage Map of Pennsylvania also confronts issues of how it displays its designated corner of the world. Some issues arise from the program in which the Map has been created, others come from the sheer quantity of material the Center has generated; still others come from the nature of some of the content to be placed on the Map.

Aspects of Presentation

The Map was created and in 2013 remains in the Flash software program, a program widely described as the proper application to use for any interactive map application. Our usage of the Flash program has been analogized to a scrapbook where each county and each town serves as a page on which we paste pictures, blurbs, or other content. Many of the display issues we face stem from this usage pattern. Overcrowding is a problem of display that affects a number of locations on the Map. Most of the medium-sized cities in the Commonwealth have reached their capacity. They include Erie, Lancaster, Johnstown, and Scranton. If any more figures are to be added, some alternative display method will need to be devised.

One similarly sized town has produced a solution to deal with its potential for overcrowding. In Centre County, the boroughs of State College and Penn State University are treated as separate towns. Moreover, the University's place marker also contains a clickable link to another Flash map of the campus on which various buildings become the equivalent of towns on a county map. Thus, neither "town" has reached its display limits. Similar solutions may await the towns previously mentioned as each has colleges that could support separate maps.

Overcrowding of an entirely different order of magnitude, however, confronts the cities of Pittsburgh and Philadelphia. The two cities do allow for some similar solutions to ameliorate the display problem. The first of these is to limit display on the Map only to a figure's most important connection in the state of Pennsylvania. Secondly, we have refined the map of each city to reflect more precise locations within the cities: neighborhoods displayed exactly as towns and cities are on county level maps. Problems do remain even with this solution as some neighborhoods have had more famed inhabitants than others.

To confront this issue in Philadelphia, the editor created several city maps depicting neighborhoods, but also added the element of time. The Center City area of Philadelphia is always the most crowded in each of the seven eras, but broken into swaths of time, more figures can be displayed. This historical approach also allows us to use locations that once were separate towns, townships, or neighborhoods, but no longer exist in the public consciousness.

A second problem with the neighborhood solution comes from the level of detail present in the biographies and in source material as a whole. While music and film star Will Smith's West Philadelphia heritage is well known (Catron, 2004), the precise residence of Kate Douglas Wiggin, author of *Rebecca of Sunnybrook Farm*, is not (McCoy, 2002). Our not entirely satisfying solution to this conundrum has been to make the name of the city a "location" connected to figures on each of the maps intended to show neighborhoods.

Another method used to display Pittsburghers and Philadelphians has been to create special thematic displays. Both cities are known for their passion for their sports franchises. After we began to include athletes, a great number of such biographies were submitted. Instead of trying to place them into geographic neighborhoods, we created a separate display box for each of the two cities' sports teams. The box has a clickable link that takes the user to a city map displaying the historic venues in which that city's present and former teams have played. Each stadium is a clickable link taking the user to a picture of the stadium, a brief history of it, and logos of the teams who played there. The logos also function as towns do on the rest of the Map, displaying the notable players from that particular team.

Precision

There are legitimate issues about locations that have caused concerns for story placement on the Map. Imprecise detail is particularly troublesome when stories or people not connected to one particular point are meant to be displayed. Our story about the Mason-Dixon Line (DeVan, 2008) is clearly important; the Line helps form the very shape of the state. Yet it does not conveniently link to a single point, rather it links to a line that we have been unable to depict. Our solution has been to place the story into the holdings of every county along the southern border.

A similar issue comes with trying to place stories connected with areas that transcend county boundaries. Stories about the growth of the territory of Pennsylvania, such as the Treaty of Fort Stanwix (Hagy, 2010) and the Walking Purchase (Gilbert, 2009), would require the ability to superimpose markings over areas that go beyond county lines. Our solution has, again, been to place the story in every county named in the story.

A different issue associated with precision is the placement of stories that have no place to connect to. Unlike lines or areas, some stories that are undeniably important to the culture of Pennsylvania do not have any precise "resident" point. Our stories about the Amish (Guss, 2007a, 2007b, 2007c, 2007d), the Pennsylvania Dutch language (Oswald, 2010), or the film industry (Bayer, 2010) have no specific place; thus, we had to arbitrarily choose counties in which to place them, trying to anticipate where the user might look for them.

Creative Additions

One in-house bit of levity turned into a Map entity. The director had long found amusing the notion of commemorating figures who had Pennsylvania connections against their will. Eventually, we realized we actually had enough such "involuntary Pennsylvanians" assembled that a location for them could be made. Thus, Jimmy Hoffa (Schmitz, 2004), Al Capone (Ackley, 2008), Alger Hiss (Walbert, 2005), and Wilhelm Reich (Stephenson, 2005) helped to make the Lewisburg Federal Penitentiary in Union County a viable "town" on the Map, complete with its own special marker, an icon of a man behind bars with a pair of handcuffs superimposed on them.

Finally, we were able to make a brief foray into mapping "imaginary Pennsylvania." In honor of the 100th anniversary of the birth of John O'Hara, we created a map distilled from his stories of the "Pennsylvania Protectorate." The Protectorate is a thinly disguised version of Schuylkill County and a number of scholars have connected the names of towns in the stories to the names of real towns; "Gibbsville" is the real-life Pottsville, "Richtersville" is the real-life Pine Grove, and so on. This early attempt included only a reused basic Schuylkill County map and redone town names. Nonetheless, the map of O'Hara's Lantenengo County was appreciated and illustrated the potential for such mapping projects in the future.

WRITING FOR THE MAP

Broadly speaking, there have been four distinct types of writers who have written biographies and essays for the Center: staff, interns, students, and volunteers. Within each group, there has been tremendous variation in their organizational origin, ability, and management requirements.

Staff

The earliest and most dependable writers for the Map project were those part-time people actually employed by the project, but it was still a struggle to produce much content until 2005 when our editor joined the staff.[6] Solely in terms of writing, the editor generated some sixty biographies and four feature articles for placement on the Map. The nature of those pieces tended to be more obscure than those solicited from the other groups of writers, largely consisting of biographies of academic authors and others for whom a surfeit of biographical information would not be available. Time the editor spent on writing feature articles could be dedicated to the filling in of gaps.

Interns

Since its earliest days, the Center has taken on well over 100 students from Penn State. They have hailed from a number of different departments, mostly English and Journalism, and all but a handful have taken their internships for course credit. In providing the internship, the Center agreed to provide the interns with a good educational experience and the intern agreed to work a specific number of hours on Center activities. Overall, interns have produced nearly four hundred biographies and features for the Map.

When additional sources of writers were cultivated, we presented our English major interns with the opportunity for editorial experiences as well. For all our interns, we began to institute individual weekly conferences discussing what they had worked on and why they had made the compositional and editorial decisions they had made. Moreover, during these conferences we would engage in quite detailed discussions about vocabulary, punctuation, and grammar. Each piece the student worked on went through this process a number of times.

We encouraged our journalism majors to go beyond the research methods customary to the writing of biographies and feature articles—digital newspaper and magazine databases and websites. We urged them to conduct interviews with people and to cover a wide array of subjects with the pieces they wrote or edited, so that, when asked by prospective employers, they could say they had indeed covered stories from many subject fields. On some occasions, we had journalism interns who had in mind what type of journalism they wished to pursue; we welcomed them to work on stories that would benefit their plans and our Map. An intern with an interest in fashion journalism wrote a biography of designer Tori Burch (Davé, 2008). Two interns interested in becoming sports journalists wrote features about historic football teams (Frankford Yellow Jackets, Pottsville Maroons) (Selway, 2008a & 2008b) and great sporting venues in Pittsburgh and Philadelphia (DeIuliis, 2008b & 2008c).

As we developed feature articles, several interns were also able to earn photojournalism credit. Allentown's Trout Hall (Fallon & Webster, 2010), Bethlehem's Musikfest (Hengeveld, 2010), Luzerne County's Lattimer Massacre (Murphy, 2010), and Mahanoy City's history in cable television (Anderson, 2010) were thus augmented.

Our best effort to enhance a journalism intern's experience came in 2008. One of our interns had written a piece on the Flight 93 National Memorial near Shanksville (DeIuliis, 2008a). While he had researched and written a nice essay, he and the editor acknowledged that his not having been to the site was really discernible to the reader. We at the Center then managed to locate sufficient funds to do on-site reporting. When they arrived at the site, the intern was encouraged to take all the pictures and to interview the ambassador who gave talks about the site. What resulted was a significant photojournalism experience for the intern and an impressive gallery of pictures to illustrate the story on the Map. Now that the permanent Memorial has since been opened, our intern's photographs of the site before that construction serve as an archive for the site's original look and feel.

Figure 9.6.   Flight 93 Memorial Site, 2008

Photo of the Shanksville, PA, crash site before the completion of the Flight 93 Memorial by Dan Deluliis, used by permission of the PA Center for the Book at Penn State University.

Students

The largest group of writers the Center cultivated consisted of students in various English classes at Penn State. Several hundred individual students have published biographies or features with the Center since 2001.

Gaining access to a source of writers like this depends on a number of factors, perhaps none as important as a personal connection to instructors. An early experiment occurred with freshman composition classes in the fall semester of 2001, and some sixty biographies were eventually published from this pilot. Each student was responsible for writing essays on two literary figures. The assignment might have proved more work than the instructors imagined because neither re-upped!

The second connection with the English department came about through the radio. The director of the Center appeared once a month on a local public radio program promoting books. The program's regular host was a well-known local independent bookstore owner who began teaching in the English department as well. Michael Svoboda offered to integrate writing for the Map into his upper-division classes in editing and this time the experiment caught on. The writing of biographies by this instructor's students was but the first stage of a lengthy process designed to give students editorial experiences of greater moment than simple classroom exercises. The first stage would be the drafting of biographies, using a style sheet the Center had devised.[7] After the initial drafts were submitted to the instructor, he would return Class A's essays to Class B and vice-versa. Students would then seek to treat each submission as a disinterested editor would, marking it up and making suggestions for improvement according to the Center's style guidelines. Manuscripts would be returned to their original writers for revision and the process would be repeated. Eventually the biographies would be submitted to the Center and published. During the editing classes' involvement with the Center, between two dozen and thirty biographies would be published each semester. The successful relationship between the Center and Dr. Svoboda ended only after he obtained a position with another university.

Our Map editor continued the collaboration between the Center and various English classes by including biographies and features as an assignment in his own classes for three years and by discussing how it worked with department colleagues who had observed his successful assignments and enthusiastic students. Thus began a two-year period of time in which the editor worked very closely with seven different instructors in five different composition classes. As we grew more experienced with working with classes, we could tell the writers of the benefits having a publication on their resumes would bring.

We found it also beneficial to visit the class for at least one and preferably more than one rough draft session. Mistakes eliminated and gaps filled by the students during the drafting process lessened the need to supplement the texts submitted on many occasions. Willingness to have voluntary conferences with students outside of their class time in the Center's office was also helpful in motivating students and in producing better-quality submissions.

One final logistical concern in working with students is the coordination of topics selected. We made clear to the students that we were not interested in judging the relative merits of several essays on the same subject. Thus, the editor served as a central clearing house for all topic claims. Moreover, a "topics claimed" web page on the Center's site was created and updated; the address was furnished to all students and their instructors so all concerned would be equally informed and on equal footing.

We also strove to make clear that any proposals of suitable people were welcomed. Some very interesting biographies came to us through such proposals, generating biographies we in the Center might never have located. One student's passion for comic books allowed him to propose the writing of Steve Ditko, cocreator of the Spider-Man character (Connolly, 2007). Another student knew that one of her school bus drivers from home, Sarah "Salty" Ferguson, had played in the All-American Girls Professional Baseball League, the organization made famous in the Penny Marshall film *A League of Their Own* (Ferro, 2007).

Volunteers

The smallest group of writers the Center has worked with is the volunteers. Over a ten-year span, we had only sixteen people who volunteered to write for us. As with the other groups, there was a wide variety of writing backgrounds. With one exception, each volunteer produced one publishable piece for the Map: twelve biographies and seven features.

Overall, this group was generally the most enthusiastic and productive. There were no rejections of pieces generated by volunteers. Once acquainted with our expectations, these writers were largely left to themselves, except when they had questions for the editor. Having volunteers creating content for the project was gratifying, but it was also a luxury we could not depend upon for a great deal of production.

More than 900 people have written biographies or feature articles for the Map since 2001. They have filled the Map with content that covers the length and breadth of the Commonwealth from the time of its founding to the present day. They have added to the store of knowledge through unique photographs, through interviews, and the unearthing of forgotten history.

ILLUSTRATING THE MAP

The Literary and Cultural Heritage Map of Pennsylvania has required a great number of illustrations. Many institution-based projects will start with a collection of illustrations and work to frame narratives around them. On some occasions, we have been able to use pictorial assets of our host institution. Having access to images from campus sources has allowed us to illustrate stories otherwise impossible to publish like that of the first Driver's Education course in the country (Peatman, 2011), Hammermill Paper Company (Ingold, 2010), and the Penn State Creamery

(Kattas & Webster, 2010). The Map project has more typically started with content and then has striven to illustrate it.

Challenges in Illustration

Illustrating either type of article for the Map has been confronted with two distinct issues that projects working with their own collections do not typically face: cost and permissions. The Center has never had a budget for illustrations. A number of cultural institutions were willing to allow the Center to use imagery, for a price. Our inability to pay for such images, however, did not derail our efforts to find images for stories on Benjamin Franklin's original lightning rod (Daniel, 2010; blanket permissions having been granted to the public as part of the Franklin tercentenary website), a museum in Pittsburgh (Bergstein, 2008; images made available to the public and media by the Pennsylvania Visitors and Convention Bureau), and a medical history museum in Philadelphia (Roberts, 2009; images found via a social media website).

Such creativity was further encouraged by the difficulties connected with obtaining permissions to use imagery from web-based sources or even finding the appropriate institution to contact to ask for that permission. For stories about the Big Mac (invented in the Pittsburgh area), Planters Peanuts (founded in Scranton), and home-shopping giant QVC (based in suburban Philadelphia), we sought assistance from and/or permission to use corporate images. Each of the companies involved proved difficult in a variety of ways.

To solve our dilemma of having promised publication to the author of a story on the Big Mac, the editor took a field trip to the Big Mac Museum to take pictures of exhibits. As the Museum is also a fully functioning restaurant and taking pictures was encouraged, our conundrum was solved (Fox, 2009).

Illustrating the article about Planters Peanuts presented a different challenge. Unlike the Big Mac, which continues to be a presence in the Commonwealth, Planters Peanuts was only located in Pennsylvania at the very beginning of its existence (Ng, 2010). Finding historical images would thus, very likely, require corporate assistance. After many promises from the company, we located an image of the Mr. Peanut logo that had been painted on the Scranton factory before its demolition from a collector of corporate wall art. To complete the story, one of our interns took pictures of surviving memorabilia in the area while on a university break.

Finally, there is the case of QVC (Murr & Ruland, 2011). Unlike the other companies mentioned thus far, QVC was relatively quick and direct in its response. Unfortunately, their response was that QVC did "not wish to participate" in the project. By this point, however, we were able to locate on a social media photography site images by a company who had exhibited its products on the network, posted pictures of its experience, and released the pictures to the public under terms with which the Map would be in compliance.

It must be observed that these experiences are very much in the minority of experiences the Center had with outside agencies of all sorts. Positive examples of cooperation are noted in another section of this chapter. They do, however, represent the types of problems that an organization seeking outside assistance with what may be regarded as institutional assets may encounter.

Sourcing Illustrations

We believed from the outset that various principles of the use of borrowed materials—fair use, nonprofit, educational purpose—would shield us from any difficulties in using images from whatever source could provide them. Eventually, however, we decided that prudence dictated a more proactive stance regarding image usage. From that point, as well as retroactively, permissions would be sought and documented.

To facilitate the more rapid posting of articles and biographies on the Map, we also began to place a premium on sources of images that would not require affirmative permission from the site hosting them—images for which a blanket permission for use had been granted to our kind of project either explicitly or implicitly.

One of the most useful of the explicit permission sites for our project has been the social media website Flickr. A great number of images eventually used by the Center for illustrating feature articles on the Map were those posted under the provisions of a Creative Commons License. Version 2.0 reads: "Attribution—You must attribute the work in the manner specified by the author or licensor (but not in any way that suggests that they endorse you or your use of the work); Noncommercial—You may not use this work for commercial purposes; and No Derivative Works—You may not alter, transform, or build upon this work" (Creative Commons, n.d.). This source has been most useful in illustrating contemporary subjects or landmarks that are extant. A number of institutions have placed some of their image holdings on a "Flickrstream" for public use; the stream of Dickinson College allowed us to complete the illustration of the Carlisle Indian School article (Yu, 2009).

A source we have treated as giving a blanket permission to use images is Wikimedia. Each image, graph, or map found on Wikimedia (and used on Wikipedia) is augmented by the Wikimedia Foundation's justification for using that particular image (Wikimedia Foundation, 2013). We have used a number of different types of images from Wikimedia, most especially images of paintings that they believe to be in the public domain. The use of various paintings from the seventeenth to nineteenth centuries has been most helpful in illustrating articles primarily concerned with historical actions and subjects for which extant imagery is impossible to locate. Portraits of Benjamin Latrobe and Benjamin Rush in the article about the Yellow Fever epidemic of 1793 (Gum, 2010) and diagrams of the conflicting territorial claims of Pennsylvania and Maryland that resulted in the surveying of the Mason-Dixon Line (DeVan, 2008) are just some of the materials used from this source.

Other sources of images unencumbered by rights issues have been government websites of all kinds. We have considered images posted on various government websites to be in the public domain and have used them wherever appropriate. To illustrate articles about various inventions, we have, for example, used the diagrams that accompany all applications for U.S. patents. The U.S. Patent and Trademark Office maintains a readily searchable and detailed database of patent applications available to the public, as such applications are public documents (Office of Chief Communication Officer, 2013). Patent diagrams include: soldering guns (Segal, 2010), individually wrapped cheese slices (Lee & Jalowitz, 2010), pencils with erasers (Phillips, 2010), the Monopoly game (Casey, 2010), perforated toilet tissue (Earley, 2010), and many others. We have also treated state and local government imagery in a similar fashion.

As a state affiliate of the Center for the Book at the Library of Congress, we also made use of the collections in the Library of Congress Prints and Photographs Catalog Online (Library of Congress, 2013). Their holdings have proven invaluable to illustrating various articles and invariably are accompanied by a "rights advisory," allowing us to use images legally.

Clearly, the most entanglement-free illustrations available are those taken by the Center's staff and by authors submitting stories for consideration. Examples would include the stories about Fulton County's Burnt Cabins Historic Grist Mill (Jalowitz, 2010), Bethlehem's Musikfest (Hengeveld, 2010), and Clearfield County's Bilger's Rocks geologic formation (Shok, 2009).

On occasion, Center staff have even been compelled to make illustrations where none were available, or when the rights holder would be too difficult to find. Smiley and frowny faces were made for the story on the creation of the emoticon (Zavalla, 2010). An image of the copyright sign and a transcription of legal text were created to illustrate a story on the formation of copyright law (Gilbert & Hawthorne, 2011). A few biographies were also written about figures for whom no images were available so word images in time-appropriate fonts were created for them.

A great number of photographs have accompanied many submissions for feature articles, particularly in more recent years when writers were actively encouraged by both the editor and their instructors to identify appropriate imagery for their submissions and to secure such images if they could. At least thirty stories were either fully or largely illustrated in this fashion. Students in classes took a number of pictures of various buildings and landforms all across the Commonwealth to illustrate stories on the Slate Belt of Northampton County (Miller, 2010), Steamtown USA in Scranton (Caterson, 2010), and the Coffee Pot building in Bedford (Miller & Capone, 2011), among others. Other students arranged with owners of images to help illustrate stories about Lanesboro's Starrucca Viaduct (Navickas, 2010), Gettysburg's Shriver House Museum (Ducato, 2010), and Altoona's Mishler Theatre (Zeak, 2010).

Gaining Permissions

Though using public domain images, staff-created pictures, or illustrations for which approvals have been prearranged is, perhaps, ideal, it is not the normal experience. A large majority of images required not only the time to search for them, but also the effort to locate and contact the presumed rights holder for those images.

Figure 9.7. Burnt Cabins Grist Mill, 2009

Photo of Burnt Cabins Grist Mill, Fulton County, PA, by Alan Jalowitz, used by permission of the PA Center
  for the Book at Penn State University

Key to our efforts in obtaining permissions from various rights holders was the development of a request letter. We believe that such a letter needs to include a number of elements designed to elicit approval from the recipient. Seemingly obvious elements include descriptions of who we are and of what we wanted. We stressed our nonprofit status, our educational goals, and our affiliation with the Library of Congress. We also promised the rights holder a photo credit of their choice and a link to their website if they so chose.

As indicated earlier, contacting companies for approval to use images for which they own rights could be a much more difficult process. Aside from the types of uncooperativeness described above, contacting the relevant department within a company could be exceptionally difficult. This was especially true with subjects related to national media. Three were particularly troublesome: stories on the film industry in Pennsylvania (Bayer, 2010), in Pittsburgh (Lipovich, 2010), and the Robot Hall of Fame (Tsang, 2010). We naturally wanted to use images that reflected the subject matter in the accompanying text, but contacting studios for permissions proved impossible. We then had to turn to the Film Commissions of Pennsylvania and Pittsburgh for their assistance. While they were not the ideal pictures we had envisioned, they did suffice. The Robot Hall of Fame was able to give us permission to use photographs of the "real" robots in their Hall, but images of the fictional robots also enshrined there were beyond the Hall's ability to grant approval. Again, we "made do" with a picture of Cmdr. Data's uniform from *Star Trek: The Next Generation* taken at a convention and with a picture of C3PO taken at the American History Museum. While such solutions are not ideal, creative captioning and diligent searching can work around difficulties of this sort.

Many organizations surprised us with their helpfulness. Special collections at major research universities were very accommodating, requiring only a very precise photo credit be used (see stories about the electric watch [Fyock, 2010] and the treaty of Fort Stanwix [Hagy, 2010] for examples). Libraries within the Commonwealth were exceptionally helpful, including Lehigh University and the University of Pennsylvania. Nonprofits like Barnes Foundation, the Holley Foundation, and the Johnsville Centrifuge and Science Museum were most forthcoming in support of articles about them.

For-profit companies were overwhelmingly positive in their responses to our requests for assistance. While no company representative ever stated it, it seems quite likely that companies regarded stories about them as bits of free advertising to be cooperated with and enhanced. KDKA Radio of Pittsburgh (Davis, 2010), Accu-Weather of State College (DiNardo, 2009), and Zambelli Fireworks of New Castle (Gurley & Hawthorne, 2011) are just some of the companies who provided us with a multitude of images for pieces about them.

Assistance went beyond granting permissions to use photographs and even beyond providing photographs for us. In several cases, these organizations offered to read through the texts of the articles about them to ensure accuracy. While some might attribute the motivations for such generosity to a desire to control the story, our communications with such companies seemed much more altruistic.

The Stetson Company helped the Center to create a uniquely informative essay with their assistance (Cartaxo, Holdsworth, & Jalowitz, 2011). After a lengthy search to find the relevant portion of the company, its historian was remarkably enthusiastic about the prospect of the company's history in Philadelphia being documented on the Map. The historian was quite pleased with the article upon reviewing it and sent us a number of images of vintage advertising and poster quality artwork. The historian did make a request of us; she informed the editor that they would like to see a section added about their women's mid-century millinery. With a great deal of investigation, the editor was able to craft a section about the women's hats to insert in the piece, enhancing an already fascinating article.

All told, nearly three thousand images have been used on the Map. They have helped bring our features alive and in some cases serve as archival materials for Pennsylvania's cultural heritage. Their presence on the Map is not only a necessity, but demonstrates that every problem of illustration can be answered.

LOOKING BACKWARD AND FORWARD

After twelve years of interns, students, and staff researching, writing, and editing biographies and featured essays, the Literary and Cultural Heritage Map of Pennsylvania can boast of an incredible breadth and depth of stories about the Commonwealth—1,435 illustrated pieces. We believe this collection to be the largest of its sort focusing on the cultural heritage of Pennsylvania.

While the raw numbers themselves may be striking, the breadth of coverage they represent may well be even more impressive. A project that started in an attempt to bring the best known authors of each county to a digital map has far transcended merely profiling the famous or the "famous for that area." It has not only published pieces about novelists, playwrights, and poets, but historians, journalists, academic writers, graphic novelists, cartoonists, and children's book writers, among other literary trades. After the broadening of our scope began in 2005, the number of fields that became open for biographers expanded greatly. Suddenly, we had athletes of all sorts, generals, artists, industrial magnates, inventors, social activists, and numerous other categories of people.

The development of the feature article as a portion of the Map project was even more striking. Before the expansion to include "cultural heritage" in 2005, we had one feature article on the Map, a piece about the creation of a children's book. That piece was written by author Megan Lloyd about the creation of her book *Pioneer Church* (Lloyd, 2003). It was accompanied by an audio and video supplement from a presentation she had delivered at Penn State in the fall of 2000.

In the six years after the advent of "cultural heritage," interns, students, and staff wrote 284 additional features that would be published. Some maintained our governing involvement with reading: we published features on the Book of the Month Club (Smolinsky, 2010), copyright law (Gilbert & Hawthorne, 2011), and *Poor Richard's Almanack* (Morgan, 2008). Beyond that, we covered food, military history, inventions, physical landforms, religion, science, and art.

Empirical Feedback

There are many ways to assess the reception a web-based project has had. Sheer numbers of page views, of course, are available. According to Google Analytics data provided by the University Libraries data analyst, the average number of unique page views per month in May 2013 was over 20,000 with a monthly average of 52,261 from August 2009 when the data collection began. Averages tend to soar during the school year—the three-year monthly page view average from the last three Octobers is 62,075 and the comparable March average is 74,373, while the July average comes in at 29,626.

Many individual biographies and features are viewed a handful of times in their lifetime on the web, but others are visited quite regularly. It may not be surprising to learn that Penn State's Joe Paterno has been visited over 10,000 times or *Mister Rogers Neighborhood* over 30,000, but it might be harder to predict 33,000 visits to young adult novelist Laurie Halse Anderson or an astounding 68,000 to Molly Pitcher!

These totals must be judged in part by the fact that new viewers most commonly come to the site because of word of mouth or because of biographies about figures sufficiently unknown that our essay appears on the first page of Google searches. In terms of direct searches, "literary map" and "cultural heritage map" in a Google search will bring our project up on the first page of results. A number of our biographies are also on the first page of Google searches: Christopher Sholes, inventor of the keyboard layout for typewriters (Morales, 2008); aviation pioneer Calbraith Perry Rodgers (Clark, 2010); and the "Father of Battlefield Medicine" Jonathan Letterman (Frederick, 2010). The same can be said for feature articles such as the historic Burnt Cabins Grist Mill (Jalowitz, 2010); the world's largest living thing, the Box Huckleberry Plant (McMillen & Capone, 2011); and the Sun Shipbuilding Company (Schmidt, 2010). Links to these individual stories are problematic for further browsing, however, as none of the pages contains a "back to menu" or "back to County" link. The only way for a user to get back to the main site is to manually augment the URL in the address bar, a task most users will not engage in. There is still much work to be done to make the Map a consistent first-level reference source for schools and public libraries.

Anecdotal Feedback

We have been fortunate to receive many compliments on our project from those in the literary world and from those who have worked with us in the creation of the Map and its contents. In 2005, for example, the national Center for the Book at the Library of Congress awarded the Literary Map its Daniel Boorstin Award for Creative Excellence. They lauded our transformation of the literary map from paper to the electronic form. The citation read, "The Pennsylvania Center for the Book's innovative online Pennsylvania literary map is wide-ranging in scope and historical depth and a rich resource for information about literature, history, and culture of the entire state" (Cole, 2005). In subsequent gatherings of Center representatives from throughout the country, the national Center has asked us to demonstrate once again the Map's continuing advances. Several states' centers have asked us for advice on the means and the costs for setting up maps of their own. We choose to take pride in the old adage that imitation is the sincerest form of flattery.

The work we and our writers have carried out has also been recognized by those who have wished to use some of the material we have created. Harper Perennial publishers, for example, contacted us about the biography we posted of Richmond Lattimore, famed translator of Homer's *Iliad* and *Odyssey* (Brooks, 2005). They wished to use portions of the biography as an introduction to a special edition of Lattimore's translation of the *Odyssey*. The *Cold River Review* sought our permission to reprint the body of our biography of psychologist Wilhelm Reich (Stephenson, 2005) for publication in its pages.

One of the more surprising requests for reuse of material from the Map came from the National Aeronautics and Space Administration (NASA). They have been working on creating a curriculum for middle school science courses and asked for permission to use our feature story about the Killer Donora Smog, a tragedy that the Environmental Protection Agency has called the impetus for the Clean Air Movement (Peterman, 2009).

Other examples of positive impact have been more personal in nature. In February 2011, John L. Hoke, an environmentalist and children's science book writer passed away. His son, faced with the always difficult task of writing his father's obituary, contacted us about using parts of our biography (Zell, 2002). We were pleased to be able to help him in an hour of need.

In a more upbeat case, we were able to reunite families who had fallen out of contact, separated by decades and by an ocean. In late 2008, we had received a query from a gentleman in Italy about an author whose biography we had posted on the Map: Marian Potter (Lavelle, 2007). His aged mother had been a war orphan and had received help from Ms. Potter's family through the Foster Parent Plan for Children; she wanted to renew contact with the family who had helped her so much during tough times. Unfortunately, at the time we only had an address of dubious currency to forward to him. Several months later, however, Marian Potter's daughter contacted us about her mother's biography. At that point, we were able to forward contact information to both families.

Other feedback has come from students and instructors with whom we have worked. One student told the editor that it was the mention of the possibility of a publication on the Map that convinced him to stay enrolled in that particular section of an English composition class. Later the same student told the editor that at his medical school interviews, his published biography of Dan Marino was the first item they brought up (Gerrity, 2007). The same circumstance was expressed by a different student whose biography of CBS founder William S. Paley struck his law school interviewers as impressive (Fasanello, 2006). Yet another student partially credited the award of a national scholarship in his field, supply chain management, to his having something other applicants did not: a publication of a biography of James "Cool Papa" Bell (Carelli, 2006). We believe that many other student writers have found their experience, and the credits associated with it, to have been valuable to the course of their early careers.

The faculty we worked with were very pleased with the opportunity the partnership gave them and their students. One wrote to us to say: "As a strong advocate of service learning and 'real-world' writing experiences myself, I immediately responded to the Center's exciting offer to work with me and my students to write full-length articles about noteworthy people and places in PA, and I can say—unequivocally—that this particular writing assignment was the most successful I've ever taught" (L. Waselinko, personal communication, August 9, 2012). Others expressed similar sentiments.

Our interns have also expressed their appreciation for the program we put together in a number of different ways. Some have expressed the value they placed on their time with us in individual e-mails and Facebook posts. Others have continued to ask us for letters of reference as they make their way after graduation. A few students even asked for the chance to serve a second internship with us, clearly a mark of esteem.

Cultural Tourism

Since we began the map we have had numerous occasions to discuss our potential audiences. Students from middle school up through college are certainly a primary target, as are citizens doing research on our state and its cultural figures. We have always thought about Pennsylvania communities as potential users of our Map as well. It seems fitting to encourage the local governments of the very counties and towns on our Literary and Cultural Heritage Map to use the local information to promote their important and unique history and perhaps to even attract visitors. Cultural Tourism continues to gain favor in the United States and beyond and is often seen as a means for small towns to recapture dollars that have migrated south and west with U.S. populations (Beeton, 2006).

An interesting statement often heard about Pennsylvanians is that if you are born in the Commonwealth, it is likely you will be buried here—more than in any other state! Some look at that prediction as a bit depressing, but the PA Center for the Book has always celebrated the positive aspect of that alleged phenomenon—why move away when you already live in the best of the fifty United States?

Several years ago the Center staff undertook the first steps toward a cultural tourism initiative using the Map. Encouraged by the late Joseph Kelly, the executive di-

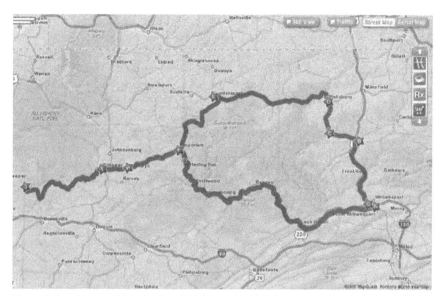

Figure 9.8.   Proposed Lumber Tourism Tour Map, 2010

Map Created for Proposed Lumber Tourism Grant by Jennifer Litz, used by permission of the PA Center for the Book at Penn State University.

rector of the Pennsylvania Humanities Council, we explored the creation of a history tour through Pennsylvania's Lumber region beginning and ending in Williamsport.

Our effort was led by Jennifer Litz, our web editor, and seemed quite promising and well-received in the locale itself when we realized we faced a problem we couldn't surmount—a lack of time—even the time to write the grant to perhaps gain a temporary employee for a year to work on the project. Anything we add to the Center's agenda beyond our current slate of programs (2), book awards (3), and online curricula (3) is unsustainable without additional personnel. That is the fork in the road we face with expanding our current Map in any major direction.

Maintaining Pennsylvania

One by-product of our editor's success is a very large number of biographies and features requiring occasional maintenance with little funding to support that maintenance. It is one thing to keep our eyes open for the death of a famous Map denizen and do a quick update, but it is another matter entirely to actually cruise the Map looking to update biographies or the bibliographies of the biographies. Facing that dilemma daily, it struck us that we might consider treating the map the way local residents treat interstate highways. Imagine the impossibility of sprucing up the entirety of Pennsylvania's 311-mile portion of Route 80. Why not divide the map up among the counties the way interstate miles are batched into ten-mile chunks?

Earlier this spring we began the first steps in putting the idea forward as a trial. History of the book scholar and associate professor of English at West Chester University of Pennsylvania Eleanor Shevlin has agreed to be the first academic site coordinator with selected English and history classes at West Chester. The director presented the notion at a faculty meeting and received a warm response. Similarly to the editor's instruction model, some students will write new essays while others will update and edit existing Map pieces. And, most importantly, West Chester and Dr. Shevlin will take command of the maintenance of a portion of the map. Additional planning will take place this fall with a start date goal of the spring semester of 2014. For the maintenance pilot portion of this experiment, we have decided to keep two approaches on the table for the present—geographic (e.g., all of Chester County or twentieth century Philadelphia only) or vocational (e.g., all of the women novelists in the Commonwealth).

An additional bonus for the association with West Chester was a chance to make contact with history professor and *Talking History* producer, Charles Hardy III. Dr. Hardy's background in history, his excellent aural history productions, and his work with *ExplorePAhistory.com* are a great match with the Center's history content, and it is hoped we will be able to share and promote each other's resources over time as the West Chester project progresses.

Two additional maintenance pilot sites are also in the planning phase—a high school in an area not served by a college or university and a historical society in a medium-sized town. When all three portions of the pilot have been in operation for a year, and if the concept succeeds, we will consider a dramatic increase in sharing the maintenance of the map. It will require a very careful and creative "franchising" operation.

Mapping on Demand

As we explore the notion of shared maintenance of the map, we are also looking at creating smaller, targeted maps by grouping and using our vast amounts of data. We are currently utilizing Oracle Database 11g to house our biographical and feature essay data. It is stored and maintained in multiple tables and used in conjunction with ColdFusion, our Map web application. Our data standardization began about seven years ago with an eye toward future data manipulation and we are on the cusp of attempting some interesting new map services. Our first new maps will be created using the Google Maps API, a no-cost web mapping service application provided by Google. Using Google Maps, we can integrate customized location icons, coordinates and metadata, and custom map image sources pertaining to Pennsylvania culture. We have always thought of our Map as interactive, but the action has been fairly one-directional and directed by the Center. What if we could use these vocational categories we have been assigning and stocking and allow our users to create their own map of Pennsylvania's cultural figures? It was a part of the dream the director had in 2000 when he called for a literary map, but well beyond what the software could do in view of all the years we put into the Map to collect this highly specific and Pennsylvania-connected data.

Our first map trial will be our collection of Pennsylvania poets. Since 2001, the Center has hosted "An Evening of Pennsylvania Poets" in which poets whose work has been selected for inclusion in our Public Poetry poster project come to campus and give a reading (Herb & Wermuth, 2013). As all selected poets have Pennsylvania connections, they have had biographies written about them by our interns or staff. Because many of the poets have read locally or have provided DVDs of a customized reading, we also have video files for about 50% of the nearly five dozen poets who have been part of the project. We managed to secure a small fund and hired a copy editor whose first goal is to update all of our Public Poetry Project poets' biographies.

Other smaller batches of people from the Map will form trials two and three and have yet to be decided. Perhaps Pennsylvania's children's book authors, an often requested reference list for schools seeking author visits, will be selected early on. Our goal is not to move a cultural grouping forward without updating all of the biographies associated with that group, so the going will be deliberate.

Coming full circle from the original idea, one notion being discussed is a new map of the 100 most famous literary and cultural heritage figures associated with Pennsylvania. We are pretty sure we already have them on the Map, we just have to identify them once more!

The Literary and Cultural Heritage Map of Pennsylvania is certainly the gift that keeps on giving. With proper editorial care and judicious additions to our data and by expanding the user's map-making options and access to additional audio/video files and other web sources, we have the potential to make the Map a go-to source in the study and exploration of Pennsylvania's literary and cultural heritage for decades to come.

NOTES

1. Both the Literary Map of Pennsylvania (approximately 2001 to 2005) and the expanded Literary and Cultural Heritage Map of Pennsylvania (2006 to present) will be referred to as the Map in this article. The citation for the map is listed under Herb & Jalowitz (2013).

2. Current Pennsylvania Center for the Book Director, Steven Herb, was a member of the Committee recommending that Penn State take on the sponsorship and cowrote the original proposal. He had been named Head of the Education Library at Penn State in 1992. His affiliation with the original PA Center for the Book was as Coordinator of Children's Services for the Dauphin County Library System in Harrisburg. The State Library had no children's library consultant in the 1980s and 1990s, and Herb sometimes served in a de facto advisory capacity on matters related to children's books and children's services. He remembers the first major program was a lecture on October 15, 1990, at the State Museum in Harrisburg by acclaimed Pennsylvania author Chaim Potok, and a reception honoring Pennsylvania authors who had published in 1989 and 1990, "They served jumbo shrimp and flowing white wine and I wondered if that opening reception could ever be topped!"

3. Nancy Eaton, Dean of Penn State University Libraries served as the initial sponsor of the second PA Center, which became the forty-first state affiliate.

4. Throughout this paper Steven Herb will be referred to as the director of the PA Center and Alan Jalowitz, as the editor of the Literary and Cultural Heritage Map of Pennsylvania.

5. For example, for many years school teacher Elsie Greathead was Fulton County's representative for her *History of Fulton County* (1936).

6. In its early years, the sponsorship of the Penn State University Libraries allowed for some programmatic and endowment funding to be directed toward PA Center for the Book activities and a twenty-hours-per-week staff position. In addition, the director's position was a 20% release time of his faculty position. All other funding was cobbled together from grants and donations. By 2013, all of Penn State's Education and Behavioral Sciences full-time staff and faculty had certain percentages released for PA Center tasks—the director (20%); assistant director (20%); second assistant director (10%); outreach coordinator (80%); web editor (10%); and collections coordinator (10%). The integration of the Center's tasks into the full-time work of the Library's three faculty and three staff is the single most important key to the Center's success and continuation.

7. One other wonderful service provided by Michael Svoboda was a thorough revision and improvement of the style sheet.

REFERENCES

Ackley, C. (2008). Al Capone. *Literary and Cultural Heritage Map of Pennsylvania*. Retrieved from http://pabook.libraries.psu.edu/palitmap/bios/Capone__Al.html

Anderson, M. G. (2010). Wired: Cable TV's unlikely beginning. *Literary and Cultural Heritage Map of Pennsylvania*. Retrieved from http://pabook.libraries.psu.edu/palitmap/Cable.html

Bayer, K. (2010). Cut and print: Film in Pennsylvania. *Literary and Cultural Heritage Map of Pennsylvania*. Retrieved from http://pabook.libraries.psu.edu/palitmap/PAfilm.html

Beeton, S. (2006). *Community development through tourism*. Collingwood, Victoria, Australia: Landlinks Press.

Bergstein, E. (2008). More than fifteen minutes of fame: The Warhol. *Literary and Cultural Heritage Map of Pennsylvania*. Retrieved from http://pabook.libraries.psu.edu/palitmap/WarholMuseum.html./

Brooks, J. (2005). Richmond Lattimore. *Literary and Cultural Heritage Map of Pennsylvania*. Retrieved from http://pabook.libraries.psu.edu/palitmap/bios/Lattimore__Richmond.html

Carelli, R. (2006). Cool Papa Bell. *Literary and Cultural Heritage Map of Pennsylvania*. Retrieved from http://pabook.libraries.psu.edu/palitmap/bios/Bell__James_Cool_Papa.html

Cartaxo, J., Holdsworth, P., & Jalowitz, A. C. (2011). Stetson: The eastern hat that tamed the west. *Literary and Cultural Heritage Map of Pennsylvania*. Retrieved from http://pabook.libraries.psu.edu/palitmap/Stetson.html

Carter, M., Ferzli, M., & Wiebe, E. N. (2007). Writing to learn by learning to write in the disciplines. *Journal of Business and Technical Communication, 21*(3), 278–302.

Casey, L. (2010). Monopoly: Financial prosperity in the depression. *Literary and Cultural Heritage Map of Pennsylvania*. Retrieved from http://pabook.libraries.psu.edu/palitmap/Monopoly.html

Caterson, C. (2010). Whooo, whoooo! All aboard to steamtown. *Literary and Cultural Heritage Map of Pennsylvania*. Retrieved from http://pabook.libraries.psu.edu/palitmap/ Steamtown.html

Catron, T. (2004). Will Smith. *Literary and Cultural Heritage Map of Pennsylvania*. Retrieved from http://pabook.libraries.psu.edu/palitmap/bios/Smith__Willard_Jr.html

Clark, P. (2010). Calbraith Rodgers. *Literary and Cultural Heritage Map of Pennsylvania*. Retrieved from http://pabook.libraries.psu.edu/palitmap/bios/Rodgers__Calbraith.html

Cole, J. (1993). *Jefferson's legacy: A brief history of the Library of Congress*. Washington, DC: Library of Congress.

Cole, J. (2005, May). Boorstin awards. *Information Bulletin, The Library of Congress, 64*(5). Retrieved from http://www.loc.gov/loc/lcib/0505/cfb.html

Connolly, D. (2007). Steve Ditko. *Literary and Cultural Heritage Map of Pennsylvania*. Retrieved from http://pabook.libraries.psu.edu/palitmap/bios/Ditko__Steve.html

Creative Commons. (n.d.). Creative commons–attribution-noncommercial-noderivs 2.0 generic. *Creative Commons*. Retrieved from http://creativecommons.org/licenses/by-nc-nd/ 2.0/deed.en

Daniel, K. (2010). The lightning rod: A not-so-shocking invention. *Literary and Cultural Heritage Map of Pennsylvania*. Retrieved from http://pabook.libraries.psu.edu/palitmap/ Lightning.html

Davé, U. (2008). Tory Burch. *Literary and Cultural Heritage Map of Pennsylvania*. Retrieved from http://pabook.libraries.psu.edu/palitmap/bios/Burch__Tory.html

Davis, B. (2010). KDKA: Broadcasting's pioneer station. *Literary and Cultural Heritage Map of Pennsylvania*. Retrieved from http://pabook.libraries.psu.edu/palitmap/KDKA.html

DeIuliis, D. (2008a). Bravery in the skies: United flight 93 and Shanksville. *Literary and Cultural Heritage Map of Pennsylvania*. Retrieved from http://pabook.libraries.psu.edu/ palitmap/Flight%2093%20Memorial.html

DeIuliis, D. (2008b). Forbes Field. *Literary and Cultural Heritage Map of Pennsylvania*. Retrieved from http://pabook.libraries.psu.edu/palitmap/Forbes_Field.html

DeIuliis, D. (2008c). Shibe Park. *Literary and Cultural Heritage Map of Pennsylvania*. Retrieved from http://pabook.libraries.psu.edu/palitmap/Shibe_Park.html

DeVan, K. (2008). Our most famous border: The Mason-Dixon line. *Literary and Cultural Heritage Map of Pennsylvania*. Retrieved from http://pabook.libraries.psu.edu/palitmap/ MasonDixon.html

DiNardo, T. (2009). Sunny skies over PA: AccuWeather. *Literary and Cultural Heritage Map of Pennsylvania*. Retrieved from http://pabook.libraries.psu.edu/palitmap/AccuWeather.html

Downing, M. (2010). John Henry "Doc" Holliday. *Literary and Cultural Heritage Map of Pennsylvania*. Retrieved from http://pabook.libraries.psu.edu/palitmap/bios/Holliday__ John_Henry.html

Ducato, K. (2010). The Shriver house: Observer at Gettysburg. *Literary and Cultural Heritage Map of Pennsylvania*. Retrieved from http://pabook.libraries.psu.edu/palitmap/Shriver.html

Duda, L. E. (2006). Louisa May Alcott. *Literary and Cultural Heritage Map of Pennsylvania*. Retrieved from http://pabook.libraries.psu.edu/palitmap/bios/Alcott__Louisa_May.html

Earley, C. T. (2010). The greatest missed luxury. *Literary and Cultural Heritage Map of Pennsylvania*. Retrieved from http://pabook.libraries.psu.edu/palitmap/TP.html

Fallon, D., & Webster, K. (2010). Allen's town and Trout Hall. *Literary and Cultural Heritage Map of Pennsylvania*. Retrieved from http://pabook.libraries.psu.edu/palitmap/TroutHall .html

Fasanello, D. N. (2006). William S. Paley. *Literary and Cultural Heritage Map of Pennsylvania.* Retrieved from http://pabook.libraries.psu.edu/palitmap/bios/Paley_William_S.html

Ferguson, S. (2008). Philly's flavorsome fight. *Literary and Cultural Heritage Map of Pennsylvania.* Retrieved from http://pabook.libraries.psu.edu/palitmap/Cheesesteaks.html

Ferro, M. K. (2007). Sarah Ferguson. *Literary and Cultural Heritage Map of Pennsylvania.* Retrieved from http://pabook.libraries.psu.edu/palitmap/bios/Ferguson_Sarah.html

Fox, J. (2009). A meal disguised as a sandwich: The Big Mac. *Literary and Cultural Heritage Map of Pennsylvania.* Retrieved from http://pabook.libraries.psu.edu/palitmap/BigMac.html

Frederick, L. (2010). Jonathan Letterman. *Literary and Cultural Heritage Map of Pennsylvania.* Retrieved from http://pabook.libraries.psu.edu/palitmap/bios/Letterman_Jonathan.html

Fyock, P. (2010). The sweep of time. *Literary and Cultural Heritage Map of Pennsylvania.* Retrieved from http://pabook.libraries.psu.edu/palitmap/ElectricWatch.html

Gavlock, E. L. (2009). Willa Sibert Cather. *Literary and Cultural Heritage Map of Pennsylvania.* Retrieved from http://pabook.libraries.psu.edu/palitmap/bios/Cather_Willa_Sibert.html

Gerrity, K. P. (2007). Dan Marino. *Literary and Cultural Heritage Map of Pennsylvania.* Retrieved from http://pabook.libraries.psu.edu/palitmap/bios/Marino_Dan.html

Gilbert, D. (2009). What ye Indians call "ye hurry walk." *Literary and Cultural Heritage Map of Pennsylvania.* Retrieved from http://pabook.libraries.psu.edu/palitmap/WalkingPurchase.html

Gilbert, D., & Hawthorne, C. A. (2011). Pennsylvania: The birthplace of copyright law. *Literary and Cultural Heritage Map of Pennsylvania.* Retrieved from http://pabook.libraries.psu.edu/palitmap/Copyright.html

Gum, S. A. (2010). Philadelphia under siege: The yellow fever of 1793. *Literary and Cultural Heritage Map of Pennsylvania.* Retrieved from http://pabook.libraries.psu.edu/palitmap/YellowFever.html

Gurley, J., & Hawthorne, C. A. (2011). Booms, blasts, and cracks heard 'round the world. *Literary and Cultural Heritage Map of Pennsylvania.* Retrieved from http://pabook.libraries.psu.edu/palitmap/Zambelli.html

Guss, J. (2007a). Amish and Mennonite groups in the Big Valley. *Literary and Cultural Heritage Map of Pennsylvania.* Retrieved from http://pabook.libraries.psu.edu/palitmap/AmishInBigValley.html

Guss, J. (2007b). Amish history: A timeline. *Literary and Cultural Heritage Map of Pennsylvania.* Retrieved from http://pabook.libraries.psu.edu/palitmap/AmishHistoryTimeline.html

Guss, J. (2007c). Humility and simplicity: The building blocks of Amish society. *Literary and Cultural Heritage Map of Pennsylvania.* Retrieved from http://pabook.libraries.psu.edu/palitmap/AmishValues.html

Guss, J. (2007d). Persecution, division, and opportunity: The origins of the Old Order Amish. *Literary and Cultural Heritage Map of Pennsylvania.* Retrieved from http://pabook.libraries.psu.edu/palitmap/OriginsAmish.html

Gutmann, M. (2006). Architectural brilliance. *Literary and Cultural Heritage Map of Pennsylvania.* Retrieved from http://pabook.libraries.psu.edu/palitmap/fallingwater.html

Hagy, C. (2010). Spoils of war: Taking PA in the treaty of Ft. Stanwix. *Literary and Cultural Heritage Map of Pennsylvania.* Retrieved from http://pabook.libraries.psu.edu/palitmap/Stanwix.html

Hengeveld, M. R. (2010). Musikfest: The musical rebirth of Bethlehem. *Literary and Cultural Heritage Map of Pennsylvania.* Retrieved from http://pabook.libraries.psu.edu/palitmap/Musikfest.html

Herb, S., & Jalowitz, A. (2013). *Literary and Cultural Heritage Map of Pennsylvania*. University Park, PA: The Pennsylvania Center for the Book, 2006–2013. Retrieved from http://pabook.libraries.psu.edu/palitmap/litmap.html

Herb, S., & Wermuth, C. (2013). *The Public Poetry Project*. University Park, PA: The Pennsylvania Center for the Book, 2001–2013. Retrieved from http://pabook.libraries.psu.edu/activities/ppp/index.html

Holmes, M., & Homol, L. (2009). Isaac Asimov. *Literary and Cultural Heritage Map of Pennsylvania*. Retrieved from http://pabook.libraries.psu.edu/palitmap/bios/Asimov__Isaac.html

Ingold, J. (2010). The best known name in paper: Hammermill. *Literary and Cultural Heritage Map of Pennsylvania*. Retrieved from http://pabook.libraries.psu.edu/palitmap/Hammermill.html

Jalowitz, A. C. (2010). Burnt Cabins: Against the odds. *Literary and Cultural Heritage Map of Pennsylvania*. Retrieved http://pabook.libraries.psu.edu/palitmap/Burnt.html

Kambhampati, S. K. (2007). Eleonora Duse. *Literary and Cultural Heritage Map of Pennsylvania*. Retrieved from http://pabook.libraries.psu.edu/palitmap/bios/Duse__Eleonora.html

Kane, J. N., Anzovin, S., & Podell, J. (2006). *Famous first facts: A record of first happenings, discoveries, and inventions in American history* (6th ed.). New York, NY: H.W. Wilson.

Kattas, K., & Webster, K. (2010). A collegiate classic: The Penn State creamery. *Literary and Cultural Heritage Map of Pennsylvania*. Retrieved from http://pabook.libraries.psu.edu/palitmap/Creamery.html

Lavelle, M. (2007). Marian Potter. *Literary and Cultural Heritage Map of Pennsylvania*. Retrieved from http://pabook.libraries.psu.edu/palitmap/bios/Potter__Marian.html

Lee, J. W., & Jalowitz, A. C. (2010). Clearfield cheese: A (pre-wrapped) slice of PA. *Literary and Cultural Heritage Map of Pennsylvania*. Retrieved from http://pabook.libraries.psu.edu/palitmap/ClearfieldCheese.html

Library of Congress. (2013). *Prints and photographs online catalog*. Retrieved from http://www.loc.gov/pictures/

Lipovich, B. (2010). From the ashes of steel . . . film stock? *Literary and Cultural Heritage Map of Pennsylvania*. Retrieved from http://pabook.libraries.psu.edu/palitmap/PGHFilm.html

Lloyd, M. (2003). Thoughts on the making of "Pioneer Church." *Literary and Cultural Heritage Map of Pennsylvania*. Retrieved from http://pabook.libraries.psu.edu/palitmap/Cumberland_church.html

McCoy, M. (2002). Kate Wiggin. *Literary and Cultural Heritage Map of Pennsylvania*. Retrieved from http://pabook.libraries.psu.edu/palitmap/bios/Wiggin__Kate.html

McMillen, N. D., & Capone, A. W. (2011). Pennsylvania's oldest citizen. *Literary and Cultural Heritage Map of Pennsylvania*. Retrieved from http://pabook.libraries.psu.edu/palitmap/Huckleberry.html

Miller, A. (2010). In pursuit of the quarry: Pennsylvania's slate belt. *Literary and Cultural Heritage Map of Pennsylvania*. Retrieved from http://pabook.libraries.psu.edu/palitmap/SlateBelt.html

Miller, J., & Capone, A. W. (2011). A coffee pot for giants. *Literary and Cultural Heritage Map of Pennsylvania*. Retrieved from http://pabook.libraries.psu.edu/palitmap/Coffee.html

Misko, S. (2008). Edgar Lee Masters. *Literary and Cultural Heritage Map of Pennsylvania*. Retrieved from http://pabook.libraries.psu.edu/palitmap/bios/Masters__Edgar_Lee.html

Morales, A. (2008). Christopher Sholes. *Literary and Cultural Heritage Map of Pennsylvania*. Retrieved from http://pabook.libraries.psu.edu/palitmap/bios/Sholes__Christopher.html

Morgan, L. (2008). The prominent and prodigiously popular Poor Richard. *Literary and Cultural Heritage Map of Pennsylvania*. Retrieved from http://pabook.libraries.psu.edu/palitmap/PoorRichardsAlmanack.html

Murphy, A. (2010). The martyred miners of Lattimer. *Literary and Cultural Heritage Map of Pennsylvania*. Retrieved from http://pabook.libraries.psu.edu/palitmap/Lattimer.html

Murr, S., & Ruland, T. (2011). They put the "home" in home shopping. *Literary and Cultural Heritage Map of Pennsylvania*. Retrieved from http://pabook.libraries.psu.edu/palitmap/QVC.html

Navickas, D. T. (2010). Solid as a rock: The Starrucca viaduct. *Literary and Cultural Heritage Map of Pennsylvania*. Retrieved from http://pabook.libraries.psu.edu/palitmap/Starrucca.html

Ng, M. (2010). The big nut. *Literary and Cultural Heritage Map of Pennsylvania*. Retrieved from http://pabook.libraries.psu.edu/palitmap/Planters.html

Office of the Chief Communications Officer. (2013, May 24). *The United States patent and trademark office*. Retrieved from http://www.uspto.gov

Oswald, M. (2010). Death of the dutchy? *Literary and Cultural Heritage Map of Pennsylvania*. Retrieved from http://pabook.libraries.psu.edu/palitmap/PADutch.html

Parker, S. (1989). *Proposal for the Pennsylvania Center for the Book*. Harrisburg, PA: State Library of Pennsylvania, Department of Education.

Pavlic, C. (2007). Wallis, Duchess of Windsor. *Literary and Cultural Heritage Map of Pennsylvania*. Retrieved from http://pabook.libraries.psu.edu/palitmap/bios/Simpson__Wallis_Warfield.html

Peatman, J. (2011). Drivers education—putting it in gear. *Literary and Cultural Heritage Map of Pennsylvania*. Retrieved from http://pabook.libraries.psu.edu/palitmap/DriversEd.html

Peterman, E. (2009). A cloud with a silver lining: The killer smog in Donora, 1948. *Literary and Cultural Heritage Map of Pennsylvania*. Retrieved from http://pabook.libraries.psu.edu/palitmap/DonoraSmog.html

Phillips, J. (2010). The pencil: The strongest tool you forgot you had. *Literary and Cultural Heritage Map of Pennsylvania*. Retrieved from http://pabook.libraries.psu.edu/palitmap/Pencil.html

Poe, M., Lerner, N., & Craig, J. (2010). *Learning to communicate in science and engineering: Case studies from MIT*. Cambridge, MA: MIT Press.

Roberts, L. (2009). The Mütter museum: A look back at the advancement of medicine. *Literary and Cultural Heritage Map of Pennsylvania*. Retrieved from http://pabook.libraries.psu.edu/palitmap/MutterMuseum.html

Schmidt, J. C. (2010). Sun ship: Vessels of progress. *Literary and Cultural Heritage Map of Pennsylvania*. Retrieved from http://pabook.libraries.psu.edu/palitmap/SunShip.html

Schmitz, J. A. (2004). Jimmy Hoffa. *Literary and Cultural Heritage Map of Pennsylvania*. Retrieved from http://pabook.libraries.psu.edu/palitmap/bios/Hoffa__Jimmy.html

Segal, K. (2010). A weapon of technology: The soldering gun. *Literary and Cultural Heritage Map of Pennsylvania*. Retrieved from http://pabook.libraries.psu.edu/palitmap/SolderingGun.html

Selway, T. (2008a). Frankford Yellow Jackets: 1926 NFL champs. *Literary and Cultural Heritage Map of Pennsylvania*. Retrieved from http://pabook.libraries.psu.edu/palitmap/FrankfordYellowJackets.html

Selway, T. (2008b). Stolen glory: The Pottsville Maroons. *Literary and Cultural Heritage Map of Pennsylvania*. Retrieved from http://pabook.libraries.psu.edu/palitmap/PottsvilleMaroons.html

Shok, H. (2009). The city of rock. *Literary and Cultural Heritage Map of Pennsylvania*. Retrieved from http://pabook.libraries.psu.edu/palitmap/BilgersRocks.html

Sidorick, M. (2001). Gertrude Stein. *Literary and Cultural Heritage Map of Pennsylvania*. Retrieved from http://pabook.libraries.psu.edu/palitmap/bios/Stein__Gertrude.html

Smolinsky, M. (2010). A new reading experience: Book of the Month Club. *Literary and Cultural Heritage Map of Pennsylvania*. Retrieved from http://pabook.libraries.psu.edu/palitmap/BOMC.html

Stephenson, H. (2005). Wilhelm Reich. *Literary and Cultural Heritage Map of Pennsylvania*. Retrieved from http://pabook.libraries.psu.edu/palitmap/bios/Reich__Wilhelm.html

Tsang, K. (2010). Best and brightest: The Robot Hall of Fame. *Literary and Cultural Heritage Map of Pennsylvania*. Retrieved from http://pabook.libraries.psu.edu/palitmap/RobotHOF.html

This is Penn State: Our history. (2013). Retrieved from http://www.psu.edu/this-is-penn-state/our-history

Walbert, E. (2005). Alger Hiss. *Literary and Cultural Heritage Map of Pennsylvania*. Retrieved from http://pabook.libraries.psu.edu/palitmap/bios/Hiss__Alger.html

Wikimedia Foundation. (2013, May 21). Retrieved from http://wikimediafoundation.org/wiki/Home

Yu, J. (2009). Kill the Indian, save the man. *Literary and Cultural Heritage Map of Pennsylvania*. Retrieved from http://pabook.libraries.psu.edu/palitmap/CarlisleIndianSchool.html

Zavalla, D. (2010). Is that a joke? Check the emoticon. *Literary and Cultural Heritage Map of Pennsylvania*. Retrieved from http://pabook.libraries.psu.edu/palitmap/Emoticon.html

Zeak, M. (2010). The Mishler: Blair County's historic playhouse. *Literary and Cultural Heritage Map of Pennsylvania*. Retrieved from http://pabook.libraries.psu.edu/palitmap/Mishler.html

Zell, R. (2002). John Lindsay Hoke. *Literary and Cultural Heritage Map of Pennsylvania*. Retrieved from http://pabook.libraries.psu.edu/palitmap/bios/Hoke__John_Lindsay.html

10

The Community Heritage Grants Program in Australia

Report of a Survey

Sigrid McCausland and Kim M. Thompson

ABSTRACT

The Community Heritage Grants (CHG) program is a small annual competitive grant scheme funded and administered directly by the Australian Government to support the management of cultural heritage at the local level. Grants fund significance assessment, preservation, and training projects in a wide range of cultural institutions, including archives, galleries, genealogical and historical societies, museums, and public libraries, among others. By the close of 2011, the program had disbursed over $4 million in funds to 888 community organizations. This paper reports on a project undertaken in 2012, Assessing the Impact of Community Heritage Grants, the focus of which was a survey of CHG applicants and recipients in regional New South Wales (NSW), Australia. The survey was designed to assess the impact of the grants on the organizations that applied for them and to document their concerns for the future of the collections they manage. The paper concludes with reflections on relationships between central government agencies and grassroots organizations as evidenced in the CHG program and offers suggestions for further research into the delivery of grant programs to local cultural heritage organizations in Australia.

INTRODUCTION

The Community Heritage Grants (CHG) program is a small annual competitive grant scheme funded and administered directly by the Australian Government to support the management of cultural heritage at the local level. The National Library of Australia (NLA) is the lead agency for the CHG program that began in 1994.

The program provides grants of up to $15,000 to not-for-profit incorporated organizations to help preserve "locally owned but nationally significant collections of materials . . . including artefacts, letters, diaries, maps, photographs, and audio visual material" (National Library of Australia, 2012a, n.p.). The types of organizations eligible to apply are archives, art galleries, community groups, genealogical societies, historical societies, indigenous groups, migrant community groups, museums, professional associations, public libraries, and religious groups. Grants are provided for significance assessment, preservation, and training projects. By the close of 2011, the program had disbursed over $4 million in funds to 888 community organizations.

This paper reports on a project undertaken in 2012, Assessing the Impact of Community Heritage Grants, the focus of which was a survey of CHG applicants and recipients in regional New South Wales (NSW), Australia. The survey was designed to assess the impact of the grants on the organizations that applied for them and to document their concerns for the future of the collections they manage. The paper concludes with some reflections on relationships between central government agencies and grassroots organizations as evidenced in the CHG program, and suggestions for further research into the delivery of grant programs to local cultural heritage organizations in Australia.

PROJECT BACKGROUND

In Australia, most grants in the arts and culture field are administered by state and territory governments, and until recently the CHG was the only national small grant scheme open to local community organizations.[1] The NLA provides the staff and office resources for the CHG and chairs the partnership of Australian Government agencies that administer the program, namely, the Department of the Prime Minister and Cabinet, Office for the Arts; the National Archives of Australia; the National Film and Sound Archive; and the National Museum of Australia. Despite its longevity and national status, there has been little published about the CHG program. Apart from the CHG website, the main source of reporting has been the *NLA News*, which from time to time has carried stories about the latest round of CHG.

In 2011, Drs. Sigrid McCausland and Kim M. Thompson, lecturers in the School of Information Studies at Charles Sturt University, Wagga Wagga, NSW, Australia, received a small internal research grant for a pilot survey to investigate how the CHG are perceived in regional areas. Regional centers were chosen because there are fewer information and cultural heritage professionals located in regional areas. As Anne Dunn (2007) has noted, "there is no coherent, Australia-wide system for the provision of support to regional collections. There are small grant programs operating nationally and in most states and territories, however these have failed to address the volume and breadth of need for support" (p. 6). There is also a documented need for more training at the local level for cultural heritage organizations (Dunn, 2007). NSW was chosen for this evaluative study because Charles Sturt University is a regional university in that state with campuses in several major towns. The years 2004 to 2011 were chosen as the time span because the current iteration of the scheme that includes a three-day workshop for successful applicants in Canberra began in 2004. The research grant of $3,300 was primarily used to pay for a research assistant and for a SurveyMonkey license.

METHODOLOGY

As noted above, there are no aggregated data documenting the experiences and perceptions of organizations that have applied for CHG funds. An evaluative study using a survey to gather a mix of factual and evaluative information was proposed, and the NLA agreed to support the research with the data sets needed for this analysis and a pre-survey letter encouraging survey recipients to participate in the study.

Determining the Survey Population

Financial and other information from recipients is required as a condition of the grant and evaluations are collected at the conclusion of the annual workshops in Canberra. The NLA provided the researchers with data sets about organizations applying for CHG between 2004 and 2011, including the names of funded and unfunded organizations, the amount awarded, and contact details. These data are maintained by state, but the NLA does not distinguish between metropolitan (Sydney, in the case of NSW) and regional (the rest of the state) location in its data. The first task was thus to refine the lists of organizations using the postcode so that only organizations in regional areas would be included in the survey population. The next task was to check the currency of contact details for the organizations. This was necessary because the NLA's data on applicants is not regularly updated. The NLA's CHG staff maintain close contact with recipients during the grant period, but do not offer ongoing support or advice once the grant has been acquitted. An e-mail address was the essential information required here, because the survey was to be delivered via a link in an e-mail. Some of the organizations applying for CHG are very small and have no paid staff. Hence some e-mail addresses supplied to the NLA were personal e-mail addresses of office-bearers at the time the grant application was received, rather than official ongoing contact points for the organization. The project team then used another more comprehensive data set, the OzCoR,[2] to verify contact details. Ultimately, a total of 176 organizations fitted the criteria for inclusion in the survey, after duplication between the lists of funded and unfunded organizations and repeat occurrences of the names of organizations that had received multiple grants were eliminated. No current e-mail addresses could be found for five organizations, so they were excluded from the survey.

Questionnaire Design

The questionnaire was divided into four sections: Section 1 asked for information about the organization, its people, and its sources of funding; Section 2 asked for assessments of the CHG; Section 3 (for funded projects only) asked about the impact of the grant on the organization; and Section 4 asked about the future management of collections.

The questionnaire consisted of thirty-four questions, nineteen of which were traditional multiple choice or yes/no questions, and fifteen of which were short re-sponse (i.e., "If you would be willing to be contacted for an interview about CHG funding, please provide your name, e-mail address, and phone number here") or open-ended questions (e.g., "How did your organisation benefit from the CHG workshop in Canberra?"). The open-ended questions in this questionnaire were written to elicit qualitative data about CHG topics that are not usually collected by the program's administrators.

Conducting the Survey

Although digital and e-mail surveys tend to have lower response rates than mail or telephone surveys (Groves et al., 2009; Sheehan, 2001), they allow a higher return on investment (Lin & Van Ryzin, 2011) because of cost savings related to printing and mailing of survey instruments as well as time for data entry once surveys are returned (Kaplowitz, Hadlock, & Levine, 2004). Studies show that response rates can be increased by sending a pre-survey notice indicating when the survey will be distributed and whom the survey will benefit. Reminder notifications are also useful for increasing response rates (Archer, 2007; Kaplowitz, Hadlock, & Levine, 2004). With this in mind, the survey was introduced to participants via an e-mail letter from the Director-General of the NLA on March 19, 2012, informing them about the study and the survey and encouraging them to take part. This was followed by an e-mail on March 23 from the researchers explaining the purpose of the survey and including a link to the SurveyMonkey questionnaire and asking the recipients to respond by April 5. On April 3, 2012, a reminder e-mail was sent, again with a link to the questionnaire, extending the final response date to April 19.

Response Rate

The CHG survey received 30 responses from the target population of 176, a re-sponse rate of 17%. This is somewhat low for quantitative analysis and prevents the study's results from being generalizable. Low response rate also has the potential to introduce nonresponse bias, which could result in misleading information about the is-sues covered in this study. However, as noted above, research on e-mail surveys suggests that low response rates are not unusual. Despite the low response rate, the geographical spread of responses across regional NSW was fairly even, providing useful qualitative data, as the objective of the survey is not to find the "truth" of the situation, but rather an understanding of the subjects' experiences with the CHG program. Responses were received from all eligible organizational types, except for migrant community groups, professional associations, and indigenous organizations. The greatest number of responses was from organizations identifying themselves as historical societies (43.3%). The next group was museums (40%), followed by archives (13.3%).

FINDINGS

Staffing, Qualifications, and Funding Sources

A large majority (73%) of survey participants reported that they had no full-time paid staff, while 70% reported that they had no part-time paid staff to manage their collections.[3] The number of volunteers involved in managing collections ranged from zero to seventy-two. Asked about the qualifications of staff, 30% responded that no member of the staff had a professional qualification in collection management. Where they did have such qualifications, these were most likely to be in librarianship or museum studies. Other qualifications reported included teaching, history, computing, business management, conservation, and archaeology. The two main sources of funding for participants were membership fees (56.7%) and grant funds (46%). Other sources of funding included donations, fund-raising, support from the parent organization, and admission charges. Sixty percent of participants said that they did not receive grants for their heritage and preservation activities on a regular basis. Some organizations were aware of and had applied for state government grants, including NSW Heritage Office grants (56.7%) and Museum and Gallery Services NSW grants (46.7%) during the 2004 to 2011 period.

Information about the CHG

The CHG program is widely advertised, and apart from knowing about the program from having previously applied, sources of information about the CHG reported by participants included Internet searches, attending a local workshop, and advice from professional associations or heritage professionals. Participants were generally unable to recall details of exactly which year they had received funding and how much they had received. Forty-two percent of participants reported that there was no one in the organization with grant writing experience to help them complete CHG applications. The response to the question, "Would you apply for another CHG?" was resoundingly positive, with 80.8% replying, "Yes." Reasons for "No" responses to this question included that the collection had been assessed as of state rather than national significance and so did not qualify for funding, the process was too time-consuming, they would apply if they thought they would succeed, and that the program was "biased towards consultancies for significance rather than practical outcomes."

Impact of the CHG

Organizations that received CHG between 2004 and 2011 nominated a range of benefits. The three main benefits can be summarized as improved understanding of the significance of their collections, receiving advice on preservation, and receiving assistance with collection management. One response was "Provides a basis for systematic data collection. Explains the significance of a very rare collection [and] provides a resource base for researchers and conservators." Other responses included "Raise profile locally. Identify priorities"; "Sound and well documented reports to base and plan future collection management projects and strategies"; and "Improved knowledge of the collection and professional reports to assist in obtaining further grants to help manage the collection." The majority (71.4%) of participants said they established a continuing relationship with the consultants they engaged for their projects. Participants who had personally attended the workshop in Canberra considered they had benefited greatly from the opportunity to learn from the practical demonstrations and visits to institutions as well as the chance to network with staff of the national cultural institutions and other grant recipients.

One purpose of the survey was to elicit information about the skills recipients had gained as a result of the grant. In answer to the survey question, "What skills has your organization developed as a result of receiving a CHG? (For example, understanding significance assessment, applying for grants, administering grants, improved collection management skills, digitization project management skills)," respondents noted that the skills included understanding significance assessment, knowing how to apply for grants, and developing collection management skills. Examples of comments received here included "the significance assessment will add to members' understanding of best practice in museums"; "applying for grants, administering grants, dealing with consultants, hosting training events"; and "improved planning and collection management skills, including identifying themes in our collection, collection gaps and how to address them."

Future Management of Collections

The questions in the final part of the survey were evaluative, seeking responses that would identify problems and potential solutions for local collections and their management into the future. The aging of the workforce, paid and volunteer, is a current issue in cultural heritage management in Australia, and 83.3% of participants said that they were concerned about the aging of the workforce, with some participants expressing concern about the difficulty of attracting younger people as volunteers. Participants considered that government initiatives to support local management of nationally significant cultural heritage collections should be primarily financial, especially through providing grants. There was also interest in ensuring that expert advice was available at the local level through encouraging professionals to share their knowledge.

Asked to nominate the three main challenges facing their organizations in the next five years, participants again identified finance, workforce, and professional assistance. Responses included: "we need more volunteers and community input especially more involvement of the youth. For smaller isolated museums, easy close access to specialists . . . is also necessary"; "funding to upgrade storage facilities"; "properly documenting the collection"; "digitizing the collection to make it available from our website"; and "finding sufficient resources, both people and money, to complete our collection management plans and strategies." CHG or other government initiatives that could help organizations meet these challenges were categorized as funding/money/grants; training/workshops; buildings/storage space; advice/guidance and volunteers/staff. These are extensive categories, suggesting that additional federal support is needed to sustain the management of nationally significant cultural heritage collections held in local hands.

DISCUSSION

Some of the survey findings confirmed existing assessments of the cultural heritage sector in Australia, such as the demand for more training opportunities in regional areas and the perception that the sector as a whole is underfunded (National Library of Australia, 2011). On the other hand, the finding that membership fees were the main source of funding for a majority of respondents was unexpected. This means that voluntary contributions received from ordinary Australians are important for maintaining local collections that are seeking recognition for their national significance. It is likely that funding profiles for collections in regional NSW are not likely to differ particularly from their counterparts in the city or interstate.

The goodwill and mutual understanding created by the relationships established through contact between Canberra and grassroots cultural heritage organizations is difficult to quantify. The value to participants of the Canberra workshop has already been noted. The CHG have become an important avenue for disseminating the principles of significance assessment that provide a rigorous and verifiable template for assessing claims of national significance for local cultural heritage collections. On the other hand, the Australian Government has been criticized for its direct delivery of small-scale funding programs, the argument being that this activity is best left to state governments (Australian Broadcasting Corporation, 2012). Cultural heritage management is an area where there are established programs run by the states, and there is a case for better coordination and targeting of grant programs.

The survey highlighted concerns about training and the need to augment the volunteer workforce, but only 15% of survey participants had received a training grant. More training for staff and volunteers is one way that local collection management capacity could be increased. The majority of grants continue to go toward significance assessment, preservation needs, or conservation or collection management activities. However, it appears that the NLA is already taking the need for more training into account, with organizations now being encouraged to submit joint applications for training projects (National Library of Australia, 2012b).

Since 1994, the priority for the CHG program has been physical rather than digital materials. Only one respondent to the survey reported that their grant was for a digitization project. Digitization projects are eligible only for digitization of original, not published, materials and only after any necessary preservation work has been undertaken. The 2013 CHG guidelines encourage potential applicants to out-source digitization as this may be more cost effective than attempting it themselves (National Library of Australia, 2013). Through its limited support for digital initia-tives, the CHG program thus appears to be sidestepping the possibility of an online cultural heritage network across Australia. There are major national programs and guidelines for digitization. For example, the NLA coordinates a successful national newspaper digitization program and the National and State Libraries Australasia (NSLA) consortium disseminates policies and guidelines on digitization and digital preservation (National and State Libraries Australasia, n.d.) The future for local cul-tural heritage is likely to change significantly with the gradual rollout of the National Broadband Network (NBN). This major national initiative promises to improve the delivery of Internet services in regional and remote areas as well as provide a means of sharing local heritage globally (Australian Government, 2013b).

CONCLUSION

The project Assessing the Impact of Community Heritage Grants provides some insight into cultural heritage practices in Australia. It suggests that over the long term the CHG program has effectively linked national institutions with local or-ganizations that manage their collections with volunteer staff and slender financial resources. The project confirms that the demand for funding and professional sup-port is unlikely to be met. The CHG are indeed small; less than $4.5 million over nineteen years is a small total spend. This figure is for the grants alone and excludes such costs as consultants' fees to assess grant applications and the time of senior staff of the national cultural institutions to oversee the program. The CHG program has nevertheless received support from successive Australian Governments whose main priority in cultural heritage is to fund the national cultural institutions. The survey and the related research point to several avenues for further investigation. These include a national study of the CHG; follow-up interviews with the twenty regional NSW respondents available for further contact; a scoping study of how the CHG could transition into an online cultural heritage space; and an analysis of policy op-tions for government support for local cultural heritage collections. It is clear that lo-cal cultural heritage collections are valued, but adequate funding and human capital are required for them to continue to be preserved and accessible to the wider world.

ACKNOWLEDGMENTS

The authors would like to acknowledge Charles Sturt University for providing Research Priority Area internal funds to support this evaluative study. We thank the National Library of Australia for their provision of the CHG data sets used to identify potential participants, and their support in introducing the project to the participants. Additional thanks to Dianne Dahlitz for her support and interest in the project and to Debra Leigo for her work as research assistant. We would like to thank each participating organization for the time and thought they put into completing the survey and to the Spatial Data Analysis Network (SPAN) of Charles Sturt University for support with data analysis.

NOTES

1. In 2011 the Australian Government (2013a) Department of Sustainability, Environment, Water, Population and Communities began another funding program entitled "Your Community Heritage" for grants in 2012 and 2013. Sub-programs funded through this granting scheme include Protecting National Historic Sites (up to $500,000), Recovering from Natural Disasters (up to $70,000), Commemorating Eminent Australians (up to $10,000), Sharing Community Heritage Stories (up to $25,000), and Celebrating Community Heritage (up to $25,000).

2. OzCoR is the Australian Collecting Organisations Register. It is a database of collecting organizations and peak bodies in Australia. OzCoR was maintained until 2010 when the Australian Government ceased funding its host, the Collections Council of Australia.

3. Statistics and quotations in this section are drawn from the survey responses.

REFERENCES

Archer, T. M. (2007). Characteristics associated with increasing the response rates of web-based surveys. *Practical Assessment, Research & Evaluation, 12*(12). Retrieved from http://pareonline.net/pdf/v12n12.pdf

Australian Broadcasting Corporation. (2012). *Sunday Profile. Terry Moran AC, former Secretary of the Department of Prime Minister and Cabinet.* Retrieved from http://www.abc.net.au/sundayprofile/stories/3417218.htm

Australian Government. (2013a). *Your community heritage: Overview.* Department of the Environment. Retrieved from www.environment.gov.au/topics/heritage-grants-and-funding/your-community-heritage

Australian Government. (2013b). *Regional Australia: Bridging the digital gap between regional Australia and the world.* Department of Broadband, Communications and the Digital Economy. Retrieved from http://www.nbn.gov.au/nbn-benefits/digital-economy-goals/regional-australia/

Dunn, A. (2007). *The Dunn report: A report on the concept of regional collections hubs.* Adelaide: Collections Council of Australia Ltd.

Groves, R. M., Fowler, F. J., Couper, M. P., Lepkowski, J. M., Singer, E., & Tourangeau, R. (2009). *Survey methodology* (2nd ed.). Hoboken, NJ: John Wiley.

Kaplowitz, M. D., Hadlock, T. D., & Levine, R. (2004). A comparison of web and mail survey response rates. *Public Opinion Quarterly, 68*(1), 94–101. doi: 10.1093/poq/nfh006

Lin, W., & Van Ryzin, G. G. (2011). Web and mail surveys: An experimental comparison of methods for nonprofit research. *Nonprofit and Voluntary Sector Quarterly, 41*(6), 1014–1028. doi: 10.1177/0899764011423840

National and State Libraries Australasia. (n.d.). *Publications—Policies and guidelines*. Retrieved from http://www.nsla.org.au/publications/policies-and-guidelines

National Library of Australia. (2011). *National cultural policy—Discussion paper*. Retrieved from http://creativeaustralia.arts.gov.au/assets/national-library-of-australia.pdf

National Library of Australia. (2012a). *Community Heritage Grants. Guidelines and application form*. Retrieved from http://www.nla.gov.au/chg/guidelines

National Library of Australia. (2012b). *2012 Community Heritage Grants assessment report*. Retrieved from http://www.nla.gov.au/sites/default/files/2012_chg_assessment_report.pdf

National Library of Australia. (2013). *Community Heritage Grant guidelines 2013*. Retrieved from http://www.nla.gov.au/sites/default/files/chg_2013_guidelines.pdf

Sheehan, K. B. (2001). E-mail survey response rates: A review. *Journal of Computer-Mediated Communication, 6*(2). doi: 10.1111/j.1083-6101.2001.tb00117

11

Toward a Study of "Unofficial" Museums

Cheryl Klimaszewski and James M. Nyce

ABSTRACT

The peasant is an important national symbol in Romania for both historical and ideological reasons. Since the 1989 revolution, a large number of rural, "unofficial" museums founded by amateur museum proprietors opened their doors to showcase peasant life in situ. Developing a better understanding of these local, "unofficial" museums may help ensure their role in the global network of cultural heritage production and preservation. Work toward a plan for the study of unofficial museums draws from field work and extant literature while considering these institutions within a library and information science (LIS) context. After an introduction situating the local, "unofficial" museum in the larger context of cultural heritage and museums in Romania, the collections, ethnic groups represented, physical spaces housing the collections, and the kinds of visitors who view the collections are described. Collection development practices and the construction of narratives around the collections are discussed and contrasted with official museum practices. Areas for further research into unofficial, local museums in Romania and elsewhere are mapped.

INTRODUCTION

The peasant is an important national symbol in Romania for both historical and ideological reasons. Consequently, the material culture of peasant life is well represented in ethnographic museums and cultural heritage collections throughout the country. Since the 1989 revolution, and especially in the more recent past (though there is precedent both under communism and in nineteenth century Romanian nationalism), a large number of local museums in rural areas have also opened their doors to the public to showcase peasant life in situ. By local museums, we mean "unofficial" museums: those collections curated and presented by private individuals, groups, or families as opposed to those found in nationally accredited museums or those cultural heritage collections curated and presented by local governments.

Though local museums often resemble miniature versions of ethnographic museums, they exist outside the museum mainstream and are often something akin to "labors of love" through which their owners set out to preserve a traditional, local way of life that is disappearing, if not already lost. Because these amateur collections are made up of local items that are no longer useful in daily life, the local museum, then, exists at least in part as an aide-mémoire to remind museum goers of the way things used to be in a particular community or region. But to think about local museums simply as an exercise in sentimentality overlooks the role these museums play in the socioeconomic lives of Romanians in the twenty-first century and in the wider cultural heritage preservation agenda.

This paper will work toward a plan for the study of these "unofficial" museums and how we might consider these institutions within a library and information science (LIS) context. We will look at ten local museum proprietors, two of which we visited during field work and eight others presented in the literature. We will briefly discuss the types of objects they collect, the ethnic groups they represent, the physical spaces that house the collections, and the kinds of visitors who see them. We will compare in more detail these collectors and curators, their collection development practices and the narratives they construct around their collections. In conclusion, we will begin to map areas for further research into unofficial, local museums in Romania and elsewhere. We begin with an introduction situating the local museum in the larger context of cultural heritage and museums in Romania.

CULTURAL HERITAGE AND MUSEUMS IN ROMANIA

When considering cultural heritage in Romania, one must begin with the understanding that the history of Romania is not one of "a" people or "a" nation, but is one of multiple histories and peoples (Boia, 2001; Verdery, 1983). Cultural or ethnic identity in Romania (as it is elsewhere) is highly dependent on when and where the question(s) of heritage and identity are asked (Hannerz, 1997; Herzfeld, 2001; Klimaszewski, Bader, & Nyce, 2012, 2013). Like most of Eastern Europe, but perhaps more so, Romania's history has been one of fluctuations in power and shifts in borders that have influenced, defined, and exacerbated political and cultural hegemony between different groups, some of which include Romanians, Saxons (ethnic Germans), ethnic Hungarians, Szekelers, Csango, Roma, Turks, Tatars, and others. Even the pursuit of studying "national" museums can lead one to trace the development of at least three such institutions: one for Saxons, one for Hungarians, and another for Romanians (Niessen, 2006). Heritage as tied to the idea of a fixed nation-state is something that Westerners often take for granted, but, in the case of Romania, operating under this assumption would overlook many of the forces that influence collectors to reassemble and preserve the past.

The quest for a Romanian national identity that eventually led to the development of the peasant as a national symbol grew out of a hegemony that began to form around the mid-nineteenth century (Turliuc, 2011). In the early twentieth century, Alexandru Tzigara-Samurcaş, the head of the Romanian National Museum, began to develop a more cohesive, narrative history of Romania that expressed the unity and continuity of Romania through time, especially as it was embodied in folk art and artifacts that became the basis for the national museum's collection (Pohrib, 2011). Romanian nationalism is rooted in the idea of family, in the concept of the indigenous, and in the idea of the common people and the agrarian lifestyle, despite the fact that all this was and still is a product of the elites (Pohrib, 2011; Schifirneţ, 2012; Turliuc, 2011; Verdery, 1995). Even communism, which was in some ways opposed to this ideal, found ways to capitalize on the "myth" of the Romanian peasant (Pohrib, 2011). For instance, the idea of the peasant embodying the "national essence" could be used as a way to control resistance to Marxist and Leninist tendencies (Verdery, 1995, p. 126).

The peasant-as-symbol appears not to have diminished since the 1989 revolution. This may be as much a reaction to a period of rapid change and modernization as it is a reaction to communism's "systemization," under which many villages faced destruction so that residents could be relocated to large-scale industrial centers. Though this plan ended with the revolution, systemization drove those inside and outside Romania to try to save the country's unique and abundant heritage. More recent developments, such as membership in the European Union (EU) in 2007, have also increased opportunities to participate in various EU-funded cultural heritage preservation initiatives. This, in turn, has helped to increase tourism to Romania, especially the type of tourism that attempts to approximate "authentic" experience for the foreign visitor (Beasley & Nyce, 2009; Closet-Crane, Dopp, Solis, & Nyce, 2006, 2009; Klimaszewski, Bader, Nyce, & Beasley, 2010).

Today, one generally finds an ethnographic museum as well as a village museum (an open-air museum of traditional buildings that contain ethnographic objects) in or near most mid-sized or larger cities. In addition, many villages or communes have a small ethnographic museum or, at least, devote some space in government buildings to display a selection of regional cultural heritage objects. In fact, fieldwork in Salaj County in 2010 (Klimaszewski, Bader, & Nyce, 2011) that studied a Bill and Melinda Gates Foundation-funded project to provide computers and Internet access in libraries revealed local plans not just to refurbish and modernize libraries; it also encouraged the libraries to develop cultural heritage displays in adjacent spaces. The growth in the number and kind of local museums seems a logical trend, especially considering the perceived economic benefits of tourism and the possibility of external EU development funding that appear to be supported at least in part by Romanian initiatives in cultural heritage preservation.

LOCAL MUSEUMS IN ROMANIA

On the surface, local museums are not dissimilar from the "official" ethnographic or open-air village museums found in Romania. They contain the kinds (though not necessarily the same quality) of objects one might expect to find in official collections. Local museums also attempt to provide an "authentic experience" for visitors, similar to accredited museums, by presenting the objects in context as opposed to employing other kinds of interpretive schemes. The 2009 issue of *Martor*, the annual review of anthropology published by the Museum of the Romanian Peasant in Bucharest, focused on local museums and collectors precisely because they have become so ubiquitous in the country's rural areas (Mihăilescu, 2009). During four field visits to Romania since 2007, we have visited a number of these museums and have on at least two occasions interviewed the proprietors at length. The following sections report on eight local collections or museums featured in the 2009 *Martor* (Andreescu, 2009; Dimcea & Turcu, 2009; Manoliu, 2009; Mateoniu & Marinescu, 2009a; Mihalache, 2009a, 2009b; Niculescu, 2009; Pascu, 2009) along with two field interviews (Campulung Muldovenesc museum proprietor, 2010; Ghimeș-Făget museum proprietor, 2008).

Some generalizations about local museums can be drawn from this literature. In the study of local museums carried out by the Museum of the Romanian Peasant, local museums were defined as being "hidden" and self-labeled by their owners (Mihăilescu, 2009, p. 11). Several focus their collections around a specific group, for example ethnic Hungarians (Andreescu, 2009; Mateoniu & Marinescu, 2009a); ethnic Turkish Muslims (Mihalache, 2009b); Csango, a mix of Hungarian and Romanian (Ghimeș-Făget museum proprietor, 2008); Momârlani, a group who consider themselves remnants of the indigenous Dacian population (Pascu, 2009); and Romanians in a mainly ethnic Hungarian area (Andreescu, 2009). The others collect with the goal of representing more of a synthesis of the way of life of a specific area or ethnographic region, which may or may not be multiethnic (Campulung Muldovenesc museum proprietor, 2010; Dimcea & Turcu, 2009; Mihalache, 2009a; Niculescu, 2009).

A collection may contain ethnographic objects, such as textiles, clothing, ceramics, tools, furniture, and even full-scale buildings, fine arts objects, icons, family heirlooms or other personal objects, photographs, books, coins, objects of natural history, and archival documents. Only one of the collections discussed here focuses on just one type of object—textiles (mainly shirts)—but even this museum provides some context because it incorporates tools and equipment used in the production of textiles (Andreescu, 2009). Some collectors also attempt to portray intangible cultural heritage activities with their material collections (Campulung Muldovenesc museum proprietor, 2010; Mihalache, 2009b; Niculescu, 2009). In all cases, the objects are housed in traditional buildings—either in the collector's home or the home of a deceased relative. It is common for these collectors to also live among their collections.

Objects are acquired through a combination of purchase, donation, inheritance, barter and, for lack of a better term, trash picking. Both Romanians (from outside the region) and international tourists seem to be the main audience for these museums, though it is more often Western tourists who are interested in the kinds of authentic experiences promised by cultural heritage and eco-tourism today. The other main audience is local schoolchildren. While none of the museums report many visits from locals, these museums do serve an important outreach service, as they educate younger generations about regional traditions that they might not be exposed to in their own homes. With these generalizations in mind, the following sections of this paper will discuss in more depth the collectors themselves and their approaches to the development and narrativization of their collections.

Collectors

While the hallmark of these local museums is their purported uniqueness, a certain set of shared characteristics emerges from this study of local collectors. Passion and a sense of duty appear to be the major linking traits, expressed as a love and desire to save objects, beauty, and old things. For instance, one collector was described as "an ordinary man with extraordinary passion" for collecting (Manoliu, 2009, p. 195). This passion is often portrayed as being pursued at any cost, with some collectors expressing their willingness to sacrifice, even to starve for the sake of their collections (Manoliu, 2009; Mihalache, 2009b; Pascu, 2009). It is also not uncommon for these collectors to be perceived as having a "mania" or "madness" for objects from the past. The same collector with the "extraordinary passion" for collecting is reported as being perceived by fellow villagers as "a strange and nonsensical man who gathers and pays for useless objects" (Manoliu, 2009, p. 195). One collector described community reactions to her and her husband's collecting activities: "At first [the villagers] said, [the collectors] are mad! They've gone mad! Why the hell do they collect the rubbish that we burn and throw away? Both are crazy! . . . They cursed us and mocked our initiative" (Pascu, 2009, p. 166).

Some of the collectors are also artisans or craftspeople, while others might be better described as amateur historians or ethnographers, though they may or may not identify themselves as such. They are all older or retired, and they have the time to pursue collecting as an avocation. However, as is evident in the comments above, simply being older members of a community or an ethnic group does not automatically mean they hold a position of respect or authority; on the contrary, the activity of collecting seem to bring to these collectors attributions of varying degrees of eccentricity, which seem to become muted only when local residents see the potential for commercial or monetary gain collecting can have. On the other hand, the negative attitude of community members seems to strengthen the resolve of these collectors, vindicating them, in fact, when it is later shown that the junk they have been collecting is found to be desirable and valuable by outsiders.

This notion of collectors as passionate eccentrics makes it perhaps too easy to romanticize the life of the collector and has the potential to overlook the challenges they face as amateur museum proprietors. Nevertheless, it should be noted that the attractiveness and uniqueness of these collections seems to stem directly from the collector's sentimental notions about tradition, family, and the past that they stir in their visitors. In particular, these kinds of amateur museums interest Western tourists who seek the "authentic" experience of a place (Klimaszewski et al., 2010), and several of the collectors reported that becoming part of the local tourism circuit was a main driver for their museum (Campulung Muldovenesc museum proprietor, 2010; Ghimeş-Făget museum proprietor, 2008; Mateoniu & Marinescu, 2009a; Mihalache, 2009a). In many cases, the collectors or others in the village also ran guesthouses marketed (and intended) to further reinforce or rekindle the authentic peasant lifestyle.

Arguably the main challenge that these collectors face, beyond a lack of monetary support, lies in the fact that they present cultural heritage from a singular point of view—their own (Mihăilescu, 2009). Though many of the collectors consult various "experts" in discussions around their collections, such as scholars, local religious leaders, other members of their ethnic group, or members of local government, and though collectors attempt to read relevant books on the topics of museums and regional traditions, it is unclear how the process of compiling information about local traditions has been carried out and to what extent others in the community are involved or want to be involved in the process. Though collection development could be described as being driven by the whims of the collectors, as we will discuss, the ability to collect is often dependent on the willingness of others in the village or region that have traditional objects to share these with the collector.

Collection Development

Though we refer to them as amateurs, these collectors all seem to have some understanding of what a museum is in the more formal sense, and most do strive as much as they can to become like "real" museums. In some cases these collectors have visited museums and/or they have read books on museum history and practice, ethnography, craftsmanship, fine art, and other relevant topics. It should also be noted that part of what drove the 2009 *Martor* study was the desire of professionals at the Museum of the Romanian Peasant to provide more professional support to these collectors through workshops and other formalized training (Mihalache, 2009c). The *Martor* survey was intended at least in part to try to figure out how these local museums might become legitimized (Mihăilescu, 2009; Mihalache, 2009c).

These interviews revealed that, though it might seem to the outsider that collection building was left to the collector's whims, most did employ some kind of collection development criteria, which generally centered on age, relevance to the ethnic group or region, uniqueness, and historical relevance. One collector selected only objects belonging to the local culture that were as old as possible (Pascu, 2009). Another gauged the relevance of objects to his collection based on authenticity, age, beauty, and "strangeness" and also because they have a history or relevance (Niculescu, 2009). The shirt collector's criteria selected only shirts that were hand sewn and characteristic of her native commune, but noted that it did not matter whether samples were considered beautiful (Andreescu, 2009). It is unclear from these interviews or even through observation when we visited these museums exactly how stringent these criteria were or how diligently they were applied in the process of collection and documentation.

It was also unclear if there were any criteria by which a collection could be considered complete. Because collection development seems to be an ongoing activity with no end, it can seem at times to approach for these collectors a type of hoarding. This is sometimes expressed in statements like: "Everything, absolutely everything must be preserved. These things must not be lost or alienated because making a collection is no easy thing to do." (Dimcea & Turcu, 2009, p. 203). This impulse seemed to be controlled mostly by the fact that one's ability to grow a collection was, not surprisingly, dependent on that collector's finances. While collectors could usually offer at least small sums for objects, they were often in competition with outsiders who could afford to pay more for objects, which often meant those items would then leave the community (Mihalache, 2009a).

One way to overcome this was to encourage others to donate to the collections. For instance, one collector relied on the trust she had built within the community of those in her ethnic group who often loaned her items for her collection (Mihalache, 2009b). Elderly members of the community were often sympathetic to the cause of saving the past and this also led to donations or loans. While local officials generally spoke positively about the presence of local museums in the villages, none were able to provide much financial support. This lack of funding has repercussions not only on the buildings where collections are housed, but on collections care and long-term preservation, as well. However, none of these collectors discussed what would happen to these collections after their deaths or in their absence, nor is it clear whether this is a question that was posed by the *Martor* interviewers.

Despite the challenges to collecting, local museums continue to appear in rural areas throughout Romania. In the next section, we will discuss how the stories that develop around these collections help reinforce their importance and make them attractive for local and international audiences.

Narrativization of Local Collections

The overarching narrative that emerges from this review of local museums is that collecting is a selfless act performed by ordinary people out of a sense of duty, driven by passion (sometimes to the extreme), and done for the betterment of an ethnic or regional group, whether that group recognizes it or not. It is about saving the past that, without the intervention of the collector, would be completely lost. This loss may simply be from the passage of time, but more likely it is the result of indifference or more overt forces, such as the looting and destruction that occurred after the revolution. The loss of artifacts can be the result of ignorance or simply the lack of knowledge on the part of others who do not know what things are truly valuable. As one collector describes:

> The post-1989 period disturbed me very much. When I saw that Sarmizegetusa (a site of Dacian ruins) was being destroyed, I mean horses and carts made their way through the amphitheaters, the museum was vandalized, broken into, the objects were stolen, a great collection of money and objects was stolen. . . . When I realized that the objects were systematically stolen by Gypsy collectors who brought them in the area of Banat and took them abroad, I decided to collect them, too. I was familiar in the way in which foreign objects were collected, as was the case of other collectors, but I focused on . . . household objects, not on heritage objects like gold and stuff like that. . . . Practically, these objects may be more precious than gold. (Mateoniu & Marinescu, 2009b, p. 161)

This saving of artifacts from destruction also helps to validate one ethnic group over another, which is especially relevant given the friction and divisions between ethnic groups and regions throughout Romania's history. As one collector stated, cultural heritage objects provide "solid proof of our existence" (Mihalache, 2009b, p. 172), especially when they are amassed and assembled into a collection that can be shared with others. Another collector asked, "Everything bears the mark of Europe, but what about our origin?" (Pascu, 2009, p. 165). This proof or validation often begins at home, with collectors keeping objects from their own families or those inherited from relatives. In one instance, a collector who inherited her aunt's home said: "This ordinary woman liked the idea of setting up a museum meant to preserve not only the memory of her death, but also the cultural context in which she lived" (Pascu, 2009, p. 165). Though collecting is not a selfish act per se, the experience of one particular family or household often seems to expand to represent the experiences of an entire community. This may help to explain why two of the collectors spoke of the potential for being "cursed" by their ancestors if they did not handle their collections properly or if they sold objects for money (Andreescu, 2009; Pascu, 2009).

The local museum, then, is a place where the history, tradition, and culture of a place or people is validated and legitimized. It is a way to provide comfort and familiarity in a rapidly changing world. It is a way for a group to have a voice and presence over which they have control. It is also strongly tied to romantic and sentimental notions about the way things were, about saving the past, and about remembrance. As the collector from Chiscau states: "Tradition means to know how to preserve the customs, the dialect and the faith: everything you inherit from your ancestors. This is tradition. Bestow the highest honour on it and respect it. . . . It is said that, 'Life was born in the countryside.'" (Manoliu, 2009, p. 196).

HOW, THEN, TO STUDY LOCAL MUSEUMS?

Interviewing the proprietors of local museums and looking at how they organize, present, and narrativize their collections does more than open up a window on the Romanian museum community. An examination of this kind of museum links aesthetics (the primary rationale used to structure these local museums) to other aspects of Romanian life that can be otherwise difficult to understand and connect. One example of this is how popular aesthetics may inform a collector's practice and vice versa. This is particularly important as cultural heritage preservation more often than not takes place in a cross-cultural context (Klimaszewski et al., 2012, 2013). In the case of Romania's local museums, it is a reminder that the term "cross-cultural" is not limited to simply the international/local dichotomy; it can just as easily apply in the context of an urban/rural interaction or to professional/amateur partnerships of individuals from even the same country or region.

A study of local museums will also enable us to look at "informal" means of organizing and framing the cognitive and social aspects of collection and classification. Currently, discussions of this kind center on tagging and folksonomy to describe activities that take place in the virtual realm. Comparing "orthodox" classification practices and those used by "amateurs" in local museums can help us to understand some important aspects of information and artifact retrieval to which LIS scholars have not been very attentive so far. Where museum studies traditionally placed the emphasis on collecting as an act that preserves the best examples of individual objects, the informal collections we see in rural Romania attempt to preserve a traditional way of life through the recreation and/or the preservation of intact households or micro-replicas of the traditional village. It is important to understand how this different approach may "change the game" in terms of selection for preservation and what implications this might have for long-term preservation, which is often the basis of formal museum collections.

Finally, a study of local museums will allow us to consider what occurs when amateurs begin doing the work of the professionals. This is relevant because the phenomenon of local museums is not unique to Romania; at least one recent article reports on "do-it-yourself" museums in Estonia (Taimre, 2013). As the Museum of the Romanian Peasant works to legitimate these local collections (Mihăilescu, 2009; Mihalache, 2009c), this will have implications for and be influenced by national and international cultural heritage policy and development efforts. While these policies, development projects, and their influence traditionally flow from the top down, it is increasingly important to see what, if any, influence is moving from the bottom up. It is likely that not only will partnerships between amateurs and professionals inform and improve the work of local collectors, but the approaches and practices of local collectors may inform, complement, and change professional museum practice. This is particularly important as the local works held by these museums continue to become situated within (as opposed to subsumed by) the global.

CONCLUSION

Local museums in Romania appear to be the work of "passionate" individuals attempting to capture and preserve a traditional but lost way of life built around the symbol or "myth" of the peasant. However, the collectors and collections examined here illustrate how amateur collecting in Romania leads to a kind of unofficial museum creation that goes beyond sentimentality and nostalgia. By examining the characteristics of collectors, their approaches to collection development, and the narratives they construct around their collections, we have uncovered several areas for research that are highly relevant to LIS. Local museums in Romania provide an opportunity to examine where, why, and how the realms of "amateur" and "professional" overlap and diverge in the process of museum making. One area where this can be observed is in studying how popular aesthetics influence collection building and display. Another is in how informal methods of classification are used to document and organize collection objects. This also has implications for the process of selection and for long-term preservation. In addition, we should consider how outside influences such as tourism and funding for cultural heritage preservation have spurred the development of local museums in rural areas where, often, few other opportunities for economic development exist. Finally, a study of "unofficial" museums can provide insight into the cross-cultural aspects of cultural heritage preservation, which includes not just local/international work, but also rural/urban cooperation or, again, amateur/professional partnerships. Such insight can shed light not just on how the influences of the elite trickle down to the local level, but also how amateur cultural heritage production might inform the work being done "at the top." Developing this kind of understanding may help to ensure that local museums will have a place in the global network of cultural heritage production and preservation.

REFERENCES

Andreescu, M. (2009). The Doina Dobrean collection. *Martor, 14*, 183–185.

Beasley, B. E., & Nyce, J. M. (2009). *A more perfect Poundbury? Prince Charles' reinvention of Viscri, Romania*. Presented at the Indiana University Romanian Studies Conference, Bloomington, Indiana.

Boia, L. (2001). *Romania: Borderland of Europe*. London: Reaktion Books.

Closet-Crane, C., Dopp, S., Solis, J., & Nyce, J. M. (2006). *The past is our only industry*. Presented at the 2006 Annual SOYUZ Symposium, Providence, RI.

Closet-Crane, C., Dopp, S., Solis, J., & Nyce, J. M. (2009). Why study up? The elite appropriation of science, institution, and tourism as a development agenda in Maramures, Romania. *Advances in Library Administration and Organization, 27*, 221–238. doi:10.1108/S0732-0671(2009)0000027016

Dimcea, A., & Turcu, D. (2009). Slaves to the beautiful: Village collections in recent Romania. *Martor, 14*, 201–203.

Hannerz, U. (1997). Borders. *International Social Science Journal, 49*(154), 537–548.

Herzfeld, M. (2001). *Anthropology: Theoretical practice in culture and society*. Malden, MA: Blackwell Publishers.

Klimaszewski, C., Bader, G. E., & Nyce, J. M. (2011). "Success stories" as an evidence form: Organizational legitimization in an international technology assistance project. *Martor, 16*.

Klimaszewski, C., Bader, G. E., & Nyce, J. M. (2012). Studying up (and down) the cultural heritage preservation agenda: Observations from Romania. *European Journal of Cultural Studies, 15*(4), 479–495.

Klimaszewski, C., Bader, G. E., & Nyce, J. M. (2013). Hierarchy, complicity and culture in the library and information science preservation agenda: Observations from Romania. *Journal of Librarianship and Information Science, 45*(1), 38–52. doi:10.1177/0961000611434998

Klimaszewski, C., Bader, G. E., Nyce, J. M., & Beasley, B. E. (2010). Who wins? Who loses? Representation and "restoration" of the past in a rural Romanian community. *Library Review, 59*(2), 92.

Manoliu, V. (2009). Horea and Auriel Flutur Ethnographic Museum. *Martor, 14*, 195–199.

Mateoniu, M., & Marinescu, R. (2009a). Doctor Kéri's Museum of Galoşpetreu, Bihor County. *Martor, 14*, 189–193.

Mateoniu, M., & Marinescu, R. (2009b). Doctor Kéri's Museum of Galoşpetreu, Bihor County (Romania): An attempt to edify proximity heritage. *Martor, 14*, 145–154.

Mihăilescu, V. (2009). Local museums? Village collections in recent Romania. *Martor, 14*, 11–18.

Mihalache, C. (2009a). The museum as a hobby: An uncommon hobby—the museum. *Martor, 14*, 159–161.

Mihalache, C. (2009b). The wealth of an ethnic group. *Martor, 14*, 171–173.

Mihalache, C. (2009c). Museums and village collections of Romania. A pleading for initiative. *Martor, 14*, 123–130.

Niculescu, C. (2009). The Constantin Niţu collection. *Martor, 14*, 177–179.

Niessen, J. P. (2006). Museums, nationality, and public research libraries in nineteenth-century Transylvania. *Libraries & the Cultural Record, 41*(3), 298–336. doi:10.1353/lac.2006.0051

Pascu, A. (2009). The Momârlan's museum (Elea Mălinese and Petru Gălăţean ethnographic collection). *Martor, 14*, 165–169.

Pohrib, I. (2011). Tradition and Ethnographic Display: Defining the National Specificity at the National Art Museum in Romania (1906–1937). In *Great narratives of the past traditions and revisions in national museums* (pp. 317–329). Presented at the EuNaMus, European National Museums: Identity Politics, the Uses of the Past and the European Citizen, Paris: Linköping University Electronic Press. Retrieved from http://www.ep.liu.se/ecp/078/ecp11078.pdf

Schifirneţ, C. (2012). Tendential modernity. *Social Science Information, 51*(1), 22–51. doi:10.1177/0539018411426518

Taimre, L. (2013, January). Do it yourself museums. Study on small museums in Estonia and the people behind them. *Museological Review*, 26–35.

Turliuc, C. (2011). Nationalism, multiculturalism, and minorities' rights in the 20th century Romania: Theoretical and methodological aspects. *Eurolimes*, sup. 2, 213–225.

Verdery, K. (1983). *Transylvanian villagers: Three centuries of political, economic, and ethnic change*. Berkeley, CA: University of California Press.

Verdery, K. (1995). *National ideology under socialism: Identity and cultural politics in Ceauşescu's Romania*. Berkeley, CA: University of California Press.

Part V

TECHNOLOGY

INTRODUCTION: TECHNOLOGY

The articles in this section reflect the paradoxical nature of technology for cultural heritage professionals. Technology may provide new tools or challenge old ones; one form of technology may become obsolete, but another provides a path to preservation; digitized heritage may prove less accessible than expected, but a new access tool might open up a collection to engaged users. The four articles in this section explore the paradox while reflecting technology's role in promoting the accessibility and preservation of cultural heritage.

The promise of technology as a tool for bringing history to life is illustrated by "Ghosts of the Horseshoe, a Mobile Application: Fostering a New Habit of Thinking about the History of University of South Carolina's Historic Horseshoe," by Heidi Rae Cooley (assistant professor, media arts, the Department of Art, University of South Carolina) and Duncan A. Buell (professor, Department of Computer Science and Engineering, University of South Carolina). *Ghosts of the Horseshoe* is a mobile interactive application deploying game mechanics, Augmented Reality, and Global Positioning System functionality to generate awareness of and questioning about the remains of the original South Carolina College (1801–1865). Opening a window onto the past through real-time images responding to touch, gesture, and location, technology provides a moment of personal interaction with the past and the opportunity to think differently about the place and work of history.

Walter Forsberg (research fellow, Moving Image Archiving and Preservation Program, New York University Libraries) and Erik Piil (digital archivist at Anthology Film Archives, video preservation technician at DuArt Film and Video) show that while one technology, analog videotape, moves to obsolescence, another technology appears to provide the path to its preservation. In "Tune In, Turn On, Drop Out:

Section 108(c) and Evaluating Deterioration in Commercially Produced VHS Collections," Walter and Erik report dropout tests of four pairs of commercially produced VHS titles and evaluate relationships between videotape deterioration, circulation statistics, and manufacturing quality control standards. Offering noninvasive evidence of videotape deterioration, quantified dropout counts appear to provide libraries and archives with objective support for invoking their rights of reproduction under the United States Copyright Act.

Sheila O'Hare (assistant professor, School of Library and Information Management, Emporia State University) and Ashley Todd-Diaz (assistant professor, curator of special collections and archives, University Libraries and Archives, Emporia State University) explore the effects of new technological tools on a long-standing cultural heritage tool—the finding aid. In "The Devils You Don't Know: The New Lives of the Finding Aid," the authors review the 2012 literature on topics related to finding aids and associated access tools while considering the future of the finding aid from four perspectives: reassessment of the traditional functions and meanings of the finding aid; online finding aid design and usability; efforts to make the "invisible" work of cocreators or information professionals in describing, organizing, and presenting resources apparent; and the impact of new developments, including interactive content and linked data.

Ashley Todd-Diaz and Sheila O'Hare continue their review of 2012 cultural heritage literature from a different focus in "If You Build It, Will They Come? A Review of Digital Collection User Studies." While digital collection access and use numbers generally appear low and challenges still remain in the areas of accessibility and usability, several intriguing trends are explored, including the impact of promotion and collection location on the use of digital materials in historical research.

12

Ghosts of the Horseshoe, a Mobile Application

Fostering a New Habit of Thinking about the History of University of South Carolina's Historic Horseshoe

Heidi Rae Cooley and Duncan A. Buell

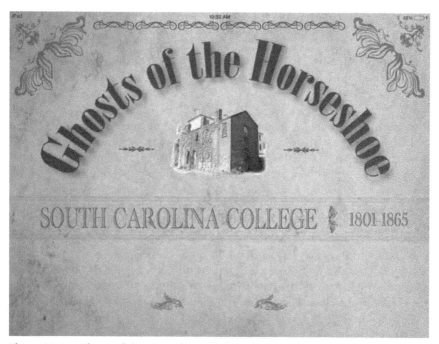

Figure 12.1. *Ghosts of the Horseshoe* **Splash Page**
Original Design by Brian Harmon.

ABSTRACT

Ghosts of the Horseshoe is a mobile interactive application deploying game mechanics, augmented reality, and Global Positioning System functionality. Drawing on American Pragmatist Charles Sanders Peirce's notion of habit-change, Ghosts was designed to generate awareness of and questioning about the historic grassy space at the center of the University of South Carolina campus that is surrounded by the remains of the original South Carolina College (1801–1865). Participants enter into a relation with history and the historical enslaved persons who built and maintained the Horseshoe through their mobile micro-screen "window" onto the past—one whose real-time image responds to touch, gesture, and location. The interaction opens moments of empathic identification and the opportunity to think differently about the place and work of history. Ghost's technology and content are described, and the application's use as an enabler of citizen archeology is highlighted. Augmented reality applications like Ghosts that invite historical reflection and sensitivity to place are surveyed.

SOUTH CAROLINA COLLEGE (1801–1865):
USC'S HISTORIC HORSESHOE

The University of South Carolina is the site of one of the most intact "landscapes of slavery" in the United States.[1] Its historic Horseshoe, situated at the heart of the modern campus, is what remains of the original South Carolina College (1801–1865). Yet the students, faculty, administrators, and visitors, who traverse these grounds today are for the most part unaware of its complex history. While the buildings comprising the campus bear the names of the men who founded, supported, attended, or taught at the institution, no plaques on site indicate that the buildings of the antebellum campus stand because of the labor of enslaved persons. No markers of any kind acknowledge that enslaved labor tended to and served the students and faculty of South Carolina College. No signs announce that enslaved labor cared for and maintained the campus. No monuments stand to remind us that the hands of enslaved labor molded, hauled, and laid the bricks that are the foundation of the site. Physically imprinted on the bricks of the buildings that still occupy the grounds and the Wall that encloses the site is evidence of the fact of these hands having been (Barthes, 1981). People habitually walk the brick paths that crisscross Carolina's historic Horseshoe without realizing that they tread on a landscape built and maintained by people who had no choice.

Certainly, no one is surprised to discover that slavery existed in South Carolina. It follows that enslaved labor would have ensured the daily functions of the institution. However, the University's prevailing self-representations actively work to minimize awareness of slavery's survival into the present. For example, the official website refers to the institution's "colorful history" and points to the Horseshoe's historic buildings

Figure 12.2.   Landscape Painting of South Carolina, 1850
Courtesy of the South Caroliniana Library.

as offering a "fascinating story" that epitomizes the enduring qualities exhibited by the "Outstanding statesmen, scholars, scientists, administrators, and business leaders" who resided, studied, and/or taught there.[2] Campus tours targeted at prospective students and their families celebrate Williams-Brice Stadium and football season and the variety of extracurricular activities available. The Horseshoe figures in these tours as a space of collegiality and community, where students gather to study, picnic, and play Frisbee. Rarely, if at all, is slavery mentioned. Moreover, the tour brochure available at the University Visitor's Center refers to the enslaved persons as "servants," the euphemism used in the antebellum period.[3] While a plaque stands at the entrance citing a period of "radical control 1873–1877," a time when South Carolina College became the first public institution of higher education in the nation with a majority black student body, this reference is oblique.[4] More direct is the message conveyed by the words "the entire student body volunteered for Confederate service 1861."

Ghosts of the Horseshoe is a mobile interactive application—or what we prefer to call a "critical interactive"[5]—that endeavors to complicate these readily digestible official representations.[6] Deploying game mechanics, as well as augmented reality (AR) and Global Positioning System (GPS) functionality, it generates awareness of and questioning about this historic grassy space at the center of a university campus. It draws participants into relation with history and historical figures by turning the mobile micro-screen into a "window" onto the past, one whose real-time image responds to touch, gesture, and location. In this way, Ghosts uses the power of the digital experience to "fill in the gaps" where institutional history and habitual thinking fall short. Not just the digital but more specifically, the mobile and, therefore, embodied experience facilitates a deeper empathy with the past that otherwise is easily overlooked. For example, it is not just that one imagines the work of slaves forming, firing, and carrying bricks and, subsequently, building a wall. Rather, one becomes capable of comprehending in situ the daily labor done by slaves to create the

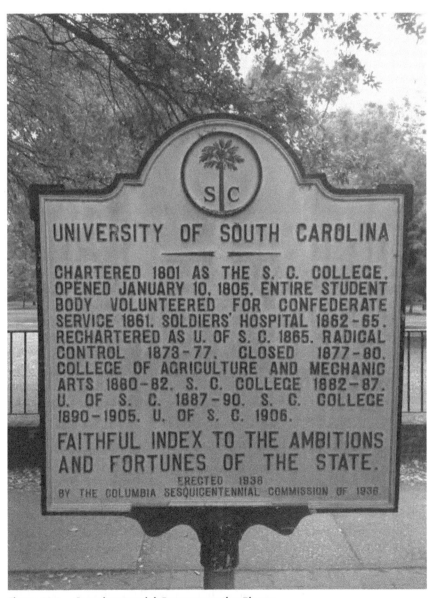

Figure 12.3. Sesquicentennial Commemorative Plaque
Courtesy of Duncan Buell.

Wall that stands physically before one today. In the process, one relates to the built environment differently. One "sees" a division of labor rather than just an old wall. The cognitive difference the app aims to introduce has to do with understanding the abiding affect of this "peculiar institution" on the landscape of the present university, and a new habit of thinking is made possible.

GHOSTS OF THE HORSESHOE: IMPLEMENTING CONTENT AND AESTHETICS FOR CRITICAL INTERACTION

The disparity in the institutional acknowledgments of the university's history is troubling. The reliance on enslaved labor for the construction and maintenance of the antebellum college would seem to be a history that must be preserved as well as communicated.[7] That it has been overlooked until very recently,[8] and perhaps deliberately obscured, makes it that much harder to present the history in a fashion that does not seem revisionist or dogmatic. Part of the goal of Ghosts, then, is not to rebut or directly assault previously official history, but rather to use the affordances of the mobile micro screen to portray a more complete (and complex) history by allowing participants to interact with digitally rendered, historically informed artifacts and information, and to do so on site in the context of the material vestiges of history. Enslaved persons would have been a pervasive presence in the life of the college, but from the records we can infer that contemporary analysis of that college life would have viewed them only through their work product. Mobilizing a new medium, Ghosts permits participants with modern eyes to arrive at a different awareness.

Indeed, Ghosts of the Horseshoe intends to provoke empathic awareness. By "empathic awareness," we mean an informed sensitivity to the history that persists— that is, is materially present—in the structures that comprise the historic site. More than a museum tour, it permits participants to explore the history of the grounds at their discretion. Rather than deploying a predetermined, linear building-by-building experience of the Horseshoe, Ghosts invites real-time, location-specific interaction with a variety of content.[9] Using the affordances of the GPS- and AR-enabled mobile device, Ghosts offers participants the ability to experience the past in situ. Three kinds of content populate the application's backend database: (1) architectural ghosts (e.g., extant but altered buildings and razed slave quarters, i.e., "outbuildings"); (2) human ghosts (e.g., faculty, students, as well as named and unnamed enslaved persons); and (3) the historic Wall (built 1835–1836). This content is called up—or "conjured"—according to a participant's position on the Horseshoe and with respect to her earlier selection of one of four twenty-year time periods.[10]

Ghosts' initial interface presents a participant with a splash screen that establishes the aesthetic for the entire application: a parchment paper backdrop (suggestive of the nineteenth century), garnet flourishes, and a typeface that echoes the font of the 1884 Sanborn Fire Insurance map that serves as the navigational interface for the application. At center screen of the splash screen appears a photographic representation of an outbuilding that once stood behind the current President's House. The words "Ghosts of the Horseshoe" arc above the outbuilding in antique black, while "South Carolina College 1801–1865" extend beneath the outbuilding below which three buttons present a participant with three options: (1) learn "About" the application, (2) activate the "Tutorial," or (3) "Start" exploring the Horseshoe. Upon selecting "Start," a participant chooses a two-decade interval: 1800–1820, 1821–1840, 1841–1860, or 1861–1880. The desired selection will populate the appropriate version of the Sanborn map with fingerprint markers that designate GPS-oriented content points.

As participants walk the grounds with a GPS- and WiFi-enabled, camera-equipped iPad or iPhone, they receive invitations to interact with content points pertinent to their location and according to their designated time periods. Some content points are merely informational—text, image, or dates. Others open onto AR layers that allow participants to see historical figures, photographs, or 3D models of buildings while looking "through" the screen at the real-time camera image of the Horseshoe. In front of Harper College, for example, an AR overlay of an image of a student appears when the camera is opened and trained onto a plaque reading, "The L. Marion Gressette Euphradian Society Hall."[11] Tapping the image of the student transports a participant three stories up to the Euphradian [Gressette] Room in Harper College. This room, usually kept locked and used only on special occasions, was one of the original two debating halls on campus where some of the student debates on slavery occurred during the antebellum period. Although we do not have actual transcripts of the debates, we know their topics and we know the conclusions drawn. The application uses audio functionality to deliver the details about one or another of the debates. At the same time, the participant can visually scan with the swipe of a finger across a panoramic image of the Euphradian Room as it exists today. We believe such multi-modal interaction to be an effective use of mobile devices for generating empathic awareness of the history of a century and a half ago, and that this can be particularly effective for locations like the Gressette room that are difficult to access or whose original configuration has been modified.

In addition to augmented reality, we have also built 3D models to assist in visualizing the antebellum Horseshoe in situ. The Sanborn map interface shows a collection of outbuildings, many of which were slave quarters, ringing the Horseshoe. Only one of these buildings remains, behind the President's House, originally built as the First Professor's House. On site at the present day President's House, the AR together with the GPS will cause a computer-generated model of a second slave quarters to appear behind the President's House—quite nearly in the spot it once stood. The model appears as a layer on the real-time image provided by the camera; the participant sees the current site through the "window" of her device along with the overlay of the architectural ghost of the now-razed second slave quarters. This is used elsewhere in Ghosts with other outbuildings and foundations no longer present; the GPS location together with the AR recognition of the camera image allows the app to bring into view the buildings that were there on site in the 1800s. Similar image effects permit the current site to be viewed in comparison to its history, both with photographic images and with the 3D models.

Figure 12.4. AR Overlay of Student at Harper College

Photograph by Heidi Rae Cooley.

Figure 12.5. Razed Outbuilding behind First Professors House on the Historic Horse-shoe (1940s)

Courtesy of South Caroliniana Library.

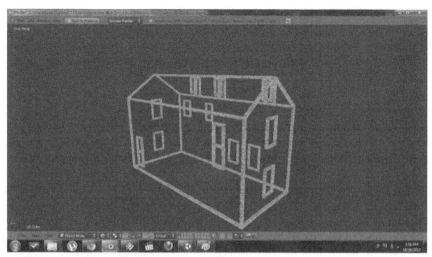

Figure 12.6. 3D Model of Ghost Outbuilding

Model by Renaldo Doe.

We use 3D modeling differently in the representation of the Wall. Originally nearly seven feet high and boasting a single main entrance, the Wall has been modified, lowered, and cut through in many places since its original construction in 1836. It has also been used for hanging banners and is in many places suffering from disrepair and erosion. We use modeling together with AR and GPS to provide an overlay image of the Wall as it would originally have appeared. Additionally, we imagine

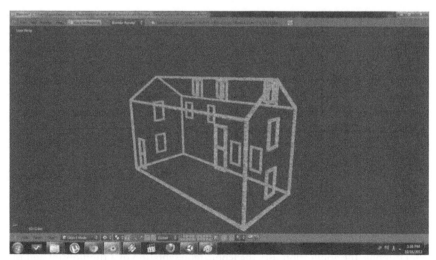

Figure 12.7. 3D Model of First Professors House

Model by Renaldo Doe.

animating the Wall model in order to illustrate the process—time and labor—of its construction in 1835–1836. At the same time, participants will be able to activate content points with a touch of their fingers. They can learn about antebellum brick making as well as current preservation efforts. Eventually, participants will be able to participate in the Wall's preservation by posting images of places where the Wall is in greatest need of care (see "The Wall and Citizen Archeology" below).

We have tried to deliver as "immersive" an experience as is possible on a small mobile device carried through public spaces. As mentioned above, we have included audio content via historically informed voice reenactments as well as period-appropriate ambient sounds (e.g., the clatter of dishes, the rumble of carriages, the gravelly sound of bricklaying) and music. All the while, the application tracks participants' engagements and traversals and offers them opportunities to review where they have gone, what they have experienced, and what they might yet encounter. Likewise, participants are able to submit comments to a community website where they can review others' comments and explore ancillary materials. This is feasible because the app is linked to a backend server that can compare a particular participant against general participation and against the orthodox participation envisioned by the app's designers. Participants do not participate independently. Rather, they participate, even if on their own individual devices, as part of the community that has gone before them and as part of the community public historians would like to create and nurture.

FINGERPRINTS AND THUMB IMPRESSIONS: REPRESENTATIONS OF ENSLAVED LABOR

No photographic evidence of enslaved persons at South Carolina College exists (as far as we know). Nor do we have any documents penned or other artifacts left by enslaved persons. What we have: one painted representation of a "black man at South Carolina College" that appears in a circa 1820 landscape painting, which currently hangs in the Caroliniana Library.[12] While portraits of the faculty exist and continue to decorate the walls of various buildings on campus, and while we can surmise what an average student matriculating at South Carolina College looked like based on the economic, social, and/or political status of the families who sent their sons to SCC, we know virtually nothing about the enslaved persons who built the campus and ensured the day-to-day functioning of the College.

We do have ledgers providing accounts of the "hire" and purchase of enslaved persons. We also have faculty papers and letters that address matters concerning "hired" servants. But these artifacts only provide for a representation of campus life according to a white enfranchised perspective. Ghosts offers an alternative view onto this history. Turning to what we do know remains of enslaved labor on the antebellum campus, the application uses the iconic representation of a thumbprint and the

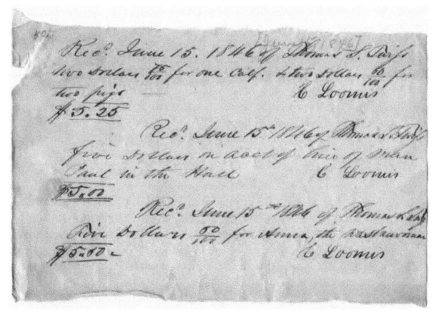

Figure 12.8.   Documentation regarding the Hire of Anna, the Washerwoman
Courtesy of South Caroliniana Library.

3D model of a brick bearing the impression of a hand. Public historians at USC have discovered bricks from the Wall that bear the impressions of the hands that molded them. Several of these bricks are housed in the McKissick Museum on the Horseshoe. And, according to scholarly assessment, similar impressions appear on various bricks that comprise the Wall. Here, the impress of a hand is an index—a physical and, therefore, immutable (theoretically speaking) trace of the existence of some hand being "there" at the time of the object's—that is, the brick's—formation. Such a sign—thumb print or impression—serves to draw attention to those who were not acknowledged, who only figured as a number (e.g., units of labor, expenditures, etc.), and who today still go unrecognized and unremembered.

We might take as an example a recent discovery. Anna, a "washer woman," was "hired" by the College for $5.00 (USD) in 1846 for an unspecified period of time.[13] The records that we have of her hire and placement only account for the work contracted. To date, we have no indication of the outcome of that work, although we can assume that this person performed domestic tasks such as washing clothing and linens. And we have no way to determine if she was kept on as a washerwoman. Having such scant evidence means that representation is complicated—especially in light of the specific context of South Carolina College. Using photographic images of another enslaved person who might have been a washerwoman was an initial suggestion. But such a design choice confronted us with the problem of substitution, wherein equivalences suggest a lack of individuality across enslaved women: that one image of an enslaved woman can stand in for any other. We also considered producing an interference of the screen image (e.g., glitch or noise) to suggest a haunting in the present. However, we soon realized that disrupting the screen might be construed as a malfunction and, thereby, produce a sense of something—or someone—being broken. What we have chosen as a representation of enslaved persons is based on the index of their manual labor.[14]

Ghosts uses thumbprint imagery and digitally rendered thumb impressions (in instances of AR interaction) to represent the enslaved persons who labored at South Carolina College from 1801 through 1865. Both fingerprint icon and 3D thumb impression use visual representation to foreground the absence of visible evidence (e.g., photographs) of slavery at South Carolina College. These images invite a participant to reach out, i.e., to touch the screen, and thereby activate an encounter with some element of the past on site and in the presence of its physical remains. The gesture of touch is essential: to touch—that is, to be in contact with—the past in situ is what matters. Each fingerprint, each thumb impression delivers to the screen specific details about daily life for those who inhabited the site now called the "historic Horseshoe." It is by means of the gesture of touch that Ghosts hopes to elicit critical awareness and empathic response to the complex history of USC's historic Horseshoe.

Figure 12.9. Demonstration of AR Functionality on December 4, 2012 (Represented: Student Andrew Ball and Dr. Susan Courtney, Professor of Film and Media Studies)
Photograph by Heidi Rae Cooley.

THE WALL AND CITIZEN ARCHEOLOGY

Ghosts of the Horseshoe also aspires to encourage what we call "citizen archeology." An analog to what is readily known as citizen journalism, citizen archeology imagines that the public might participate in the preservation of a historical site. While citizen journalism involves average citizens participating in "acts of journalism" (Glaser, 2006) by posting updates, comments, corrections, or images to personal and/or organizational blogs and forums, Ghosts will solicit evidence of the Wall's erosion, disrepair, and damage. Participants will be invited to document instances of its compromise by imaging with a mobile device and uploading to a secure online database. Part of a larger project to preserve the Wall,[15] the citizen archeology component of Ghosts intends to use the imaging functionality of the mobile device as inspired by each participant's personal awareness of and sensitivity to the local landscape.

The resulting repository of images will assist in specifying portions of the Wall in greatest need of attention and repair. When posted to the database, contributors' images will be encoded with GPS coordinates, date and time stamps, and individual comments. This data will permit submissions to be organized and presented according to location and/or date for those responsible for repairs. Additional modules in the backend server for Ghosts will display the photo stream in GPS-coordinate or date order. Likewise, a module in the mobile app will display the images in location order, triggered by GPS sensing, so that if one were to walk the perimeter of the Wall with the Ghosts app in hand, one could identify and comment on sites of ongoing or recurring wear.

Here, it is important to qualify that while Ghosts uses the camera functionality for contributing to the larger institutionally funded Wall preservation project, the image-capture capability is disabled for the AR features, which likewise require the camera. This is because Ghosts wants to encourage critical engagement and interaction, rather than general touristic encounter. Many of us are accustomed to approaching historical sites as eager consumers—and we are encouraged to be so. Wielding our cameras, we simply "point and shoot." The problem is not that we take pictures or capture a moment; the problem is that we tend not to consider what and why we are imaging that which is before the lens.[16] Informed by Susan Sontag's point that "To photograph is to appropriate the thing photographed" (Sontag, 1977, p. 4), Ghosts seeks to redefine how appropriation might operate in ways other than acquisition for the purposes of self-gratification.[17] What if imaging served a larger community? What if imaging might preserve a past at the same time that it ensured a future? What if imaging succeeded in saving a historical object—the Wall—that bears the imprints of historical individuals whose only lasting traces are, in fact, their fingerprints?

Few people, unfortunately, seem to view the Wall as a historical object to be preserved. Students use it to hang banners, nails are driven into it, and occasionally cars drive into it. This exacerbates natural deterioration of the brick and mortar that accompanies problems like tree growth that crowds out the Wall. In response, Ghosts

Figure 12.10.   3D model of Wall with Content Point

Model by Renaldo Doe. Text for Content Point by Amanda Noll. Photograph by Heidi Rae Cooley.

uses crowd sourcing to accrue information about deterioration of the Wall. By so-
liciting photographs of the Wall and permitting the uploading of those photographs
to a database that is periodically communicated to the University Archivist and to
university maintenance staff, we hope to inspire a community of people to embrace
the Wall as something more than a functional object. By emphasizing its historical
nature, and by permitting participants to contribute to its preservation, we will in-
culcate students, faculty, staff, and visitors to campus in a shared appreciation of the
Wall's significance to the university's past, its present, and its future.

INHABITING THE HORSESHOE OTHERWISE

In its effort to inspire empathic awareness, Ghosts imagines a community of participants who take responsibility for a history that has been obscured for the past
century. In the process, the app proposes to change how people habitually think
about, approach, and experience the historic Horseshoe. Such change requires new
types of relations to each other, to our surroundings, and to time. In other words,
it is not simply a matter of establishing new "ideals" that, in the end, stand apart or

transcend everyday, material existence. Rather, change "expresses" through the lived transactions that shape how people think and relate.

Our understanding of the kind of change to which Ghosts aspires draws on American Pragmatist Charles Sanders Peirce's notion of habit-change (Peirce, 1934).[18] For Peirce, habit-change is necessarily social. This is because habit-change is a process of meaning making, or interpreting. Meaning making requires—at the same time that it binds together—a community of people, that is, interpreters, so that they can communicate with one another. Moreover, meaning making (interpretation) transpires on the cusp of consciousness before we know that we know, which means that we, as interpreters, always exist in a conditional moment of "would-be."[19] This moment of "would-be" —that is, nascent habitual behavior or thought—is a moment during which, for example, a simple gesture (e.g., pointing a finger) might fundamentally open onto new insights, revised interpretations, and new ways of inhabiting a place. Ultimately, this is where Ghosts' potential lies: in the moment of the "would-be," wherein the historic Horseshoe might be experienced and understood in terms other than those that are conventionally reinforced—by institutional logic, by tradition, by routine.

We locate the greatest potential for habit-change at the site of the AR interface and the moment of the gesture it invites. When a participant lifts her device and directs its lens toward some object, she enacts what Peirce refers to as "deixis." Deixis is, as film theorist Mary Anne Doane explains, the "purest form" of index because it is the most decisive (Doane, 2006, p. 136). Proceeding in the manner of a pointing finger or the "this" of language (e.g., "this building"), deixis only exists—has a referent, or object of reference—in the now of its happening. Unlike a fingerprint or a photographic image, which are indices of a different variety, the deixical "evaporate[s]" in the very moment of its production: nothing is recorded, nothing remains. In the instance of the AR overlay, the screen presents a referent that is only here and now, in the moment of an instance of framing. Raising the mobile micro-screen and extending a finger to activate an AR overlay, a participant comes into contact with her surroundings differently. While she may merely touch a screen, what transpires as a consequence has the potential to elicit what Peirce refers to as intellectual sympathy. That is, she might experience a more resonant or intuitive relation to her surroundings.[20] Such experience runs counter to consumer-oriented AR applications, such as Layar, Junaio, and Vicinity, which work to reinforce rather than alter habit when they identify place with consumerism and tourism.

Others are pursuing AR applications that offer experiences that invite historical reflection and sensitivity to place. Perhaps the closest analog to Ghosts is Mapping Ararat: An Imaginary Jewish Homelands Project (2012),[21] which seeks to present onsite the "what-if" of Mordecai Noah's attempt to create a Jewish homeland named "Ararat" in 1825 on Grand Island in the Niagara River on the United States/Canada border. Mapping Ararat offers a "para-history" of how Grand Island might look today had Noah's plan succeeded. The AR "augments"[22] include the international border crossing on entry to the island, grave markers for the graves of Noah and his family, the monument to the original creation of Ararat, and a historical synagogue that could have been built. As with Ghosts, the AR is triggered by GPS coordinates sensed by the mobile device. Because the area covered is much larger than the Horseshoe, participants are provided with a map so they may search purposely for positions close enough for the AR to be triggered. Ghosts and Mapping Ararat are similar in their underlying programming, although Ghosts is done natively using Apple's programming tools and Mapping Ararat uses Layar, a commercial and more simplified tool. They differ in obvious ways: Mapping Ararat covers perhaps thirty times the area of the Horseshoe, and its AR features, being almost entirely pure fiction, are limited largely by the imagination and efforts of its creators. Ghosts, however, is confined to about fifteen acres still dedicated to the use to which they were put in 1801, and dense with two subsequent centuries of a real, and a complex, history to which we would like to be as faithful as possible. Mapping Ararat thus imagines what might have been; Ghosts presents "what was" but has been kept hidden.

John Craig Freeman and Mark Skwarek's Border Memorial: Frontera de los Muertos (2012) offers another example of an AR application. Referred to by its creators as an "augmented reality public art project and memorial," it pursues an overtly political intervention by bringing to visibility the human costs of the United States' enforcement of its southwestern border.[23] An application for mobile smart phone, it also uses Layar and GPS coordinates to locate and give representation to the thousands of migrant workers who have died along the United States/Mexico border in attempting to find work in the United States. Attention is focused on a triangular area whose base is the roughly seventy-five miles of national border between Sonoyta, Mexico, and Nogales, Arizona, with Phoenix at the peak about an equal distance north of the border. On-site and "live" in the Sonoran Desert of southern Arizona, individuals with the application downloaded and launched can raise their mobile devices to face the desert landscape. Scanning the desert through the camera view, one is able to "visualize the scope of the loss of life": at each GPS location where one of the thousands of deaths has been documented, a three-dimensional skeleton effigy appears on-screen as an overlay.[24] The image is reminiscent of the Oaxacan *calacas* that are traditionally used to commemorate deceased loved ones. Immigration and labor policies are currently matters of enormous political debate, and the debate is especially heated in border states like Arizona. Border Memorial is intended to make clear that these border security and immigration policies can and do have real human costs. While Ghosts is not as overtly political, it does aim to intervene in how an institutional history is framed, presented, and remembered.

CONCLUSION

Ghosts of the Horseshoe intends to demonstrate how mobile interactive applications featuring augmented reality might open onto moments of empathic identification, or in Peircean terms, intellectual sympathy. At the intersection of a con-

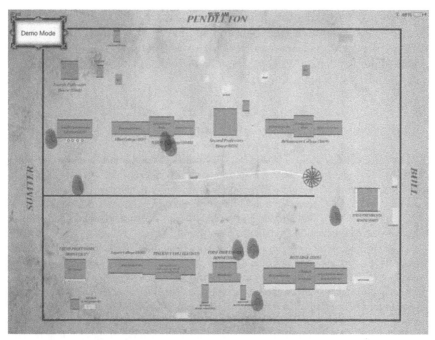

Figure 12.11. *Ghosts* **Navigational Interface with Fingerprint Icons and Participant Locative Compass Rose**

Design by Students in Critical Interactives (Fall 2012).

tinuously refreshed real-time image, the here and now of a user's deixical relation to her surroundings, and the geo-coordinated ghostly encounter, we might find the condition of possibility for thinking differently about the place and work of history. Ghosts charges its participants to acknowledge their relation to history and embrace a responsibility to a legacy that has been obfuscated—and continues to be so. As such, it aspires to intervene in how people approach, "see," and experience the physical grounds of the Horseshoe as a site of historical erasure. Our hope with Ghosts is that participants will be drawn to an acknowledgment that the complete history of the Horseshoe is in fact "their" history, that the app will help to reverse a habitual, social blindness, and in the process, the community that inhabits the Horseshoe either routinely or only occasionally will be encouraged to think toward the "would-be" of a shared future.

ACKNOWLEDGMENTS

We thank the College of Arts and Sciences for providing bridge-funding for the hire of two graduate research assistants during spring 2012 for initial conceptual development of the Ghosts application. We likewise thank University of South Carolina VP for Research for a grant to build-out the 1.0 version of Ghosts. Finally, we thank the graduate research assistants who continue to work ardently to produce Ghosts: Richard Walker (computer science), Celia Ward Galens (history), and Amanda Noll (public history).

NOTES

1. See Allison Baker, Jennifer Betsworth, Rebecca Bush, Sarah Conlon, Evan Kutzler, Justin McIntyre, Elizabeth Oswald, Jamie Wilson, and JoAnn Zeise, *Slavery at South Carolina College, 1801–1865: The Foundations of the University of South Carolina* (Columbia: University of South Carolina, Spring 2011). Accessible at http://library.sc.edu/digital/slaveryscc/index.html.

2. "University Map: Buildings as History," University of South Carolina. Accessible at http://www.sc.edu/uscmap/bldg/buildings_history.html.

3. *The Horseshoe at the University of South Carolina* (Columbia, SC: University Publications, January 2006). A more recent brochure edited by University Archivist Elizabeth Cassidy West explicitly acknowledges that slavery was central to daily life at South Carolina College. While the mention is restricted to a single section of the brochure, "Forgotten Structures of the Horseshoe," it straight-forwardly explains, for example, "Slaves were either owned by faculty or the college itself, or they were hired out from Columbia-area owners" (Allen, 2011, p. 7).

4. What goes without clarification: that 1877 marks the closing of the college at the end of Reconstruction. When reopened in 1880, it was a segregated institution that did not enroll African American students until 1963 and did not employ African American faculty again until the late 1960s.

5. We use "critical interactive" to underscore what is fundamental to the projects we are developing: engaging participants in ludic interaction with socially and politically sensitive, indeed controversial, subject matter. Informed by Mary Flanagan's scholarship on "critical play" (2009) and Ian Bogost's work on "procedural rhetoric" (2007), the term proposes that there is another viable way to impart knowledge, build awareness, and provoke thinking and raise questions. Specifically, we imagine a mode of scholarship that invites people to imagine themselves as active participants in conversation with the materials of intellectual inquiry.

6. At the time of this writing, Ghosts runs on iPad and iPhone. Later versions will allow interaction by means of other platforms (e.g., Android).

7. Ghosts of the Horseshoe is based on the robust scholarly website "Slavery at South Carolina College, 1801–1865: The Foundations of the University of South Carolina" (see note 1, above). A prototype of the Ghosts application was presented and demonstrated on December 4, 2012, by undergraduate and graduate students enrolled in a cross-college course called Critical Interactives. The project has received bridge funding (USC College of Arts and Sciences) and an internal ASPIRE II grant (USC Office of the VP for Research). The University Libraries hosts the server that houses the Ghosts database and website (http://calliope.tcl.sc.edu). Please see the website to view a short video and a local WIS television segment about the project.

8. One of the more curious observations made by Dr. Weyeneth about his class in history was that apparently the study of slavery at the antebellum college had never before been done.

9. Content points are indicated on the maps displayed on the screen, but it is the GPS triggering of location awareness that "pushes" the app's content to the participant, instead

of having the experience go the other way around. The app can guide; it can suggest similar content at other locations. Recording dwell-time at particular locations, it suggests other (i.e., "like" or similar) locations to visit.

10. The application's logic of periodization begins in 1800, in keeping with the founding of South Carolina College in 1801, and ends in 1880 with the reopening of the college as a resegregated institution in the post-Reconstruction era.

11. The Euphradian and Clariosophic Societies were the two debating societies of the antebellum period in which students practiced the debate techniques that they would use later as political and social leaders in South Carolina. The Euphradian Society is still active on campus.

12. See http://library.sc.edu/digital/slaveryscc/campus-slaves--slavery.html.

13. Graduate research assistant for Ghosts Celia James, a PhD candidate in history with an MA in public history, recently discovered documents in the archives at South Caroliniana Library. Evidence of the hire of Anna, the washerwoman, is among one of her finds.

14. We thank our colleagues in the departments of history, art, and film and media studies for conversations that challenged us to think more complexly about representation of enslaved persons: Lydia Brandt, Susan Courtney, Bobby Donaldson, Laura Kissel, Simon Tarr, and Robert Weyeneth. We also thank the students who enrolled in Critical Interactives, a cross-college course that we co-taught in fall 2012.

15. According to university archivist Elizabeth West, the University has allocated $1.5 million to fund a preservation plan for the Wall. The work will involve the university architect Derek Gruner, facilities, and a committee that will be formed soon (e-mail correspondence between Duncan Buell and Elizabeth West on May 19, 2013).

16. For media theorist Richard Grusin, this is not a surprise in the twenty-first century: that we so readily imagine places, people, and happenings can be explained by the fact that nearly everyone carries a camera phone (or similar device). Nearly always in-hand and almost always "on"—connected to other entities by means of cellular provider and/or WiFi functionality—our devices make it routine to image and share our images via social networking services quite nearly in real time. In other words, the inclination to "point and shoot" has become enmeshed and habitual—automatic. Which means, according to Grusin (2010), it happens at an affective, non-conscious level prior to any conscious recognition or interpretation. Ghosts wants to trouble such "automatic" response to things that fascinate or captivate.

17. In more explicit terms, Sontag describes picture taking as "predatory" (1977, p. 14)—an act of violence. It "violate[s]" (p. 14) those who are photographed. Likewise, she lays bare the brutality—because bureaucratic in nature—of the catalogs that frequently keep or house photographs.

18. Heidi Rae Cooley addresses habit-change in *Finding Augusta: Habit and Governance in the Digital Era* (Cooley, 2014).

19. According to Peirce (1934), meaning making is always conditional: If certain conditions pertain, then a particular meaning is likely to result. Because cognition is both social and conditional, it is never necessarily certain. It "works" through habitual repetition, and change is always possible.

20. Karl-Otto Apel, describing Peircean intellectual sympathy, uses the term "mediated immediacy" (Apel, 1995). Relatedly, philosopher John Protevi has posited the notion of an "affective cognition" that enables "empathic solidarity" among a body politic, and media theorist Rita Raley has considered how tactical media practices, intervening in the status quo, endeavor to effect a "shared sensibility." Both concepts are in keeping with what *Ghosts* aims to accomplish (Protevi, 2009; Raley, 2009).

21. The *Mapping Ararat* project team includes Melissa Shiff, Louis Kaplan, and John Craig Freeman. See: http://www.mappingararat.com.

22. This is the term the Mapping Ararat team use to refer to the digital assets that overlay the real time image on-screen.

23. See Border Memorial: Frontera De Los Muertos, http://bordermemorial.wordpress .com/border-memorial-frontera-de-los-muertos/.

24. In October 2010, the Museum of Modern Art (NY) hosted a version of *Border Memorial*, whose skeleton effigies appear in a virtual desert setting overlaying a real-time image of the museum's courtyard.

REFERENCES

Allen, K. T. (2011). *The University of South Carolina Horseshoe: Heart of the campus*. E. C. West (Ed.). Columbia, SC: University of South Carolina Archives, University Libraries.

Apel, K.-O. (1995). *Charles S. Peirce: From pragmatism to pragmaticism*. (J. M. Krois, Trans.). New York, NY: Humanity Books.

Baker, A., Betsworth, J., Bush, R., Conlon, S., Kutzler, E., McIntyre, J., . . . Zeise, J. (2011, Spring). *Slavery at South Carolina College, 1801–1865: The foundations of the University of South Carolina*. Retrieved from http://library.sc.edu/digital/slaveryscc/index.html

Barthes, R. (1981). *Camera lucida: Reflections on photography* (1st American ed.). New York, NY: Hill and Wang.

Bogost, I. (2007). *Persuasive games: The expressive power of videogames*. Cambridge, MA: MIT Press.

Cooley, H. R. (2014, forthcoming). *Finding Augusta: Habit and governance in the digital era*. Interfaces Studies in Visual Culture. Hanover, NH: Dartmouth College Press.

Doane, M. A. (2006). Information, crisis, catastrophe. In W. H. K. Chun & T. Keenan (Eds.), *New media old media: A history and theory reader* (pp. 251–264). New York, NY: Routledge.

Flanagan, M. (2009). *Critical play: Radical game design*. Cambridge, MA: MIT Press.

Glaser, M. (2006, September 27). What is citizen journalism? Retrieved from http://www.pbs .org/mediashift/2006/09/your-guide-to-citizen-journalism270

Grusin, R. A. (2010). *Premediation: Affect and mediality after 9/11*. Basingstoke, UK: Palgrave Macmillan.

Peirce, C. S. (1934). *Collected papers of Charles Sanders Peirce* (Vol. 5). Cambridge, MA: Harvard University Press.

Protevi, J. (2009). *Political affect: Connecting the social and the somatic*. Minneapolis, MN: University of Minnesota Press.

Raley, R. (2009). *Tactical media* (Vol. 28). Minneapolis, MN: University of Minnesota Press.

Sontag, S. (1977). *On photography*. New York, NY: Farrar, Straus and Giroux.

13

Tune In, Turn On, Drop Out

Section 108(c) and Evaluating Deterioration in Commercially Produced VHS Collections

Walter Forsberg and Erik Piil

ABSTRACT

Analog videotape, an imperfect moving image technology format since its introduction, is reaching the end of its life cycle. However, large quantities of out-of-print and irreplaceable VHS titles still comprise significant portions of library and archival collections and circulations. Given the need to preserve this content, this study investigates the use of the "dropout" metric (counts of disruptions in the video signal) for determining whether libraries and archives can invoke their rights of reproduction under the United States Copyright Act. Videotape technology and deterioration problems are explained and prior deterioration studies are reviewed. Dropout tests of four pairs of commercially produced VHS titles are conducted and relationships between videotape deterioration as measured by dropout counts, circulation statistics, and manufacturing quality control standards are evaluated. Offering noninvasive evidence of videotape deterioration, quantified dropout counts appear to provide libraries and archives with an objective measure to meet the vague "deterioration" standard of the Copyright Act.

INTRODUCTION

Particularly among research-level university institutions, circulating library collections still consist of large amounts of VHS videotape. With the advent of "peak-VHS" sales in 1998, and the 2008 announcement of commercial discontinuation by its "final supplier" (wholesaler Distribution Video and Audio), university libraries defaulted to become some of the most significant North American entities still

213

annually dealing with substantive quantities of the videotape format (Simon & Kugler, 2008). Faculty preferences, budgetary limitations, and the unavailability on subsequent formats of content originally held and acquired on VHS, all contribute to these institutions' continued reliance on this practically obsolete format. As one example, the Avery Fisher Center for Music and Media at New York University (NYU) Libraries recorded 4,371 checkouts of VHS tapes from 2011 to 2012, representing nearly 15% of its total circulation for video materials. Four years prior, VHS circulation stood at half of that of titles on DVD.

During this decade-long period of decline for VHS as a moving image user format in consumer spheres, the landscape of media use in libraries radically changed. Information management and delivery mechanisms met a period of rapid technological development and deployment. Impacted directly by the Internet, library patron expectations expanded across diversifying technological strata where speed of delivery, facility of discovery, and digital access became the new normal. The trending obsolescence of VHS "fast-forwarded" alongside these shifts, as content became available on DVD and BluRay, and as digital files through internal and external streaming services. Citing the growing unavailability of VCRs, a wave of quiet notifications by institutional information technology (IT) departments now inform media librarians and faculty that support of VHS playback will soon draw to a close. As one recent contributor to the VIDEOLIB listserv characterized it, "VHS death went from a lingering, gradual one (to which we seem to be slowly adapting) to a quick bullet to the head."[1]

This "VHS death" in libraries is troubling for a host of reasons. Immense resources have been expended on growing libraries' research and teaching collections in a format they are being told will soon be unusable. Furthermore, a significant portion of content held on VHS is out-of-print or unavailable on other formats (though, few libraries have undertaken the required research to systematically determine what the scope of this unavailability is). Many librarians are ill-equipped with limited institutional support, financial budgets, specialized hardware, or technical knowledge needed to perform preservation of their videotape collections in-house, or through a third-party vendor. For these reasons, and others, circulating videotape collections in libraries are critically threatened.

What is frustrating, in the face of these circumstances, is the fact that fair use rights afforded under Section 107 of the United States Copyright Act actually exist to make copies for the sake of preservation. Congress, even, explicitly mentions that preservation of deteriorating moving images on aging formats is an activity that "certainly" qualifies as a fair use.[2] Furthermore, Section 108 of the United States Copyright Act explicitly provides an additional special exemption for libraries and archives to make copies of material held on obsolete formats, and for material that is "damaged, or deteriorated." Yet, many libraries have remained timid and inert about preservation reformatting for commercially produced circulating VHS collections.

This chapter is an attempt to buoy the confidence of libraries in their present (or, yet unrealized) efforts to digitally preserve their at-risk analog circulating VHS collections. With specific attention to deciphering the vague and format-agnostic legal qualification of "deteriorating" required under Section 108(c), this paper presents a survey of magnetic media deterioration studies. Considering dropout as a key practical metric for deterioration determination, we propose and employ a methodology, and present results from technical tests undertaken at DuArt Film and Video with VHS videotapes from New York University Libraries collections at the Avery Fisher Center for Media (AFC), conducted as part of the Andrew W. Mellon Foundation-funded project, Video At Risk: Strategies for Preserving Commercial Video Collections in Libraries.

SECTION 108(c) AND MAKING COPIES

Aside from fair use rights of reproduction for preservation purposes set forth in Section 107 of the Copyright Act, under specific circumstances libraries and archives possess additional legal rights for making copies of material for which they do not own copyrights. Section 108(c) of the United States Copyright Act provides an exemption for libraries and archives to make copies of copyrighted material if a copy of a work belonging to a library or archive is "damaged, deteriorating, lost or stolen," provided no replacement copy can be found in the marketplace, and resultant (no more than three) new copies are not circulated to the public outside the premises. These copies can be digital copies. As the statute states:

> (c) the right of reproduction under this section [i.e., § 108] applies to three copies or phonorecords of a published work duplicated solely for the purpose of replacement of a copy or phonorecord that is damaged, deteriorating, lost or stolen, or if the existing format in which the work is stored has become obsolete, if—
>
>   (1) the library or archives has, after a reasonable effort, determined that an unused replacement cannot be obtained at a fair price; and
>
>   (2) any such copy or phonorecord that is reproduced in digital format is not made available to the public in that format outside the premises of the library or archives in lawful possession of such copy.
>
> For purposes of this subsection, a format shall be considered obsolete if the machine or device necessary to render perceptible a work stored in that format is no longer manufactured or is no longer reasonably available in the commercial marketplace. (17 U.S.C. § 108(c))

The existence of manufacturers still producing combination VHS/DVD playback machinery likely disqualifies VHS from being safely considered an "obsolete" format, according to a conservative interpretation of legal language. Thus, while the terms "lost" and "stolen" conditions are self-evident (if paradoxical, in practical terms of the ability to make a copy of an absent item), and the term "damaged" somewhat less so, the statute's failure to define the term "deteriorating" prompts the current inquiry.

VIDEOTAPE TECHNOLOGY

Articulating the aspects of deterioration in analog VHS tapes first requires a brief recap of what videotape technology is, and how it basically works. Analog videotape stores magnetically encoded electrical information to represent recorded sound and moving images. Through a complex technological language of electromagnetic engineering, a magnetizable layer of (most often) ferric oxide in polyurethane binder is evenly applied to a thin film polyester base and serves as a carrier for every manner of content in broadcast, educational, and home theater markets. Other binder materials have been employed; however, those described above have been the most common and widespread methods with regards to the VHS format considered in the experimental study, below.

For a half-century, across dozens of video format platforms, magnetic tape manufacturers sought to improve videotape stability and performance by experimenting with various "recipes" for this magnetic binder. From several metal particle formulations of ferric oxide, cobalt ferrite, and chromium dioxide, to other metal-evaporated tape formulations, these variations in binder makeup largely remain undisclosed trade secrets. While manufacturers made advances in binder density capacity, and introduced many subsequent analog and digital tape formats, the imperfections inherent in magnetic videotape recording were never completely eliminated; attempts at alleviating them continue to this day in the field of magnetic storage for data. As an organic carrier, videotape naturally experiences some degree of physical change of state with use and over time. The stability of information stored using this technological memory system—a kind of semi-hard "rust soup" on plastic strips—is subject to a wide array of liabilities and potential points of failure that can contribute to deterioration.

WHAT CONSTITUTES DETERIORATION
IN MAGNETIC VIDEOTAPE?

Relevant Previous Deterioration Testing

A modest body of scientific scholarship exists relating to experimentation employing chemical analyses of videotape binders, documenting their instability and susceptibility to breakdown caused by moisture absorption, known as "hydrolysis." One 1993 publication saw British scientists and the Agfa Gevaert company collaborating on measuring naturally and accelerated-aged tapes using Fourier Transform infrared (FTIR) spectroscopy to determine the resilience of polymer chains in the magnetic binder, with specific emphasis on the impact of hydrolysis. Their work scientifically reiterated the central role binder hydrolysis plays in videotape deterioration (in lieu of organic breakdown in the polyester film base), yet did not specifically consider the factor of repeated playback (Edge, Allen, Hayes, Jewitt, Brems, & Horrie, 1993, pp. 207–214). A recent Institute for Museum and Library Services grant awarded to researchers at the University of South Carolina in collaboration with the Library of Congress supports the development of a rapid, nondestructive, degradation-identification tool using infrafed (IR) spectroscopy and an IR spectral database for determining deterioration. Other studies often also document hydrolysis breakdown of tape binder via optical magnification, using scanning electron microscopes (SEMs) (Gilmour, 2000). Such SEM-based approaches can provide visual evidence of changes in the surface of the videotape binder, including impurities on the tape surface caused by binder breakdown and deterioration.

Other studies consider the role of repeated playback in precipitating physical videotape binder deterioration. A 1992 peer-reviewed published test by several engineers at Sony considered the effects of repeated video head wear on an immobilized videotape track in "still mode." Their test methodology revealed physical portions of the tape binder to be removed by rotary heads of a three-head VTR spinning over the same surface area at ninety cycles per second, citing several physical stress responses of the inherently uneven surface of magnetic tape (Osaki, Oyanagi, Aonuma, Kanou, & Kurihara, 1992, pp. 76–83). The repeated physical contact between head and tape in this test parallels some use concepts for the current study we describe; however, the authors' detail in describing their metric for documenting performance loss in the videotape is vague.

In a 1999 paper, a United Kingdom-based police unit considered the effect multiple recording passes had on diminishing ability to remagnetize tape binder with different recorded content. Using visual test pattern charts, the Police Scientific Development Branch sought to determine the number of times closed-circuit television (CCTV) systems might reuse a single videotape to record new (and, not merely repeatedly playback the same) security camera footage, determining that after an average maximum of twelve recording passes deterioration of the videotape binder resulted in unacceptable visual quality. Again, it is worth noting that their methodology was dependent on subjective human visual assessments of the test charts they employed (Mather & Neil, 1998, pp. 220–224). While such rerecording and magnetic remanence investigations are less pertinent to investigating playback performance of material recorded only once, they serve to reiterate the complexity of the chemical and organic processes with regard to videotape performance.

One playback-based study by the British Broadcasting Corporation in 2000 found that over 45% of the 2,800 ¾-inch U-matic videotapes digitized required that "technical comments" be made during transfer (Lee, Prytherich, & King, 2000, pp. 177–186). This study, however, did not speculate as to whether problematic playback issues (such as incorrect audio levels, "low RF," and "noisy/low-quality pictures") were by-products of the original recording process, or the age of the tapes at the time of transfer (all of which were between eleven and eighteen years old).

As Jean-Louis Bigourdan, James M. Reilly, Karen Santoro, and Gene Salesin of the Image Permanence Institute observed in a 2006 National Endowment for the Humanities final report, articulating and documenting videotape degradation with any degree of specificity is a challenging and under-sophisticated reality (Bigourdan,

Reilly, Santoro, & Salesin, 2006, p. 15). Across the extant scholarship, at some point along the spectrum of testing, analysis, and comparison, a lack of condition assessment (most often, at the moment of creation or acquisition) renders any subsequent condition without a comparative counterpoint.

One of the most in-depth studies on videotape deterioration to date is the 2005 PrestoSpace report, *Report on Video and Audio Tape Deterioration Mechanisms and Considerations about Implementation of a Collection Condition Assessment Method.* Its authors define "deterioration" as resulting from "an alteration process" in the magnetic tape (Thiebaut, Vilmont, & Lavedrine, 2006, p. 15). Such an alteration process can be identified by four symptoms that lead to loss of performance during playback, including: tape-transport instability, a decrease in signal strength, loss of signal, and/ or dropout. The PrestoSpace report echoes comments by Bigourdan, et al. on the complexity of deterioration evaluation processes, alluded to above, concluding that deterioration of videotape:

> depends not only on the intrinsic material stability but also on the player specifications and tolerance to media deterioration as well as tape handling. In addition, the complexity of mass-manufactured tapes with numerous formulations and manufacturing practices result in a variety of deterioration mechanisms. As a consequence, finding a unique deterioration marker is highly challenging and would probably involve much more consequent research efforts. (Thiebaut, Vilmont, & Lavedrine, 2006, p. 42)

The complexity of the magnetic recording processes with regards to deterioration is also found in, arguably, the most authoritative publication on magnetic media tribology—the study of interacting surfaces in relative motion: Bharat Bhushan's 1990, *Tribology and Mechanics of Magnetic Storage Devices.* In it, Bhushan categorizes six distinct kinds of wear mechanisms resulting from playback: adhesive wear; abrasive wear; fatigue; impact by erosion, or percussion; corrosive wear; and electrical-arc-induced wear (Bhushan, 1990, p. 412). Bhushan's analysis of wear is extensive, and he categorizes tape wear as having functional problems rooted in: high friction, loss of reproduced signal amplitude, and excessive dropouts caused by debris adhered to the tape surface (p. 462).

Establishing a Practical Deterioration Metric

The experiment and results presented in this paper engage the complex issues surrounding videotape deterioration as a starting point to establish a practical method and potential justification for libraries and archives to reformat their deteriorating VHS collections. As Legal Counsel Robert Clarida commented in a white paper for the Video At Risk project,

> Because the process of deterioration is very context-dependent, and viewing tapes for visible deterioration is extremely time-consuming, it could be very helpful for the Library to prepare and publish a formal study of the degree to which various factors about

a VHS tape correlate to the degree of deterioration, even of unplayed VHS tapes. Factors such as age, tape stock used, storage conditions (temperature, humidity), number of plays, and type of playback equipment might all contribute to the speed at which tapes deteriorate, and if a sufficiently large sample of tapes could be analyzed as to these variables the Library might be able to develop a set of reliable criteria for knowing, in advance, how seriously compromised a given tape's condition would be at a given point in the future. This could help the Library plan its digitization efforts more effectively.

Drawing from Clarida's recommendation, PrestoSpace's testing methodology, the facility of machine-based dropout quantification, and its status as both a videotape manufacturing quality-assurance metric and a visually evident on-screen phenomena, the authors chose dropout counts as a point of inquiry and deterioration metric for playback testing of several used, circulating, commercially produced VHS videotapes, as well as in unused, shrink-wrapped, new duplicate VHS copies of the same titles.[3] Importantly, the imperative that deterioration testing be noninvasive and nondestructive—a requirement not normally held to by other scientific inquiries—was another reason for selecting dropout as a testing metric. Nondestructive chemical analyses of circulating VHS tapes in libraries may prove viable and feasible in the future, but were not so at the time of this testing. Unlike analyses of chemical changes in tape binders (for which no information related to their original chemical state is available), dropout affords a means of physical condition assessment of tapes based on the assumption that they were originally in a state of acceptable quality and performance. Other metrics, specifically signal-to-noise ratios, may also prove useful but were not employed here.

Measuring Dropout

Videotape manufacturer literature and specification documentation indicates that dropout count measurements were one of several key quality-assurance metrics by which manufacturers assessed blank VHS videotape. Dropouts result from disruptions in the video signal, caused by an interruption of contact between the videotape recorder (VTR) playback head and the videotape (such as debris clog), or by missing portions of the tape binder that should hold signal information but fail to because of a manufacturing or recording defect. Physical damage such as creasing or crinkling can cause dropout, as well.

As interruptions of the video signal, dropouts are measured by the degree to which they cause the video signal to drop below its nominal decibels (dB) value (Braithwaite, 1989, pp. 3–14). Most tape manufacturers considered a decrease of 20 dB as constituting a dropout, and categorized dropouts by the amount of time required for the signal to return to its nominal value, as measured in microseconds (µs). Here, *Video Magazine*'s editor-in-chief Lancelot Braithwaite explains his methodology's measurement rate of 15 µs:

> In our NTSC video system it takes 63.5 microseconds to make each line of a picture of which 52.5 microseconds actually contain picture information. So a dropout of 15

microseconds causes a bit more than a quarter of a line to lose information. If the results of each dropout were visible, we would have a very patchy picture, but all VCRs have circuits called dropout compensators. They reduce the effects of dropouts, but they don't eliminate them. (Braithwaite, 1989, pp. 3–14)

Dropout compensator circuitry can replace missing information with stored information about nearby preceding lines of video, which is temporarily stored by the compensator circuitry, often built into a VCR or VTR. While dropout compensators offer replacement chrominance (color) information—but not luminance (achromatic) information—the effect on the viewing experience is less disrupting than a "raw" dropout that appears as a brief horizontal white flash in one of the lines of the onscreen video image. In some cases, even with the presence of compensator circuitry, significant enough amounts of dropout experienced during playback can exceed the compensator's error concealment ability and visually persist as horizontal white flashes. As Dave Rice and Stefan Elnabli point out in their discussion of similar compensation techniques in digital videotape, assessment of error concealment is a "meaningful aspect of the preservation process," as it reveals the extent to which difficulties in reading magnetically encoded signal information can compromise picture integrity (Rice & Elnabli, 2010, p. 5). Again, dropout compensators do not eliminate the existence of dropouts, they merely mask them from the viewer. A VTR's dropout compensator circuitry can be bypassed when the radio frequency (RF) signal of videotape playback is measured through an RF output. This is the method by which accurate dropout counts can be electronically quantified using a specialized piece of dropout counter machinery.

DROPOUT TESTING METHODOLOGY

Investigation Rationale

By employing professional-grade tape signal processing and evaluation equipment, this investigation sought to discover whether a moving image work held on the VHS format might be demonstrated to be "deteriorating" based on quantitative measurement. In the case of still-playable VHS tapes in circulating media collection, what was the correlation between the number of circulations counts and such damage or deterioration, if any? Did tapes with higher amounts of playback register higher dropout counts? Did older tapes perform worse than newer ones? Could such characteristics of age and playback counts be established as contributing to greater deterioration? And: if there were such clear thresholds after which point the tape could be characterized as deteriorating, what were those outer limits?

Technical Approach

Four pairs of commercially produced VHS titles were employed as test tapes in the course of these experiments: Disney's *Bambi*,[4] the educational title *Child-*

hood: Great Expectations,[5] the live-action feature film *Kids,*[6] and Disney's animated feature *Snow White and the Seven Dwarfs.*[7] To measure dropout counts on each of the eight tapes, a calibrated ShibaSoku VH01BZ Dropout Counter at DuArt Film and Video's Restoration Department was employed to measure the RF output of the VTR. All tape playback occurred on a professional-grade JVC BR-S610U S-VHS VTR. Once received by DuArt, the tapes under analysis were acclimatized to the facility's controlled environmental conditions for a period of thirty days, at an average temperature of 69°F. Tapes of matching titles were played sequentially. During playback, each tape was simultaneously monitored for dropout counts per minute using the ShibaSoku Dropout Counter. Two dropout measurements (–20 dB at 5 µs; and –20 dB at 15 µs) were taken at minute intervals for all tapes under testing. All tape playback was also digitized to a Quicktime-wrapped 10-bit un-compressed v210 file for future visual reference. No cleaning of the tapes occurred prior to playback (to ensure condition authenticity and to mimic the circulating library use environment), but video and audio heads on the VTR were cleaned before each playback pass with trichlorotrifluoroethane (CAS 76-13-1), isopropyl alcohol (CAS 67-63-0l), and nitromethane (CAS 75-52-5).

To address the lack of an initial condition assessment, as described above by Big-ourdan et al., this experiment tested four used and four unused pairs of the same titles: one taken from the circulating VHS collection at the Avery Fisher Center for Media at NYU Libraries; and, the second a new, unused copy, from the same era, in original shrink-wrap, purchased from after-market vendors via Amazon.com. Great care was taken to ensure that new duplicates were of the same edition, produced by the same distribution company, and with identical packaging. It was impossible to verify if duplicates were made at identical commercial tape duplicator locations; however, similar machine identification and barcode markings on the physical VHS carriers suggest that they were, at least, made by the same duplication company. Combined with the expense of such testing, the difficulty in finding matching pairs of videotape titles (used and unused) in the marketplace significantly limited the experiment's test set of tapes.

Comparing used, circulating copies against new, unused copies, was thought to hold promise in isolating the effects of playback (documented by library cataloging systems as circulations) on tape deterioration. A third set of metrics for condition assessment comparison were measurements taken from published manufacturer quality-control standards and literature regarding dropout counts of new, blank videotape stock.

Acknowledged Test Liabilities

Environmental Storage

Temperature and humidity conditions for storage of each tape may well have been different, and this difference may sway test result accuracy.

Differences in Packaging

While both used and unused *Kids* tapes were 1996 Vidmark releases, and both contain similar white machine-inscribed markings on their tape spines (suggesting they were duplicated by the same manufacturer), these markings are also not identical. The etched pattern on each tape's physical carrier shell differs slightly.

Limited Manufacturer Information

As with the guarded details of manufacturer recipes for tape binder compositions, there is relatively limited manufacturer literature on the technical details of videotape. The manufacturer dropout count measurements cited in this study come from only two manufacturers (Sony and 3M) from 1991 to 1992, and it cannot be determined which manufacturer's tape stock was employed in the creation of the titles under testing.

Back-Coating

In higher-quality tape stock, the back surface of the tape (opposite the emulsion side that faces the video playback and recording heads) is usually coated with carbon to reduce static generated by friction when travelling through the cassette past the metal tape guides. A preliminary inspection of each test tape for carbon-backings yielded interesting results: both the new, unused tapes for *Childhood: Great Expectations* and *Snow White and the Seven Dwarfs* featured carbon-backed videotape, while their circulated counterparts did not. This finding revealed important realities about the consistency of tape stock during large duplication runs of commercially created titles in processing plants. As with the preceding acknowledged test liabilities, however, these are unavoidable realities that contravene ideal experiment control environments.

DROPOUT TESTING RESULTS AND DISCUSSION

The following charts depict dropout counts for each of the four pairs of titles at both measured dropout sensitivities (–20 dB at 5 µs; and –20 dB at 15 µs). Readers will note that each title's pair of graphs represent measurements performed simultaneously, at different sensitivities. Used, circulated tapes appear as light gray bars. Unused, new tapes appear as black bars. Minute-by-minute dropout counts can be found in the appendices.

I. *Bambi*

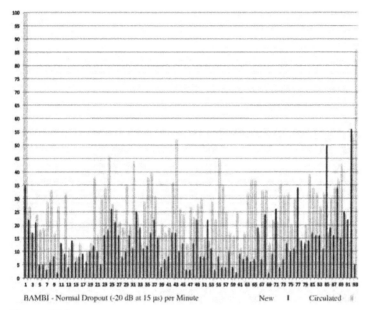

Figure 13.1.

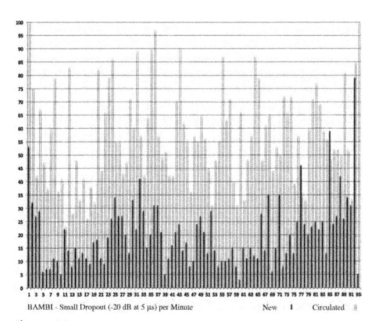

Figure 13.2.

II. *Childhood: Great Expectations*

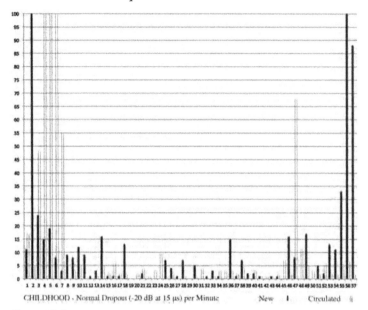

CHILDHOOD - Normal Dropout (-20 dB at 15 µs) per Minute   New ▮   Circulated ▯

Figure 13.3.

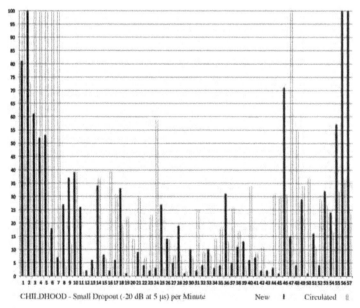

CHILDHOOD - Small Dropout (-20 dB at 5 µs) per Minute   New ▮   Circulated ▯

Figure 13.4.

III. *Kids*

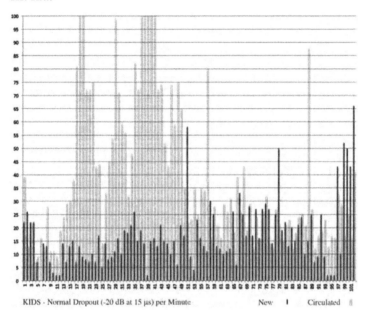

Figure 13.5.

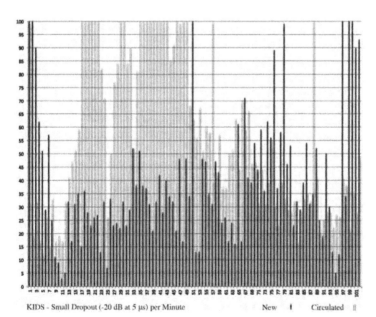

Figure 13.6.

IV. *Snow White and the Seven Dwarfs*

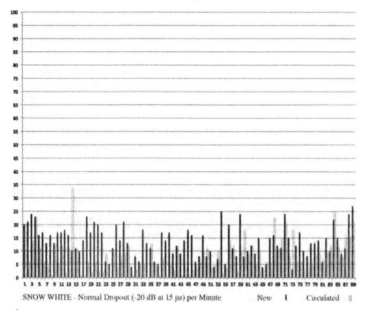

SNOW WHITE - Normal Dropout (-20 dB at 15 μs) per Minute   New   Circulated

Figure 13.7.

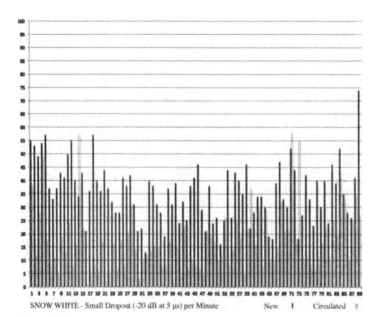

SNOW WHITE - Small Dropout (-20 dB at 5 μs) per Minute   New   Circulated

Figure 13.8.

Comparing Test Results with Blank Tape Stock Manufacturer Literature

Taken from original manufacturer tape stock specification pamphlets, below are some examples of dropout count acceptability standards for new tape stock:

Video Performance for Sony's Professional Grade VHS Video Cassettes,[8] dropouts (–20dB, 15 μs): 10 per minute.

Video Performance for Sony MQST-120 S-VHS,[9] dropouts (–15dB, 20 μs): less than 5 per minute (average).

Video Properties for 3M Broadcast VHS videocassettes,[10] dropouts (–20 dB, 15 μs): maximum average: 6 per minute. Typical average: 3 per minute.

Video Properties for 3M Master Broadcast S-VHS Videocassettes,[11] dropouts (–12 dB, 30 μs): 8 per minute.

By the early 1990s, the era from which these standards are available, it appears that fewer than ten dropouts per minute was an acceptable threshold of quality that dropout counter sensitivity metrics (in dBs and μs) may have been adjusted to achieve. Acceptability thresholds for videotape also appear to have changed over time. According to *Video Magazine*, "in 1982, fewer than 15 blemishes per minute was considered excellent. [In 1990] a tape must have fewer than five blemishes per minute to be rated excellent" (Woodcock, 1989, p. 16).

Likely due to a combination of deterioration contributing factors—age, possible hydrolysis, suboptimal environmental conditions, and (for some) amount of play-back wear—all tapes tested in our experiment failed manufacturer quality standards for acceptable dropout counts. If we are to assume that these tape copies were originally created during the duplication/recording process on manufacturer tape stock that met quality standards quoted above, the tapes under testing can be understood to have experienced some manner of "alteration process" and should be seen to qualify as deteriorating.

Comparing Test Results with Third-Party Blank Tape Stock Tests

As a service to its readership, an exhaustive 1989 quality survey test of tape manufacturers blank stock by *Video Magazine* (1989, p. 12) established the following ratings hierarchy for dropout count testing of blank videotape stock (measured at –20dB, 15 μs):

0–5 dropouts per min.	=	Excellent
6–10 dropouts per min.	=	Very Good
11–20 dropouts per min.	=	Good
21–30 dropouts per min.	=	Average
31–40 dropouts per min.	=	Fair
41–50 dropouts per min.	=	Weak
over 50 dropouts per min.	=	Poor

Of the sixty-five stocks from twenty-one manufacturers *Video Magazine* tested, most manufacturers' blank stocks fell in the upper half of this hierarchy, supporting the validity of manufacturer-stated measurement literature. Only two stocks satisfied the "Poor" rating for dropout counts, none satisfied the next category of "Weak," and only one qualified as "Average" (*Video Magazine*, 1989, pp. 18–23).

Using this hierarchy for comparison, the tapes under testing in this experiment averaged the following dropouts per minute (measured at –20dB, 15 μs):

Bambi (used, circulating)	27.0 dropouts per min. [Average]
Bambi (new, unused)	13.3 dropouts per min. [Good]
Childhood: Great Expectations (used, circulating)	38.3 dropouts per min. [Fair]
Childhood: Great Expectations (new, unused)	13.7 dropouts per min. [Good]
Kids (used, circulating)	17.2 dropouts per min. [Good]
Kids (new, unused)	41.1 dropouts per min. [Weak]
Snow White and the Seven Dwarfs (used, circulating)	8.3 dropouts per min. [Good]
Snow White and the Seven Dwarfs (new, unused)	13.4 dropouts per min. [Good]

Dropout measurements for all of the tapes under testing in this experiment, with the exception of one, fail to surpass the "Good" categorization and two of them rate in the lower rungs of this hierarchy.

Comparing Test Results with Third-Party Tests of Commercially Produced Tapes

While instructive, charting dropout counts in commercially produced tapes in this experiment against dropout measurements of blank, new videotape stock is somewhat of an imperfect comparison. Ideally, commercially produced tapes would be measured against commercially produced tapes, and a 1990 investigation by the trade publication *Video Review* makes such a comparison possible.

Titled, "Video's Dirty Secret," this study by author Ron Goldberg (1990) uses quantitative and qualitative testing to reveal defects in over 60% of the commercially produced tapes tested, finding that even tapes of titles duplicated for larger Hollywood studio releases evidenced excessive dropout counts—the principal evaluation metric employed by Goldberg (pp. 36–39).

None of the Video At Risk (VAR) test tape titles overlap with those tested by *Video Review*, but Goldberg's findings are especially relevant, as the VAR test strategically selected two Disney animated feature titles that carried the THX label of quality—a quality certification system bestowed on only the highest-quality duplicated material. Among the new, unused copies of those titles, *Bambi* failed to perform significantly better than its used, circulated counterpart, and *Snow White and the Seven Dwarfs* actually performed worse than its used, circulated counterpart.

Goldberg's conclusion is akin to an indictment of videotape duplicators looking to save money by using inferior-grade blank tape stock in the duplication process. The notion that the tape duplication industry could utilize substandard tape stocks is not surprising. As one former tape duplication industry employee described it, "tape duplication was a penny-pinching business."[12] Goldberg's study found that of the thirty-six tapes tested (pairs of eighteen titles) more than one-third of them exceeded dropout rates of fifty per minute (measured at −20dB, 15 μs).[13]

The suggested inconsistency among duplicators' quality-assurance processes that Goldberg uncovered may be echoed by our experiment. The two THX-certified Disney titles had discrepancies in each tape's physical characteristics: only one of the Disney titles (new, unused *Snow White and the Seven Dwarfs*) contained anti-static back-coating on the tape—a quality measure intended to extend the life of the tape and protect against damage. Moreover, if inferior tape stock was, in fact, so commonly employed by tape duplicators, the authors believe that the case for deterioration qualification is strengthened: tape stock of inferior manufacturing quality is likely to result in decreased stability and performance, over time, when compared with tape stock that meets the high manufacturer quality-control standards cited above.

Impact of Playback and Circulation Counts on Deterioration

The circulation statistics for tapes tested in this experiment appear below:

Bambi (used, circulating)	45 circulations
Bambi (new, unused)	0 circulations
Childhood: Great Expectations (used, circulating)	248 circulations
Childhood: Great Expectations (new, unused)	0 circulations
Kids (used, circulating)	203 circulations
Kids (new, unused)	0 circulations
Snow White and the Seven Dwarfs (used, circulating)	17 circulations
Snow White and the Seven Dwarfs (new, unused)	0 circulations

Looking at the two highest-circulated titles, *Childhood: Great Expectations* and *Kids*, a pattern may be said to corroborate claims that tapes experiencing high levels of playback experience a burnishing or "calendaring" effect whereby the videotape binder becomes so well-worn that the rate of subsequent physical deterioration diminishes, or plateaus. The specifics of calendaring resulting from VTR head-to-tape physical contact are reflected in the research of Osaki et al., and Bhushan, cited above. But, for the purposes of this inquiry it can be stated that highly circulated tapes are likely to have already experienced such a degree of physical wear and deterioration that by their 200th-odd pass the microscopic roughness of the tape binder has been significantly worn down—in essence, polished. This fact may be reflected by the dropout counts in *Childhood: Great Expectations*, yet inconsistency in tape backing between the used and the unused copies makes such a determination difficult to definitively assert.[14] What this calendaring effect does directly suggest is that libraries wishing to detect deterioration in their circulating VHS tapes begin such evaluations with the most highly circulated titles in their collections.

Impact of Age on Deterioration

For tapes under testing in this experiment no noticeable trend can be asserted with regard to the impact of age alone on quantifiable deterioration factors, such as dropout counts. However, insofar as both used and unused copies of all titles failed manufacturer quality-control standards, age likely plays a core contributing role in the deterioration-associated "alteration processes" taking place in the tape binder. While this may not be so surprising a finding, it does directly suggest that libraries wishing to detect deterioration in their circulating VHS tapes begin such evaluations with the oldest titles in their collections.

Impact of Environmental Conditions

The possibility that NYU-Libraries' environmental conditions played a corrupting role and contributed to potential tape hydrolysis remains. It is clear that such environmental conditions may fall short of ISO 18934 recommendations for temperature, relative humidity, and stability (which should not exceed 73°F for 20% RH and should not exceed 52°F for 50% RH) (ISO, 2006). However, the conditions at NYU-Libraries are most likely in keeping with those conditions at other circulating video libraries, and it is unlikely that many other libraries store their circulating VHS collections in ISO 18394 compliant conditions.

GENERAL IMPRESSIONS AND CONCLUDING OBSERVATIONS

The dropout count testing results of these experiments demonstrate that all tapes considered failed quality standards set by tape stock manufacturers. These test results were surprising as the authors did not foresee such resulting high dropout counts for the tapes, and as we had originally anticipated some manner of specific correlation between circulation and dropout—namely, that highly circulated tapes would demonstrate a more contextual trend in dropout counts. While the small data set from this testing may make it difficult to definitively assert such trends or offer definitive conclusions about the deterioration status of other videotapes in the AFC circulating collections, it is clear that these tapes no longer meet any of the available quality and performance documentation that they were believed to have met in their original state at the time of production and/or manufacture.[15] Whether or not a tape under testing in its original state adhered to such standards seems moot, as such a retroactive determination is impossible for these (and most other) tapes. Most importantly, the authors strongly believe that all evidence suggests that the complex factors involved in the "alteration processes" of deterioration will only serve to intensify the deteriorating condition of any given videotape with time. The evident deterioration relative to dropout counts is likely only the first in a litany of deterioration factors for all tapes tested in the course of this experiment.

Unlike myriad other potential deterioration factors, dropout count thresholds specified by tape manufacturers actually do exist. As such, we believe that such quantified dropout counts offer one of the least subjective forms of noninvasive evidence for videotape deterioration currently available. From the legal perspective of justifying preservation reformatting under Section 108(c), we would recommend such dropout count measurement, as it can at least enable contrast with subsequent physical condition states, even if only at future points in time. While one can, perhaps, never know an original dropout count measurement for a specific videotape item at the point-of-creation, documenting current dropout rates for library collections can be seen as invaluable data for deterioration assessments down the road. The authors also concur with the legal analysis of Counsel Robert Clarida that, given the absence of a specific requisite quantity of deterioration in the language of the law, as small a spike in dropout counts as those lasting even a few minutes would certainly qualify a tape as "deteriorating."

ACKNOWLEDGMENTS

This testing was carried out under the auspices of the Andrew W. Mellon Foundation-funded project, Video At Risk: Strategies for Preserving Commercial Video Collections in Libraries. The authors would like to thank Counsel Robert Clarida; DuArt Film and Video's Chief Engineer, Maurice Schechter; NYU Libraries' Melissa Brown, Carol Mandel, Craig Michaels, Ben Moskowitz, David Perry, Michael Stoller, Kimberly Tarr, and Kent Underwood; as well as VAR interns Federica Liberi and Kristin Mac-Donough for their research contributions, feedback, and assistance. Special thanks to Howard Besser for his continued support in the research of moving image preservation.

APPENDIX A: VHS DROPOUT DATASETS, NEW AND CIRCULATED: *BAMBI, CHILDHOOD, KIDS, SNOW WHITE*

Table 13.1.

UNIT TIME (H:MM:SS)	BAMBI—NEW DROPOUT		BAMBI—CIRCULATED DROPOUT	
	(15μ/20dB)	(5μ/20dB)	(15μ/20dB)	(5μ/20dB)
0:00:00–0:01:00	35	53	109	267
0:01:00–0:02:00	22	32	27	75
0:02:00–0:03:00	17	27	17	42
0:03:00–0:04:00	21	29	24	67
0:04:00–0:05:00	5	6	18	47
0:05:00–0:06:00	5	7	19	37
0:06:00–0:07:00	3	7	29	60
0:07:00–0:08:00	6	11	33	79
0:08:00–0:09:00	8	10	17	36
0:09:00–0:10:00	2	5	27	41
0:10:00–0:11:00	13	22	11	23
0:11:00–0:12:00	9	14	32	83
0:12:00–0:13:00	4	8	11	28
0:13:00–0:14:00	14	15	13	48
0:14:00–0:15:00	6	11	8	33
0:15:00–0:16:00	8	13	13	41
0:16:00–0:17:00	9	11	4	26
0:17:00–0:18:00	6	9	10	38
0:18:00–0:19:00	10	17	13	32
0:19:00–0:20:00	12	18	38	82
0:20:00–0:21:00	10	11	16	44
0:21:00–0:22:00	5	9	30	66
0:22:00–0:23:00	16	19	34	79
0:23:00–0:24:00	18	26	46	86
0:24:00–0:25:00	26	34	28	55
0:25:00–0:26:00	21	27	26	55
0:26:00–0:27:00	16	27	21	43
0:27:00–0:28:00	8	20	19	47
0:28:00–0:29:00	10	13	35	71
0:29:00–0:30:00	16	33	20	60
0:30:00–0:31:00	11	22	44	89
0:31:00–0:32:00	25	41	24	57
0:32:00–0:33:00	19	29	13	42
0:33:00–0:34:00	11	15	29	64
0:34:00–0:35:00	12	20	38	90
0:35:00–0:36:00	17	31	40	97
0:36:00–0:37:00	22	31	31	57
0:37:00–0:38:00	15	21	16	49

UNIT TIME (H:MM:SS)	BAMBI—NEW DROPOUT		BAMBI—CIRCULATED DROPOUT	
	(15μ/20dB)	(5μ/20dB)	(15μ/20dB)	(5μ/20dB)
0:38:00–0:39:00	4	5	20	51
0:39:00–0:40:00	7	11	17	42
0:40:00–0:41:00	8	16	19	42
0:41:00–0:42:00	17	21	36	70
0:42:00–0:43:00	17	24	52	90
0:43:00–0:44:00	10	14	26	62
0:44:00–0:45:00	13	17	24	55
0:45:00–0:46:00	3	8	13	36
0:46:00–0:47:00	3	10	27	57
0:47:00–0:48:00	13	24	23	55
0:48:00–0:49:00	22	27	28	65
0:49:00–0:50:00	8	21	30	56
0:50:00–0:51:00	8	13	15	45
0:51:00–0:52:00	22	29	14	31
0:52:00–0:53:00	11	14	29	48
0:53:00–0:54:00	3	8	22	55
0:54:00–0:55:00	8	10	45	87
0:55:00–0:56:00	4	10	35	63
0:56:00–0:57:00	4	11	25	71
0:57:00–0:58:00	10	15	17	40
0:58:00–0:59:00	4	8	16	31
0:59:00–1:00:00	2	3	25	66
1:00:00–1:01:00	9	15	11	33
1:01:00–1:02:00	7	11	17	48
1:02:00–1:03:00	8	15	32	57
1:03:00–1:04:00	6	12	37	87
1:04:00–1:05:00	7	11	37	79
1:05:00–1:06:00	19	28	17	48
1:06:00–1:07:00	7	14	33	61
1:07:00–1:08:00	24	35	33	65
1:08:00–1:09:00	2	6	13	44
1:09:00–1:10:00	9	15	22	53
1:10:00–1:11:00	26	35	21	50
1:11:00–1:12:00	4	8	35	72
1:12:00–1:13:00	7	13	31	66
1:13:00–1:14:00	13	20	32	72
1:14:00–1:15:00	10	13	20	39
1:15:00–1:16:00	11	25	30	57
1:16:00–1:17:00	34	46	15	35
1:17:00–1:18:00	14	24	11	33
1:18:00–1:19:00	13	20	20	60
1:19:00–1:20:00	14	23	39	71

(continued)

Table 13.1. (continued)

| UNIT TIME (H:MM:SS) | BAMBI—NEW | | BAMBI—CIRCULATED | |
| | DROPOUT | | DROPOUT | |
	(15μ/20dB)	(5μ/20dB)	(15μ/20dB)	(5μ/20dB)
1:20:00–1:21:00	17	25	34	77
1:21:00–1:22:00	16	22	32	69
1:22:00–1:23:00	16	25	27	59
1:23:00–1:24:00	11	13	32	56
1:24:00–1:25:00	50	59	17	48
1:25:00–1:26:00	19	24	30	52
1:26:00–1:27:00	16	27	34	52
1:27:00–1:28:00	34	42	37	50
1:28:00–1:29:00	15	26	43	81
1:29:00–1:30:00	25	34	24	52
1:30:00–1:31:00	22	31	14	33
1:31:00–1:32:00	56	79	54	85
1:32:00–1:33:00	5	5	86	151
Total	1240	1874	2511	5549

Table 13.2.

| UNIT TIME (H:MM:SS) | CHILDHOOD—NEW | | CHILDHOOD—CIRCULATED | |
| | DROPOUT | | DROPOUT | |
	(15μ/20dB)	(5μ/20dB)	(15μ/20dB)	(5μ/20dB)
0:00:00–0:01:00	11	81	17	731
0:01:00–0:02:00	122	293	5	73
0:02:00–0:03:00	24	61	48	781
0:03:00–0:04:00	15	52	667	8975
0:04:00–0:05:00	19	53	1052	17659
0:05:00–0:06:00	8	18	146	1940
0:06:00–0:07:00	3	7	55	501
0:07:00–0:08:00	9	27	0	4
0:08:00–0:09:00	8	37	3	12
0:09:00–0:10:00	12	39	5	40
0:10:00–0:11:00	9	26	0	2
0:11:00–0:12:00	1	2	0	0
0:12:00–0:13:00	3	6	1	3
0:13:00–0:14:00	16	34	5	37
0:14:00–0:15:00	1	8	2	7
0:15:00–0:16:00	1	2	6	40
0:16:00–0:17:00	1	6	2	31

UNIT TIME (H:MM:SS)	CHILDHOOD—NEW		CHILDHOOD— CIRCULATED	
	DROPOUT		DROPOUT	
	(15μ/20dB)	(5μ/20dB)	(15μ/20dB)	(5μ/20dB)
0:17:00–0:18:00	13	33	2	19
0:18:00–0:19:00	0	1	0	22
0:19:00–0:20:00	0	0	2	14
0:20:00–0:21:00	2	9	4	30
0:21:00–0:22:00	0	4	1	7
0:22:00–0:23:00	0	2	3	23
0:23:00–0:24:00	0	3	10	59
0:24:00–0:25:00	7	27	0	3
0:25:00–0:26:00	4	14	2	14
0:26:00–0:27:00	1	5	0	8
0:27:00–0:28:00	7	19	1	8
0:28:00–0:29:00	0	1	0	2
0:29:00–0:30:00	5	10	1	7
0:30:00–0:31:00	0	2	4	25
0:31:00–0:32:00	1	4	0	9
0:32:00–0:33:00	3	10	1	8
0:33:00–0:34:00	1	3	3	14
0:34:00–0:35:00	0	4	3	18
0:35:00–0:36:00	15	31	3	13
0:36:00–0:37:00	1	5	2	26
0:37:00–0:38:00	7	11	4	17
0:38:00–0:39:00	2	13	0	4
0:39:00–0:40:00	2	6	3	34
0:40:00–0:41:00	1	7	1	9
0:41:00–0:42:00	0	2	1	11
0:42:00–0:43:00	1	2	0	0
0:43:00–0:44:00	1	3	2	31
0:44:00–0:45:00	0	1	7	30
0:45:00–0:46:00	16	71	2	31
0:46:00–0:47:00	8	15	68	1114
0:47:00–0:48:00	0	4	11	55
0:48:00–0:49:00	17	29	5	34
0:49:00–0:50:00	0	1	3	37
0:50:00–0:51:00	5	16	2	11
0:51:00–0:52:00	2	4	6	29
0:52:00–0:53:00	13	32	2	27
0:53:00–0:54:00	11	24	2	16
0:54:00–0:55:00	33	57	4	32
0:55:00–0:56:00	251	1075	7	35
0:56:00–0:57:00	88	350	2	24
Total	781	2662	2188	32746

Table 13.3.

UNIT TIME (H:MM:SS)	KIDS—Tape A NEW		KIDS—Tape B CIRCULATED	
	DROPOUT		DROPOUT	
	(15μ/20dB)	(5μ/20dB)	(15μ/20dB)	(5μ/20dB)
0:00:00–0:01:00	22	230	39	99
0:01:00–0:02:00	26	220	13	19
0:02:00–0:03:00	22	90	22	32
0:03:00–0:04:00	22	62	7	17
0:04:00–0:05:00	7	51	9	12
0:05:00–0:06:00	0	29	16	26
0:06:00–0:07:00	14	57	13	15
0:07:00–0:08:00	13	25	28	33
0:08:00–0:09:00	7	11	11	17
0:09:00–0:10:00	3	9	11	19
0:10:00–0:11:00	2	3	9	17
0:11:00–0:12:00	2	5	19	32
0:12:00–0:13:00	14	32	24	41
0:13:00–0:14:00	7	17	29	47
0:14:00–0:15:00	13	31	30	51
0:15:00–0:16:00	15	35	38	59
0:16:00–0:17:00	7	15	81	140
0:17:00–0:18:00	13	36	178	284
0:18:00–0:19:00	9	28	138	211
0:19:00–0:20:00	8	23	72	103
0:20:00–0:21:00	7	26	72	103
0:21:00–0:22:00	10	27	75	115
0:22:00–0:23:00	7	13	43	82
0:23:00–0:24:00	17	32	44	71
0:24:00–0:25:00	5	7	14	26
0:25:00–0:26:00	14	33	33	50
0:26:00–0:27:00	8	23	45	77
0:27:00–0:28:00	9	24	54	84
0:28:00–0:29:00	11	22	99	156
0:29:00–0:30:00	16	32	71	121
0:30:00–0:31:00	10	23	59	84
0:31:00–0:32:00	19	29	56	90
0:32:00–0:33:00	18	52	32	52
0:33:00–0:34:00	21	38	48	81
0:34:00–0:35:00	26	51	82	148
0:35:00–0:36:00	15	38	72	110
0:36:00–0:37:00	19	37	113	169
0:37:00–0:38:00	14	31	110	158
0:38:00–0:39:00	2	21	155	246
0:39:00–0:40:00	15	32	134	218
0:40:00–0:41:00	16	42	111	190

UNIT TIME (H:MM:SS)	KIDS—Tape A NEW		KIDS—Tape B CIRCULATED	
	DROPOUT		DROPOUT	
	(15μ/20dB)	(5μ/20dB)	(15μ/20dB)	(5μ/20dB)
0:41:00–0:42:00	13	28	72	123
0:42:00–0:43:00	21	40	74	130
0:43:00–0:44:00	15	34	52	85
0:44:00–0:45:00	14	32	43	91
0:45:00–0:46:00	10	21	74	126
0:46:00–0:47:00	15	48	59	99
0:47:00–0:48:00	6	17	75	129
0:48:00–0:49:00	21	48	65	108
0:49:00–0:50:00	17	34	35	68
0:50:00–0:51:00	58	170	22	63
0:51:00–0:52:00	9	13	23	56
0:52:00–0:53:00	4	13	35	67
0:53:00–0:54:00	23	48	25	51
0:54:00–0:55:00	16	47	35	60
0:55:00–0:56:00	13	35	34	58
0:56:00–0:57:00	11	31	80	142
0:57:00–0:58:00	30	47	16	43
0:58:00–0:59:00	25	43	28	57
0:59:00–1:00:00	13	24	21	37
1:00:00–1:01:00	12	26	16	37
1:01:00–1:02:00	10	17	29	50
1:02:00–1:03:00	11	24	26	51
1:03:00–1:04:00	12	16	31	63
1:04:00–1:05:00	26	61	18	44
1:05:00–1:06:00	6	17	39	70
1:06:00–1:07:00	33	71	26	59
1:07:00–1:08:00	25	41	43	66
1:08:00–1:09:00	17	39	19	46
1:09:00–1:10:00	28	54	29	47
1:10:00–1:11:00	17	44	12	31
1:11:00–1:12:00	27	59	24	44
1:12:00–1:13:00	16	36	16	31
1:13:00–1:14:00	27	62	26	39
1:14:00–1:15:00	29	56	32	55
1:15:00–1:16:00	27	89	14	30
1:16:00–1:17:00	14	37	12	23
1:17:00–1:18:00	25	58	27	39
1:18:00–1:19:00	50	99	21	33
1:19:00–1:20:00	19	46	15	29
1:20:00–1:21:00	22	53	21	28
1:21:00–1:22:00	13	23	23	32
1:22:00–1:23:00	20	32	12	17

(continued)

Table 13.3. (*continued*)

UNIT TIME (H:MM:SS)	KIDS—Tape A NEW DROPOUT		KIDS—Tape B CIRCULATED DROPOUT	
	(15μ/20dB)	(5μ/20dB)	(15μ/20dB)	(5μ/20dB)
1:23:00–1:24:00	15	29	18	28
1:24:00–1:25:00	21	39	24	33
1:25:00–1:26:00	24	54	25	35
1:26:00–1:27:00	10	31	21	32
1:27:00–1:28:00	15	35	88	116
1:28:00–1:29:00	25	52	27	41
1:29:00–1:30:00	7	25	12	20
1:30:00–1:31:00	9	19	17	25
1:31:00–1:32:00	25	50	19	28
1:32:00–1:33:00	9	30	23	28
1:33:00–1:34:00	2	13	13	22
1:34:00–1:35:00	2	5	17	27
1:35:00–1:36:00	2	12	16	26
1:36:00–1:37:00	43	129	33	41
1:37:00–1:38:00	10	34	29	38
1:38:00–1:39:00	52	135	17	21
1:39:00–1:40:00	50	103	25	35
1:40:00–1:41:00	43	90	16	28
1:41:00–1:42:00	66	93	41	49
Total	1755	4453	4189	6935

Table 13.4

UNIT TIME (H:MM:SS)	SNOW WHITE— Tape B NEW DROPOUT		SNOW WHITE— Tape A CIRCULATED DROPOUT	
	(15μ/20dB)	(5μ/20dB)	(15μ/20dB)	(5μ/20dB)
0:00:00–0:01:00	20	55	20	38
0:01:00–0:02:00	21	53	6	12
0:02:00–0:03:00	24	49	14	28
0:03:00–0:04:00	23	54	23	49
0:04:00–0:05:00	16	57	11	18
0:05:00–0:06:00	17	37	6	8
0:06:00–0:07:00	13	33	5	11
0:07:00–0:08:00	16	37	1	5
0:08:00–0:09:00	13	43	13	19
0:09:00–0:10:00	17	41	6	13
0:10:00–0:11:00	17	50	12	24

UNIT TIME	SNOW WHITE—Tape B NEW		SNOW WHITE—Tape A CIRCULATED	
	DROPOUT		*DROPOUT*	
(H:MM:SS)	(15μ/20dB)	(5μ/20dB)	(15μ/20dB)	(5μ/20dB)
0:11:00–0:12:00	18	55	2	8
0:12:00–0:13:00	16	40	11	16
0:13:00–0:14:00	10	34	34	58
0:14:00–0:15:00	11	43	11	22
0:15:00–0:16:00	10	21	1	1
0:16:00–0:17:00	14	36	1	5
0:17:00–0:18:00	23	57	6	8
0:18:00–0:19:00	17	40	2	6
0:19:00–0:20:00	21	36	6	17
0:20:00–0:21:00	20	44	2	2
0:21:00–0:22:00	17	37	2	5
0:22:00–0:23:00	6	32	9	16
0:23:00–0:24:00	5	28	0	7
0:24:00–0:25:00	11	28	11	18
0:25:00–0:26:00	20	41	4	8
0:26:00–0:27:00	14	38	8	20
0:27:00–0:28:00	21	42	9	31
0:28:00–0:29:00	13	31	12	14
0:29:00–0:30:00	4	21	1	3
0:30:00–0:31:00	8	22	3	10
0:31:00–0:32:00	6	13	5	12
0:32:00–0:33:00	18	40	5	14
0:33:00–0:34:00	13	38	0	15
0:34:00–0:35:00	11	31	13	15
0:35:00–0:36:00	6	28	5	8
0:36:00–0:37:00	5	19	1	8
0:37:00–0:38:00	17	37	7	18
0:38:00–0:39:00	14	31	0	2
0:39:00–0:40:00	17	39	5	15
0:40:00–0:41:00	9	24	3	5
0:41:00–0:42:00	12	32	12	23
0:42:00–0:43:00	9	25	1	7
0:43:00–0:44:00	14	38	4	10
0:44:00–0:45:00	18	41	1	8
0:45:00–0:46:00	16	46	3	7
0:46:00–0:47:00	6	29	4	5
0:47:00–0:48:00	8	21	6	21
0:48:00–0:49:00	16	38	10	19
0:49:00–0:50:00	8	24	11	17
0:50:00–0:51:00	10	26	4	10
0:51:00–0:52:00	4	16	5	12

(continued)

Table 13.3. *(continued)*

| UNIT TIME (H:MM:SS) | SNOW WHITE— Tape B NEW | | SNOW WHITE— Tape A CIRCULATED | |
| | DROPOUT | | DROPOUT | |
	(15μ/20dB)	*(5μ/20dB)*	*(15μ/20dB)*	*(5μ/20dB)*
0:52:00–0:53:00	7	25	10	26
0:53:00–0:54:00	25	44	2	8
0:54:00–0:55:00	5	26	4	14
0:55:00–0:56:00	20	43	14	25
0:56:00–0:57:00	11	40	12	19
0:57:00–0:58:00	8	35	2	5
0:58:00–0:59:00	24	46	10	22
0:59:00–1:00:00	8	22	18	37
1:00:00–1:01:00	10	28	9	16
1:01:00–1:02:00	12	34	12	30
1:02:00–1:03:00	9	34	5	8
1:03:00–1:04:00	15	30	10	29
1:04:00–1:05:00	4	19	3	10
1:05:00–1:06:00	5	18	6	10
1:06:00–1:07:00	15	39	6	14
1:07:00–1:08:00	16	47	23	32
1:08:00–1:09:00	12	33	11	21
1:09:00–1:10:00	11	30	15	21
1:10:00–1:11:00	24	52	21	58
1:11:00–1:12:00	15	44	8	18
1:12:00–1:13:00	3	18	18	55
1:13:00–1:14:00	12	27	6	10
1:14:00–1:15:00	17	42	6	11
1:15:00–1:16:00	10	33	3	8
1:16:00–1:17:00	8	23	4	7
1:17:00–1:18:00	13	40	6	11
1:18:00–1:19:00	13	30	9	17
1:19:00–1:20:00	14	40	10	22
1:20:00–1:21:00	6	24	7	10
1:21:00–1:22:00	15	46	10	25
1:22:00–1:23:00	10	39	12	19
1:23:00–1:24:00	22	52	25	41
1:24:00–1:25:00	15	35	12	33
1:25:00–1:26:00	9	28	8	10
1:26:00–1:27:00	11	26	16	25
1:27:00–1:28:00	24	41	16	35
1:28:00–1:29:00	27	74	21	27
Total	1198	3178	747	1540

NOTES

1. October 10, 2012. "[Videolib] Confronting a campus wide VHS DEATH Deadline."

2. See H. Rep. 94–1476 at p. 73, under the heading "Reproduction and uses for other purposes":

> A problem of particular urgency is that of preserving for posterity prints of motion pictures made before 1942. Aside from the deplorable fact that in a great many cases the only existing copy of a film has been deliberately destroyed, those that remain are in immediate danger of disintegration; they were printed on film stock with a nitrate base that will inevitably decompose in time. The efforts of the Library of Congress, the American Film Institute, and other organizations to rescue and preserve this irreplaceable contribution to our cultural life are to be applauded, and the making of duplicate copies for purposes of archival preservation certainly falls within the scope of "fair use."

3. The term "new" should be understood as meaning an unused copy of the same title, purchased in its original shrink-wrap packaging, and manufactured at the same time and era as the used, circulating copies. As VHS videotapes are no longer manufactured, references to such "new" tapes do not mean tapes that were recently manufactured.

4. *Bambi* [Fully Restored 55th Anniversary Edition], directed by David Hand (1942; Burbank, CA: Walt Disney Home Video, 1997), VHS.

5. *Childhood: Great Expectations*, directed by Geoff Haines-Stiles (1991; New York: Ambrose Video, 1991), VHS.

6. *Kids*, directed by Larry Clark (1995; Marina Del Rey, CA: Vidmark Entertainment, 1997), VHS.

7. *Snow White and the Seven Dwarfs* [Platinum Edition], directed by David Hand (1937; Burbank, CA: Walt Disney Home Video, 2001), VHS.

8. Sony Professional Grade VHS Video Cassettes, Sony Corporation specifications sheet, 1991. Catalog no. ACG-5140-TKY-9109-P1-005.

9. Sony MQST S-VHS videocassettes, Sony Corporation specifications sheet, 1992. Catalog no. ACG-5164-TCS-9206-010.

10. Broadcast VHS tapes, specifications Sheet, 3M, 1991. Catalog no. 84-9811-4338-5. According to the Test Notes, "during playback of a 50% gray level signal, the unlimited RF signal is monitored for dropouts exceeding 20 dB in depth and 15 microseconds in length."

11. Master Broadcast S-VHS Videocassettes, specifications sheet, 3M, 1991. Catalog no. 84-9811-4340-1. Defined in Test Notes as, "any tape defect that produces a 12dB [for] 30 m sec or greater is electronically counted as a dropout."

12. Maurice Schecter, in conversation with the authors, December 2012.

13. While Goldberg's investigation does not specify dropout dB size measured, past *Video Review* dropout count testing employed a –18 dB measurement (Measuring tape, 1990, 31–36).

14. The severe spike in dropout at the beginning of the used copy of *Childhood: Great Expectations* can be attributed to physical crinkling damage—affirmation of the dropout metric's ability to document videotape problems.

15. Indeed, the potential data set encompassing any representative percentage of VHS tapes and stocks ever produced would be far too enormous and unscalable.

REFERENCES

Bigourdan, J. L., Reilly, J. M., Santoro, K., & Salesin, G. (2006). *The preservation of magnetic tape collections: A perspective*. Final Report to National Endowment for the Humanities Division of Preservation and Access, NEH Grant #PA-50123-03. Rochester, NY: Image Permanence Institute.

Bhushan, B. (1990). Tribology and mechanics of magnetic storage devices. New York, NY: Springer-Verlag.

Braithwaite, L. (1989). Introduction. In *Video Magazine's official blank tape tests* (pp. 3–14). New York, NY: Reese Communications Inc.

Edge, M., Allen, N. S., Hayes, M., Jewitt, T. S., Brems, K., & Horrie, V. (1993). Degradation of magnetic tape: Support and binder stability. *Polymer Degradation and Stability, 39*, 207–214.

Gilmour, I. (2000). Media testing in audiovisual archives: Why is my tape falling to bits? In M. Aubert & R. Billeaud (Eds.), *Image and sound archiving and access: Challenges of the 3rd millennium* (pp. 79–87). Paris: CNC.

Goldberg, R. (1990). Video's dirty secret. *Video Review, 10*, 36–39.

(ISO) International Organization for Standardization. (2006). *ISO 18934 Imaging Materials— Multiple media archives—Storage environment* (1st ed.). Geneva: International Organization for Standardization.

Lee, A., Prytherich, R., King, A. (2000). U-Matic preservation. In M. Aubert & R. Billeaud (Eds.), *Image and sound archiving and access: Challenges of the 3rd millennium* (pp. 177–186). Paris: CNC.

Mather, P. B., & Neil, D. C. (1998). Assessing video tape degradation. In *Proceedings, 32nd Annual 1998 International Carahan Conference on Security Technology* (pp. 220–224). New York, NY: IEEE.

Measuring tape. (1990, November). *Video Review, 11*(8), 31–36.

Osaki, H., Oyanagi, E., Aonuma, H., Kanou, T., & Kurihara, J. (1992, January). Wear mechanism of particulate magnetic tapes in helical scan video tape recorders. *IEEE Transactions on Magnetics, 28*(1), 76–83.

Rice, D., & Elnabli, S. (2010, October). *Barcode scanners, miniDV decks, and the migration of digital information from analog surfaces*. New York, NY: AudioVisual Preservation Solutions. Retrieved from http://www.avpreserve.com/wp-content/uploads/2010/11/Migration-of-Digital-Information-from-Analog-Surfaces.pdf

Simon, S. (Interviewer) & Kugler, R. (Interviewee). (2008, December 27). Ode to VHS [Interview transcript]. Retrieved from NPR: http://www.npr.org/templates/story/story.php?storyId=98754557

Thiebaut, B., Vilmont, L. B., Lavedrine, B. (2006, September 1). *Report on video and audio tape deterioration mechanisms and considerations about implementation of a collection condition assessment method*. Retrieved from http://www.prestospace.org/project/deliverables/D6-1.pdf

Video Magazine. (1989). *Video Magazine's official blank tape tests*. New York, NY: Reese Communications Inc.

Woodcock, R. (1989). How to rescue a damaged tape. In *Video Magazine's official blank tape tests* (p. 16). New York, NY: Reese Communications Inc.

14

The Devils You Don't Know

The New Lives of the Finding Aid

Sheila O'Hare and Ashley Todd-Diaz

ABSTRACT

The nature and purpose of the "finding aid" in cultural heritage institutions has become the focus of considerable scholarly examination. As much of the literature of 2012 devoted to the subject indicated, finding aids are still at the heart of the cultural heritage enterprise, but questions surround their future design and ultimate relevance in the digital era. This review of the 2012 literature on topics related to finding aids and associated access tools considers the future of the finding aid from four perspectives: reassessment of the traditional functions and meanings of the finding aid; online finding aid design and usability; efforts to make the "invisible" work of cocreators or information professionals in describing, organizing, and presenting resources apparent; and the impact of new developments, including interactive content and linked data.

INTRODUCTION

Over the last few years, the "finding aid" in cultural heritage institutions has become a focus of scholarly attention and criticism. Is a finding aid per se necessary at all in a digital era? Are finding aids cumbersome, biased, user-unfriendly, partial at best, hopelessly static, structurally archaic, and arcane? As much of the scholarly literature of 2012 devoted to the subject indicated, finding aids are still at the heart of the cultural heritage enterprise—much as, in some instances, we wish they were not. Further, as much as standard finding aids may be necessary evils, they have the virtues of familiarity and consistency. Should they be changed, and, if so, in which particulars?

From a special issue of *Archival Science* devoted to finding aids as representative of sociological and rhetorical genres, to online finding aid design and usability (as treated in *RBM: A Journal of Rare Books, Manuscripts and Cultural Heritage*), to efforts to make the "invisible" work of museum professionals in describing, organizing, and presenting resources transparent, finding aids/access tools were in the spotlight in 2012. The continuing transfer from print to digital format clearly prompted some of the discussion, but developments in metadata, the inclusion of interactive content, and the expected benefits of linked data also led to a reassessment of the scope and purpose of traditional finding aids.

THE FINDING AID IN A DIGITAL WORLD

The growing pains associated with a move from physical to digital collections, and from print to electronic finding aids, are familiar to archivists and other information professionals. In 2012, a number of archival scholars tackled the issue of the continuing utility of the finding aid or its possible obsolescence. The August 2012 issue of *Archival Science* examined the finding aid as a sociological and rhetorical genre. Trace and Dillon (2012) provide a thorough discussion of genre as representation communicative construct, coupled with an overview of the history of the American finding aid. While genre theory has frequently assumed that genres emerge slowly and without conscious examination, and then remain relatively stable, the authors note that the rapid analog-to-digital shift in documentation presents key opportunities: a chance to assess genre change deliberately, and a chance for purposeful modification of the form.

The latter is, of course, easier said than done. Trace and Dillon acknowledge that the finding aid as genre embodies the shared assumptions and practices of the archival profession; it is "perhaps the most canonical genre form" (p. 502), both as document type and symbol of the archivist's work. Two approaches to the paper-to-digital transformation represent different goals: (1) to mimic print forms to maintain stability for users and creators, and (2) to exploit new possibilities for improved exposure, discovery, and interaction. Understanding the finding aid in the light of genre theory, the authors argue, allows archival scholars to place the finding aid in context and to identify the relationships, expectations, and purposes that lie beneath its rhetorical form. These are not stable, especially in the print-to-digital setting. For the finding aid to be a useful communicative construct, we need to know more about the user behavior, information seeking, and current information practices in the archival setting. (See also Dancy, 2012, and Yeo, 2012a, for discussions of the historical background of the Canadian Rules for Archival Description and recommendations for change.)

Two other articles in the same issue examined archival sense making or meaning making. Bazerman (2012) poses his version of the ultimate question: "Are we on the way to doing away with texts and documents, left only with a non-hierarchical mega-server with a database of all information, to be queried with a universal interface?"

(p. 382). This, he avers, is unlikely, simply because the human user needs to make sense of the information, and, not so incidentally, the provenance, genre, activity context, and social and institutional structures around which the information arises and is used. The finding aid *as genre*, as a tool to orient the user to time, situation, and system, is fundamental to sense making (see also Mandell, 2013). Duff, Monks-Leeson, and Galey (2012), in a pilot study of archival meaning making by book history graduate students, asked their subjects to report on their use of finding aids. For some, a finding aid provided a useful frame for their investigation; for others, conversely, it was a constraint, steering them into a predetermined assessment. In fact, the authors concluded that finding aids contribute to meaning because of "their capacity to foreground certain connections and background others" (p. 85). However, the expectations routinely brought by users to their archival reference tools were not apparent in the diary and interview data collected in the study. For additional discussion, see Rhee (2012; genre repertoires in the records management setting) and MacNeil (2012; conceptualizing archival description as rhetorical genre).

One theme across the theoretically based literature was a call for critical reflexivity. Anderson (2012) analyzes the archival concept of a "record" as a sociocultural construct, proposing a shift from specific forms to "intentional, stable, semantic structure[s]" that are understood in social and technological contexts. Solberg (2012), in an article titled "Googling the Archive," raised the issue of the digital finding tool and its relationship to researcher positionality. Online keyword searches, Solberg opines, helped her to develop a more nuanced view of her subject, but digital technologies bring with them their own "structural biases and limitations for the scholarly work we deem important" (p. 66). Using several archival examples, she proposes that historians and other scholars should reflect on the role of digital technologies in the research process—if only to engage in the dialogue about future development and the needs and structures of academic libraries and archives.

What is at stake here? McCausland (2011) reviewed literature related to the impact of online finding aids and archival records access on users, archivists, and institutions. She summarized a number of issues previously noted by scholars, including the privileging of online content, the unfamiliarity of archival terminology to lay users, and the need for contextualization and reference guidance in finding aid use. In short, McCausland states, "It seems as if there are multiple conversations happening: one advising caution about abandoning mediation, one warning that access online needs to remember issues of sensitivity in the content of records, and another exploring and encouraging the potential for a different future for archival research in an online world" (p. 316). The final question: will the future of archival research be a disintermediated one? The author's answer is "not yet."

DESIGN AND USABILITY STUDIES

If the articles described above tended to conclude that more practical, user-centered analyses of finding aids would benefit archives and special collections, several others addressed the issue more directly. Hu (2012) provided an overview of usability assessment methods for online finding aid and web design. Beginning with a summary of the initial forays into usability testing in archives, she described heuristic evaluation techniques that are well established in other settings, but may not be familiar to archivists.

As Hu's article did not include a case study, the application of usability techniques to archival finding aids was left to other parties. DeRidder, Presnell, and Walker (2012) detailed the method they developed for linking digitized items into an Encoded Archival Description (EAD) finding aid. As demonstrated in the Septimus D. Cabaniss Papers digitization project, partially funded by the National Historical Publications and Records Commission (NHPRC), the authors developed scripts to add links to EAD records, to generate minimal Metadata Object Description Schema (MODS) records, and to upload scanned content to the web. By planning for access to the collection via the EAD finding aid rather than by item-level description, the expected cost and time savings were realized. DeRidder et al. also describe a subsequent usability study of twenty participants, looking at time on task and number of clicks for four known-item searches. The tasks were performed on both the Cabaniss EAD finding aid and a digitized item-level collection searchable through a search box. Somewhat surprisingly, the item-level collection required 35% less time to search and 48% fewer interactions than the Cabaniss collection, with more experienced special collections users having less difficulty with the finding aid interface, and novice special collections users having more difficulty with it. The usability study results, the authors conclude, indicated that their method of web delivery—at least at present—might be more suitable for scholars than for students.

Jackson (2012) reported the results of a usability study on digital finding aids from the North Carolina Collection Photographic Archives at the University of North Carolina at Chapel Hill. After a finding aid redesign that permitted links to digitized content, nine users participated in an eight-task search session. The study looked at the use of two search methods: the traditional "Find" command versus a new search box for digital content. As in the DeRidder et al. study, the level of user prior experience was relevant; users with some archival background found the finding aid text easy to use, and novices preferred searching via the digital content search box. None of the subjects rated the finding aids as "user-friendly."

In addition, the Jackson subjects were surveyed regarding their interest in proposed Web 2.0 features for archival finding aids; their level of interest in those features was low. Similarly, the use of Web 2.0 tools to improve the browsability of online archives catalogs was the subject of a study by Gresham and Higgins (2012). Only 17% of the seventy-nine catalogs reviewed at UK repositories used at least one of the Web 2.0 technologies studied (RSS feeds, tagging, social bookmarking, mashups, collaborative filtering, and user ratings or comments). Interviews with staff at three archives indicated that they took a fairly dim view of Web 2.0 tools, as they neither wished to maintain them nor to collect data on their use. See also

Meyerson, Galloway, and Bias (2012) regarding the operationalization of a user-centered design framework in archives.

Other studies in 2012 addressed finding aid design elements, running the gamut from improved flexibility and interactive capabilities to affective presentation (see, e.g., Anderson and Allen's wiki-based "Malleable Finding Aids"; Linge et al.'s mi-Guide, a multimedia museum and gallery guide for mobile devices; MacDonald, Park, and Chae's AMARA, a search system for online art collections using an embedded interactive agent). The goals of these projects were varied, but recurring elements included: increased adaptability in arrangement, incorporation of nonstandard contribution or annotation, an expanded definition of provenance, linked data and associated collections, and visualization. See also Daigle (2012), noting the benefits of digital technology in iterative uses of digital objects.

A preference for the use of a library catalog as an archival access tool, instead of a finding aid, was apparent in some case studies. These included Brenner, Larsen, and Weston's (2012) report on an adaptation of electronic resources management (ERM) for the Oregon Sustainable Community Digital Library—a collection of "key planning documents and reports, maps, and other ephemeral materials that have high value for Oregon citizens and for scholars around the world" (p. 67). The access tool for the collection was Portland State University Library's catalog, based on the rationale that patrons would be able to find the digitized original documents and other library materials simultaneously.

Finally, a finding aid is only useful and usable if it is accessible. LaBarre (2012), describing her own archival research at the American Society for Information Science & Technology (ASIS&T), noted the less-than-exemplary state of the organization's own online finding aid; it did not correspond to box contents at all. As LaBarre eventually discovered, the finding aid had been superseded by an updated version, but the latter had never been uploaded or placed in the physical backup of finding aids.

REVEALING THE INVISIBLE

Another common topic in the 2012 literature was the need to reveal the hidden role—be it physically or intellectually inaccessible collections—of cultural heritage and information professionals in describing, organizing, and presenting collections, or the heretofore neglected contribution of "cocreators." This topic had implications for archival understandings of provenance, processing, and, yes, promotion. As stated by Marty (2012), "Invisibility is a problem in particular for information professionals working in libraries, archives and museums, in part because the information profession is at its core a service industry. . . . [Its members] are happy if someone is simply using the resources they have created, and often the last things they think about are money, credit, and other economic realities" (p. 30).

Several articles in the September issue of *RBM: A Journal of Rare Books, Manuscripts and Cultural Heritage* discussed processing levels and description, including workflow and assessment issues (see Gustainis, 2012; Carter, 2012; Chapman & Yakel, 2012). Most relevant to the finding aid is Altermatt and Hilton's (2012) case study of the processing of the "hidden collection" of printed ephemera at New York University's Tamiment Library. The authors noted that the collection began as a partly processed agglomeration in file cabinets and boxes that was "wildly uncontrolled, largely inaccessible, and dauntingly repetitive" (p. 172). Print ephemera is often described at the item level or classified as vertical file material; neither approach was working at Tamiment. A National Endowment for the Humanities (NEH) grant allowed project staff to take an archival approach in organizing the material in aggregations (by organization, trade union, or subject), rather than at an item level. This allowed them to make the new aggregated "Printed Ephemera" collections available in less than twenty-four months via forty-four EAD finding aids posted online. Patron response was immediate; the collections are now among the most heavily used at Tamiment. Altermatt and Hilton concluded that the inclusion of printed ephemera in finding aids both streamlined processing and made the material much more accessible. In the same issue, Fell (2012) described a project to create bibliographic records for Yale University's cartographic materials, improving access and security while also identifying and describing rare and unique items.

Issues of nonprofessional participants in description, and the ways in which stakeholders could add depth and dynamism to cultural heritage collections, were treated in several articles over the year. Of course, the potential impacts on standards of provenance and authority control were part of the conversation as well. As set out by Zhang (2012a), archival description traditionally includes source (provenance), order of organization (hierarchy), and additional access points (archival content). In her examination of three digital archival collections, Zhang noted that this traditional configuration appears to be changing; for example, access points may be independent of the representation of archival order, and hierarchical order may be replaced by content-oriented access. She described the faceted representation of two of the collections as "a variety of virtual series," rather than the traditional finding aid's representation of the physical order of a collection. This makes records more accessible to users, but it also decontextualizes (and thus, potentially devalues) them.

The theme persists through much of the archival literature of 2012: do the benefits of user access and participation outweigh the costs to archival evidentiary and contextual principles? Gilliland (2012) discussed the ethical responsibility of archivists to pursue descriptive mechanisms to represent the needs and concerns of both creator and cocreator (the latter encompassing those involved in the creation of the record as contributors, subjects, victims, or legatees). This violates the traditional principles of provenance, but, as Gilliland details, several expanded conceptualizations (e.g., "functional provenance," "multiple provenance") have provided room for the acknowledgment of cocreators. Developments in archival theory, including the "community of records" model and the potential for metadata to document plural relationships, have challenged conventions of archival description. The author references the Aboriginal and Torres Strait Islander Data Archive (ATSIDA), a multisite archive that is based on indigenous protocols and supports additional forms of descriptive access. However, the archive also poses challenges in dealing with diversity, cultural nuance, and consultation. For other recent discussions of the changing definition of provenance, see Bunn, 2013; Groth, Gil, Cheney, and Miles, 2012; Wells, 2012; Lehane, 2012; Zhang, 2012a, 2012b; White, 2012.

In the museum setting, Stein (2012) discussed the effects of the rise of public participation on the museum professional's work, noting the "immense and potentially seismic issues" the institutions will face. In order to embrace typically marginalized "non-audiences," a level of commitment and collaboration is vital. Cairns (2013) looked at the role of folksonomies in the museum setting as a potential bridge between expert and nonexpert, creator and cocreator, and static catalog and "living historical document." Again, the direct engagement of the user with digital collection records is contrary to established curatorial practice. Cairns notes that "whenever the museum uses hierarchical classifications to provide object interpretations that align with its own curatorial knowledgebase, the opacity of the institutional voice will be maintained" (p. 116). Conversely, interaction will promote diverse responses, engagement, complexity—and, yes, messiness. The transition, as Cairns acknowledges, will be "uncomfortable."

Folksonomies, tagging, and participatory cataloging as tools to increase accessibility were also explored by Flanagan and Carini (2012) in their pilot study of the Metadata Games software system; Newman (2012), in his discussion of the Mandeville Legacy Project and the Revisiting Archive Collections (RAC) cataloging methodology; and Nodler (2012) in an examination of the particular challenge of access to museum video archives and the potential for emerging tools involving crowdsourcing to ameliorate the problems. Caron and Kellerhals (2012) added a caution to the discussion, noting that archives are also facing their own information overload via a "memory politics" supporting the preservation of more and more documentary evidence in the interests of representations of diversity. Finally, Eveleigh's (2012) review of participatory archives and crowdsourcing projects in archives concluded that "whilst the Archival Commons remains a source of inspiration, it seems current practice is more constrained by organisational reality" (p. 4).

All of the above may operate in tandem with a "more product, less process" (MPLP) approach to description: more large-scale digitization projects that are "based on the MPLP-oriented belief that it is in the best interests of users to have less detailed access to more content" (Sutton, 2012, p. 53). Sutton's recommendation is moderation; archives and special collections need to avoid a project-by-project approach, but they also need to avoid inflexible standards for all phases of the digitization process.

A second article by Zhang (2012b) on digital archival representation also advocated a balanced approach. Based on a discussion of the ethical responsibilities of the archivist—which, she noted, are codified in vague and general terms—she set out several approaches to the traditional finding aid/metadata–driven access dilemma. First, archivists can "embed" metadata below the surface of their main access interface (the finding aid), thus keeping it hidden; they can use multifaceted metadata as the main access tool, and effectively "segregate" the finding aid (and context) by making it available by a link; they can run "parallel" representational systems, each suitable for different user groups (an example being the California Digital Library's parallel sites: the Online Archive of California (OAC) for researchers, and Calisphere for K–12 use); and they can, somehow, bring the two together. It is a knotty problem, but, to Zhang, a vitally important one:

> To obtain the status of relevancy in the digital world, archivists cannot afford an "all context and no content" or "more context and less content" approach. The issue may become so crucial with an ethical dimension that requires careful deliberation to maintain the balance—going to the extreme of either direction would be doing harm to the profession. There would be no archival profession without an appropriate control of archival context, and there would be no future of archival profession if no effective effort could be made to optimize access to digital content in digital archival collections. (p. 338)

How will this work on a practical level? Zhang concludes that archivists have an ethical obligation to make their descriptive systems more inclusive of descriptive metadata, and to do so at the item level; this is both integral information and what future users will depend upon to locate what they need. See also Beaudoin (2012a, 2012b), describing an exhaustive framework for cultural objects across eight dimensions: technical, utilization, physical, intangible, curatorial, authentication, authorization, and intellectual.

Bak (2012) also makes a case for the item-level management of electronic records as a way of capturing typical Web 2.0 uses of material in an archival system. The resulting accretion of metadata "would underwrite a much more sophisticated understanding of records use and repurposing" (p. 313), and, in turn, support improved user service. Resource discovery at the item level could be user driven through a combination of full-text searching and metadata manipulation, thus obviating the need for a single mandatory means of access. Archivists would maintain control of records in the aggregate and manage the necessary technical and preservation metadata; then, as Bak puts it, "archives will escape the metaphor of the lifecycle, no longer saddled with dead records, frozen as if by rigor mortis into particular configurations and presented to the public like fish on the fishmonger's slab—salmon here, trout there" (p. 315). Of course, Bak also admits that supporting item-level data accumulation would be "neither cheap nor easy."

ABOVE AND BEYOND THE COLLECTION

The finalization of the Functional Requirements for Bibliographic Records (FRBR), its companion documents, and the Resource Description and Access (RDA) standards in the realm of library description drew the attention of cultural heritage scholars as well. The goal of placing bibliographic data from all sources in a linked data network is appealing, as it promotes sharing and enriching data, as well as reducing duplication of effort. However, as Nimer and Daines (2013) note, FRBR states that it may be used with archival materials, but it presents some difficulties in practice; further, multiple standards for manuscript collections, rare books, and photograph collections complicate the mix. Thus "institutional decisions on how to implement the standards often depend on user needs, potentially placing them at odds with efforts to improve the interchange of standardized descriptions" (p. 547).

In some instances the "discovery" of cultural heritage collections moves away from the home repository entirely. Hogsden and Poulter (2012) used examples of projects at the University of Cambridge Museum of Archaeology & Anthropology and the British Museum to illustrate the benefits of a digital contact network in which ownership and control of content remains with each location, but reciprocal links provide a platform for engagement. While the unique properties of the physical objects are absent, there are some benefits to the digital encounter (i.e., the absence of the frame of an institutional display). Interaction with digital museum objects is not "better" or "worse," the authors argue; instead, they can be active and transformative in their own ways.

Europeana (http://www.europeana.eu/portal/) and the Europeana data model (EDM) were referenced in a number of sources dealing with access issues. A discussion of Europeana, which is intended to be a single access point for European digital culture, is beyond the scope of this article (see Peroni, Tomasi, & Vitali, 2012; Agenjo, Hernández, & Viedma, 2012; and Casarosa, Meghini, & Gardasevic, 2012, stating flatly, "The use of online finding aids has proved to be too complicated for non-specialists," p. 153). However, a few details are worth stating here. Ivacs (2012) noted some areas for improvement:

> Current digital library technologies applied in project HOPE—and in many similar ones funded by the European Union—tend to take the "union catalogue" approach by relying on aggregator services to provide data to different portals including the centralized cultural heritage site, such as Europeana. More precisely, this means that digital content and data curation happens locally, and the portal only displays a limited set of information to describe the digital object without showing the archival finding aid and related information about where the digital object resides in the highly complex archival hierarchy. Moreover, Europeana stores the harvested metadata in various languages in a standardized format, but no requirements exist to provide parallel, multilingual bibliographic records in favour of cross domain searching. (p. 492)

As Zhang (2012b) noted, "Archival hierarchical structure and digital descriptive metadata are representation systems of a different nature that may be difficult to accommodate each other" (p. 337). Europeana is still attempting to work out this dilemma (its Task Force on Hierarchical Objects published a report in 2012). See also, among others, Kilkki, Hupaniittu, and Henttonen (2012) regarding new Finnish rules for archival description (which are based on parallel provenance); the authors note the influence of Europeana, the shared interface, and open linked data as the future of information services.

New rules and realities for archival description were explored in several other articles. An issue of *Archivaria* was devoted to arrangement and description; it included Dancy's (2012) examination of the Canadian Rules for Archival Description (RAD), several case studies, and Yeo's (2012b) article on aggregate records in the digital age. Yeo adopts Weinberger's "third order" trope, which is shorthand for the ability of the user to arrange resources in any sequence desired, without the limitations of analog systems. As is apparent in other discussions, the third order is unsettling to archivists. Multiple representations have, however, become the de facto norm, and the series as a single definitive aggregation is moot. Still, Yeo recognizes the value of the traditional finding aid, noting that "some cultural critics have envisaged a kind of techno-utopia where archival materials can be retrieved and examined without verbal labels or semantic indexing. Their dream is of the computer as a transparent medium, providing unmediated access to 'texts' unsullied by curatorial intervention or the forces of hegemony" (p. 86). This, he argues, is impractical and unrealistic. The finding aid as we know it may have deficiencies, but it is still the best way to provide indications of the scope, significance, and appropriate research use of a collection. While new tools built on multidimensional relational models may be a solution, their benefits will only be known when they are widely available.

One of the new tools may be the archival use of digital forensics. Lee, Chassanoff, Woods, Kirschenbaum, and Olsen (2012) described the BitCurator Project developed at the University of North Carolina at Chapel Hill that incorporates digital forensic tools into a repository's digital collections workflow. BitCurator could, the authors note, support "properly mediated" public access to forensically acquired data, at a user-controlled level of granularity. Knight (2012) discussed the use of digital forensics in handling donated personal digital collections. As Yeo stated, the wider utility of these tools is yet to be determined.

CONCLUSION

The literature of the finding aid in 2012 reflected very real concerns about the role of the archivist, the significance of the finding aid, and the notion—assumed or explicit—of the replacement of either or both by metadata-driven and systems-oriented tools. This goes to the heart of archival representation as we know it. As Morgan, Smith, and Evans (2012) asked, "Are our finding aids documents to be read from start to end, or are they databases to search and explore from any entry point?" (p. 7). Are we prepared for the consequences of an adherence to either approach, or can we find a middle ground that holds the advantages of both?

To say that the finding aid is entering a transitional phase is to state the obvious. Many archivists appear to be eager to embrace the possibilities, though a note of caution is usually present. There are intriguing ideas, not yet fully realized; there are also pitfalls, the worst of which show up in association with rallying calls to prepare for dramatic and dangerous change. The good news is that discussion, assessment, and planning is going forward within the profession. The new life—or lives—of the finding aid are undetermined at this point, but if the literature on the subject in 2012 is any indication, archivists fully intend to be involved in coming up with sound and realistic solutions.

REFERENCES

Agenjo, X., Hernández, F., & Viedma, A. (2012). Data aggregation and dissemination of authority records through linked open data in a European context. *Cataloging & Classification Quarterly, 50*(8), 803–829. doi: 10.1080/01639374.2012.711441

Altermatt, R., & Hilton, A. (2012). Hidden collections within hidden collections: Providing access to printed ephemera. *American Archivist, 75*(1), 171–194.

Anderson, K. (2012). The footprint and the stepping foot: Archival records, evidence, and time. *Archival Science*, 1–23. Advance online publication. doi: 10.1007/s10502-012-9193-2

Anderson, S. R., & Allen, R. B. (2012). Malleable finding aids. In P. Zaphiris, G. Buchanan, E. Rasmussen, & F. Loizides (Eds.), *Theory and practice of digital libraries: Proceedings, second international conference, TPDL 2012* (pp. 402–407). Berlin, Germany: Springer.

Bak, G. (2012). Continuous classification: Capturing dynamic relationships among information resources. *Archival Science, 12*(3), 287–318.

Bazerman, C. (2012). The orders of documents, the orders of activity, and the orders of information. *Archival Science, 12*(4), 377–388.

Beaudoin, J. E. (2012a). Context and its role in the digital preservation of cultural objects. *D-Lib Magazine, 18*(11/12). Retrieved from http://www.dlib.org/dlib/november12/beaudoin/11beaudoin1.html

Beaudoin, J. E. (2012b). A framework for contextual metadata used in the digital preservation of cultural objects. *D-Lib Magazine, 18*(11/12). Retrieved from http://www.dlib.org/dlib/november12/beaudoin/11beaudoin2.html

Brenner, M., Larsen, T., & Weston, C. (2012). *Digital collection management through the library catalog.* Retrieved from http://www.ala.org/lita/ital/sites/ala.org.lita.ital/files/content/25/2/brenner.pdf

Bunn, J. (2013). Questioning autonomy: An alternative perspective on the principles which govern archival description. *Archival Science*, 1–13. Advance online publication. doi: 10.1007/s10502-013-9200-2

Cairns, S. (2013). Mutualizing museum knowledge: Folksonomies and the changing shape of expertise. *Curator, 56*(1), 107–119.

Caron, D. J., & Kellerhals, A. (2012). Archiving for self-ascertainment, identity-building and permanent self-questioning: Archives between scepticism and certitude. *Archival Science*, 1–10. Advance online publication. doi: 10.1007/s10502-012-9189-y

Carter, L. R. (2012). Articulating value: Building a culture of assessment in special collections. *RBM: A Journal of Rare Books, Manuscripts and Cultural Heritage, 13*(2), 89–99.

Casarosa, V., Meghini, C., & Gardasevic, S. (2012). Improving online access to archival data. In M. Agosti, F. Esposito, S. Ferilli, & N. Ferro (Eds.), *Digital libraries and archives: 8th Italian research conference, IRCDL 2012* (pp. 153–162). Berlin, Germany: Springer.

Chapman, J., & Yakel, E. (2012). Data-driven management and interoperable metrics for special collections and archives user services. *RBM: A Journal of Rare Books, Manuscripts and Cultural Heritage, 13*(2), 129–151.

Daigle, B. J. (2012). The digital transformation of special collections. *Journal of Library Administration, 52*(3–4), 244–264.

Dancy, R. (2012). RAD past, present, and future. *Archivaria, 74*, 7–41.

DeRidder, J. L., Presnell, A. A., & Walker, K. W. (2012). Leveraging encoded archival description for access to digital content: A cost and usability analysis. *American Archivist, 75*(1), 143–170.

Duff, W. M., Monks-Leeson, E., Galey, A. (2012). Contexts built and found: A pilot study on the process of archival meaning-making. *Archival Science, 12*(1), 69–92. doi: 10.1007/s10502-011-9145-2

Europeana Task Force on Hierarchical Objects. (2012). *Recommendations for the representation of hierarchical objects in Europeana.* Retrieved from http://pro.europeana.eu/documents/468623/4a6eb2ec-4cc6-48b1-8824-92a1e564a279

Eveleigh, A. (2012). Welcoming the world: An exploration of participatory archives. Paper presented at the International Council on Archives Congress, Brisbane, Australia. Retrieved from http://www.ica2012.com/files/pdf/Full%20papers%20upload/ica12Final00128.pdf

Fell, T. (2012). Maps as special collections: Bibliographic control of hidden material at Yale University. *RBM: A Journal of Rare Books, Manuscripts and Cultural Heritage, 13*(1), 27–37.

Flanagan, M., & Carini, P. (2012, Fall/Winter). How games can help us access and understand archival images. *American Archivist, 75*(2), 514–537.

Gilliland, A. J. (2012). Contemplating co-creator rights in archival description. *Knowledge Organization, 39*(5), 340–346.

Gresham, E., & Higgins, S. (2012). Improving browsability of archive catalogues using Web 2.0. *Library Review, 61*(5), 309–326.

Groth, P., Gil, Y., Cheney, J., & Miles, S. (2012). Requirements for provenance on the web. *International Journal of Digital Curation, 7*(1), 39–56. Retrieved from http://www.ijdc.net/index.php/ijdc/article/view/203

Gustainis, E. R. N. (2012). Processing workflow analysis for special collections: The Center for the History of Medicine, Francis A. Countway Library of Medicine as case study. *RBM: A Journal of Rare Books, Manuscripts and Cultural Heritage, 13*(2), 113–128.

Hogsden, C., & Poulter, E. K. (2012). The real other? Museum objects in digital contact networks. *Journal of Material Culture, 17*(3), 265–286.

Hu, R. (2012). Methods to tame the madness: A practitioner's guide to user assessment techniques for online finding aid and website design. *RBM: A Journal of Rare Books, Manuscripts and Cultural Heritage, 13*(2), 175–190.

Ivacs, G. (2012). The pervasiveness of archives. *LEA—Lingue e letterature d'Oriente e d'Occidente, 1*(1), 468–497.

Jackson, T. M. (2012). I want to see it: A usability study of digital content integrated into finding aids. *Journal for the Society of North Carolina Archivists, 9*(2), 20–77.

Kilkki, J., Hupanittu, O., & Henttonen, P. (2012, August). *Towards the new era of archival description—the Finnish approach.* Paper presented at the International Council on Archives Congress, Brisbane, Australia. Retrieved from http://www.ica2012.com/files/data/Full%20papers%20upload/ica12Final00361.pdf

Knight, G. (2012). The forensic curator: Digital forensics as a solution to addressing the curatorial challenges posed by personal digital archives. *The International Journal of Digital Curation, 7*(2), 40–63.

LaBarre, K. (2012). Spelunking in the archives: Or how I learned to love the art of the unexpected. *Bulletin of the American Society for Information Science and Technology, 39*(1), 32–34.

Lee, C. A., Chassanoff, A., Woods, K., Kirschenbaum, M., & Olsen, P. (2012). BitCurator: Tools and techniques for digital forensics in collecting institutions. *D-Lib Magazine*, *18*(5/6). Retrieved from http://dlib.org/dlib/may12/lee/05lee.html

Lehane, R. (2012). Documenting sites of creation. *Archives and Manuscripts*, *40*(3), 171–180.

Linge, N., Bates, D., Booth, K., Parsons, D., Heatley, L., Webb, P., & Holgate, R. (2012). Realising the potential of multimedia visitor guides: Practical experiences of developing mi-Guide. *Museum Management and Curatorship*, *27*(1), 67–82.

MacDonald, C. M., Park, S. J., & Chae, G. H. (2012). AMARA: An affective agent to enhance users' enjoyment and engagement with online art collections. In *Proceedings of the Association for Information Science & Technology Annual Meeting (ASIS&T 2012)* (pp. 1–4). Hoboken, NJ: Wiley. doi: 10.1002/meet.14504901303

MacNeil, H. (2012). What finding aids do: Archival description as rhetorical genre in traditional and web-based environments. *Archival Science*, *12*(4), 485–500.

Mandell, L. (2013). Digitizing the archive: The necessity of an "early modern" period. *The Journal for Early Modern Cultural Studies*, *13*(2), 83–92.

Marty, P. F. (2012). Unintended consequences: Unlimited access, invisible work and the future of the information profession in cultural heritage organizations. *Bulletin of the American Society for Information Science and Technology*, *38*(3), 27–31.

McCausland, S. (2011, December). A future without mediation? Online access, archivists, and the future of archival research. *Australian Academic & Research Libraries*, *42*(4), 309–319.

Meyerson, J., Galloway, P., & Bias, R. (2012). Improving the user experience of professional researchers: Applying a user-centered design framework in archival repositories. In *Proceedings of the Association for Information Science & Technology Annual Meeting (ASIS&T 2012)* (pp. 1–7). Hoboken, NJ: Wiley. doi: 10.1002/meet.14504901208

Morgan, H., Smith, A., & Evans, J. (2012, August). *Standing the test of time: Building better resilience into online archival descriptive networks*. Paper presented at International Council on Archives Congress, Brisbane, Australia. Retrieved from http://www.ica2012.com/files/pdf/Full%20papers%20upload/ica12Final00185.pdf

Newman, J. (2012). Revisiting archive collections: Developing models for participatory cataloguing. *Journal of the Society of Archivists*, *33*(1), 57–73.

Nimer, C. L., & Daines, J. G., III (2013). The development and application of U.S. descriptive standards for archives, historical manuscripts, and rare books. *Cataloging & Classification Quarterly*, *51*(5), 532–549.

Nodler, H. (2012). A haystack full of needles: Scholarly access challenges in museum video archives. *Bulletin of the American Society for Information Science and Technology*, *38*(3), 32–37.

Peroni, S., Tomasi, F., & Vitali, F. (2012). Reflecting on the Europeana Data Model. In M. Agosti, F. Esposito, S. Ferilli, & N. Ferro (Eds.), *Digital libraries and archives: 8th Italian research conference, IRCDL 2012* (pp. 228–240). Berlin, Germany: Springer.

Rhee, H. (2012). Genres and genre repertoires of user and use information sources in U.S. state archival and records management appraisal practice. *Archival Science*, *12*(4), 461–483. doi: 10.1007/s10502-012-9176-3

Solberg, J. (2012). Googling the archive: Digital tools and the practice of history. *Advances in the History of Rhetoric*, *15*(1), 53–76.

Stein, R. (2012). Chiming in on museums and participatory culture. *Curator*, *55*(2), 215–226.

Sutton, S. C. (2012). Balancing boutique-level quality and large-scale production: The impact of "More Product, Less Process" on digitization in archives and special collections. *RBM: A Journal of Rare Books, Manuscripts and Cultural Heritage*, *13*(1), 50–63.

Trace, C. B., & Dillon, A. (2012). The evolution of the finding aid in the United States: From physical to digital document genre. *Archival Science*, *12*(4), 501–519.

Wells, E. (2012). Related material: The arrangement and description of family papers. *Journal of the Society of Archivists*, *33*(2), 167–184.

White, S. (2012). Crippling the archives: Negotiating notions of disability in appraisal and arrangement and description. *American Archivist*, *75*(1), 109–124.

Yeo, G. (2012a). The conceptual fonds and the physical collection. *Archivaria*, *73*, 43–80.

Yeo, G. (2012b). Bringing things together: Aggregate records in a digital age. *Archivaria*, *74*, 43–91.

Zhang, J. (2012a). Archival representation in the digital age. *Journal of Archival Organization*, *10*(1), 45–68.

Zhang, J. (2012b). Archival context, digital content, and the ethics of digital archival representation. *Knowledge Organization*, *39*(5), 332–339.

15

If You Build It, Will They Come?

A Review of Digital Collection User Studies

Ashley Todd-Diaz and Sheila O'Hare

ABSTRACT

As more and more cultural institutions have begun curating digital collections, it is a priority to examine how users are interacting with digital objects. Recent scholarship has focused on data (e.g., web analytics, use statistics, number of citations) and user feedback to gauge how often users are accessing digital collections and to what extent they are using the objects—considering that viewing, downloading, and citing are all different activities. This article reviews studies focusing on digital collection use in practice published in 2012. Generally, access and use numbers appeared to be fairly low. However, results also uncovered intriguing trends, including the impact of promotion and collection location on number of views and citations of digital materials in historical research over the last decade. The challenges still confronting the accessibility and usability of digital collections are explored.

INTRODUCTION

As technology has developed and advanced, moving society toward a mobile culture focused around concepts of accessibility, immediacy, and user interaction, more and more cultural heritage institutions have begun curating digital collections. However, in rushing to create these collections and make digital objects available, many institutions have overlooked the important processes of reflecting on and evaluating use and accessibility. It has now become a priority to examine how users interact with digital collections, either by browsing and viewing objects or incorporating them into their research. Recent scholarship has focused on quantitative data (e.g., web analytics, use statistics, number of citations), as well as qualitative user feedback (e.g., survey responses, and social tags) to gauge how often users are viewing, downloading, and citing digital collections. Despite a wide range of techniques that examine different aspects of use and activity, a consistent result among studies is low overall usage of collections with a few spikes for specific objects. Research has also helped identify areas that are influencing use both positively and negatively, including the degree of promotion, collection location, and the promise of increased accessibility.

This article reviews literature and studies focusing on digital collection use in practice published in 2012. It is broken into four sections to compare various aspects of the studies more closely. The first section examines the range of qualitative and quantitative methods currently employed to track and evaluate user activity. The second section analyzes the studies' results to identify the users and their behavior, as well as the effects promotion and location have on use. The third section focuses on some of the challenges still confronting accessibility and usability. Finally, we discuss suggestions and reflections resulting from the studies to improve accessibility and increase use in the future.

USER STUDIES: MANY METHODS

For almost twenty years a primary motivation for establishing digital collections has been increased accessibility and use (Gorny & Mazurek, 2012; Gracy, 2012; Harkema & Nygren, 2012; Heradio, Fernandez-Amoros, Cabrerizo, & Herrera-Viedma, 2012; Petrelli & Clough, 2012; Sinn, 2012; van Vliet & Hekman, 2012). In turn, as researchers and scholars become accustomed to increased accessibility, they expect more resources will be available digitally (Ellis & Callahan, 2012; Heradio et al., 2012; Smith & Rowley, 2012; Southwell & Slater, 2102). In theory, by providing digital access free from restraints of distance, staffing, and time of day, it can be reasoned that use would be expected to also increase. However, in the current environment of tighter budgets and limited resources, a greater emphasis is being placed on assessment and evaluation to determine whether this assumption is accurate and users are satisfied with the end products (Eccles, Thelwall, & Meyer, 2012; Hughes, 2012; Schlosser & Stamper, 2012). Within the last year a number of studies have been conducted to take a closer look at the use of digital collections. Since use can be defined in a number of ways, including browsing through digital objects, the equivalent of visiting a library, archives, or museum to view a traditional collection; downloading an object, the equivalent of receiving photocopies or scans of a physical item; and citing an object or collection in a scholarly work—there are different ways to approach the analysis.

Web Analytics

Web analytics is the collection and analysis of data pertaining to how a particular website or web page is accessed and used, including how often a site or page is viewed, how long a visitor stays on the site/page, how they arrived at the site/page, and which links are clicked. This method can also provide much of the same information collected when a patron visits a traditional library, archives, or museum, including how many patrons are new or returning, where they are from, and what objects they are accessing. Considering that there are many free programs that will track and report web analytics automatically, this is an easy, low-effort, and cost-effective way to collect data.

Schlosser and Stamper (2012) utilized this method when evaluating the use of a digital photograph collection posted in both Ohio State University's institutional repository and a media sharing site. Using statistics provided by the repository's software, they tracked both page views and downloads for individual items to generate a history of use and determine which platform received more activity. Other institutions utilized Google Analytics to monitor activity within web pages; however, although this software is free and easy to access, it also has limitations (Ellis & Callahan, 2012; Hess, 2012). Hess (2012) used Google Analytics to study user behavior at the Illinois Harvest Portal. Hess observed two shortfalls: the program's failure to track (1) the activity of links to external sites, (2) and object downloads. To remedy these problems, he enabled event tracking to monitor these types of activities, as well as "site search," to track how users were navigating and searching the digital collection site and better discern trends in their behavior.

Eccles, Thelwall, and Meyer (2012) took another approach to studying usage data generated by online activity. They studied the use and impact of five prominent digital collections by utilizing webometrics to conduct a comparative link analysis, through which they examined and compared links to each of the primary sites with those of comparable sites.[1] Webometric Analyst (Statistical Cybermetrics Research Group, 2013), their program of choice, collects data via search engines to analyze and create reports about the impact of websites, documents, and search terms across the Internet. Their results indicated this method was useful in determining how widely a particular collection is promoted and supported by observing the amount and breadth of URLs and domains contributing links to the collection. Webometrics provided a more distanced view of use by studying how users and fellow institutions are referring users to a site. Although on the one hand this represented the network of institutions that are assisting one another to gain user awareness, it can also be used to form an approximate idea of user support for a particular collection through the *type* of link that is used. For example, Eccles et al. (2012) noted links to the full URL displayed in the browser window suggest a user generated them by copying and pasting the page's URL. Although this only provided a projected idea of user activity founded on behavioral assumptions, it offered another viewpoint from which to observe use.

Citation Analysis

Citation analysis is a more labor-intensive method of evaluation, but one that provides a more precise and deeper understanding of exactly which digital objects are being used for scholarly activities. Sinn (2012) approached the question of use by conducting a citation analysis to examine how frequently digital collections have been used within historic research over the decade. She reviewed issues of *American Historical Review* published between 2001 and 2010 and tracked the types and frequency of cited resources. Harris and Hepburn (2012) conducted a similar citation analysis focusing on the frequency of digital images included in historical research articles between 2000 and 2009. They reviewed five peer-reviewed, core journals rated as having the largest impact on the history field and seven peer-reviewed, open access journals to compare the differences between print and online journals.[2]

User Feedback

Although quantitative data has the benefit of being objective and straightforward, it lacks the depth of human insight. Fletcher and Lee's (2012) study of social media use among museums noted that while analytics and use statistics provide evidence of activity and use, they do not tell us if users' experiences are meaningful. User feedback offers a qualitative dimension of use that analytical data simply does not possess; however, the tradeoff is that the researcher is dependent on users to provide that insight, whereas analytical data is collected automatically without user effort.

Gorny and Mazurek (2012) pursued user feedback by developing a survey to collect information about Polish digital library users. In Poland, digital libraries contain a wide range of textual documents, including books as well as historic ephemera and records, which are often difficult to access in analog form. The survey, which collected information about demographics, what materials are being used, and what the motivations are to use the collections, was placed on all thirty-one Polish digital library websites for three months to target users as they conducted their normal activities. Ross, Terras, and Motyckova (2012) also conducted a survey to gain a better understanding of user activity and experience with the British Museum's Collection Database Online. They used SurveyMonkey software to develop the survey and deployed it as a pop-up survey on the collection's website for one month. This method allowed them to present the survey to a random sample of users.

Social tagging presented another opportunity to examine user activity within digital collections. Within the last decade, social tagging has become an accepted way for cultural institutions to engage users by asking for their assistance to interact with and describe objects. Although it is a practice that carries with it potential downsides, including the risk of inappropriate or overly personalized tags being added to items or the loss of authority control, it offers the benefits of sharing a common feature with other social media sites, emphasizes user-interaction, and has the potential to increase accessibility and retrieval by adding new perspectives to metadata (Ercegovac, 2012; Flanagan & Carini, 2012). Considering that users must access digital objects to tag them, examining social tagging activity within a digital collection is another way to view evidence of use. Van Vliet and Hekman (2012) and Petek (2012) conducted studies of social tagging as interaction with cultural collections.

Evaluating user comments and reviews was also a source of information about user activity. Mitchell and Suchy's (2012) study of mobile access to digital collections revealed that institutions were eager to assess users' experiences and overall opinion of their mobile apps. One institution the authors interviewed developed a built-in feedback feature to help users communicate their thoughts and suggestions, but they reported only a few users had taken advantage of it. Instead the institution noted that it received more feedback through user comments and ratings submitted through the Apple App Store, where its app is available.

MULTIPLE ANGLES, CONSISTENT THEMES, AND PARALLEL RESULTS

A Pattern of Low Usage

Regardless of the method of study chosen, the results the authors reported were relatively similar; suggesting that overall use of digital collections was fairly low. Schlosser and Stamper's (2012) web analytics indicated that the digital materials chosen for their study were rarely viewed. The data also revealed that there was no significant difference between the number of times users viewed objects or downloaded them (five to thirty-eight views per item, versus five to thirty-four downloads per item). The low rate of downloads could indicate users are either casually browsing or are not locating materials of long-term usefulness; however, the fact that object views are also low suggests that overall discoverability of the collection is limited and reducing access. Likewise, Hess's (2012) study reported that the majority of digital materials in the Illinois Harvest Portal were never viewed or downloaded. He also noted the site search tracker revealed users rarely utilized the site search function and instead accessed the collection from external search engines, the catalog, or direct in-links to object pages. This suggests that while users are discovering specific individual digital materials, the overall digital collection is not recognized. Discoverability also seemed to be a factor within the Eccles et al. (2012) study. Their data revealed a low rate of link creation for each of the primary digital collections examined, ranging from 16 to 187 URLs and 14 to147 domains over the six-month study period. The results of Sinn's (2012) study reflected a low frequency of citations for digital collections within history articles. Her data showed that while all of the articles she examined contained citations for secondary resources (86.83% of all citations) and 49% contained citations for archival resources (10.54% of all citations), only 17% cited digital objects (.39% of all citations). Likewise, Harris and Hepburn's (2012) analysis of digital images showed no increase or decrease in the inclusion of digital images between 2000 and 2009, despite the considerable increase in availability of digital images over that time period. In fact, they found that use of digital images in core, print journals remained steadier throughout the decade (36.19% in 2008 to 48.48% in 2000) than the use of images in open-access, born-digital journals (4.17% in 2009 to 26.32% in 2002). Harris and Hepburn attributed these results to the possibility that historians are not finding the images they require digitally. This is not to say that these collections do not exist, but rather that a lack of awareness and discoverability of specific collections is keeping useful materials hidden from potential users.

A Few Spikes

Not all results followed this trend; some data reinforced the expectation that users are accessing and becoming more comfortable with digital collections. Hess's (2012) Google Analytics data showed the Illinois Harvest Portal received 15,000 unique visitors over a six-month period, yet the event tracker revealed most of the use was restricted to specific objects within the collection. He observed that the most-viewed pages were object-landing pages, with individual number of views ranging from 270 to 219. Comparing these spikes of usage with the previously discussed lack of usage, Hess noted that further evaluation will be conducted of user behavior to determine if a collection's size affects how users navigate through it and successfully locate objects.

Sinn's (2012) citation analysis revealed a promising trend through the rise of citations for digital objects between 2006 and 2010. Of the 138 digital objects that were cited, 122 appeared within the latter five years of the study and 82 within the final year. This indicates that although historians still rely very heavily on secondary resources and to a lesser, though consistent, extent on archival materials, digital materials are becoming more common and are steadily gaining acceptance as time progresses.

Van Vliet and Hekman's (2012) study offered another positive set of results. Over the course of one year of social tagging, they witnessed nearly three thousand six hundred tags made by 935 users regarding all objects in the study (379). Of those, nearly one thousand nine hundred were unique tags. Data revealed the average user added thirteen tags and spent approximately 13.5 minutes on the site. While van Vliet and Hekman did not directly address the topic of general usage, their study of how users interact with social tagging directly reflects evidence of use. Although the digital collection examined was constructed for the purposes of the study and only contained 379 objects, the fact that all objects were accessed and tagged reveals a high level of engagement and dedication among users. This could be attributed to the structured nature of the study, but it may also be a reflection of users' positive response to the interactive nature of social tagging. Harkema and Nygren (2012) point out that in today's technology-driven world where information is everywhere, cultural institutions need to be highly aware of how users interact with information and what attracts them. They asserted, "Many of the activities commonly associated with the information age blur the line between work and play" (p. 2), so keeping an interface familiar, interactive, and inviting may assist in providing the user with a positive, active experience.

Who Are the Users?

The ability to identify users of digital collections varied, based on how the studies were conducted. As one would expect, the studies using web analytics were not able to collect much data relating to specific users. Eccles et al. (2012) examined the links' domain and country of origin to discern broad trends in what user groups were accessing and promoting various digital collections. They noted that webometrics provides insight into what types of domains were utilizing the collections; for example, a high amount of ac.uk domains revealed a following among the British academic community, while a high amount of .edu domains indicated a strong user base in the American academic community. Their results also revealed certain collections had gained a presence within the blogging community based on links to the sites, which promoted the use of particular collections.

In the studies that took a more active role in collecting data from users, the researcher often targeted specific user groups. Harris and Hepburn (2012) and Sinn's (2012) studies focused on academic use of digital collections, specifically within the history discipline. Van Vliet and Hekman (2012) opened their study to the public, but also specifically directed solicitations to students, professors, and museum staff.

Alternatively, Gorny and Mazurek (2012) and Ross et al.'s (2012) surveys targeted all users of specific digital collections, the prior allowing all users to decide if they wanted to participate and the latter offering random users the opportunity to participate. Gorny and Mazurek received 964 responses over a three-month period. Their results revealed that approximately half of the users self-identified as members of academia: students (20%), academic researchers (17%), teachers (7%), school pupils (2%). The other 54% of respondents identified as belonging to "other professions;" the largest subgroup in that category was "non-workers" (18%), including retirees, housewives, and unemployed people. The results showed that nearly 60% of respondents used the digital collections for research into local history or genealogy. By far the majority of users (89%) lived in Poland, about half of whom lived in cities with populations of one hundred thousand or more. These responses provide clear usage trends for the Polish digital libraries, suggesting a primary group of users who belong to academia and/or possess an interest in local history, but nearly all reside within the country of origin. It is worth noting, however, that while Gorny and Mazurek received a considerable amount of feedback directly from users, it was not representative of all users. During the test period the server transcription logs for just one of the thirty-one libraries showed three thousand to four thousand visitors per day and Google Analytics for the same library revealed ninety thousand unique visitors.

Ross et al.'s (2012) survey received 2,657 responses over a one-month period. Just over half the respondents (50.2%) self-identified as scholars or students using the collection for academic research. The next largest group of respondents stated that they use the collection for personal interest, followed by non-academic research. Considering age, the largest group of users was aged twenty-one to thirty (27.7%), followed by thirty-one to forty (22.3%). Interestingly, respondents identified fifty-seven countries of origin, with the most hailing from the United Kingdom (29%), United States (17.6%), Germany (9%), and France (5.7%). Much like Gorny and Mazurek's (2012) survey, it is clear there is a strong usage trend among users belonging to academia; however, the global use of this digital collection is striking. This result might be related to language accessibility, size, subject matter, or extent of promotion. It is worth noting the majority of respondents stated that they use the collection to find specific objects, indicating that they are accessing the collection with a goal in mind. This also suggests that users are being referred or directed to the collection from an external source rather than discovering an object by browsing.

Use by Format

The format of the digital collections and objects was a focal point of several studies. Sinn's (2012) analysis showed that of the 138 digital resources cited, 99 were text resources, 24 were aggregated databases, 13 were visual resources, one was an audio resource, and one was a multimedia resource. Hess's (2012) study of analytics revealed the top three objects downloaded from the Illinois Harvest Portal were text objects. Gorny and Mazurek's (2012) survey results showed their biggest group of respondents, users interested in local history and genealogy, most frequently accessed diaries, address and name lists, photographs, and newspapers. These results show users are accessing text objects; however, it is noteworthy that many structured studies chose to examine use of visual collections and objects. For example, Schlosser and Stamper (2012) selected a photograph collection they believed would be of broad interest as the subject of their study, and van Vliet and Hekman (2012) selected three little-known collections of digitized artwork for their social tagging study. Harris and Hepburn (2012) also examined use of digital images, hypothesizing that scholarly articles would include more digital images over time due to the increased availability of digital collections. They additionally hypothesized that born-digital open-access journals would include more digital images than print journals due to authors taking advantage of the possibilities inherent in a web environment. They found neither hypothesis to be entirely accurate, but rather observed that inclusion of digital images has neither increased nor decreased considerably.

Another format-related discussion that wove through a number of studies focused on whether users were more apt to use digital or analog versions of a collection. In many cases the development of digital collections allows inaccessible and previously unknown collections to become available to users (van Vliet & Hekman, 2012; Gorny & Mazurek, 2012). For many institutions, accessibility and preservation are the driving benefits of digitization. However, Newell (2012) expressed a concern that an increase in digitizing collections could result in limited access to the analog materials due to a potential rise in policies promoting exclusive use of digital surrogates over analog originals for increased preservation. From the opposite perspective, Hudson (2012) expressed a concern that an increase in digitization would decrease the number of visitors at cultural institutions since digital collection users would not need to see the analog materials. Studies showed, however, that the use of analog collections was still high, and at times potentially higher than use of digital collections. Eccles et al.'s (2012) study showed in some cases the web pages for the analog collection possessed more links than the digital collection pages. The authors concluded this was likely related to how long the web page had been live and how familiar users and institutions were with the resource. Sinn (2012) noted that some citations she reviewed during her study did not specify the format of the object cited. In these cases, she checked to see if a digital version existed, and if it did she attributed the citation to the digital collection. Although she admits this may have introduced errors into the data, she still observed a firm reliance on analog collections. Ross et al.'s (2012) survey revealed the experience with the British Museum's Collections Database Online inspired 73.9% of respondents to visit the physical museum; however, many noted the purpose of the physical visit would be more for pleasure and entertainment, whereas the online visit was more for scholarly pursuits.

Collection Location

When establishing a digital collection, the decision of where to locate it is an important factor regarding use, since location choice has the potential to influence a user's opinion of the collection. One attribute collection location can affect is perceived authenticity or authority. As independent researchers unattached to a particular institution, Sinn (2012) and Harris and Hepburn (2012) were able to examine collection location, which in some cases indicated its host institution or creator, from a unique perspective. Of the 121 digital collections cited in the articles Sinn reviewed, the three highest concentrations were provided by commercial vendors (26), followed by libraries (22) and, surprisingly, individual websites (17). These independent, personal collections were cited more often than collections provided by museums (16), institutions of higher education (15), the government (9), and archives (4), among others. Sinn noted that these collections were often the result of family history or other personal research. This indicates that scholarly users are either not considering authenticity when citing digital collections, or are not seeing any details that make them question the authenticity of the digital collections provided by individuals. Harris and Hepburn (2012) observed the opposite; citations for noninstitutional digital materials were very low in both print and open-access history journals. They speculated this may be due to the collections being "too new, or not of sufficient historical value" (p. 11) to interest historians. Their data also showed more than half the images appearing in open-access articles fell into a category of "no source" (65.07%). In many cases these images were attributed to the article's author, leading Harris and Hepburn to suggest that the interactive web environment and ease of uploading content had assisted authors to utilize their personal image collections to enhance their writing.

Another factor related to location is discoverability, since if users are unable to locate a collection they will also be unable to use it. Due to today's robust online and mobile environments there are a number of platform options available to create and share a digital collection, including an institution's website, an institutional repository, a media-sharing site (such as Flickr or YouTube), or a social media site (such as Facebook). Each platform has its own pros and cons, such as increased chance of discoverability and accessibility, familiarity with different user groups, opportunities for user interaction and community development, sustainability, and cost (Chen, Chen, Hong, Liao, & Huang, 2012; Fletcher & Lee, 2012; Harris & Hepburn, 2012; Kamble, Raj, & Sangeeta, 2012; Lihitkar & Lihitkar, 2012). Petek (2012) conducted a study comparing how users describe and tag objects within the Digital Library of Slovenia and Flickr. To better understand use of Flickr, participants were asked to share their motivation for visiting Flickr. Results revealed the majority of participants use the site to upload and tag their personal photos (29.2% and 19.4%, respectively) or share photos with family and friends (18.8%). This indicates that posting digital collections on a popular and socially focused site might increase casual browsing and discovery. In some cases developing a multiplatform foundation for a digital collection is a good way to increase its chances of accessibility and reach different user groups (Sabharwal, 2012; Schlosser & Stamper, 2012; van Vliet & Hekman, 2012).

Gracy (2012) conducted a survey regarding the digitization, accessibility, and use of moving images within academic libraries, archives, and museums that revealed repositories possessing digital moving image collections were utilizing a combination of the above options. Of the twelve respondents who answered the question about distribution, six noted they share digital videos on their institution's website, five noted sharing them on a media sharing site, three reported posting them to the institution's Facebook page, and only two noted sharing them via an institutional repository. It is apparent from the amount of responses that many of the institutions provide multiple access points to their digital videos. Institutional websites and media sharing sites were more common than Facebook or institutional repositories, but the distribution between internal and external locations shows an awareness of increasing the potential of user discovery by placing collections within familiar web environments.

Harris and Hepburn (2012) conducted a study over the course of a year to compare the use of the CARLI Digital Collection on its website and in Flickr. They hypothesized that posting objects to two locations, one of which is a popular social networking site, would provide increased exposure and a higher rate of spontaneous usage through browsing and searching while not detracting from the authenticity and authority offered by the collection's website. Their results showed the images in Flickr received many more views than the collection's website (5.29 versus 0.74). They noted that the dual posting successfully drew attention from two different types of users: the public who may not be actively seeking images on a library website but is interested to find them through browsing, and the historian or scholar who is actively seeking authentic resources. They concluded that more institutions should "exploit the ubiquity and ease-of-use of social networking sites to broadcast their holdings" (p. 19).

Schlosser and Stamper (2012) conducted a similar study that compared use of a photograph collection housed in both the university's institutional repository and Flickr. Their results showed the images located in Flickr were viewed one hundred to six hundred times each, whereas the images in the institutional repository were viewed five to thirty-eight times each. In this case discoverability was clearly higher in Flickr, possibly due to its familiarity with the browsing and viewing audience. Despite the higher rate of object views in the Flickr collection, Schlosser and Stamper noted they did not observe much spontaneous discovery of objects on either platform and that users were discovering the digital collections organically through the search and browse functions. They concluded there was another influence affecting the number of views: unbalanced promotional efforts. Van Vliet and Hekman (2012) also uploaded their digital collections to Flickr in addition to their website. Similarly, their data revealed few spontaneous tags were added, but they came to a different conclusion than Schlosser and Stamper. Rather than looking to user search behavior to explain these results, they questioned how discoverable a small collection is among the massive selection of other objects available via Flickr. The Flickr community includes over eight billion photos contributed by over seventy million "photographers" (Flickr.com, 2013). Considering these figures, it is understandable that a collection of 379 images might be challenging to locate among the abundance of other images on the site—particularly if users do not know it is there.

Impact of Promotion

The presence or lack of promotion was also observed by a number of studies as having a considerable effect on whether users discover and utilize digital collections. Schlosser and Stamper (2012) were able to discern the launch of promotional efforts for their collection within the study data through a modest, but distinct rise in object views. This trend was evident in both the Flickr and the institutional repository's user statistics. They admitted, however, that the promotional tactics utilized may have affected their overall results since the promotional e-mails and announcements only publicized the instance of their collection in Flickr. Although Schlosser and Stamper observed distinctly higher rates of viewing among the objects in Flickr than the ones in the institutional repository, they were unable to draw any clear conclusions due to this imbalance of promotion.

Van Vliet and Hekman (2012) also observed peaks in their data following promotion of their digital collection website featuring the social tagging tool. Their promotional efforts included announcements at conferences and in publications as well as directed communication with university students and museum staff to provide a range of responses from laymen and experts. Their data, like Schlosser and Stamper's, revealed there were very few instances of spontaneous discovery and tagging. Since promotion proved to have a considerable impact on usage data in these studies, it would seem that increasing promotion is an effective way to increase usage by actively informing users of a collection and directing them to discover it.

From the opposing standpoint, Wagner and Smith's (2012) study of digital collection use among university students revealed that lack of promotion and, consequently, lack of awareness of digital collections was impeding use. Among the 470 students who participated in their survey, 63% admitted to being unaware of the university's archives or its digital collections, and 86% stated they had never used the digital collections. However, when survey participants learned which materials were available digitally, 87% expressed interest in using them. This implies that it is not lack of interest that is preventing some users from accessing digital collections, but rather it is lack of knowledge that the collections exist.

Of course, initial discovery is not the only situation where promotion can be useful. Once a user has discovered a collection, it is the responsibility of the host institution to promote any changes to the collection to maintain its continued accessibility. Eccles et al.'s (2012) webometrics study observed the importance of promotion if a collection is going to relocate to a new website or URL. Their data revealed collections that had undergone relocation during the study experienced a decline in links from external URLs and domains. For example, the British Library Sound Archive was moved during the course of the study due to a website restructuring project. Prior to the relocation, the collection had received links from 814 URLs and 733 domains; however, in the second segment of the study the new website only received links from 47 URLs and 37 domains. This reinforces that a permanent URL is highly favorable for the continued discovery of a digital collection; however, if relocation is necessary it must be appropriately promoted to ensure established users will continue to locate and recommend the collection.

ACCESSIBILITY CHALLENGES

Curators of digital collections have long contended that sharing a digitized collection increases its accessibility by removing the constraints of distance, staffing, and business hours. It is true that a computer and Internet access now offer patrons the ability to visit and conduct research at institutions across the world from the comfort of their own home or office. However, while increased accessibility is a valuable and beneficial aspect of digital collections, it is also vague and difficult to measure. It suggests that more users are being served, but not all of them—thereby raising questions of universal accessibility and inadvertently creating unexpected challenges.

Multilingual Functionality

Considering that images and visual materials have the potential to be understood and appreciated around the world to a greater extent than textual materials (due to freedom from language limitations) it is logical that many of these types of materials are available in digital collections. What is not often considered when digitizing and making visual collections available is the cross-language accessibility of the metadata and descriptive information that accompanies the objects (Petrelli & Clough, 2012; Wu, He, & Luo, 2012). For a user who is not fluent or familiar with the native language of the digital collection, searching for images may be challenging due to translation issues or lack of familiarity with descriptive terms, which might contain colloquialisms or regionalisms. Petrelli and Clough (2012) organized a study to test the practice of cross-language image retrieval among users of a digital image collection at St. Andrews University. They conducted an analysis of user queries by showing sixteen images from the collection to a small group of native Italian speakers and then asking them to find the same images in a database using a search function. The queries were submitted in Italian and translated into English via an automated translation tool to conduct the search. Once the results were compiled, they were translated back into Italian in the form of a list. The automated translation aided the users and also provided insight for the authors into the accuracy of the translation tool. The study produced 618 queries across all participants. Their results revealed a varied number of queries per image (8 to 68 queries per image, four to ten terms used per query), yet there was no correlation between success rate and number of queries or terms. However, a correlation was discerned between success rate and how much metadata accompanied the image, leading Petrelli and Clough to conclude that increased granularity in metadata and descriptive fields, with particular care to not use colloquial terms, will aid users in successfully locating relevant digital objects. Regarding translation, 83% of terms were translated properly; however, 11% of translations failed and 6% were mistranslated. Petrelli and Clough related this rate of mistranslation to the tendency for participants to search with keywords rather than phrases. Since users' search behavior is unlikely to change, working to develop a tool that will be more adept at translating keywords may be helpful.

Wu et al. (2012) surveyed a group of academic digital library users from different countries regarding their multilingual use and expectations regarding digital libraries and discovered a strong interest in more advanced translation tools. When asked what multilingual services and retrieval functions they would like to see offered in collections, 74% of respondents expressed a desire for digital libraries to provide search capabilities for retrieving multilingual content; 63% showed interest in the translation probability so users could filter out mistranslations; 62% thought it would be helpful for digital libraries to display search results with automatically translated summaries in a specified language; 59% requested full translation of content, 57% requested embedded translation software, and 52% requested the ability for users to correct translation errors. Considering the high percentages of users who expressed an interest in increased multilingual functionality, it is apparent that patrons are interested in utilizing collections that may currently be intellectually inaccessible to them due to a language barrier.

Alternative Text Functionality

Another group of users who would benefit by additional attention being focused on achieving universal access is the visually impaired. Southwell and Slater (2012) argue that despite an awareness of the need for digital collections to be accessible to a range of diverse user groups, many collections are still inaccessible to visually impaired users. Their study of textual documents from digital collections at sixty-nine academic libraries belonging to the Association of Research Libraries (ARL) reveals this widespread lack of accessibility. A sample of textual objects was chosen for the study by selecting a document at random from each ARL institution's digital collection, resulting in a group of thirty-eight handwritten and thirty-one typed objects. Southwell and Slater sought to determine whether the digital objects were accessible to patrons using screen-reading technology. Their findings revealed only twenty-nine of sixty-nine documents (42%) were readable by at least one of the tested screen reading methods. A defining characteristic of the readable documents was the presence of a transcript or associated alternative text that conveyed the content of the object to the user. However, Southwell and Slater note that merely providing a transcript or alternative text did not always make the object readable. If the transcript was buried within a catalog record or included links throughout the text, the screen-reading technology was less effective. The study showed the remaining forty unreadable documents were often presented only as an image and therefore did not provide any content for the screen readers to convey to the user. Although it is potentially time consuming to include a transcript or text alternative for every object included in a digital collection, it is time well spent, considering how much this additional step contributes to an object's overall accessibility.

Davis (2012) performed a similar study to examine the accessibility of archival repository websites by analyzing their home pages.[3] She incorporated quantitative and qualitative methods by first testing the pages' compliance with the Website Content Accessibility Guidelines (WCAG) 2.0 and color contrast/luminosity standards with validators, and then evaluating the pages from a user's perspective. For comparative purposes, Davis also analyzed the home pages of five non-archival sites that appeared at the top of Google's list of most-visited sites.[4] The validators reported the average error ratio for the archival sites was 0.0074 and 0.0075 for the non-archival sites, revealing the general accessibility of both groups was consistent. Davis noted that the errors reported by the validators were not always equivalent, so the qualitative analysis provided additional insight. For example, the home page ranked most accessible by the validators only contained two errors; however, both resulted from the failure to provide text alternatives for nontext content. In this case, since the majority of the page was a slideshow advertising events and programs, this one error rendered nearly the entire page inaccessible to users with screen readers.

MOVING FORWARD

Reflecting on the study results, each author or group of authors was aware of the need to continue refining digital collections to better serve the users and attract more of them in the future. Prominent themes included spending additional time developing collections to increase accessibility, remembering to promote collections to increase discoverability, and paying attention to user activity and feedback to inform decisions about improvements.

A number of studies emphasized spending more time following through on the development and extended accessibility of digital collections, rather than stopping once the materials are minimally accessible. Southwell and Slater (2012) suggest taking the extra time to ensure all digital materials are as accessible as possible by supplementing objects with transcripts and alternative text, and offering magnification tools when possible. They also suggest ensuring all departments from a given institution follow the same policies so all materials are presented in a cohesive manner with the same level of accessibility. Although adding these tools may be time-intensive, they round out a digital object by complementing its visual aspect with a readable textual aspect and help it approach the desired status of universal accessibility. Similarly, Petrelli and Clough (2012) recommend developing the metadata and descriptive information accompanying digital objects to provide nonnative speakers a better chance of discovering materials via searching.

Placing an emphasis on promotion was also a resounding lesson learned. Schlosser and Stamper's (2012) study helped them realize posting digital objects to a website is the first step, but sharing their existence with researchers and potential users is just as important. Wagner and Smith (2012) and Harris and Hepburn's (2012) results led them to suggest the importance of actively introducing information about digital collections into their target users' environments to ensure potential users are aware of what they have to offer. Considering a number of studies showed a strong user base in academia, sharing collections on social networking and media sharing sites could potentially attract a wide range of other users. Eccles et al.'s (2012) study reinforced the importance of continued promotion, particularly in the case of a collection's relocation, to ensure returning users are able to maintain access once they have discovered a collection.

Although many of the studies discussed were self-reflective, there were a few conducted by independent researchers interested in emphasizing the benefit of assessment and self-evaluation. Gracy's (2012) survey revealed only one of sixteen respondents was actively pursuing self-study, and in that case the repository was only reviewing statistics provided by the Internet Archive rather than actively collecting user data through a web analytics program or user survey. Schlosser and Stamper (2012) emphasized it is up to the educational and cultural institutions to advocate the importance and benefit of their collections and the access they offer, particularly in this climate of limited budgets and increased assessment. Likewise, Eccles et al. (2012) stressed assessment is a way to offer funding agencies, stakeholders, and even project staff a factual view of the success and value of a digitization project. Heradio et al. (2012) noted that the digital collection community must arrive at a "consensus on standard definitions for usability and usefulness" so everyone can work together to evaluate the success and quality of users' experiences with digital collections. Hughes (2012) noted assessment and user testing may be challenging in some cases, since digital collections are often developed using short-term funding and temporary staff; however, she suggests institutions look to more cost-effective methods, such as recruiting volunteers or interns to tackle these projects or calling on users to provide feedback on their experiences.

A final, but important recommendation was for institutions to pay attention to user activity and feedback when making changes and improvements to current and future collections. Meyerson, Galloway, and Bias (2012) note that previously user studies have been employed to provide evidence of activity, but not to serve as a basis for improvements. They recommend working with usability performance metrics, which are already collected by many institutions, to approach making modifications from a user-centered standpoint. Harris and Hepburn (2012) note that collection developers and curators need to understand both their audience and its interests, since it does not make sense to focus efforts on a project that will not be used. Agnosti and Orio's (2012) study showed collections often cater to more than one audience, so the ability to listen to, balance, and address differing requests is sometimes necessary. Ellis and Callahan (2012) reflected that developing prototypes to examine "imagine if" scenarios would provide curators and developers with "the freedom to test, fail and improve along the way" (n.p.). They reflected institutions must learn to "accept user habits as they are, rather than as [they] would like them to be" (n.p.). With this in mind, it is important to embrace evidence of users' activities and experiences to make informed decisions about helpful improvements and modifications rather than what a development team might think will be helpful or technologically appealing. If certain collections, types of materials, or subject areas are consistently not being used, it will benefit the institution to review who their target audience is and which objects are being used in order to best refocus efforts on what will attract users and provide them with a satisfying experience.

CONCLUSION

Although the user studies published in 2012 utilized a variety of quantitative and qualitative approaches and examined different aspects of use, there were a number of recurring themes among them. Many revealed low user activity with spikes in use for specific objects, suggesting that despite knowledge of or referral to some objects, general discoverability and awareness of whole collections is lacking. Survey data and link analyses showed a strong user base within the academic sphere, both in self-reported responses and examinations of web domains. A citation analysis of history articles supported these results, revealing a slow but steady increase in references to digital materials indicating that scholars are beginning to accept digital collections as reliable sources. Collections that were actively promoted experienced distinct increases in object views and downloads, but those that were not promoted suffered from lack of user awareness. Likewise, location of the collections was observed to have a distinct impact.

Although a common location for digital collections is on the institution's own website or institutional repository, many authors acknowledged the benefit of also sharing collections within the familiar web environment of social media to attract the attention of additional users. Additionally, studies revealed digital collections have a long way to go before they are universally accessible. Currently, many collections do not feature multilingual or alternative text functionality to allow foreign or visually impaired users the ability to successfully access all objects within a collection.

Reflecting on the study findings, authors suggested a number of recommendations for improving usage in the future. An emphasis was placed on fully developing collections in the initial project phase to round out each object with additional functionalities to enhance overall accessibility. Promotion was also highlighted as an important area to focus on to increase awareness and use of collections. Finally, authors stressed the importance of curators taking an active role in assessing and evaluating user experiences, both as evidence of a collection's value and as vital data to inform future developments and progress.

Although most of these studies are small-scale and exploratory, they demonstrate the engagement of cultural heritage professionals in the active promotion and improvement of digital collections. As with any cultural heritage institution, a digital collection needs to find a balance between the best interests for the materials and the needs of the users in order to succeed and thrive. Conducting assessment and user studies provides professionals with evidence toward achieving this goal; however, it is the next, and often more challenging, step of actively listening to and responding to user experience and input that leads to the realization of success and the advancement of digital collections.

NOTES

1. The five digital collections studied were Histpop–Online Historical Population Reports; nineteenth-century British Library newspapers; British Library archival sound recordings; Eighteenth-Century Official Parliamentary Publications Portal 1688–1834 at the British Official Publications Collaborative Reader Information Service (BOPCRIS); and the Wellcome Trust medical journals backfiles.

2. Core journals analyzed were *American Historical Review; Comparative Studies in Society and History; Ethnohistory; European History Quarterly;* and *History Workshop Journal.* Open access journal were *49th Parallel; Electronic Journal of Vedic Studies; Heroic Age; ERAS; E-Journal of Portuguese History; Digital Medievalist;* and *Journal of Historical Biography.*

3. The five pages analyzed were the home pages of the National Archives, Mid-Atlantic Region; the Athenaeum of Philadelphia; the Free Library of Philadelphia's Rare Book Department; the University of Delaware Library Special Collections; and Bryn Mawr College Special Collections.

4. These sites, identified by Google's February 2011 list of most-visited websites, included Wikipedia, YouTube, Yahoo!, Live.com, and Facebook.

REFERENCES

Agnosti, M., & Orio, N. (2012). User requirements for effective access to digital archives of manuscripts. *Journal of Multimedia, 7*(2), 217–222. doi: 10.4304/jmm.7.2.217-222

Chen, C., Chen, Y., Hong, C., Liao, C., & Huang, C. (2012). Developing Taiwan library history digital library with reader knowledge archiving and sharing mechanisms based on the DSpace platform. *The Electronic Library, 30*(3), 426–442.

Davis, L. J. (2012). Providing virtual services to all: A mixed-method analysis of the website accessibility of Philadelphia Area Consortium of Special Collections Libraries (PACSCL) member repositories. *American Archivist, 75*(1), 35–55.

Eccles, K. E., Thelwall, M., & Meyer, E. T. (2012). Measuring the web impact of digitised scholarly resources. *Journal of Documentation, 68*(4), 512–526.

Ellis, S., & Callahan, M. (2012, October). Prototyping as a process for improved user experience with library and archives websites. *Code4Lib, 18*. Retrieved from http://journal .code4lib.org/articles/7394

Ercegovac, Z. (2012). Digital image tagging: A case study with seventh grade students. *School Libraries Worldwide, 18*(1), 97–110. Retrieved from: http://www.iasl-online.org/pubs/slw/

Flanagan, M., & Carini, P. (2012). How games can help us access and understand archival images. *American Archivist, 75*(2), 514–537. Retrieved from http://www2.archivists.org/american-archivist

Fletcher, A., & Lee, M. J. (2012). Current social media uses and evaluations in American museums. *Museum Management and Curatorship, 27*(5), 505–521. Retrieved from: http://dx.doi.org/10.1080/09647775.2012.738136

Flickr.com. (2013). *Welcome to Flickr—Photo sharing.* Retrieved from http://www.flickr.com/

Gorny, M., & Mazurek, J. (2012). Key users of Polish digital libraries. *The Electronic Library, 30*(4), 543–556.

Gracy, K. F. (2012). Distribution and consumption patterns of archival moving images in online environments. *American Archivist, 75*(2), 422–455.

Harkema, C., & Nygren, C. (2012). Historypin for library image collections: New modes of access for unique materials at the University of Saskatchewan Library. *Partnership: The Canadian Journal of Library and Information Practice and Research, 7*(2). Retrieved from https://journal.lib.uoguelph.ca/index.php/perj/

Harris, V., & Hepburn, H. (2012). Trends in image use by historians and the implications for librarians and archivists. *College and Research Libraries.* Advance online publication. Retrieved from: http://crl.acrl.org/content/early/recent

Heradio, R., Fernandez-Amoros, D., Cabrerizo, F. J., & Herrera-Viedma, E. (2012). A review of quality evaluations of digital libraries based on users' perceptions. *Journal of Information Science, 38*(3), 269–283.

Hess, K. (2012, June). Discovering digital library user behavior with Google Analytics. *Code4Lib, 17.* Retrieved from http://journal.code4lib.org/articles/6942

Hudson, C. (2012). The digital museum. In L. M. Hughes (Ed.), *Evaluating and measuring the value, use and impact of digital collections* (pp. 35–48). London: Facet Publishing.

Hughes, L. M. (2012). Introduction: the value use and impact of digital collections. In L. M. Hughes (Ed.), *Evaluating and measuring the value, use and impact of digital collections* (pp. 1–10). London: Facet Publishing.

Kamble, V. T., Raj, H., & Sangeeta, S. (2012). Open source library management and digital library software. *DESIDOC Journal of Library and Information Technology, 32*(5), 388–392. Retrieved from http://www.publications.drdo.gov.in/ojs/index.php/djlit

Lihitkar, S. R., & Lihitkar, R. S. (2012). Open source software for developing digital library: Comparative study. *DESIDOC Journal of Library and Information Technology, 32*(5), 393–400. Retrieved from http://www.publications.drdo.gov.in/ojs/index.php/djlit

Meyerson, J., Galloway, P., & Bias, R. (2012). Improving user experience of professional researchers: Applying a user-centered design framework in archival repositories. In *Proceedings of the Association for Information Science & Technology Annual Meeting (ASIS&T 2012)*. Hoboken, NJ: Wiley.

Mitchell, C., & Suchy, D. (2012). Developing mobile access to digital collections. *D-Lib Magazine, 18*(1/2). doi: 10.1045/january2012-mitchell

Newell, J. (2012). Old objects, new media: Historical collections, digitization and affect. *Journal of Material Culture, 17*, 287–306. doi 10.1177/1359183512453534

Petek, M. (2012). Comparing user-generated and librarian-generated metadata on digital images. *OCLC Systems & Services: International Digital Library Perspectives, 28*(2), 101–111. doi: 10.1108/10650751211236659

Petrelli, D., & Clough, P. (2012). Analysing user's queries for cross-language image retrieval from digital library collections. *Electronic Library, 30*(2), 197–219.

Ross, C., Terras, M., & Motyckova, V. (2012). Measuring impact and use: Scholarly information-seeking behaviour. In L. M. Hughes (Ed.), *Evaluating and measuring the value, use and impact of digital collections* (pp. 85–102). London: Facet Publishing.

Sabharwal, A. (2012). Digital representation of disability history: Developing a virtual exhibition. *Archival Issues: Journal of the Midwest Archives Conference, 34*(1), 7–26.

Schlosser, M., & Stamper, B. (2012). Learning to share: measuring use of a digitized collection on Flickr and in the IR. *Information Technology & Libraries, 31*(3), 85–93.

Sinn, D. (2012). Impact of digital archival collections on historical research. *Journal of The American Society for Information Science & Technology, 63*(8), 1521–1537. doi: 10.1002/asi.22650

Smith, L., & Rowley, J. (2012). Digitisation of local heritage: Local studies collections and digitisation in public libraries. *Journal of Librarianship and Information Science, 44*(4), 272–280. doi: 10.1177/0961000611434760

Southwell, K. L., & Slater, J. (2012). Accessibility of digital special collections using screen readers. *Library Hi Tech, 30*(3), 457–471.

Statistical Cybermetrics Research Group. (2013). *Webometric Analyst 2.0.* Retrieved from http://lexiurl.wlv.ac.uk/index.html

van Vliet, H., & Hekman, E. (2012). Enhancing user involvement with digital cultural heritage: The usage of social tagging and storytelling. *First Monday, 17*(5). Retrieved from http://www.firstmonday.org/htbin/cgiwrap/bin/ojs/index.php/fm/article/view/3922/3203

Wagner, J. L., & Smith, D. A. (2012). Students as donors to university archives: A study of student perceptions with recommendations. *American Archivist, 75*(2), 538–566.

Wu, D., He, D., & Luo, B. (2012). Multilingual needs and expectations in digital libraries: A survey of academic users with different languages. *The Electronic Library, 30*(2), 182–196.

Part VI

REVIEWS (NASCENT)

INTRODUCTION: REVIEWS (NASCENT)

Our nascent Reviews section promises to flower into a wide-ranging examination of the themes and concepts featured in conferences, seminars, workshops, books, and blogs, among other forms of discourse, during the past year. Inaugurating our venture into this topic, we feature "Memories of a Museum Visit" by Carol Lynn Price, a Cultural Heritage Informatics doctoral student at the School of Library and Information Science at the University of South Carolina. Carol examines the museum visitor's experience through a review of two books by John Falk and Lynn Dierking. Published twenty years apart, the books chronicle the authors' realization that museum visitors seek to fill identity-related needs—a theme echoed throughout this volume.

16

Memories of a Museum Visit

Carol Lynn Price

The Museum Experience by John H. Falk and Lynn D. Dierking, 1992, Washington, DC: Whalesback Books, 205 pages, hardcover, $34.88, ISBN 978-0-9295-9006-6.

The Museum Experience Revisited by John H. Falk and Lynn D. Dierking, 2013, Walnut Creek, CA: Left Coast Press, Inc., 416 pages, hardcover, $94.00, ISBN 978-1-6113-2044-2.

John Falk and Lynn Dierking are leading museum professionals and pioneers of the research to explore the museum experience from the visitor's perspective. Together they have over seventy years of experience studying the behavior that motivates museum visitors. Their research has delved into why people go to museums, whom they go with, how they learn, and what they remember from their visit. Falk has written several books and more than a hundred scholarly articles on museum visitors in addition to serving fourteen years as the director of education research at the Smithsonian Institute. Dierking's research has highlighted the significance of lifelong learning, specifically out-of-school learning, for youth and families, communities, and historically underrepresented groups. Both award-winning authors are proponents of free-choice learning; learning not confined to a structured environment such as a classroom. Free-choice learning can include reading books; surfing the web; or visiting science centers and museums, zoos, or state parks. Falk and Dierking are currently Sea Grant Professors of Free-Choice Learning at the College of Education Center for Research and Lifelong Learning at Oregon State University.

As education-oriented museum professionals, Falk and Dierking have devoted their careers to studying the public use of museums. By "museum" they mean everything from art or history museums to science centers, zoos, and aquariums. In *The Museum Experience*, published in 1992, and the 2013 revised edition, *The Museum Experience Revisited*, they present their own research findings and information from other studies to explain the museumgoer's expectations and explore how this information can improve the sustainability of museums.

In 1992, Falk and Dierking wrote *The Museum Experience* to examine the "public aspect of the museum world." In the last quarter century, museums have become popular. This new interest created an increase in museums, visitors, and financial support. The financial support came with the expectation that museum activities must be "highly visible to the public," and place an emphasis on learning and education. Museums that traditionally placed their emphasis on exhibits and collections now had to redefine their focus to consider the public or the "visitor's" needs.

Twenty years after the first edition, and at the request of their publisher, Falk and Dierking wrote *The Museum Experience Revisited*. One wonders after reading the first edition if there is anything left to investigate about the museum experience, but the authors will undoubtedly say, "yes." They prove this by expanding the new edition to a staggering 416 pages—200 pages longer than the first edition. More impressively, they discuss new research on the visitor's perspective, present a new theory, and provide insight on how the Internet's digital tools and virtual worlds will impact visitors to the twenty-first-century museum.

Falk and Dierking present the argument in both books that the museum visitor's experience is as crucial, or more so, than the museum exhibits and collections. Their books present a framework of research to view the overall museumgoer's experience and to provide recommendations for museums to develop strategies to grow and prosper.

The Museum Experience Revisited is essentially a guidebook for museum professionals. Every chapter includes practical strategies to enhance the museum visitor's experience and suggestions for programming and marketing strategies. Falk and Dierking's informal writing style will appeal to the layperson, volunteer, or teacher who is interested in understanding how visits to cultural heritage institutions become memorable events for individuals and families. The authors continue to examine the museum from the visitor's perspective; however, they add discussions on the long-term effects of a museum visit, how learning occurs in museums, and what opportunities exist within the digital landscape of twenty-first-century museums.

Falk and Dierking believe that most museum practitioners come into the industry "through the back door from another profession other than museum studies" and have no experience and little understanding of the impact of the visitor's perspective. Libraries, corporations, and shopping malls have increased competition by setting up "museum-like" exhibits that could hurt visitor attendance at museums (Falk, 2010). With the prospect of losing potential customers, the authors' argument for writing this book is their belief that fulfilling the museum visitor's expectations is still the best way to ensure museums' success and growth in attendance.

Museums are not only an integral part of a country's cultural heritage; they have a significant impact on the economy. According to the American Association of Museums (AAM), Americans view museums as a vital resource for educating children and a reliable source of information. Museums directly contribute $21 billion to the United States economy each year, with billions more generated indirectly by their visitors. Today there are 17,500 museums in the United States, with a museum in at least nine out of ten counties. In 2010, eight hundred million people visited museums in the United States (Highbeam Business, 2013). Worldwide, the number of museums has doubled since 1992 and museum visitors have tripled. In China alone, a new museum opens every three days (Falk, 2013).

Falk and Dierking examine the museum visitor's experience, or "journey," as they define it, from the visitor's perspective. Both books are exhausting but fascinating summaries of the research on museumgoers' motivational behavior. Research has been analyzed to describe how visitors decide to go to a museum, how they feel about the visit, and what they remember after it. Every detail, idea, and suggestion by the authors is substantiated with research evidence. The average reader will be in awe of their thoroughness, but intrigued with their findings. The veteran museum director as well as the novice student will learn something from the books and appreciate the implications of a museum visitor's perspective.

A significant development in *The Museum Experience Revisited* is Falk's discovery that the reason people go to museums is to satisfy a "personal, identity-related need." In 2009, just after Falk completed his book, *Identity and the Museum Visitor Experience*, he admitted that there were problems with much of the museum visitor research, including his own. Falk's discovery is that it may take days, weeks, or longer to form memories. Consequently, museum visitors need time to think about what they remember from their visit. However, most of the museum research was collected at the very end of visitors' museum visit. As a result, visitors had not had time to form memories of their museum visit and, therefore, could not truly describe what they learned (Falk, 2010). Falk and his colleagues interviewed hundreds of museum visitors "weeks, months and years" after their actual museum visit. What they found was that museum visits are "deeply tied to an individual's sense of identity." What museumgoers remember about their visit is based on their own personal goals for initially making the decision to visit the museum. It has little to do with the type of museums or the contents of the exhibits. These needs may be something as basic as: (1) a family outing to share a good time together, (2) to support a child's learning experience, or (3) to learn more about a favorite artist (Falk, 2010).

The authors seem to have thought of every aspect of a museum visit. A good portion of the book deals with what is going on inside the museum—everything from parking and the gift shop to museum fatigue. The book has a textbook-like format with summary points and suggestions for practitioners at the end of each chapter. This information is full of marketing and programming recommendations to help museums develop strategies that are more in line with the research findings on the visitor's perspective. The critical issue is for museums to figure out why people choose to visit their museums. Museums cannot think solely about the needs of their institution—they must consider visitors' identity-related needs that will be satisfied by their institution.

Falk believes that identity-related needs never go away. Visitors use museums to meet their needs, and consequently this is what they will remember from their visit.

The relevance of this book is in whether museums can take this information and apply it to their marketing messages and programs to create an environment that meets visitor needs. They may only have one chance, since most museumgoers usually visit a museum one time (Falk 2013).

REFERENCES

Falk, J. H. (2010, August 18). *The museum visitor experience: Who visits, why and what affect?* Balboa Park Cultural Partnership. Retrieved from http://www.learningtimes.net/bpcp/wp-content/uploads/2010/11/Falk-The-Museum-Visitor-Experience.pdf

Falk, J. H., & Dierking, L. D. (1992). *The museum experience.* Washington, DC: Whalesback Books.

Falk, J. H., & Dierking, L. D. (2013). *The museum experience revisited.* Walnut Creek, CA: Left Coast Press, Inc.

Highbeam Business (2013). *Museums and art galleries.* Retrieved from http://business.highbeam.com/industry-reports/business/museums-art-galleries

Index

About the Editor

Dr. Samantha K. Hastings joined the faculty at the University of South Carolina, School of Library and Information Science, as director and professor in August 2006. Previously she directed the digital image management program of study at the University of North Texas, School of Library and Information Sciences, and served as interim dean 2004–2005. She holds an MLIS from USF Tampa and a PhD from Florida State. Sam's research interests in the retrieval of digital images, cultural heritage, telecommunications, and evaluation of networked information services influence how she views the changing roles for information professionals. "Without library and information scientists, there is little hope that people will be able to find the information and knowledge needed to flourish in the digital environment." Sam tries to integrate real-world experiences as reflected by teamwork and product development in all of her classes, which range from research methods to digital image management. Sam has worked as a consultant and built full-text and image databases for accountants, dentists, doctors, lawyers, and county and state governments. Along the way, Sam has worked to help public libraries and museums connect to the Internet and share their cultural objects in a digital environment. Her current research explores the use of 3D digital objects in learning environments. She served as president of the American Society for Information Science and Technology (www.asist.org) in 2004 and served five years as the acquisitions editor for the ASIS&T Monograph series, published by Information Today, Inc. She will be president of the Association for Library and Information Science Educators (ALISE) in 2015. Recently she launched a new annual review for cultural heritage informatics with editor Charles Harmon of Rowman & Little-field, and you are holding the first issue of this important publication partnership.

Dr. Samantha K. Hastings
Director & Professor
University of South Carolina
School of Library and Information Science
Davis College, 1501 Greene Street
Columbia, SC 29208
803-777-3858, hastings@sc.edu
http://www.libsci.sc.edu/